Medical misadventure in an age of professionalisation, 1780–1890

MANCHESTER 1824
Manchester University Press

SOCIAL HISTORIES OF MEDICINE

Series editors: *David Cantor and Keir Waddington*

Social Histories of Medicine is concerned with all aspects of health, illness and medicine, from prehistory to the present, in every part of the world. The series covers the circumstances that promote health or illness, the ways in which people experience and explain such conditions, and what, practically, they do about them. Practitioners of all approaches to health and healing come within its scope, as do their ideas, beliefs, and practices, and the social, economic and cultural contexts in which they operate. Methodologically, the series welcomes relevant studies in social, economic, cultural, and intellectual history, as well as approaches derived from other disciplines in the arts, sciences, social sciences and humanities. The series is a collaboration between Manchester University Press and the Society for the Social History of Medicine.

Previously published

The metamorphosis of autism: A history of child development in Britain *Bonnie Evans*

Payment and philanthropy in British healthcare, 1918–48 *George Campbell Gosling*

The politics of vaccination: A global history *Edited by Christine Holmberg, Stuart Blume and Paul Greenough*

Leprosy and colonialism: Suriname under Dutch rule, 1750–1950 *Stephen Snelders*

Medical misadventure in an age of professionalisation, 1780–1890

Alannah Tomkins

Manchester University Press

Published by Manchester University Press
Altrincham Street, Manchester M1 7JA

www.manchesteruniversitypress.co.uk

British Library Cataloguing-in-Publication Data
A catalogue record for this book is available from the British Library

Library of Congress Cataloging-in-Publication Data applied for

ISBN 978 1 5261 1607 9 hardback

First published 2017

Typeset in 11 on 12 pt Arno Pro Regular
by Toppan Best-set Premedia Limited
Printed in Great Britain
By Lightning Source

For Cliff and Joyce, Meg and Tommy

Contents

Figures

Tables

Acknowledgements

A book written over the course of a decade incurs a lot of debts, not least among colleagues in libraries and archives. In particular I want to thank staff at the Royal Medical Benevolent Fund who made the charity's records available to me, and Bobbie Judd at the St Andrew's Healthcare archives for the tea and biscuits, among other things. Similarly, staff at county and city archives produced volume after volume of asylum records, including those in Berkshire, Birmingham, the Borthwick Institute, Cheshire, Derbyshire, Devon, Gloucestershire, Leicestershire and Rutland, Lincolnshire, Nottinghamshire, Staffordshire, Warwickshire, and Worcestershire. Staff at the National Archive helped me to understand the idiosyncrasies of the bankruptcy and Chancery papers, while staff at the British Library assisted me with images. I was supported in researching Chapters 4 and 5 by two MRes students, namely Harriet Wallis and Jennie Hubbard, who identified their own research areas but also helped me to flesh out my own. Colleagues at Keele have listened to some rather gruesome papers under the heading of 'research in progress' and offered critical friendship. Chris Adams generously shared his research on the Hoyle family of Lincolnshire, while David Helm must be credited with tracking down patient information for Barnwood House: without his research I would not have been able to include a private licensed house among my consideration of medical asylum patients. Heartfelt thanks also go to Hilary Ingram, Marie-Andree Jacob, Steve King, Lisetta Lovett, Michael Myers, and Keir Waddington who commented on drafts of chapters.

The most significant research assistance I have received in the last ten years has come from my mother. Molly Tomkins has been tireless in tracking down references, reading drafts, visiting archives, and generally agreeing to investigate any new avenues of research that cropped up over the decade. Without her commitment this book would still have been written, but it would have taken me much longer. Thanks to her for unfailing enthusiasm and energetic assistance.

Introduction

Victorian medical men could suffer numerous setbacks on their individual paths to professionalisation, and Thomas Elkanah Hoyle's career offers a telling exemplar. Hoyle was the son of a surgeon and the brother of another in his native Lincolnshire, was registered with the General Medical Council (GMC) in 1859, and married the following year.[1] He worked as a public vaccinator and poor-law district medical officer up to 1864 and died at a rather young but respectable age of fifty-nine.[2] Taken as a potted biography, this represents the outline of a modest but solid career. It is contradicted, however, by reference to alternative sources for a history of a medical professional, namely the local press and the records of the Lincolnshire County Lunatic Asylum. Hoyle's career was anything but secure. He had bought into his father's practice, but was effectively bankrupted by his parent in 1862.[3] His marriage broke down in the same year following threats of violence to his wife, and this appeared to inaugurate a pattern of aggressive behaviour.[4] Ultimately, in 1873 after an affray at an inn, he was admitted to the Lincolnshire Asylum where the case notes amplify his history of *de facto* alcoholism and sense of persecution. At the heart of his distress was a sense of infringement on his medical identity. He accused unnamed 'detectives' of having stolen copies of *The Lancet* from his railway luggage, and of 'talking about him in the town to injure his character'.[5]

Hoyle offers a concentrated vignette of 'medical misadventure' in the sense it is construed here. Men might benefit from all of the traditional markers of professional success, including inheritance of an established practice and GMC recognition, plus attributes of Victorian middle-class masculinity including a respectable marriage, and still have fallen short. Admittedly Hoyle was probably disadvantaged or disturbed by his father's example – Hoyle senior was also a practitioner and had faked his own abduction and murder in 1845 – but the two different accounts of his life illustrate the positive ways that even problematic medical careers might have been read in the past.[6] A better understanding of the professionalising process in medicine requires attention to halting and truncated careers.

This book addresses a range of the financial, professional, and personal challenges that faced and sometimes defeated the aspiring medical men of England and Wales. Spanning the decades 1780–1890, approximately from the publication of the first medical directory in 1779 to the second Medical Registration Act in 1886, it considers both their careers in England and Wales, and in the Indian Medical Service.[7] These years saw the practitioners of orthodox medicine shift from a self-defined group loosely or barely represented by London Colleges and Companies to a self-conscious profession asserted and recognised by specialist publications, collective organisations, regulated training, public service, and the law. Duty to observe the boundaries for membership of the group, particularly in respect to tests of competence, was balanced by recognition of the value of autonomy over working practices and investment of public trust. Consequently, this era was an age of economic opportunity and social aspiration for professional men across different medical specialities. Yet opportunity was no guarantee of upward social mobility for all who sought it in a highly crowded market, and fear of failure was sometimes the prelude to actual failure. Jeanne Peterson wrote of medicine nearly forty years ago that 'Shared occupational status meant shared problems and joint efforts'; but not all problems were shared, and not all careers were transformed in positive ways.[8] Therefore, unlike other histories of the profession, what follows is a sustained consideration of the career turbulence, disappointment, and curtailment that beset some men who were not able to secure full advantage from professionalising trends.

Practitioners were not unique among the professions more broadly in risking or suffering forms of failure. All of the same negative phenomena might beset representatives of the other learned professions, or men pursuing aspiring occupations which were moving towards professional status during the nineteenth century. Lawyers, for example, were much more likely than doctors to be declared bankrupt, and bankers struggled in their moves towards a 'newly confident ideal of professional morality'.[9] Yet medical men experienced these forms of failure in some professionally specific ways. In particular the twin pressures of professionalisation and a persistent and highly competitive medical market for medicines and expertise had profound consequences for specifically medical forms of masculinity.

Similarly, Scottish, Irish, continental European, and extra-European practitioners were not immune to failure either. The importance of Scotland and Ireland in supplying men to the British medical profession is very well established, so the decision to concentrate on England and Wales may look misplaced. What is more, some notably lurid medical crimes were played out in the wider British context and made a strong negative impression on public perceptions of the profession as a whole.[10] Nonetheless, the legal and structural differences distinguishing medical careers lived out beyond England and Wales imposed their own methodological constraints, such as their different legal systems and contrasting poor laws.[11] Therefore, Irish and Scottish practitioners do feature here but only where their turbulent careers were played out in England and Wales, or (in the case of Chapter 2) among English and Welsh colleagues in India.

The study of medical 'failure' within these parameters construes failure as central to the professionalisation process. Medical professionalisation was not exceptional in any respect: failure is the rule in any social project but, as in other spheres of inquiry, it has only been considered in passing in the history of medicine as a temporary staging post on the route to success. Failure needs to be reconceived 'as itself serving to direct and shape the process of governance', in this case the imposition of new occupational norms.[12] Only by appreciating the ubiquity and experiential features of failure can we recognise the specific functions it performed.

Professionalisation, reform, and legitimation

Medical professionalisation in this period went hand in hand with drives for reform.[13] Most formally trained practitioners were agreed that a priority for the reform agenda was the eradication of quackery; however, beyond this goal reform meant different things to different parts of the sector in different decades. Debate arose in part because orthodox practitioners could not agree on what quackery comprised, but consensus also foundered on the best strategy for legitimating medical authority. Recommendations for reform action from within cited variously occupational representation, education, and raising professional status, all of which were plausibly susceptible to statutory definition. Countervailing pressures from without held that only market deregulation and eradication of privilege could hope to set the seal on professional power.[14]

Medical journals were at the forefront of disseminating calls for reform. For Thomas Wakley and *The Lancet*, or at least *The Lancet* of the second quarter of the nineteenth century, reform entailed the formation of a self-disciplined meritocracy and the eradication of occupational advantage based on wealth and nepotism.[15] Other periodicals tended to be more placatory, but the absence of a homogeneous tone was not necessarily a significant problem for medical journalism *per se*; practitioners going into print at any angle of the reform debate found 'a means of signalling their occupational ascendancy and establishing their legitimacy as professionals'.[16] Together, the journals supplied medical men with a combination of updated medical knowledge and information about the options for reform, while their existence reassured the lay public of the norms and competencies of orthodox medical practice.[17]

Regulation of medical education lay at the heart of the reform project. Reformers wanted to take the intelligence of aspiring practitioners and, with the right educational structures, fashion their scientific medical expertise and examine them in rigorous ways. Awkwardly, these intentions had to map onto a shifting notion of where expertise lay. Educative primacy was shifting in the period 1750 to 1825 from ancient texts to dissection, observation, and clinical experience, preferably by walking the wards in a teaching hospital.[18] Medical education became the subject of lay scrutiny in a Parliamentary inquiry of 1834 and one anticipated advantage of public interest, it was hoped, would be a decline in justified accusations of malpractice. Yet the timing was wrong for the fulfilment of any such hopes; from the 1830s onwards, the pressures of service introduced by the New Poor Law meant that rank and file practitioners struggling with individual pride, heroic workloads, and structural disadvantage ran up against charges of neglect and consequent dismissal from public office as a matter of routine.[19]

Moves towards professional oversight of medical education went hand in hand with an enhanced reputation for medical science, where each benefited from the other. By the mid nineteenth century, Michael Brown argues that 'medical men had come to think of themselves as scientific professionals'.[20] While the status of science itself was not assured, the symbiotic relationship between intellectual command and specialised inquiry was theoretically advantageous.[21]

In addition to purely occupational reform, some recognised the necessity for practical *social* legitimation: 'professional authority, however defined, rests on more than professional assertion ... it requires some measure of cultural acceptance as well'.[22] A disinterested personal investment in the advance of knowledge and public service, quite aside from pecuniary gain, was an essential component of any reformist vision that looked beyond the confines of medicine to wider public support. Honourable service in the best interest of patients was tendered in exchange for interpersonal trust and professional privilege in law.[23] Uncomfortably, as medical aspirations encompassed a fully professional identity that was beyond reproach, men were caught up in the requirement to assert irreproachability while simultaneously striving to deserve the label.[24] The rhetoric of disinterest came to have a strong hold on the profession by the end of the period, but it is more questionable whether the majority of practitioners felt secure in their professional identity by the same date. Also, the rhetoric had an uncertain impact on day-to-day practice, both in relations with poorer patients and in instances of professional rivalry. Self-sacrifice and treating the poor without charge was all very well in theory, but there was the strong temptation to give less regard to pauper patients, particularly in the promotion of collective rather than individual professional gains. Anatomy Inspector George Cursham, for example, reproached the moral punctiliousness of a house surgeon in Manchester who made sure that poor patients were aware of their right to avoid dissection; he thought this conduct unbecoming to a medical professional.[25] In this instance, then, professionalism was unequivocally allied with interest and with concealment of the provisions of law.

Yet medical status was not wholly or necessarily tied to medical ideologies and behaviours around vested interest or the cultivation of disinterest. Historiographical perceptions of medical status have fluctuated instead around expertise and statutory recognition. Early works saw professional authority as an extension of specialisation and scientific advance, which Foucault refined as a translation of knowledge into overweening power.[26] Latterly, historians have stressed instead provisionality, uncertainty, and discontinuous advance. Ian Inkster has argued that medical men had no established social status up to 1850, but Michael Brown sees the second decade of the nineteenth century as formative.[27] The increasing role for medical witnesses in insanity trials would seem to locate the 1830s as critical in cementing practitioners' legal status.[28] Even so, Roberts identifies the 1858 Medical Registration Act and the thirty years that followed as pivotal to the increase in lay respect for and deference to medical authority. He attributes this to three developments, namely the capacity of the GMC to contain intra-professional dispute, a perception from outside medicine of potential scientific advances to come, and a rebalancing of professional attributes to acknowledge the value of patient interpretation.[29] This book confirms the importance of the third quarter of the nineteenth century, and particularly the 1860s, in fostering lay respect, but also points to additional background cultural trends in perceptions of medical practitioners as integral to changing perceptions; 'the process by which the medical men achieved this respect encompassed so much more than medicine', and certainly more than successful medical practice.[30] Respect was manifested in different ways specific to the locality or decade, and not just on the plausibility of claims to authority but on the substantial investment of a non-medical public in medical claims of social status.

By the late 1880s, the concept of the professional medical man had acquired numerous potential attributes. These did not all necessarily have to be represented in one man, but individuals needed to display a suitable range to qualify. Criteria included education and qualification by recognised bodies, membership of learned or professional societies, holding public office, subscription to dedicated journals, and espousing values indicative of participation in a collective community of doctors. This concept was forged in the face of considerable internal difficulty and dissent, generated by a dilemma at the heart of medical practice. Yet disinterested professional judgement was jeopardised on a daily basis by the need to make a viable living.

Markets, ethics, and professional honour

To appreciate the intensity of this dilemma, it is important to consider the dimensions of the medical marketplace.[31] At the end of the eighteenth century, this market comprised a mixed bag of orthodox practitioners, irregulars who did not make their whole living from medicine, quacks, and sellers of patent medicines. Without falling into the error of thinking that all participants in the marketplace were ideologically alike, it is necessary to reflect on the impact of orthodox practitioners' dependence on fee income. To date, the impact of this dependence has been construed fairly generally or within a tight time-frame, and with the emphasis on prosperity.[32] Mary Fissell has argued that around the late eighteenth century there was a sense that something valuable had been lost to professional medicine, in that commercialisation had undermined medical manners.[33] More recently, Michael Brown has taken issue with the dominance of marketplace narratives and has offered instead a picture of a co-operative, sociable profession, where attitudes only hardened in the second quarter of the nineteenth century.[34] This book establishes that there was certainly a new urgency to intra-professional relations and economic motivations by the 1830s, and that marketplace relations were not wholly superseded by 'professionalisation' at any point in the nineteenth century. What is more, visions of the market have been one-sided and culturally narrow; we can understand much more about failure to make money, about other forms of failure, and about the experience of fear in advance of such failures.[35]

Market concerns persisted because, throughout the period 1780–1890, medical integrity was founded on a paradox: it was a necessity for practitioner–patient relations that clients' best interests (and not money) were presented as the prime motivator for medical men. Norms of professional demeanour developed in such a way as to promote prestige for medical altruism but undermine receipts of hard cash. Actions expressive of largesse, that restrained practitioners from demanding payment from impoverished patients for example, or which prompted them to offer their services *gratis* to a local institution, were widely adopted.[36] As Anne Digby has shown, institutional affiliation conferred status while establishing a man's credentials as a trusted practitioner and a selfless citizen. It also advantaged men who were intent on keeping their rivals out of the public eye.[37] At the same time, money patently remained essential and of abiding interest to men who were, among other things, self-employed entrepreneurs.[38] What changed across the period was the increasing gentlemanly imperative to suppress any allusion to medical incomes beyond guarded occupational circles. Separation from a physical shop counter became important for self-perception, and doctors were not alone among medically related fields in this attempt to shed 'a commercial rather than a professional morality'.[39] However, by 1890, most practitioners remained unsalaried or regarded any paid position as a channel for private practice rather than a sole professional outlet. Payment by fees required extension of credit and dignified trust in clients, which inevitably meant short-term cash-flow problems and entrenched difficulties in reclaiming outstanding debts.[40] At the same time, any public expression of concern about fee income became repugnant, and remained so into the twentieth century.[41]

Other sorts of conflict might be used to disguise fee competition. Medical disagreements about therapeutic utility were notionally acceptable or even a necessity when multiple consultations were the right of the patient.[42] Practitioners theoretically acknowledged the requirement for discretion over arguments about honourable practice and etiquette, but in reality discretion only lasted until the individuals concerned decided that public exposure was unavoidable or at any rate in their interests. Disagreement typically generated responses of disquiet and generalised calls for restraint. *The Lancet* suggested a labour-intensive model for medical tribunals to resolve points of etiquette, with little effect.[43] Avoidance of the implications of quarrels between practitioners, and their wider significance for the profession, stretched well beyond 1890.[44] Protecting and augmenting one's private patient list was certainly a constant throughout the period covered here.

Medical reformers recognised the social disadvantage of public enmity; an early president of the Provincial Medical and Surgical Association confessed a hope that 'jealousy and hatred, that unseemly speck and blemish, shall [be] washed from the fair face of our humane and charitable profession'.[45] Public unanimity and expressions of personal disinterest became explicit goals for medical practitioners, and the pressure to maintain appearances intensified from the mid nineteenth century. From 1858, the GMC was formally charged with reprimanding or striking off practitioners found guilty of attracting patients, and this included advertising, canvassing, and deprecation of colleagues.[46] The distinction between advertisements and 'public announcements' was a subtle one, and collective self-policing of sly promotional agendas became increasingly vocal.[47] Yet these intentions were drastically at odds with the broader occupational and social context: 'The Victorian bourgeois world was highly competitive.'[48] Consequently, most if not all organs of medical journalism were complicit in forms of personal or group advancement; alluding to the *British Medical Journal*, for example, James Mussell has concluded that 'all of its textual spaces belied the myth that professionals did not advertise.'[49]

From the patients' perspective, there was a long history to suspicions that medical practitioners were periodically guilty of avarice or self-advancement. Hard evidence is anecdotal and chronologically dispersed, as much evident from attempts by doctors to counter these impressions as from clear-cut cases of profiteering.[50] It was hardly surprising, though, if practitioners' concerted drive to present themselves as professionally disinterested accelerated patient expectations. It is difficult to avoid the conclusion that medical men unwittingly set themselves entirely unachievable standards in this respect that might provide a goal which could never decisively be reached. Throughout the chapters that follow, medical ideals on marketplace behaviour and other matters are often seen to be untenable.

The paradox of 'interest' in promoting or undercutting medical professional and social legitimacy underlay the emergence of medical ethics, and so provided an additional source of personal conflict for practitioners.[51] Traditional sociological literature about the professions confirms that the ethical practitioner–client relationship will be built on a form of trust absent from the relationship between buyer and seller. Since the professional enjoys the advantages of knowledge and skill, which the client is not competent to judge on the grounds of equal knowledge and skill, the latter is vulnerable to exploitation. Internally enforced integrity minimises this risk and enhances professional trust.[52] Early nineteenth-century medicine did not follow the 'internal integrity' model very closely. Historians have recently been debating whether medical ethics were largely or wholly viewed as coterminous with professional duties, and chief among these duties were the obligations owed to other professionals.[53] The ethic of collegiality over-rode ethical duties to patients.[54] This book analyses the fates of practitioners who struggled to manage their collegial duties in relation to their own and their patients' best interests. The strain of surviving as 'competitive entrepreneurs who also shared remarkably strong communal loyalties', or at least aspired to share them, was acute.[55]

Such loyalty, in the form of occupational solidarity, was most confidently expressed in opposition to competition from irregular practice, and while the historiographical focus on opposition to quackery has rested on the period up to 1858 it continued to supply a regular presence in medical journalism throughout the 1860s. As the threat of quackery receded it was supplanted by the prospect of competing with female practitioners. Clare Brock has pointed to the complicated response of medical commentators to university training for women as indicative of a lack of security in the masculine profession.[56] Female practitioners represented on one level the unwelcome introduction of a new sort of non-traditional (if not entirely 'irregular') competitor for medical work that threatened male incomes, but vocal opposition to female students, activists, and qualified practitioners risked a different sort of social detriment. Men who were too keen to denigrate female medical aspirations risked displaying a passionate and public form of self-interest that was both ungentlemanly and increasingly seen as unprofessional. The protectionism of practitioners was nothing new, but the scope for its expression or defence was narrowing across the final quarter of the nineteenth century.[57]

By the 1880s, practitioners' occupational competence and personal integrity were inseparable, the former fostered by education and regulated by statute, with policing devolved to the GMC, and the latter by the gentlemanly etiquette and self-command required of a self-regulating profession from within and without.[58] The result was a notionally exacting prescription for medical behaviour that demanded men be not only skilled but also friends to their patients and united with colleagues.[59] In defending his brother Joseph's posthumous reputation, Thorold Rogers may well have overstated his case, but he claimed that the professional doctor was held to higher standards than other men, eschewing evident rivalry with colleagues and being required to be wholly open on matters of treatment; 'It is no easy matter to win position and fortune in a calling which is regulated by the strictest rules of professional honour.'[60] Rogers was tacitly recognising the enhanced tensions between the still-active medical marketplace and the multiple emergent yardsticks of professional conduct.

Ironically, no amount of punctilious politeness towards fellow medical people and apparently open-handed disinterest towards patients *could* have insulated the profession from continued external suspicions of unethical conduct and mercenary motives, but in any event such perfection was not forthcoming.[61] Ongoing expression of divergent sentiments, on a spectrum from disquiet at professional differences to choked fury at professional trespasses, generated satirical, angry, or fearful lay responses. Divisions in the profession over the Contagious Diseases Acts, for instance, inspired outrage in the repeal campaign towards medical supporters of the Acts.[62] What was more, an impression of smooth public unanimity risked a different sort of reproach, in the form of strident criticism for professional arrogance as seen for example in the searing anger expressed in Frances Power Cobbe's 'The Medical Profession and It's Morality' in 1881.[63] The fraught relationship between medical finances and ethical behaviours proved impossible to navigate for some if not most men, and created disastrous conflicts for a minority. The external pressures to expunge open competition with colleagues, in addition to only partial success, led unsurprisingly to the development of means for covert competition between practitioners. Covertly competitive behaviours were a feature of both 'the hard pressed rank-and-file' and the more established members of the profession.[64] They also induced an additional stress, fear of exposure, at the same time that the imperatives of middle-class masculinity sought to govern the range of men's acceptable expressions.

Manliness and medical masculinity

The same decades that saw the 'rise' of the medical profession also witnessed an intense focus on what it was to be appropriately masculine. Prominent ideas about stereotypical or hegemonic manliness from the late Georgian to the late Victorian periods altered substantially and with surprising speed. In the eighteenth century, masculinity had been generated or undermined by politeness and social performance. In the late century this was inflected by the notions of sensibility, whereby easy verbal sociability was increasingly modulated by displays of sympathetic feeling.[65] The early nineteenth century saw masculinity become more strongly associated with privacy than sociability. The inherent superficiality of politeness was supplanted by a serious and purposeful manliness, characterised by personal integrity and expressed by direct, succinct or even taciturn interaction with peers.[66] In turn this required an altered attitude to domestic life; 'Men's stance towards the home was influenced not only by the particular web of relationships they found themselves in, but by their sense of what was right and proper for themselves as men.'[67] Experience of family was varied, as individual men either extolled homeliness or were defeated by its demands, but in either case the relationship with the domestic was key and potentially disciplinary.[68] In the longer term, though, the *rejection* of home became definitional. In the second half of the nineteenth century, muscular Christianity was purveyed by British public schools and the school story giving rise to even secular athleticism; 'a neo-Spartan ideal of masculinity was diffused throughout the English-speaking world'.[69] By the end of the period the rhetorical emphasis had shifted to distance from home, whereby 'images of frontier manliness were fed back into the metropolis' to foster militarism, stoicism, and discipline among British boys and men.[70]

Practitioners of medicine either aspired, or emphatically belonged, to the middling sort and later the middle class throughout the late eighteenth and the nineteenth centuries. The evolution of medical masculinity across the period was therefore dependent on the consolidation of particular types of authority, some of which derived from middle-class householder or gentlemanly status – 'good practitioners must "feel and act as gentlemen"' – but where others were specifically medical in tone.[71] In terms of middle-class norms, John Tosh and others have argued for the centrality of the domestic sphere and an ideological allegiance to the values of domesticity for middle-class, mid-Victorian manliness. This gave precedence to marriage, not as a right but as a goal to struggle towards; to 'form a household, to exercise authority over dependents, and to shoulder the responsibility of maintaining and protecting them – these things set the seal on a man's gender identity'.[72] The production or recruitment of dependents in the form of children and servants extended the remit of his control. Therefore, financial stability and (after marriage) sexual continence were as much a part of the medical persona as they were that of other middle-class professionals.

The additional, personal qualities which were essential to the successful medical man as a gentleman went beyond the external enactment of propriety and demanded an equal commitment to appropriate internal states.[73] These included the mindset born of 'breeding, and a cultured education'.[74] This looked beyond the merely masculine mind to foster a properly manly mind, comprising an intellectual power that was presented as beyond the reach of most adult men. These ideas crystallised in the 1880s in the social-Darwinist writings of Edward Cope, Karl Pearson, and George Romanes among others: as Boddice explains 'The manly mind was … not simply a scientific reinforcement of the opposition between the sexes, but an expression of extreme exceptionalism, in which only a small coterie of select men were fitted by natural law to lead, invent, philosophise, judge, and generally be at the vanguard of progress. All of society fell in behind the gentleman.'[75] By the end of the period, the pressure was decisively on professional and medical men to occupy this elite social and intellectual space, as well as to fulfil the demands of middle-class masculinity more broadly.

Further medical inflections on masculine status derived from a shared experience of training, work-life identification, and pursuit of occupational fulfilment. This entailed not just collective participation but also ideological commitment and an appropriate expression of ambition – energetic but honest. One physician thought medical men were perhaps best placed to secure 'the attainable portion of the Divine Idea', in preference even to clergymen, arising from doctors' combination of duty and practical benevolence.[76] Medically specific knowledge, skill, and vocational fervour were adjuncts to both the public and domestic persona, since a medical identity entailed being always on duty, not being a slave to work but wholly fulfilled by it.[77] This meant that a practitioner's family was dependent on him for physical health in addition to safety and financial security, and that the public had a right to expect medical assistance to be proffered in public emergencies. In the ongoing overlap between medical work and the practitioner's own home, there was a less rigid boundary observed between work and domestic spaces than was (notionally at least) emerging for other trading and professional people, because home and surgery typically occupied the same premises.[78] What was more, other people's homes comprised doctors' occupational contexts and 'their destination was perhaps the most unprofessional and gendered of all spaces: the bedroom.'[79] Did this complex relationship with the domestic damage practitioners' ability to become fully engaged with mainstream bourgeois culture?[80] Medical men might feel that it did, even where lay people were prepared to excuse them for domestic evidence of professional activity, and masculinity in other professions like education may also have suffered from an 'inherently critical relation to conventional domestic arrangements'.[81] At the same time there was a risk that practitioners would fail to find the succour at home that was available to other middle-class men because they could not view home as a refuge from professional demands.[82] Participation in both private tragedies and famous cases took their toll on practitioners' peace of mind.[83]

The later Victorian period brought additional challenges. Muscular Christianity's implied disparagement of the feminine conflicted with the medical role as carer. Attentive, almost doting, concern was idealised for practitioners in cultural formats, most obviously perhaps in the painting 'The Doctor' by Luke Fildes, which significantly was first exhibited in 1891. Here the doctor waits anxiously and almost wistfully at the bedside of a child patient, where otherwise the child's mother might sit; the mother is relegated to the background.[84] Such professional tenderness and stillness was essentially irreconcilable with the physical action and emotional stoicism associated with *fin-de-siecle* manliness.

Just as early historians of masculinity queried the deforming force of stereotypes and ideals, we can by extension consider the potentially deforming nature of medical professional manliness.[85] The same process of estrangement from complex individual identities placed discernible and sometimes unbearable pressures on men, meaning that they could not sustain the required image either in their own eyes or according to external markers. This was the price paid for forging an authoritative professional identity by the late Victorian period, and some men fell short, although the visibility of their shortcomings depended quite heavily on the willingness of the lay public to acknowledge them.

Falling short

The combined forces of professionalisation and the evolution of manly identities were enormously challenging, and opened up new possibilities for failure. Recognition of 'failure' across the late eighteenth and nineteenth centuries arguably shifted from perfunctory and occasionally comic to complex and serious. In the Victorian period, 'Failure was, perhaps unsurprisingly, a significant preoccupation of an age fascinated with success.'[86] Financial failure was treated most prominently, but the era was highly attentive to different forms of failure in all walks of life and all stages of a career.[87] In medicine, the combined imperatives of professionalisation, the market, and medical masculinity together constructed a mutable but stringent ideal, which was the object of many but the attainment of rather fewer. Medical careers and personal lives rarely ran so smoothly as to permit a steady acquisition of multiple positive attributes without delay or interruption. Students might fall at the first clear hurdle, namely by failing their examinations or falling prey to examination stress. Once secure in their qualifications they might struggle to obtain a remunerated post. The strains of juggling private practice, public responsibility, domestic solvency, and personal ambition could and did wreak havoc on individual men's physical and mental health, and prompted hundreds of medical suicides.[88] The evolution of a professional ideal ensured the emergence of its antithetical counterpart, giving rise to the anxious, overworked, disappointed or fearful practitioner, who could not consistently withstand the pressures imposed by their professional and personal goals.

Failure could in theory be given a positive cast, in the close ideological proximity between striving, failing, and potential greatness; as influential author John Ruskin put it, 'no great man ever stops working till he has reached his point of failure'.[89] Defeat could be faced bravely, and so supply an opportunity to augment the masculine identity rather than undermine it.[90] Browning's 'aesthetic of failure' found supportive echoes in Victorian biography which placed 'emphasis on the quiet heroism and courage present in perseverance in the face of failure'.[91] But Victorian biography tended to be written posthumously, inevitably some time after shortcomings are realised. It was much more difficult to secure such dispassionate sympathy in the immediate aftermath of crushed hopes, self-reproach or public exposure. Localised expressions of support can be inferred in the case of men who suffered financial disaster, where their recovery and return to practice can be proven, and were palpable in the face of accusations of serious sexual crime. Other sins took longer to mitigate or might never be redeemed.[92]

Naturally, failure and success were never fixed entities, and the attributes of the professionalising process meant that the criteria for either state were constantly shifting. The spectrum of difficulty encompassed financial, occupational, personal, and legal grounds, and each variety of misfortune might be experienced as either mild or acute, short-lived or permanent. At the same time, the moral basis for blame over failure was calibrated by context: an innocent mistake could be exonerated where a wilful error was reproached, but the definition of either depended very heavily on the construction of the failing by family members, peers, and lay observers, and from one decade to the next. Finally, the extent to which a person fell short was partially measured by their personality and character in advance of the fall. In this way, both self-conception and public reputation contributed to the perceived severity of failure. Historical analyses of failure *versus* success are therefore hedged about with qualification and can only be pursued using some fairly crude markers. The best that can be said of those markers is that they strive for internal consistency of application over relatively short periods.

Historians of medicine have paid only very modest attention to 'acknowledgement of failure'.[93] Historians began by considering the difficulties of establishing an income with the related threat of financial failure.[94] Treatments of other forms of failure were piecemeal, suggestive of closure rather than opening up a new field of inquiry.[95] Even Brown, who problematises traditional marketplace readings of the social history of medicine, highlights failure in the eighteenth century but does not extend the possibility forward into the nineteenth. He observes that 'For every fabulously wealthy practitioner ... there were literally hundreds of others who either eked out a meagre existence, or fell by the wayside.'[96] What of these hundreds of men and, more importantly, what of their generational successors?

Medical men fell short of expectations inadvertently or intentionally, in private or exposed to public criticism. The most emphatic (but not necessarily the most personally damaging) public disappointment was probably removal from the *Register* of the General Medical Council after its first publication in 1859. The GMC adjudicated on 160 professional conduct cases up to 1890, but commentators have agreed that this is a poor indicator of 'medical sin'.[97] Financial considerations and/or fear of losing credibility have inhibited the Council from drawing all potential cases into its remit.[98] Also, the nineteenth-century cases were not always framed to undermine a medical identity decisively. Statutory misconduct around false certification (of births and deaths, qualifications, vaccination or for the purposes of elementary education) could be dismissed as accidental or as technical infringements that were not permanently discrediting.[99] Finally, deregistration was not necessarily irrevocable as re-registration applications were heard favourably from the 1870s.[100] Therefore, those men who were selected for investigation and were struck off functioned as a small subset of 'bad apples', removed to demonstrate the functioning of the system and provide reassurance about the competence and rectitude of practitioners remaining on the list.

The most common form of public inadequacy, where specifically *medical* reproach was only implied rather than explicit, was that of financial failure in the form of either insolvency or bankruptcy. Far more medical men were caught up in one of these processes than in any of the other forms of career turbulence considered here. Both procedures were a matter of public record, advertised nationally in the *London Gazette* and then excerpted for the provincial press. Medical bankrupts and insolvents may be found throughout the period 1780 to 1890, but in much greater numbers after 1820. As a consequence, Chapter 1 considers the full span of years but the case studies of individual men are concentrated within 1805–55.

Personal perceptions of falling short, which undercut the medical masculine identity beyond that of financial provider, are more difficult to uncover. Given the necessity to be wholly fulfilled by one's career, it seemed important to consider thwarted ambition; men who aimed high patently did not always secure the illustrious professional paths they sought. Expressions of regret, disappointment, frustration, or depression may be found across the period and across occupational labels and specialisms, but here they have been gathered specifically from men whose careers took them overseas in the service of the East India Company. Extensive global travel supplied an obvious and inevitable career interruption to men who were born and trained in Britain, but also seemed liable, at first glance, to attract men whose opportunities had been narrowed or evaporated elsewhere. An older historiography frequently repeated the claim, for example, that military or naval service recruited the less well-qualified practitioners.[101] While this was often an unjustified slur, it does suggest a concomitant experience on the part of medical men, that they were reluctant or regretful that their skills might not secure them a better or more lucrative practice. Army and navy doctors, though, have enjoyed a recent resurgence of interest, while literature on the Indian Medical Service is yet to be substantially updated.[102] Therefore Chapter 2 addresses medical service in India from 1780, but stops short in 1858 owing to structural alterations to governance, recruitment, and the terms of service after that date; additionally, the surviving narrative sources for medical men compel closest attention to private perception of disappointment in the decades 1810–40.

Falling short in public, in terms of gentlemanly demeanour or professional competence that did not necessarily generate GMC action, is more difficult to locate. Public censure without formal criminal prosecution was a common experience of alleged failing, and for purposes of this research it was most often visible in the verdicts of Victorian coroners' courts and the unofficial riders given to verdicts by indignant juries. In this way, many more men were caught up in public reproach as a consequence of their work for Poor Law Unions than were ever investigated by professional or lay searches for justice.[103] Therefore the chronology observed in Chapter 3 of necessity concentrates in the years after 1834 and the Poor Law Reform Act.

Men who chose to fall short in one area in order to maintain their status in others were explicitly or unintentionally testing the boundaries of viable medical identities and behaviours in order to serve their own best interests. Personal preference and a sense of asserting the power of the group might even align in some instances: it has been suggested by Milligan that a rising phenomenon of medical opium addicts in the late nineteenth century can be traced to a collective desire to assert authority over the drug, and addiction enjoyed the advantage of privacy in both its practice and treatment.[104] At the other end of the spectrum of exposure, the most scandalous and public were those cases where practitioners were prosecuted for murder. A handful of cases have been repeatedly surveyed in both historical and popular literature, with Palmer the Rugeley poisoner leading the way towards Dr Crippen in the early twentieth century.[105] Yet these cases have provided a narrative of lurid exceptionalism on the part of doctors, when in fact they should rather be seen as part of a continuum of violence emanating from the legitimated bodily invasions of medical practice.[106] By consulting less infamous cases of medical prosecution for both murder and serious sexual assault, all of which happen to fall after 1840, Chapter 4 uncovers unexpected potential in allegations of wrong-doing, both for shaping the medical profession and responses to it from without.

From a more domestic and personal perspective, individuals' masculinity was challenged by barriers to householder and breadwinner status, particularly in the form of chronic illness: doctors might be patients too. Most bodily illness among middle-class families was managed privately and gives rise to highly dispersed notice in the historical record, but mental illness was different in that it prompted institutional admission of patients across the social spectrum. Medical men were admitted to nineteenth-century asylums in significant numbers, and their case notes reveal an array of detail about the way that professional drivers interacted with poor mental health and underlay the occasional breakdown of doctors' home lives.[107] By these means, Chapter 5 is able to consider the *de facto* surrender of household authority and medical identity inherent in such admissions for the years when asylum case notes survive, starting with sporadic reports in the 1820s through to clumps of evidence in the 1870s and 1880s.

The fear of opprobrium stemming from cash crises and the risk of mental imbalance from any cause were in some cases so severe that they precipitated suicide. Practitioner suicide plainly took place in all decades, so the rise in reporting seen after 1840 is as much a function of newspaper practice as it was an indication of intensifying stress. Even so, Chapter 6 does not present a static picture; the ramifications of doctors killing themselves intensified for both profession and public, such that one specific death in December 1882 became a national scandal.

The chronological parameters for each variety of falling short dealt with in successive chapters will vary, partly in accordance with the availability of the underlying sources but also with changes to the law and the significance with which contemporaries invested each failing. These fluctuations damage the ability to chart change over time in relation to each form of failure. Bankruptcy offers the most consistent and lengthy coverage, but here changes in the law render a declaration in 1780 very different to its equivalent in 1890. Topics are typically considered in most detail from 1840 onwards. Collectively, however, the overlapping chronologies at work in each chapter compile a picture of medical misadventure with key pressure points across the nineteenth century.

An unexpected feature of this picture is the emergence of the 1860s as a notably precarious decade for medical reputations, and this echoes findings elsewhere beyond the historiography of medical professionalisation. Sheila Sullivan has identified this decade as critical for both displays of masculine failure and the consequential development of a professional masculine identity. She deploys evidence from men's writings, including sensation novels, to argue that the phenomenon of sensationalism was profoundly interested in 'the failures of supposedly normal men'.[108] By rendering failures 'spectacular' such writing contributed to the consolidation of a new, authoritative form of masculinity invested in professionalism, 'which is gradually freed from its mooring in specific jobs to become the qualities that allow Englishmen to exercise power from a variety of positions'.[109] Attributes such as financial disinterest, control of the energetic self, and control of women's bodies, are all germane to this realignment. Doctors' presentation and self-presentation in the newspaper press can offer confirmatory narratives for this process, played out in the public and sometimes 'spectacular' coronial and criminal courts.

Methodology, digitised newspapers, and occupational terms

To explore the scope for medical men to 'fall short' of their own or others' expectations, this book conducts a species of cohort study where different, overlapping, cohorts provide a series of foci depending on variant types of career turbulence. The majority of these cohorts have been defined by close analysis of late eighteenth- and nineteenth-century newspapers for doctors suffering financial failure, allegations of wrong-doing, or suicidality. Newspaper reports were hardly neutral in that they were active participants in generating scandal, by flagging unconventional behaviour and so guiding public perceptions of, in this case, practitioners who fell short in public.[110] In turn, lay reporting of medical career turbulence contributed to 'setting the agenda for public and private discussion', and consequently the negotiation of professional status or modification of medical conduct.[111] The account written from such research is therefore partly concerned with cause and effect, but is more attentive to how different types of story functioned. At the same time it heeds Bingham's call for more research on newspapers' construction of gender, in this case specifically medical masculinity.[112]

Recent online publication of digitised newspapers means that it is now possible to search extensive bodies of text for genres of information which would otherwise remain hidden in plain sight.[113] The main database used here is the British Library Newspapers resource hosted by Gale.[114] Newspapers enjoyed diverse constituencies of readers across

England and Wales (including London but very far from confined to it), so a database which included metropolitan and provincial journals appealing to both elite and popular readerships was essential. The titles incorporated in the British Library collection range from the London daily *Morning Post* to the much more popular Sunday publication *Lloyds Weekly Newspaper*, and across numerous county and city periodicals.[115] This database has the advantage of permitting proximity searches, making location of relevant material much more precise. It also helps to mitigate the risk of the (hitherto) distorting predominance of *The Times* in historical enquiry.[116]

Nonetheless, it is important to acknowledge the limitations of the British Library Newspapers database. The most significant generic warning for the purposes of this research was that 'The accuracy of optical character recognition (OCR) software is (quite literally) hit and miss.'[117] Another fundamental characteristic of the database is its instability and partiality. It initially comprised forty-eight or forty-nine newspapers with different spans of extant copies, but has been augmented such that at the time of writing, parts II, III, and IV contain an additional twenty-two, thirty-five, and twenty-two titles respectively.[118] When the bulk of the research for this book was completed, part II was available via institutional university library subscription but parts III and IV were not. This means that a protracted research timetable will give rise to different numbers of crude hits at the start and end of a project, but at no time will the research given in the following chapters include hits from newspapers digitised for the third and fourth phase of the database. Furthermore, all hits will remain fewer on the British Library Newspapers database than they would on the British Newspaper Archive which comprises over seven million newspaper images but which, unlike its counterpart, is not licensed by JISC and so is currently viewable only at the British Library or via subscription.[119]

Identifying relevant men entailed devising a list of occupational labels that might reasonably hope to sweep up all of the practitioners deemed by most contemporaries to be formally qualified, or *en route* to formal qualification, but with the proviso that some labels put health workers beyond the reach of the project. 'Physician' is generally a reliable indicator of professional inclusion. 'Surgeon' is more equivocal given the number of potential occupations which integrated the term. Dental surgeons, veterinary surgeons, and others whose professional trajectories differed significantly from that of formal medicine were excluded. 'Doctor' required similar care; doctors of laws, economics or divinity were disregarded. The most generic term was 'medical', since this prefix was used to identify medical men, officers, gentlemen, students, assistants, and practitioners.

Medical assistants were not always or decisively professionals, but their presence here is thanks in some measure to Arthur Dix. Dix was a surgeon in Stourbridge in Worcestershire who came from a good Northamptonshire family and had been sent to Oundle public school but was admitted to the Worcester asylum in 1863.[120] Asylum personnel ascribed his violence and self-aggrandising ideas to his over-consumption of opiates and spirits: 'he has for some time past taken 36 grains of Morphia in 24 hours. His habits have been active but intemperate and vicious.'[121] Gradual improvement in his symptoms allowed him to be discharged after three and a half months, but he was subsequently admitted to the St Andrew's asylum in Northamptonshire for two months in 1865.[122] Dix's career was substantially disrupted by his poor mental health, such that by 1871 he had removed from Worcestershire to Hampshire, and his occupational designation had been downgraded from surgeon to assistant.[123] In other words, the assistant's role might be taken by aspiring practitioners, but also by qualified men suffering social and occupational decline.

The most obvious omission from this list of occupational labels is 'general practitioner'. The term was in widespread use by the 1840s, and the 1881 census grouped physicians, surgeons, and general practitioners together as emphatic representatives of the 'medical profession' in its occupational tables. Even so, the phrase does not generate many hits in contemporary newspapers and journals.[124] This suggests that, even if the profession was increasingly categorising itself in terms of general practice from within, the reading public and journalists were adhering to more traditional terminology in characterising practitioners from without.

A sequence of structured searches of digitised newspapers for this delimited range of occupational descriptors permits an analysis of career disruptions of one form or another for over 1,500 practitioners across the period 1780–1890, with a clustering of cases after 1840. The information and attitudes displayed in the collective articles naming these men are rarely available from other sources, and certainly would not be retrievable in similar numbers. The patchy survival of coroners' court records, for example, would be unlikely to yield similar returns even if all survivals were to be digitised, and the extant searchable versions of medical journals such as *The Lancet* and the *British Medical Journal* merely reveal laudatory histories of practitioners as great, or at least respectable, men. Therefore, scrutinising the incidence and reception of medical misadventure must hinge on digitised lay newspapers.

Collective biography and resisting 'great men'

This book represents the latest in a short line of medical cohort studies examining the working experiences, private lives, and deaths of practitioners.[125] Unlike these, it is not chiefly concerned with the ways that professionalisation was promoted and consolidated, but instead foregrounds the ways in which it was halted, retarded or undermined. The criteria for falling short helped to define the boundaries of acceptable behaviour and practice every bit as decisively as criteria for achievement. Furthermore, it is not dealing with a discrete group of men (such as students in Scotland, recruitment to the armed services or workhouse medical officers), but with participation in certain types of event, where only some of the evidence for each event can be compiled systematically; in other cases searches might be applied logically but discoveries are more hit and miss.[126]

As such it represents in part an ongoing desire, deep-rooted but a widespread and explicit objective from the 1960s, to move away from the history of medicine as the biography of great men.[127] The 'individual-and-idea, biobibliographic approach' has been stifling in two ways, because it probably conferred undue credit on some men while certainly inhibiting histories of the profession more broadly.[128] Initial attempts to move away from this model found expression in a variety of social history that brought patients to the fore, among other things by charting the fall and rise of the patient narrative. Recognition of the full potential of this trend is still being unpacked; seeing practitioners *as* patients, or as fallible humans who may be subject to the law rather than as expert witnesses, remains exceptional.[129] Development of the field will involve additional sceptical investigation of how doctors emerged at or near the top of the Victorian hierarchy of credibility, and how notions of exemplary lives or medical heroism were generated.[130]

To undertake this work is not to attack medicine as a profession, in the way perhaps exemplified by some sociological writers of the 1960s and 1970s or periodically expressed as part of the general decline of orthodox medical authority across the second half of the twentieth century.[131] The intent here is not so much to question the greatness of some individual men or to undermine medical authority further, as to address the implied applicability of greatness and power inherent in late Victorian conceptions of medical professionals. Not only is it the case that not everyone can be great, it is also evident that inadequacy can take many forms and be expressed variably over a career and life-cycle. This involves more than merely showing the weaknesses of heroes in order to magnify the achievement of their greatness, by subordinating evidence of their humanity to the larger project of lauding their ideas or scientific discoveries.[132] Imperfection functions in multiple ways; the stress here is on a series of recorded frailties that shed direct light on turbulent careers, but that also indirectly focus attention on the way that medical status was, and is, constructed.

This is important to the ongoing historical study of the medical profession because any public stridency or power expressed by the late 1880s was matched by the continuation of private fragility, of medical authority and identity. Historians of masculinity have observed that 'the very process of acquiring social dominance may be subjectively experienced as oppression', and collectively and cumulatively this is what has happened in medicine.[133] Recognition of practitioners past and present as human beings first and medical practitioners second will serve to alleviate the pressures imposed by presumptions of skill and authority from both within and outside the profession. Unrealistic expectations in the twenty-first century are in part a product of nineteenth-century handling of evidence for falling short.

Notes

1 General Medical Council, *The Medical Register* (London: General Medical Council, 1859), p. 151; General Medical Council, *The Medical Register* (London: General Medical Council, 1863), p. 196; National Archives (N.A.) HO 107/624/4; London Metropolitan Archives P90/PAN1, Saint Pancras Parish Church register of marriages item 127, marriage of

18 December 1860; I am indebted to Chris Adams for additional information concerning the wider Hoyle family.

2 'Smallpox', *Lincolnshire Chronicle* 20 November 1863, p. 5 and 'Board of Guardians' 23 April 1864, p. 5; Lincolnshire Archives, HOSP/ST JOHNS/2/13/3 Lincolnshire Lunatic Asylum male case book G-O 1870–82, f. 440 and 440r for Hoyle's death on 14 December 1893.

3 [Untitled] *London Gazette* 7 February 1862, p. 697; 'Nottingham Bankruptcy Court', *Lincolnshire Chronicle* 28 February 1862, p. 7.

4 [Untitled] *Lincolnshire Chronicle* 17 October 1862, p. 5, and 'Borough Police', *ibid.* 26 November 1869, p. 7.

5 Lincolnshire Archives, HOSP/ST JOHNS/2/13/3 Lincolnshire Lunatic Asylum male case book G-O 1870–82, f. 163.

6 [Untitled] *Lincoln, Rutland and Stamford Mercury* 30 May 1845 p. 3, 'The Mystery', *ibid.* 6 June 1845 p. 3 and [untitled] *ibid.* 8 August 1845 p. 3.

7 S.F. Simmons, *The Medical Register for the year 1779* (London: J. Murray, 1779); 49 & 50 Vict c 48.

8 M.J. Peterson, *The Medical Profession in Mid-Victorian London* (Berkeley: California University Press, 1978), p. 2.

9 T.L. Alborn, 'The moral of the failed bank: professional plots in the Victorian money market', *Victorian Studies* 38:2 (1995), pp. 199–226, on p. 220; see Chapter 1 for a comparison of the numbers of late-nineteenth century medical and legal bankrupts.

10 See among others the conviction for murder of Edward Pritchard in Glasgow, 1865, treated briefly in Chapter 4.

11 This distinction is also necessitated by the risk that practitioners' national identity or place of origin might not be revealed alongside revelations of career turbulence; unlike with cohorts of practitioners in the Army Medical Department studied by Ackroyd et al., it is not possible to know country of birth for the majority of men discussed in these chapters. See A. Crowther and M. Dupree, *Medical Lives in the Age of Surgical Revolution* (Cambridge: Cambridge University Press, 2007) and M. Ackroyd, L. Brockliss, M. Moss, K. Retford, and J. Stevenson, *Advancing with the Army. Medicine, the Professions and Social Mobility in the British Isles 1790–1850* (Oxford: Oxford University Press, 2006) for the centrality of Irish and Scottish practitioners to medical professionalisation.

12 J. Malpas and G. Wickham, 'Governance and failure: on the limits of sociology', *Australian and New Zealand Journal of Sociology* 31:1 (1995), pp. 37–50, on p. 43.

13 Professionalisation in medicine is a wide field, but see particularly M. Brown, *Performing Medicine: Medical Culture and Identity in Provincial England, c.1750–c.1850* (Manchester: Manchester University Press, 2011);

Crowther and Dupree, *Medical Lives*; A. Digby, *Making a Medical Living: Doctors and Patients in the English Market for Medicine, 1720–1911* (Cambridge: Cambridge University Press, 1994); I. Loudon, *Medical Care and the General Practitioner, 1750–1850* (Oxford: Oxford University Press, 1986); H. Marland, *Medicine and Society in Wakefield and Huddersfield 1780–1870* (Cambridge: Cambridge University Press, 1987); Peterson, *Medical Profession*.

14 M.J.D. Roberts, 'The politics of professionalisation: MPs, medical men, and the 1858 Medical Act', *Medical History* 53:1 (2009), pp. 37–56, on pp. 39, 44.

15 Wakley was of course not the sole driver of reform, see I. Waddington, 'The development of medical ethics – a sociological analysis', *Medical History* 19:1 (1975), pp. 36–51, nor necessarily a righteous figure, see R. Porter, *Disease, Medicine and Society in England, 1550–1860* (Cambridge: Cambridge University Press, 1995), p. 48; for his dependency on radicalism of the period more broadly, see M. Brown, '"Rats, bats, and barristers": *The Lancet*, libel and the radical stylistics of early nineteenth century medicine', *Social History* 39:2 (2014), pp. 182–209.

16 T.A. Lee, 'The professional journal as a signal of movement to occupational ascendancy and as legitimation of a professional project: the early history of *The Accountant's Magazine* 1897–1951', *Accounting History* 11:1 (2006), pp. 7–40, on p. 10.

17 Lee, 'The professional journal', p. 35.

18 S. Lawrence, *Charitable Knowledge. Hospital Pupils and Practitioners in Eighteenth-century London* (Cambridge: Cambridge University Press, 2002), pp. 337–8; I. Loudon, 'Medical Education and Medical Reform', in V. Nutton and R. Porter (eds), *The History of Medical Education in Britain* (Amsterdam: Rodopi, 1995), pp. 229–49, on p. 231–2.

19 K. Price, *Medical Negligence in Victorian Britain. The Crisis of Care under the English Poor Law, c.1834–1900* (London: Bloomsbury, 2015).

20 Brown, *Performing Medicine*, p. 226.

21 P.C. Kjaergaard, 'Competing allies: professionalisation and the hierarchy of science in Victorian Britain', *Centaurus* 44 (2002), pp. 248–88, on p. 249.

22 Roberts, 'Politics of professionalisation', p. 38.

23 Roberts, 'Politics of professionalisation', p. 40. The informal and unwritten history of practitioners treating the poor freely was superseded in the eighteenth century by the formalised, public honorary positions that medical men took with charitable infirmaries and dispensaries; M. Brown, 'From the Doctors' Club to the Medical Society: Medicine, Gentility, and

Social Space in York, 1780–1840' in M. Hallett and J. Rendell (eds), *Eighteenth-Century York: Culture, Space and Society* (York: Borthwick Society, 2003), pp. 59–69, on p. 63.

24 I. Inkster, 'Marginal Men: Aspects of the Social Role of the Medical Community in Sheffield 1790–1850', in J. Woodward and D. Richards (eds), *Health Care and Popular Medicine in Nineteenth Century England* (London: Croom Helm, 1977), pp. 128–64, on p. 129.

25 H. MacDonald, 'Procuring corpses: the English anatomy inspectorate 1842–1858', *Medical History* 53:3 (2009), pp. 379–96, on p. 388.

26 M. Foucault, *The Birth of the Clinic: An Archaeology of Medical Perception* (London: Tavistock, 1973).

27 Inkster, 'Marginal Men', p. 128; Brown, *Performing Medicine.*

28 J.P. Eigen, '"I answer as a Physician": Opinion as Fact in pre-McNaughtan Insanity Trials', in M. Clark and C. Crawford (eds), *Legal Medicine in History* (Cambridge: Cambridge University Press, 1994), pp. 167–99.

29 Roberts, 'Politics of professionalisation', pp. 53–5.

30 Inkster, 'Marginal Men', p. 152.

31 The historiography of the concept is summarised in M.S.R. Jenner and P. Wallis, 'Introduction', in M.S.R. Jenner and P. Wallis (eds), *Medicine and the Market in England and its Colonies, c.1450–c.1850* (Basingstoke: Palgrave Macmillan, 2007), pp. 1–23.

32 Digby, *Making a Medical Living,* chapter five.

33 M. Fissell, 'Innocent and Honourable Bribes: Medical Manners in Eighteenth-century Britain', in R. Baker, D. Porter, and R. Porter (eds), *The Codification of Medical Morality Volume One: Medical Ethics and Etiquette in the Eighteenth Century* (Dordrecht: Kluwer Academic Publishers, 1993), pp. 19–45, on pp. 38–9.

34 Brown, *Performing Medicine.*

35 Brown, *Performing Medicine,* p. 5.

36 See, for example, an early reference in T. Percival, *Medical Ethics* (Manchester: S. Russell, 1803), p. 47 and later discussions in, *inter alia,* the *British Medical Journal* in 1864 on the wisdom or otherwise of tendering gratuitous medical services.

37 Digby, *Making a Medical Living,* pp. 249–53.

38 M.S. Larson, *The Rise of Professionalism: A Sociological Analysis* (Berkley: California University Press, 1979), p. x; J.M.T. Ford, 'John Gorham 1814–1899. Victorian Medicine in Tonbridge' unpublished PhD thesis (Exeter, 2009), pp. 38–9, 131, 179, 186.

39 Quote from C. Stebbings, 'Tax and Pharmacy: A Synergy in Professional Evolution', in P. Harris and D. De Cogan, *Studies in the History of Tax Law* 7 (2015), pp. 153–69, on p. 163.

40 W.J. Reader, *Professional Men: The Rise of the Professional Classes in Nineteenth-century England* (London: Weidenfeld and Nicolson, 1966), p. 37.
41 R.H. Major, *A History of Medicine* (Springfield: Charles C. Thomas, 1954) volume I, pp. 320–1, commenting on the medieval French practitioner Henri de Mondeville.
42 D. Helm, 'The beauty of a sick room: family care for the dying in the english upper and middle class home, c. 1840-c. 1890', *Family and Community History* 16:2 (2013), pp. 100–12, on p. 104.
43 'Courts medical', *The Lancet* 48:1203 (1846), p. 334.
44 J.C. Burnham, *How the Idea of Profession Changed the Writing of Medical History* (London: Medical History Supplement, 1998), p. 50.
45 Andrew Carrick in 1833, quoted in W.H. McMenemy, *The Life and Times of Sir Charles Hastings, Founder of the British Medical Association* (Edinburgh: Livingstone, 1959), p. 99.
46 R.G. Smith, *Medical Discipline. The Professional Conduct Jurisdiction of the General Medical Council, 1858–1990* (Oxford: Clarendon Press, 1994), p. 101.
47 Peterson, *Medical Profession*, p. 252.
48 J. Tosh, 'Gentlemanly politeness and manly simplicity in Victorian England', *Transactions of the Royal Historical Society* 12 (2002), pp. 455–72, on p. 467.
49 J. Mussell, 'Telling Tales about Secret Remedies: the Case of Chlorodyne', unpublished paper delivered at the conference Working with Nineteenth-Century Medical and Health Periodicals, 30 May 2015; I am indebted to James Mussell for confirmation of the wording in his paper.
50 Brown, 'Doctors' club', p. 63; Ford, 'John Gorham', pp. 37–8 for an instance of financial manipulation for personal gain.
51 Percival, *Medical Ethics*.
52 Waddington, 'Development of medical ethics'.
53 A-H. Maehle, 'Medical Ethics and the Law', in M. Jackson (ed.), *The Oxford Handbook of the History of Medicine* (Oxford: Oxford University Press, 2011), pp. 543–60, on p. 545.
54 Burnham, *How the Idea*, p. 65.
55 Crowther and Dupree, *Medical Lives*, p. 2.
56 C. Brock, 'The *Lancet* and the Campaign against Women Doctors, 1860–1880', in A.M. Caleb (ed.) *(Re)Creating Science in Nineteenth-Century Britain* (Newcastle: Cambridge Scholars Publishing, 2007), pp. 130–45.
57 Brock, 'The *Lancet*', p. 132.
58 See Peterson, *Medical Profession*, chapter 2 for practitioners' collective identity as students plus their pride and loyalty in professional affiliations,

endorsed by Rosner's conclusions of education conferring medical unity; see L. Rosner, *Medical Education in the Age of Improvement. Edinburgh Students and Apprentices 1760–1826* (Edinburgh: Edinburgh University Press, 1991). Sophia Jex-Blake denigrated the behaviour of her fellow (male) medical students as unworthy of 'a body of men claiming the name of gentlemen'; quoted in Brock, 'The *Lancet*', p. 140.

59 Peterson, *Medical Profession*, p. 131 quoting Dr Isaac Ashe in the Carmichael Prize essay of 1868.

60 J. Rogers, *Reminiscences of a Workhouse Medical Officer* (London: T. Fisher Unwin, 1889); preface by Professor Thorold Rogers, p. vii.

61 Peterson, *Medical Profession*, pp. 132, 196.

62 J.R. Walkowitz, *Prostitution and Victorian Society. Women, Class and the State* (Cambridge: Cambridge University Press, 1990), pp. 108–9.

63 F.P. Cobbe, 'The medical profession and its morality', *Modern Review* 2 (1881), pp. 7–42.

64 Peterson, *Medical Profession*, p. 226 and *passim* has discussed evidence of protectionism and failures of intra-professional co-operation at the macro level of the Royal Colleges. This book is concerned rather with the deleterious effects of competitive behaviour at the individual and personal level.

65 P. Carter, *Men and the Emergence of Polite Society, Britain 1660–1800* (Harlow: Longman, 2001), pp. 209–11.

66 Tosh, 'Gentlemanly politeness'.

67 J. Tosh, *A Man's Place. Masculinity and the Middle-Class Home in Victorian England* (New Haven: Yale University Press, 1999), pp. 1–2.

68 M. Weiner, 'Domesticity: A Legal Discipline for Men?', in M. Hewitt (ed.), *An Age of Equipoise? Reassessing Mid-Victorian Britain* (Aldershot: Ashgate, 2000), pp. 155–67.

69 J.A. Mangan and J. Walvin, 'Introduction', in J.A. Mangan and J. Walvin (eds), *Manliness and Morality. Middle-class Masculinity in Britain and America, 1800–1940* (Manchester: Manchester University Press, 1987), pp. 1–6, on p. 3.

70 J.M. MacKenzie, 'The Imperial Pioneer and Hunter and the British Masculine Stereotype in Late Victorian and Edwardian Times', in J.A. Mangan and J. Walvin (eds), *Manliness and Morality. Middle-class Masculinity in Britain and America, 1800–1940* (Manchester: Manchester University Press, 1987), pp. 176–98, on p. 177.

71 R.B. Baker, 'The Discourses of Practitioners in 19th- and 20th-Century Britain and the United States', in R.B. Baker and L.B. McCullough (eds), *The Cambridge World History of Medical Ethics* (Cambridge: Cambridge University Press, 2009), pp. 446–64, on p. 450.

72 Tosh, *A Man's Place*, p. 108.

73 S. Broomhall and D.G. Barrie, 'Introduction', in D.G. Barrie and S. Broomhall (eds), *A History of Police and Masculinities 1700–2010* (London: Routledge, 2012), pp. 1–34, on p. 22.
74 K. Waddington, 'Mayhem and medical students: image, conduct and control in the Victorian and Edwardian London teaching hospital', *Social History of Medicine.* 15:1 (2002), pp. 45–64, on p. 49.
75 R. Boddice, 'The manly mind? Revisiting the Victorian "sex in brain" debate', *Gender and History* 23:2 (2011), pp. 321–40, on p. 334.
76 Thomas Laycock, quoted in Brown, *Performing Medicine*, p. 193.
77 A. Jaffe, 'Detecting the beggar: Arthur Conan Doyle, Henry Mayhew, and "The Man with the Twisted Lip"', *Representations* 31 (1990), pp. 96–117, on p. 113.
78 A. Digby, *The Evolution of British General Practice, 1850–1948* (Oxford: Oxford University Press, 1999), p. 278.
79 M. Fitzwilliam, '"Mr Harrison's Confessions": a study of the general practitioner's social and professional dis-ease in mid-nineteenth century England', *The Gaskell Society Journal* 12 (1998), pp. 28–36, on p. 30.
80 Tosh, *A Man's Place*, pp. 4–5.
81 S. Sullivan, 'Spectacular Failures: Thomas Hopley, Wilkie Collins, and the Reconstruction of Victorian Masculinity', in M. Hewitt (ed.), *An Age of Equipoise? Reassessing Mid-Victorian Britain* (Ashgate: Aldershot, 2000), pp. 84–108, on p. 96.
82 Alborn, 'The moral of the failed bank', p. 222.
83 See Chapter 5 for the cases of Angus Cameron and William Gibson; A.E. Tomkins, 'Casenotes and Madness', in M. Jackson (ed.), *The Routledge History of Disease* (London: Routledge, 2016) for the case of Charles Beard.
84 Anxiety was the characteristic identified by Fildes' son and biographer; L.V. Fildes, *Luke Fildes RA, A Victorian Painter* (London: Michael Joseph, 1968), p. 114. The print was one of the most successful ever printed by Agnews; www.tate.org.uk/art/artworks/fildes-the-doctor-n01522/text-summary viewed 15 January 2015.
85 M. Roper and J. Tosh, 'Introduction', in M. Roper and J. Tosh (eds), *Manful Assertions: Masculinities in Britain since 1800* (London: Routledge, 1991), pp. 1–24, on p. 6.
86 J. Atkinson, *Victorian Biography Reconsidered. A Study of Nineteenth-century 'Hidden' Lives* (Oxford: Oxford University Press, 2010), p. 112.
87 D.M. Evans, *Facts, Failures, and Frauds: Revelations Financial Mercantile Criminal* (Groombridge: London, 1859); Alborn, 'The moral of the failed bank'.

88 Practitioners' physical inadequacies raised comment among campaigners for female medical training such as Emily Davis; Brock, 'The *Lancet*', p. 133. See Chapters 5 and 6 for fuller treatment of practitioners' mental fragility.
89 J. Ruskin, 'The Nature of Gothic', in D. Birch (ed.), *John Ruskin: Selected Writings* (Oxford: Oxford University Press, 2004), pp. 32–63, on p. 39.
90 J. Richards, 'Passing the Love of Women: Manly Love and Victorian Society', in J.A. Mangan and J. Walvin (eds), *Manliness and Morality. Middle-class Masculinity in Britain and America 1800–1940* (Manchester: Manchester University Press, 1987), pp. 92–122, on p. 105.
91 Atkinson, *Victorian Biography*, p. 114.
92 See, for example, the posthumous readmission of Francis Fox to the medical fold in Derby, outlined in Chapter 5, following his support for working-class causes and alleged mental instability.
93 Peterson, *Medical Profession*, p. 126. This book alludes to a bi-partite profession, distinguishing between the successes of the London medical elite and the struggles of the overcrowded rank-and-file, p. 246.
94 Loudon, *Medical Care*, pp. 256–66.
95 See, for example, Digby, *Evolution*, pp. 281–2 for a rapid treatment of professional stress, propensity to suicide, alcohol or drug addiction, and sexual misconduct.
96 Brown, 'Doctors' club' p. 63; the stresses of the medical marketplace in the nineteenth century are given only generalised treatment in his book, see Brown, *Performing Medicine*, p. 115.
97 Smith, *Medical Discipline*, pp. 99, 238–45. It is also a poor guide to erasures from the *Register*, as only 31 percent of cases generated this result.
98 Smith, *Medical Discipline*, p. 99.
99 Smith, *Medical Discipline*, p. 100.
100 Smith, *Medical Discipline*, p. 200. Only 6 percent of cases lead to re-registration up to 1890, pp. 238–45.
101 C. Kelly, *War and the Militarization of British Army Medicine, 1793–1830* (London: Pickering and Chatto, 2011), pp. 4–5.
102 Ackroyd et al., *Advancing with the Army*; M.J. Cardwell, 'Royal Navy Surgeons, 1793–1815: A Collective Biography', in D.B. Haycock and S. Archer (eds), *Health and Medicine at Sea 1700–1900* (Woodbridge: Boydell Press, 2009), pp. 38–62.
103 Price, *Medical Negligence*.
104 B. Milligan, 'Morphine-addicted doctors, the English opium eater, and embattled medical authority', *Victorian Literature and Culture* 33 (2005), pp. 541–53.

105 I.A. Burney, *Poison, Detection and the Victorian Imagination* (Manchester: Manchester University Press, 2006).
106 The same exceptionalism has been used to illustrate related developments, such as the evolution of responses to murder, to press reporting, or to the conduct of coroners' courts; see J. Flanders, *The Invention of Murder: How the Victorians Revelled in Death and Detection and Created Modern Crime* (London: Harper Press, 2011); Burney, *Poison.*
107 A.E. Tomkins, 'Mad doctors?: The significance of medical practitioners admitted as patients to the first English county asylums up to 1890', *History of Psychiatry* 23:4 (2012), pp. 437–53; Tomkins, 'Casenotes'.
108 Sullivan, 'Spectacular failures', p. 85.
109 Sullivan, 'Spectacular failures', p. 85.
110 K.O. Garrigan, 'Foreword: Decorum, Scandal, and the Press', in K.O. Garrigan (ed.), *Victorian Scandals. Representations of Gender and Class* (Athens: Ohio University Press, 1992), pp. 1–8, on p. 5.
111 A. Bingham, 'Reading newspapers: cultural histories of the popular press in modern Britain', *History Compass* 10:2 (2012), pp. 140–50, on p. 142.
112 Bingham, 'Reading newspapers', p. 144.
113 A. Bingham, 'The digitization of newspaper archives: opportunities and challenges for historians', *Twentieth Century British History* 21:2 (2010), pp. 225–31, on p. 228.
114 British Library Newspapers, find.galegroup.com/bncn/, accessed from 1 May 2005 onwards. The database is used particularly heavily in Chapters 3, 4 and 6. Chapter 1 also uses the digitised *London Gazette* to identify bankruptcies and insolvencies.
115 The editorial complexion of some newspapers and the impact of policy upon reporting of medical issues are discussed at more length in relevant chapters, particularly Chapter 6.
116 A. Hobbs, 'The deleterious dominance of *The Times* in nineteenth-century scholarship', *Journal of Victorian Culture* 18:4 (2013), pp. 472–97, on pp. 472, 479; *The Times* would also have been a poor choice given its relative sparsity of non-political news, pp. 481, 484.
117 Nicholson, 'Counting Culture', p. 242.
118 J. Shaw, 'Selection of newspapers', *British Library Newspapers* (Detroit: Gale Cengage Learning, 2007); http://find.galegroup.com/bncn/page.do?page=/bncn_about.jsp&prodId=BNCN&userGroupName=keele_tr viewed 11 November 2014 specifies forty-eight titles, but the website's own title list gives forty-nine titles for part I of the database. The title list also supplies the number of periodicals chosen for parts II, III, and IV of the project.

119 A. Prescott, 'I'd rather be a librarian. A response to Tim Hitchcock, "Confronting the Digital"', *Cultural and Social History* 11:3 (2014), pp. 335–41, on p. 340.
120 N.A. HO 107/808/42.
121 Worcestershire Record Office, B/A 10371 Ref 499:9, parcel 4: Powick Hospital patients' case book volume 9 1863–72, patient number 1339.
122 St Andrew's Heathcare archive, CL4 St Andrew's asylum case notes from 1863, p. 401.
123 N.A. RG 10/1200/13.
124 P.J. Corfield, *Power and the Professions in Britain 1700–1850* (London: Routledge, 1995), p. 149 observes that in the early nineteenth century the composite noun first acquired currency within the medical community. The British Library Newspapers database displayed 2,312 hits for the phrase 'general practitioner' but 1,008,962 hits for 'surgeon' on 15 January 2015; very few of the hits for general practitioner were substantive for the proximity searches conducted here.
125 Brown, *Performing Medicine*; Ackroyd et al., *Advancing with the Army*; Crowther and Dupree, *Medical Lives*; Cardwell, 'Royal Navy Surgeons'.
126 Price *Medical Negligence*, which treats workhouse medical officers, is the only other historical work to consider medical career turbulence at length.
127 Narrow biographical histories were attacked by writers in the field from the first decade of the twentieth century, but the reach and impact of the attacks was only effective much later; Burnham, *How the Idea*, pp. 42, 113–14.
128 Burnham, *How the Idea*, p. 46 and *passim*.
129 A. Gawande, 'Why Do Doctors Fail?' (Reith lecture 25 November 2014); H. Marsh, *Do No Harm: Stories of Life, Death, and Brain Surgery* (London: Weidenfeld and Nicolson, 2014); Tomkins, 'Casenotes'.
130 S. Nenadic, 'Portraits of Scottish professional men in London, c. 1760–1830', *Journal for Eighteenth-Century Studies* 34:1 (2011), pp. 1–17; M. Brown, '"Like a Devoted Army": medicine, heroic masculinity, and the military paradigm in Victorian Britain', *Journal of British Studies* 49:3 (2010), pp. 592–622.
131 Burnham, *How the Idea*, pp. 112–14.
132 G. Sarton, *The Study of the History of Mathematics and the Study of the History of Science* (New York: Dover, 1957) quoted in T. Soderqvist, '"No genre of History fell under more odium than that of biography": the delicate relations between scientific biography and the historiography of science', in T. Soderqvist (ed.), *The History and Poetics of Scientific Biography* (Aldershot: Ashgate, 2007), pp. 241–62, on pp. 249–50.
133 Roper and Tosh, 'Introduction', p. 15.

1

Financial hardship: bankruptcy, insolvency, and medical charity

Debt is an unequivocal signal of career turbulence, yet very little is known about medical bankruptcy. This is partly determined by the limited data on occupational bankruptcy available in aggregate form. Indeed it is not even possible to calculate a simple total of bankrupts that occurred among all occupations in England and Wales in all years across the nineteenth century without multiple caveats.[1] This is particularly ironic given the intense interest in financial solvency evinced throughout the century, at national, institutional, and individual levels.[2]

What is more, practitioners' hardship in particular cannot be pursued through bankruptcies alone but must be examined alongside other forms of financial failure. Lester's indispensable analysis of Victorian insolvency and bankruptcy assumes that, by and large, some occupations will have had access to bankruptcy, but that others which did not were forced to undergo insolvency.[3] This implies an either/or scenario, whereby one's means of making a living largely dictated the form of process that one experienced after falling irrevocably into debt. Medical practitioners did not enjoy a clear-cut pathway through the law, however, because they could feasibly take advantage of bankruptcy law but they did not always do so (or were not permitted to choose this option, either by their level of indebtedness or their creditors' actions).

Financial difficulty was not of course peculiar to medical men, since Victorian professionals, businessmen, and bankers widely and even notoriously underwent insolvency and bankruptcy in very visible ways which might precipitate personal or public crises.[4] 'Facing the discouragement of an empty order book' was a test of character, and as with all tests it carried the risk of failure.[5] An inability to make ends meet, to support one's family, and to maintain a literally creditable identity, cut across the core features of middle-class masculinity and could prove very damaging to mental health.[6] But while practitioners were subject to the same vicissitudes of financial fortune as their peers, they also underwent additional challenges. The random processes at work for small tradesmen were augmented for medical men by the pressures of the medical market working in tandem with the specifics of medical professionalisation.[7] In the case of medical debt, for example, the balance between professional income and expenditure was naturally important, but it was also the case that conspicuous household consumption was presumed to have a direct and beneficial correlation with medical income. There is significant anecdotal evidence from across the nineteenth century that inspiring confidence among patients was vital for practitioners in private practice.[8] Just as 'The legal procedures governing indebtedness were ... the key to sustaining confidence in the credit system that underlay the British economy', so too was the display of prosperity by doctors with a private practice key to sustaining patient confidence in their skill (and thus to the maintenance of their list of paying patients).[9] A falling income would of necessity restrain a practitioner's expenditure, and so risk generating a vicious cycle of diminishing confidence and thereby patients' fees. What other options were open to them, given that practitioners were inhibited or from 1858 prohibited from advertising their services explicitly?[10] Arguably competitive medical behaviours were forced into non-standard channels, and it is possible to uncover detailed evidence of the promotion or protection of medical practices, including the steps taken by individual men to shore up or insulate their financial position.

There are two ways to achieve a finer-grained analysis of medical financial hardship and failure, via a digitised periodical and serendipitous manuscript survivals. The *London Gazette* was central to the implementation of both bankruptcy and insolvency law because it advertised notice of legal process to creditors. Throughout the eighteenth and nineteenth centuries it warned people on the occasion of bankruptcies, reported meetings to appoint assignees and prove debts, and notified interested parties about distributions of dividends.[11] It also featured petitions from insolvent debtors seeking release from prison, and from 1862 it advertised compositions or other arrangements, including liquidations, that avoided full bankruptcy. Consequently, the digital publication of the *Gazette* has changed the landscape. It is now possible to identify multiple named bankrupts and insolvents by reference to occupational labels, and so to chart exposure to risk for different trades and professions. These individuals can be checked against the online catalogue of the National Archives' bankruptcy case files, which since 2013 has included occupational labels.[12] Case files only survive for around 5 percent of bankruptcies, and it is not known how the extant files were selected for retention. Even so, the identification of multiple case files in occupational cohorts makes it possible to unpick some of the pathways into debt taken by medical men, and to weigh the significance of different financial and professional burdens.

This chapter will first consider the impact of the law and legal change on medical men who fell into debt, and will then examine both bankruptcy and insolvency as discrete processes in more detail. What impact did changes to the law of debt have upon doctors' chances of experiencing hardship? What was the scale of medical debt? Do experiences of bankruptcy and insolvency reveal new perspectives on the medical marketplace and the ability to secure financial recovery? Finally, this chapter will consider an additional indicator of financial hardship: the need to draw on medical charity. Were medical charities available to support medical men seeking to re-establish themselves after public exposure as a debtor, or were they exclusively directed to the relief of other sorts of hardship?

Legal change and medical financial failure

If a medical man could not pay final demands for bills against him, his creditors might either seek his bankruptcy, entailing the determination and redistribution of all his assets, or have him arrested for debt. In the late eighteenth and early nineteenth century, bankruptcy required men to owe substantial sums (at least £100 to a single creditor, or higher sums if more than one creditor was involved).[13] The bankrupt's full, technical co-operation was required in the realisation of his assets. The produce of this exercise would be distributed equally amongst all creditors in the form of a dividend, typically some shillings for every pound of proven claim on a bankrupt's estate. When creditors had been legally 'satisfied' that they had secured the maximum return that they might expect from the bankruptcy, the medical man might be discharged and permitted to re-establish his practice or another enterprise without any further burden from the former debt liability.[14] Yet the process could be quite drawn out: the man might be permitted to draw an allowance to enable him and his family to pay for rent and food during the period of bankruptcy administration, which was necessary because calling in debts could be a protracted business. Furthermore, some debts were 'bad', with little or no hope of collection.[15] It is not clear whether such men continued to engage in practice during bankruptcy and to augment the sum available for creditors via their earnings. If they could not or would not act in this way, bankruptcy might impose a lengthy career break in doctors' application of their skill.

The alternative of imprisonment for debt could take place on mesne process (after default of payment but before trial) or final process (after a trial had established the debtor's liability). In theory, imprisonment could be for life if the debts incurred prior to and during imprisonment were never paid. In practice, mechanisms came into play in the eighteenth century allowing 'honest' debtors to seek release from prison periodically, and by 1800 few prisoners languished in confinement for more than six months at a time.[16] Reliable access to the means for release was available from 1813 when a Court for the Relief of Insolvent Debtors was established. The debtor could petition for release on certain conditions, albeit the costs of a successful petition could be prohibitively high.[17] After 1813, the names, occupations, and former addresses of petitioners to courts around England and Wales were routinely listed in the *London Gazette* to give creditors the chance to protest against their debtors' release.

Thus, the likelihood of being bankrupted or imprisoned was somewhat governed by the financial threshold required for bankruptcy, but for practitioners it was also potentially controlled by the nature of their work. Legislation from as early as 1571 had limited the scope of bankrupt status to 'traders', defined as those who made their living by buying and selling things, who had been guilty of specific 'acts of bankruptcy' (such as the concerted evasion of creditors).[18] This nicety gave some practitioners a practical problem – they had to prove that at least some of their activity was commercial and not based solely on giving advice. On its own, the label 'surgeon' was considered 'doubtful' as a qualification for trading status, but surgeons and apothecaries could, like other occupations, attach the catch-all suffix 'dealer and chapman' to their working title to ensure they were eligible for bankruptcy.[19] Apothecaries were in any case included under a new definition of traders from 1844.[20] Physicians had more trouble in theory, although, as will be seen in the following, very few men describing themselves as physicians, MDs or doctors of medicine suffered from either process in any year from 1780 onwards. The 'trader' distinction gave professionalising practitioners in the early nineteenth century an awkward social dilemma, however. On the one hand men might reasonably be anxious to take advantage of bankruptcy law because it protected them from imprisonment as an insolvent debtor, and because a certificate of discharge would release them from future liability against their catalogue of debt. On the other, by 1800 practitioners with formal qualifications in surgery or medicine were increasingly anxious to separate themselves from mere tradesmen and to reject the label 'apothecary' as a lone descriptor of medical expertise, with its implications of the shop counter.[21] The meanings of insolvency versus bankruptcy were complicated further by the social cachet adhering to imprisonment for debt. Prisoners were 'depicted as innocent victims of misfortune and counting men of considerable property among their ranks', so practitioners' preferences when facing debt after 1800 were overburdened with social and professional freight.[22]

The bankruptcy laws underwent some modifications in the second and third quarters of the nineteenth century.[23] An Act of 1825 permitted those in debt to work with creditors to have themselves declared bankrupt. The necessary declaration of insolvency from the debtor that was required to prompt bankruptcy thereafter become a feature of the financial notices placed in the *London Gazette,* and doctors made their share of these declarations, although success in the form of a Commission of Bankruptcy required a creditor to act on a declaration. Creditors did not necessarily see their own best interests in acting to initiate or further bankruptcy, particularly when they feared that the distribution of assets would generate a very small dividend. The 1825 Act also permitted a bankruptcy to be superseded by a 'composition'. This was possible where nine-tenths of creditors agreed to a specified proportional payment. The device allowed the bankrupt to resume business, safe in the knowledge that they need only meet the terms of the composition (whether from within their assets at the time of bankruptcy or from their earnings subsequent to the composition). This provided a way to satisfy all parties without potentially long and costly bankruptcy proceedings, and compositions were used 'extensively'; unfortunately there is little enough evidence about compositions *per se* until the 1860s, and none at all discovered concerning the discharge of medical debt.[24]

The Bankruptcy Act of 1831 made little direct impact on practitioners, despite its enforcement of 'officialism' on the process.[25] It did amend the terminology of the law, because commissions of bankruptcy were from 1831 termed 'fiats' (dubbed 'petitions for adjudication' from 1853). The drive for reform and the desire to see eradication of all imprisonment for debt were promoted by Acts of 1838 and 1844, which effectively prevented anyone from being imprisoned for a debt of under £20.[26] It is not clear, though, whether any doctors benefited from these interim measures, since the scale of medical debt in insolvency cases of the 1830s and 1840s is unknown. Acts from the 1860s were much more significant for medical men. An Act of 1861 spliced the parallel bankrupt and insolvency laws, and after that date no one in England or Wales could be subjected to separate laws of insolvency.[27] This means that all practitioners after 1861 were subject to the bankruptcy law alone, and could become bankrupt on either their own or their creditors' petition. It also made private arrangements or compositions more visible, since notices of these were now published in the *Gazette*. Imprisonment for debt in perpetuity was formally abolished in 1869, although detention for a fixed period of up to six weeks remained a possibility.[28] The opportunity for bankruptcy on one's own petition was rescinded at the same time. An Act of 1883 signalled the end to substantive legal change until the twentieth century. It reimposed 'officialism', and once again permitted people to become bankrupt on their own petition.[29]

The Act of 1861 necessarily extended bankruptcy to non-traders and the impact of the distinction lessened, although it was not erased entirely until the Act of 1883. Ironically, the *British Medical Journal* engaged in some discussion of whether doctors *could* be regarded as traders, but only after the question had become irrelevant.[30] In 1888 the *Journal* gave brief notice to a case whereby Alfred Peskett MD, who was also a Licentiate of the Apothecaries Society, became bankrupt in 1883 prior to the legislation of the same year taking effect. Peskett's case was presumably one of the last which required the determination of 'trader' status for a practitioner, in this case to find whether a post-nuptial settlement was invalidated by a practitioner's swiftly subsequent bankruptcy.[31] The *Journal* confidently commented 'Medical men are generally considered to belong to one of the learned professions, and not to be, strictly speaking, traders.' This was perhaps disingenuous, but also an indication of how far the specifically medical learned profession had come in a short space of time. In the 1820s, practitioners had still been relatively keen to denote themselves 'dealer and chapman' in order to ensure they could be counted as 'traders' and therefore take advantage of bankruptcy over penal insolvency. The nineteenth-century law reports were alleged by the *Journal* to be historically silent on the question of whether practitioners were traders. This was quite possibly a pragmatic silence on the part of legal commentators, given the numbers of medical men who took advantage of bankruptcy each year from the second quarter of the nineteenth century onwards. Peskett's case came down to a judgement about whether he had sold medicine discretely, or whether the cost of medicines he supplied to patients were only ever rolled into his charges for attendance per visit. Ultimately, he was deemed not to have been a trader under the meaning of the 1869 Act. This outcome allowed the *Journal* to reflect complacently 'It may … be a source of gratification to some members of the profession to know that they may dispense the medicines they prescribe without necessarily by so doing constituting themselves tradesmen.' In this way, at least one change in the bankruptcy laws was co-opted by medicine and mobilised as a marker of professionalism.

Legal changes clearly made a qualitative difference to practitioners' general experiences of prosecution for debt. They also made an impact on the ability or eagerness of creditors to obtain redress from medical men; there was no period when the law applied automatically or was independent of creditors' preferences. Creditors will have been driven by their perception of the efficiency of different processes, the likelihood of a remunerative return, and by their own sense of financial security. It is also possible that creditors weighed social status in the balance; did some creditors stay their hand, and withhold legal process, because their debtor was a medical man? Creditors' finer motives for pursuing one course of action or another are rarely available from the historical record, but the quantitative consequences of their actions are retrievable.

Occupational bankruptcy and the *London Gazette*

Returns to Parliament by the Board of Trade made some occupational analysis of bankruptcy from 1885 onwards, by which time medical practitioners were apparently not a group significantly at risk in comparison to other job titles, or in comparison to other 'professions'. Grocers, publicans, farmers, and builders routinely headed the list in the later 1880s, with 200–300 casualties in each trade. Physicians and surgeons were not represented on the list at all in 1885 and 1886. By 1888 physicians had crept on to the lower reaches of the list, while physicians and surgeons combined suffered between nine and eighteen bankruptcies per annum between 1887 and 1890. Other professional or professionalising groups were more vulnerable in numbers and in relative terms, with Clerks in Holy Orders, architects, and particularly solicitors routinely outnumbering doctors.[32]

The division of physicians from surgeons for these purposes presumably meant that there were very low numbers of each in 1885 and 1886 which, counted discretely, did not qualify for inclusion in Table 1.1, whereas if they had been counted together they would have been more prominent.

Earlier attempts to gauge the risk of bankruptcy for different occupations were sporadic, such as the tabulation conducted by *The Standard* in a one-off 'bankruptcy analysis' for the twelve months from 1 February 1829 to 31 January 1830.[33] Here, surgeons accounted for fifteen in a list technically headed by merchants (numbering 100, from a total of 1,677 individuals). There was a run of similar analyses published by the Society for the Diffusion of Useful Knowledge 1833 to 1850 pertaining to bankruptcies across twelve-month periods from 1 November each year, 1831–32 until 1848–49.[34] Typically these counts reveal between ten and twenty bankruptcies for surgeons each year up to the late 1830s, and between five and fifteen to the late 1840s, from a total of around 1,000–1,500 bankruptcies in all.[35]

These figures pertaining to the 1830s, 1840s, and 1880s provide a starting point for considering medical bankruptcy across the nineteenth century, and imply that it diminished in relative significance in the population as a whole – which grew from around 16 million to around 30 million in the same period – and also declined in terms of all bankrupts in the sixty years from 1829 to 1889. This is in contrast to Digby's

Table 1.1 Bankruptcy in selected professions, 1885–90

	1885	1886	1887	1888	1889	1890
Medical men	–	–	12 physicians	9 physicians/17 surgeons	15 surgeons	18 surgeons
Clerks in holy orders	15	20	16	13	14	14
Architects/surveyors	16	20	16	16	17	18
Solicitors	41	46	34	46	53	46
Total	4,348	4,859	4,838	4,843	4,570	4,008

Table 1.2 Total 'hits' in a digitised, combined-keyword search of the *London Gazette*, 1780–1890

	Bankrupt	Insolvent	Composition/Liquidation
Physician	177	105	230
Surgeon	5204	3018	2608
Doctor	959	563	736
Medical	313	441	283

finding that financial uncertainty increased in the late nineteenth century, albeit that uncertainty was not a simple proxy for full bankruptcy.[36] There are no equivalent counts demonstrating the level of occupational insolvency, or the number of private arrangements or compositions reached. This means that further examination of medical financial failure can only be tackled by a close reading of the *London Gazette*.

In line with other digitised searches undertaken for this book, the words 'bankrupt', 'insolvent', 'composition', and 'liquidation' were sought in conjunction with one of four occupational indicators, namely 'physician', 'surgeon', 'doctor', and 'medical' for the years 1780 to 1890 inclusive (Table 1.2).

Given the initial volume of hits, which far exceeded the number of medical men involved in each of these processes, and the consequential need for manual checking, it seemed pragmatic to sample them at regular intervals rather than attempt to survey them all. Therefore the terms bankrupt and insolvent were sought for every five years between 1780 and 1890, and for every year 1815–35 because this quickly emerged as a period of significant change. The terms composition and liquidation were sought at five-year intervals 1865–80 only, owing to the limited period when these were consistently reported (namely between the acts of 1861 and 1883). These processes yielded 340 occasions of medical bankruptcy, 590 insolvencies, and 145 compositions. There was no way to validate the success of the searches on insolvents and those making a composition, but it is possible to make a very rough check on how the digitised searches of the *London Gazette* perform against the known totals of bankrupt practitioners by comparing the

Table 1.3 Totals of medical bankrupts: digitised searches compared with contemporary counts in selected years*

	Contemporary counts	Digital search of *Gazette*
1829–30	15 (surgeons only, Feb–Jan)	15 (all practitioners, 1829)
1831–32	13 (surgeons only, Nov–Oct)	15 (all practitioners, 1832)
1832–33	12 (surgeons only, Nov–Oct)	8 (all practitioners, 1833)
1833–34	15 (surgeons only, Nov–Oct)	17 (all practitioners, 1834)
1834–35	14 (surgeons only, Nov–Oct)	9 (all practitioners, 1835)
1839–40	14 (surgeons only, Nov–Oct)	13 (all practitioners, 1840)
1844–45	6 (surgeons & dentists, Nov–Oct)	10 (all practitioners, 1845)
1890	18 (surgeons only, Jan–Dec)	7 (all practitioners, 1890)

* 'Bankruptcy Analysis', *The Standard* 11 February 1830, p. 3; *The British Almanac of the Society for the Diffusion of Useful Knowledge 1833* and subsequent editions dated 1834, 1835, 1836, 1841, and 1846; PP. *Eighth report by the Board of Trade under section 131 of the Bankruptcy Act, 1883* (1891), p. 44; counts for 1836–39, 1841–44, 1846–69 and 1886–89 are available in Almanacs and Parliamentary Papers but are omitted here, because corresponding digital searches of the *London Gazette* were not made for these years. Unfortunately the Almanac count for 1844–45 does not disaggregate surgeons from dentists, whereas my own designation 'all practitioners' includes physicians, surgeons, medical men, and medical 'doctors' but excludes dentists.

results with the count in *The Standard* for 1829–30, returns in the *Companion to the British Almanac* 1831–49 and official returns to Parliament from the late 1880s (Table 1.3).

The efficacy of the digital search process for bankrupts is demonstrably quite high for 1829–45, but appears to decline by 1890. This is notable given that both the analyses published in the serial press 1830–50 and the totals published by the Board of Trade from the 1880s onwards also derived from the same source as my own searches, namely orders published in the *Gazette*.[37] It is unclear whether the propensity for medical bankrupts to be found via digital searches declined at a constant rate, or whether it fluctuated in line with changing terminologies or other factors that influence the bankruptcies securing 'hits'. One clear reason for declining success is probably to be found in the *Gazette*'s use of tables from the 1880s, whereby the word 'bankrupt' (signifying that processes are taking place under the 1883 Act) only appears on the first page of the table and not in subsequent pages. This means that practitioners who did not happen to feature in the first page of the table may not register among the 'hits' for that year. On balance, this search methodology is a valuable way to identify exposure to financial legal process for practitioners, particularly before the very end of the period under study, and it provides a basis for further analysis.

Medical bankruptcy

The numbers of medical men undergoing bankruptcy were negligible in decades before 1815, but thereafter they were subject to general increase, and some very marked annual variations (Figure 1.1).

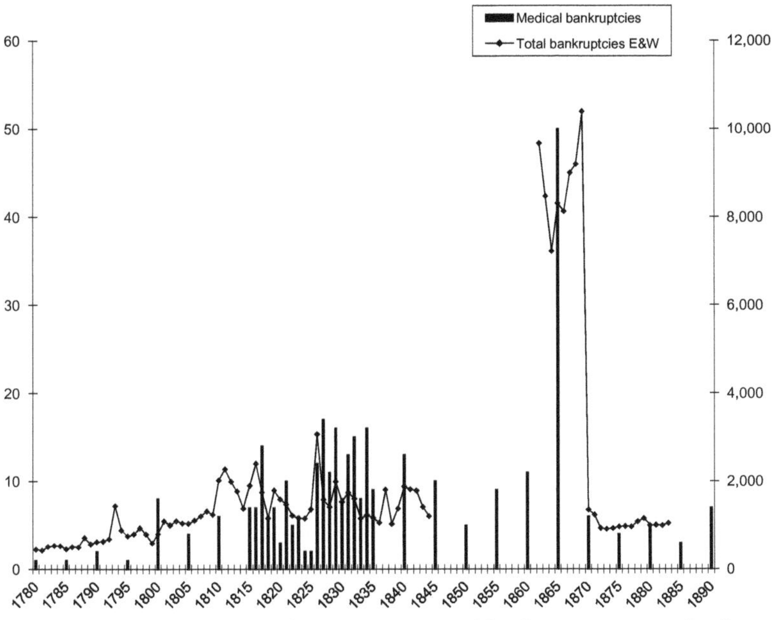

Figure 1.1 Medical bankrupts against total bankruptcies in England and Wales

It is clearly necessary to consider these figures in relation to trade cycles and the exposure of different occupational categories to the economic context. There are some years where context seemingly made a discernible difference to medical bankruptcy, as in 1817: this was a year of post-war crisis in the English economy, and medical bankruptcy certainly went up. Yet the relationship between cycles and aggregate levels of bankruptcy in the wider economy has proved difficult to unpick; for example, in the period 1888–1913. Very broadly, when economic activity declined the number of bankruptcies increased, but the link between cycles and individual occupations is much less visible, and specific/random factors independent of trade cycles are equally or more important.[38] Further, the propensity of one occupational group to fall bankrupt could clearly diverge from general, background or cyclical trends.[39] Contemporary commentators were certainly accustomed to ascribing occupationally determined bankruptcy to factors inherent to that trade or its client group: the *Liverpool Mercury*, for instance, focused on the bankruptcy analysis for 1843–44 with particular reference to trades reliant on sales of alcohol, and saw in their increased bankruptcies the influence of the Temperance movement.[40] There seems little justification in trying to peg medical bankruptcy to wider economic trends rather than to those inherent to the profession.

The numbers involved in medical bankruptcy crept up after 1800, but the 1820s were a defining decade. Whereas the annual total for all practitioners was typically ten or fewer up to 1825, the total was routinely between ten and twenty in the succeeding decade. There were at least two processes driving this change. One was the short-term impact of the 1825 Bankruptcy Act, which prompted a doubling of all bankruptcies between 1825 and 1826.[41] The other was the enhanced risk faced by all practitioners in an increasingly overcrowded profession. Complaints of overcrowding were palpable at the time and have been endorsed by historians subsequently, so the upswing in bankruptcies in the later 1820s comes as no surprise.[42] On these figures, practitioners experienced modest amelioration in their propensity to suffer bankruptcy after the early 1830s and into the 1850s.

The scale of the increase in medical bankruptcies in the 1860s arises from the impact of the 1861 Act but was not out of line with the increase in all bankruptcies in that decade. The conflation of bankruptcy and insolvency law in 1861 meant that individuals who would previously have been dealt with as insolvents were now added to the total of bankrupts. Since between thirty and thirty-five medical men had been declared insolvent between 1855 and 1860, it was always likely that their successors would boost the number of medical bankrupts in similar numbers after 1861. Add to this the fact that all classes of debtors could now petition for their own bankruptcy in order to escape from a burden of indebtedness via the prospect of 'discharge', and it is only surprising that the number of medical bankrupts did not rise even higher. Therefore the spike in medical bankrupts in 1865 represented a temporarily raised likelihood of exposure to bankruptcy, but medical men were not alone in this and may have been willing participants in the phenomenon.

In a similar manner, the drop in bankruptcies seen from 1870 onwards signalled a decline in exposure to bankruptcy, but not necessarily a marked improvement in practitioners' finances. The 1869 Bankruptcy Act abolished the official assignee and placed bankruptcy administration entirely in the hands of creditors who were more likely to pursue large debtors than small ones. It is not clear why this would have any significant effect on doctors *per se*, or at least why it would have a depressing effect on their rate of bankruptcy. As will be seen, practitioners from the 1820s to the 1850s whose dealings can be known tended to have larger rather than smaller debts. The Act also deprived debtors of the chance to petition for their own bankruptcy, and this might have had a deleterious effect on practitioners' experience if, when in difficulty, they had been used to inviting the process to escape a burden of unmanageable debt. Furthermore, compositions had a role to play in accommodating cases that would have been dealt with under bankruptcy in other years (and for their numbers, see Figure 1.3).

The totals of practitioners who experienced bankruptcy may be notionally determinable, but this is an admittedly narrow basis for considering the financial vulnerability of the developing profession. There is no way at all to assess the probability of failure, or the perception of financial jeopardy by practitioners as individuals or groups (except in its most extreme manifestation: for practitioner suicide arising from financial worry, see Chapter 6). In selected instances, however, it is possible to consider the scale of losses and the factors which contributed to bankruptcy via case files.[43] These documents survive for thirty doctors who suffered bankruptcy between 1815 and 1854 and provide a window on to the specific financial circumstances which precipitated failure, despite the variety of their content. They may comprise only a few papers, or be substantial volumes replete with all of the paperwork typically generated by a bankruptcy case. The doctors' files, like others in the holdings of the National Archive, 'are recorded in moderate detail, though many are not closed in a tidy conclusive way – they convey the impression of being abandoned before the final curtain had fallen'.[44] Consequently, not all information is available for each man (Table 1.4).

Debts owed by the bankrupts to their creditors are usually taken from the 'bankrupt's balance sheet' which accompanied many case files. This was not always the final word on debt, as the total given on the balance sheet might be an interim calculation of creditors' assertions and not the amount which could be 'proved'. Therefore, the amount of indebtedness could go up or down depending on whether creditors' allegations were verifiable. In some instances where a balance sheet was missing, the calculation of proved debt at the time of a dividend is the only source for the information in this column. In one man's case, James Maximilian Cornwall, his debts are given in neither context, but his file contains two lists of debts proved on different days, meaning that his total of £1,096 is likely to be the minimum amount of his total provable debt.

Twenty-three of the twenty-six individual medical bankrupts whose total debts are calculable owed an average of £3,100. The level of indebtedness required to invoke a bankruptcy was £100 from 1831, falling to £50 in 1842, and after the definitive Act of 1883, 75 percent of all bankrupts 1883–1914 owed less than £200.[45] Even allowing for the fact that the post-1883 figure includes people who might previously have undergone insolvency for low debts, this suggests that medicine could induce drastic indebtedness in advance of bankruptcy. The most compromised medical bankrupt, Samuel Fox, ran up debts ranging from £4,763 to a single creditor, a stationer called Richard Birkett, to the £10 he owed to the milk woman. But even if his anomalous liability for £14,397 is stripped out of the calculation, the average amount that practitioners owed to their creditors was £2,587. That some medical men were able to run up vast debts in comparison to other 'traders' is perhaps less surprising when two factors are taken into consideration. First, these men with surviving case files may not be representative of all bankrupt

Table 1.4 Debts and dividends of medical bankrupts*

Medical bankrupts with case files in year order	Debts incurred by the bankrupt	Money due to the bankrupt's estate†	1st dividend per £	Additional dividends
Steight 1811	£1,064		3s 0d	
Lankshear 1814	Bankruptcy 'renewed' 1827, see below			
Barry 1815			3s 0d	Y
Chapman 1819	£648	£1,302	2s 6d	
Grant 1819	£4,463		0s 5.75d	
Sutton 1826	£813		1s 6d	Y
Lankshear 1827	£1,168		8s 9d	Y
Shepherd 1827	£3,621	£548		
Chaldecott 1828	£849	£377	[1s 7.75d]‡	
Scriven 1828	£2,401	£3,164		
Edwards 1829	£5,873	£422		
Jameson 1829	£1,102	£297		
Travis 1829	£6,168	£1,661		
Fox 1830	£14,397			
Lerew 1831	£2,466	£805	1s 1d	
Robertson 1831	£2,156	£1,085		
Sleigh 1831	£3,500	£314	0s 6d	
Wordingham 1831	£7,134	£774	2s 0d	Y
Anderson 1832	£3,801	£710	0s 4.5d	Y
Ayckbourn 1832	£844	£466	4s 0d	
Pitt 1833	£3,159	£474	0s 7.5d	
Nixon 1837	£1,384	£207	1s 7d	
Latham 1838	£1,279	£240	2s 0d	
Cornwall 1839	£1,096+			
Franks 1853	£1,929	£946	2s 4.5d	
Clarke 1854			0s 5.5d	
Evans 1854			0s 0.75d	

* N.A., B 3/365, 938, 1098, 1235, 1630, 1962, 2755, 2967, 2968, 3128, 3158, 3784, 4116, 4117, 4374, 4721, 4730, 4813Q, 4488, 4693, 5045, 5368, 5501; N.A., B 9/1, 3, 124, 136, 140. This table excludes three men with surviving case files, on the grounds that their files contain no reliable data under any of these headings. See B 3/ 5467 John Ellis Brown (1830), B 3/4084 George Peskett (1830) and B 3/5074 William Taylor (1835).

† This was the amount of cash due to the bankrupt by people indebted to him for medical and other services, not the total value of all of his assets such as the amount realisable from the sale of household goods.

‡ The dividend is not given explicitly in the case file, but the amount available for distribution divided according to the debts proved against Chaldecott suggest that this level of dividend can be inferred.

practitioners. It is entirely possible that these specific files were kept because the scale of the debts was so large, and that apparent levels of medical indebtedness in bankruptcy are overstated as a result. Second, and a more interesting possibility, is that medical men had the capacity to run up inordinate debts in pursuit of a visibly respectable lifestyle partly because their emergent professional status secured high levels of trust among creditors, trust that was itself fostered as a component of the confidence necessary for a professional persona. This suggests that the conspicuous consumption mentioned in the introduction to this chapter did not merely have implications for potential indebtedness, but could be directly responsible for the sizeable scale of medical failure. This was categorically the case for some men with case files containing detailed estimates of expenditure for the years preceding the bankruptcy. William Hopeful Lerew (sic) had kept a horse and carriage for over three years when he fell bankrupt, which on its own added 5 percent to his outgoings.[46] In this light, a reputation for financial probity might have proved a double-edged sword, for practitioners and their creditors alike, if it encouraged unrealistic hopes on both sides. Furthermore, where did optimism end and outright misdirection begin? Richard Chapman was explicitly caught out in an act of financial bravado. He was required to admit to the bankruptcy commissioners that, when he told one of his acquaintances in September 1818 that he had £2,000, he had 'merely said it in joke'.[47]

The depth of these men's indebtedness can be shown by reference to the money their bankrupt estate might still hope to collect, because practitioners were paid retrospectively by patients rather than in advance. The money theoretically due to seventeen of the same men from credit they had themselves extended averaged £811, equivalent to just £1 of potential income for every £4 of debt. The situation in practice was even more acute, because a proportion of the money owed to practitioners was admitted to be 'bad' debt that could not be collected (from patients who had died or left the country). This means that while the money due to bankrupts' estates should on average have been sufficient to support dividends equal to around a quarter of their debts, irrespective of any additional funds deriving from property or other assets, the results were rarely as positive as this.[48]

Dividends were paid in proportion to a creditor's liability, in equal shares per pound sterling of the credit they had extended to the bankrupt. The depth of practitioners' financial difficulty is therefore further illustrated by the levels of dividends payable on their estates. Admittedly, dividends from all bankruptcies were fairly low in 1817, when one commentator put the average dividend arising from bankruptcies among all occupations at under five shillings in the pound.[49] Even so, the creditors of medical bankrupts were markedly disadvantaged. Only one case listed paid a first dividend of more than four shillings in the pound, and the estate of Owen Evans, bankrupt in 1854, paid a miniscule three farthings in the pound. The average for the eighteen cases, where a first dividend is given or can be inferred, was two shillings. There was the scope for subsequent and final dividends in cases which were protracted over years or decades, but of course the chances that creditors would be genuinely recompensed for their wait was slim, given that creditors, like practitioners, might prove mortal. William Miller Anderson's troubles were soon over, in that he fell bankrupt in 1832 and died in 1834; his creditors received a meagre dividend of four and a half pence in the pound in 1834, but this was not quite the end of the story. Twenty years later there was a second dividend – this time of three and a quarter pence. Not surprisingly, more than half of the letters sent to creditors in 1854 were returned unanswered.[50] It is ironic, then, that the creditors of Augustus Ayckbourn, who received four shillings in the pound, complained that their dividend was too small.[51]

Aside from supplying the raw data common to most bankruptcies, case files can be deployed to unpack the causes of individuals' bankruptcy wherever detailed accounts effectively chart the course of financial crisis. Common causes of failure *per se* towards the end of the nineteenth century included over-extension of the business, paying too much to buy out a partner's interest, and losses attributable to the dishonesty of employees or partners.[52] All of these factors are present in practitioners' bankruptcy case files and in this way they speak to the men's involvement in productive activity within and beyond medicine, but also help to uncover some of the aggression of the medical marketplace. Thus, Henry Edwards suffered bankruptcy in 1829 because although his household income and annual turnover were vast, his outgoings were regrettably still higher. Edwards enjoyed an estimated income from his practice of £800 a year, and he was also in the enviable position of charging (and receiving) average premiums of £216 for apprentices, of whom he recruited four. But he was tempted into business beyond his medical practice, and suffered badly as a consequence. He had entered into partnership with John Warwick, a refiner and stereotype founder, but Warwick absconded to America leaving company debts of £3,000 behind him. Edwards paid the company debts, but bankrupted himself in the process.[53]

Not all bankrupt practitioners were stung quite as badly as Edwards in respect of losses unconnected to medicine, but dabbling in business was a contributory cause in a number of cases. James Grant had no one to blame but himself, and the market in commodities from the East, for his financial downfall. During his travels between India and China he bought quantities of cotton, opium, tea, cloves, and other goods, and was disappointed in his hopes of trading at a profit.[54] Others could pin the blame on someone else. George Franks protested that he had been 'induced to join several persons in an attempt to form a Cab Company'.[55]

In a more scientific vein, Augustus Ayckbourn spent £300 equipping himself to experiment with the artificial incubation of duck's eggs for a profitable return. Unfortunately, Ayckbourn seems to have been a quixotic man whose enthusiasms and subsequent aversions evidently undermined his solvency. In accounting for his recent expenses, for example, he freely admitted to spending £200 in sending his apprentice William Wormsley out to India, 'my object being to get rid of him'. Perhaps not surprisingly his costs also included an allowance to Mrs Ayckbourn of £40 a year for the previous seven years, by reason of their separation.[56]

A handful of the case files supply an alternative view of the medical marketplace in action. Emergent professional etiquette in the 1820s and 1830s already inhibited the practitioner from explicitly advertising his services, or from trespassing on another man's practice. This meant that active self-promotion necessarily entailed rejecting the niceties of etiquette. Alternatively, medical men had to find covert means for challenging or ousting competitors.

The downfall of William Wilcocks Sleigh might have been attributable to conspiracy by professional rivals, but Sleigh's evidently grandiose ambition may also have been his main problem. As founder and proprietor of the short-lived Royal Western Hospital in Bryanston Square, in the late 1820s Sleigh was determined to secure recognition for his institution as a 'school' by the Royal College of Surgeons. Correspondence was repeatedly exchanged about the number of beds, the proportion of cases that could be called 'surgical', and other topics, apparently without the College approving of the hospital as a site of surgical education.[57] Sleigh took the view that the hospital had quickly attracted jealous attention from his medical peers in Marylebone, which consequently embroiled him in financial disaster: 'The present embarrassed state of my affairs may be *justly* attributed to the *unprovoked, cruel* and *malicious* exertions (commenced in 1829) by one Jonas Hall Pope and his accomplices, to get possession of my anatomical school at the Royal Western Hospital by which exertions they have brought both it and me to ruin.'[58] This might look like a clear example of medical competition that got out of hand were it not for the additional evidence available for Sleigh's life. He was a man of multiple, strong passions resulting in numerous publications on religious, medical, and political topics. He also took out at least one rather fanciful patent.[59] None of this proves that Sleigh's own view of his affairs was unbalanced, but it certainly raises the possibility of an alternative interpretation of the causes of his financial woes.

A clearer instance of bankruptcy arising from competitive practise is afforded by the case file of John Steight.[60] Steight was a surgeon in Richmond who entered a partnership with Richard Hunter in 1807 to work together as surgeons, apothecaries, and male midwives. The partnership was dissolved in 1810, as Hunter protested that he had been prevailed upon by fraud and misrepresentations as to the likely yield from their joint practice. Steight then suffered the dual misfortune of breaking his leg and falling bankrupt in 1811, and the cutthroat nature of medical competition in Richmond was brought into focus in the evidence collected by the bankruptcy commissioners. Steight protested that he thought that the original articles of partnership specifically prohibited Hunter from continuing to practise medicine in Richmond (or even within a 10-mile radius) after the dissolution of 1810. Hunter had always said that he would leave Richmond and travel to Portugal to join his brother in the army, when instead he remained in the neighbourhood and took advantage of Steight's bankruptcy to poach patients. Hunter also tried to register himself as one of Steight's creditors, claiming that money he had paid to buy a half share in the business should be repaid, on the grounds that it had been obtained fraudulently. Steight denied any misrepresentation, and the Bankruptcy Commissioners agreed, refusing to acknowledge the debt to Hunter. They confirmed that Hunter had breached the partnership terms by continuing to practise in Richmond after the partnership broke up in 1810.

Whatever the truth of these opposing claims, there are some general points to make about this dispute. First, Steight had from the outset tried to insure himself against a source of future competition. The articles of agreement were designed to preclude a partner from capitalising on privileged exposure to the local medical marketplace to acquire patients later on his own account, either in Richmond or anywhere in the near vicinity. It looks very much as though Steight was highly alert to the risk that his own practice might act as a channel for the promotion of his future rivals. Moreover, this is not merely a single instance of an otherwise unknown tactic; it was tried by other practitioners, with varying success.[61] Territoriality was a normal feature of building a practice, but this sort of pre-emptive clause is rather more surprising.[62] Second, Steight's bankruptcy tendered two sorts of opportunity to Hunter, both of which he tried to seize. He took advantage of Steight's temporary absence from business in 1811 to secure patients, and he used the bankruptcy process to try to retrieve a lost investment.[63] Both men were making calculations about the value of the other's goodwill, and finding it much less persuasive than the prospect of concrete advantage in the form of territorial control or monetary gain.

These bankruptcy case files offer some detailed insights into the very substantial scale of medical debt and otherwise concealed features of the evolving medical market. The latter did encourage both covertly competitive behaviour and heightened fears of what forms this might take. Nonetheless, not all medical men were granted damaging access to expansive credit and consequential bankruptcy as a 'trader'. Some were held accountable at lower levels of debt, or had insufficient visible assets to tempt creditors to seek bankruptcy, and so were dealt with by the law of insolvency.

Medical insolvency and imprisonment for debt

Doctors who were imprisoned for insolvency but did not (or could not) seek protection of their person in bankruptcy did at least have one advantage; they retained control of whatever assets they possessed. Bankrupt practitioners routinely gave up their gold or silver watches at the time of their bankruptcy examination, or had to sell the contents of their surgeries, but their insolvent colleagues could choose to await release without the prospect of having to re-equip themselves for business.

It is possible to estimate a minimum figure for the number of doctors who went to prison for debt by reference to the men whose petitions for release were printed in the *London Gazette* (Figure 1.2). As with their bankrupt colleagues, insolvent practitioners were sought at five-yearly intervals between 1780 and 1890, with all years 1815–35 being checked (partly because rising numbers in this twenty-year period attract obvious interest, but also to ensure chronological coincidence with searches for bankrupts).

By this mode of analysis, medical insolvency afflicted fewer than ten men per year before 1820, but thereafter the annual total rose significantly to between twenty and thirty men. By the 1840s this had risen again to forty men or more per year, falling back to thirty or more immediately prior to the amalgamation of the bankruptcy and insolvency processes effected by the Act of 1861. The chances of a practitioner experiencing insolvency are therefore exactly what might have been expected from the 'overcrowding' narrative that both contemporaries and historians have linked to the medical profession for these decades. Practitioners formed a very small proportion of all

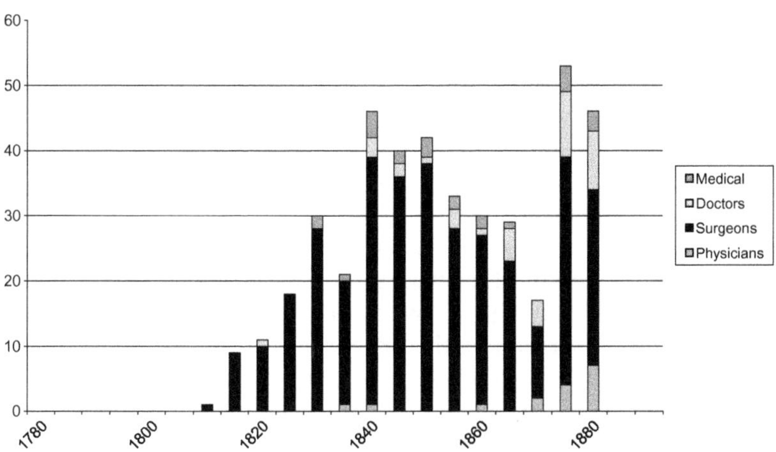

Figure 1.2 Numbers of medical insolvents

imprisoned debtors, who numbered between 3,814 and 9,030 in the period 1798–1818.[64] Naturally, insolvency loomed larger in the population of all practitioners, where there was perhaps one case of insolvency per 400 men per year.[65]

Counts of insolvent medical men reveal their distribution across prisons in the forty-five years between 1815 and 1860. These can be set against a one-off count of 1826 giving the distribution of all debtors across prisons. In 1826, 60 percent of all debtors were being held in one of four London prisons (the Debtor Prison for London and Middlesex, the Fleet, King's Bench Prison, and the Marshalsea). Of the 195 practitioners whose place of imprisonment is known for certain, half were also clustered in the same institutions.[66] The remaining men were incarcerated across a large number of provincial prisons, where Lancaster gaol was the most prominent – as it was for non-medical insolvents.[67]

There are no detailed records equivalent to the bankruptcy case files that may shed light on the extent of practitioners' debts at the point of insolvency. There are, however, two tabulations of debt available for men who either took immediate advantage of the 1813 Act or who were counted in 1820–21 preparatory to planned statutory amendment in 1822. Parliamentary accounts for 1813–14 list twenty-four men with medical occupational labels, alongside their total debt liability.[68] The average total debt was again high at over £792, echoing the deep indebtedness of bankrupts.[69] It was also high in comparison to the debts of other occupations, because only around 25 percent of those listed in 1813–14 had debts of even £500 or more.[70] The 1820–21 data confirms a difficult and worsening situation for practitioners, with twenty-five men exhibiting an average debt of £1,059.[71]

For further insight into practitioners' insolvency it is necessary to turn to the evidence of prisons embedded in Parliamentary papers. This yields two brief testimonies from insolvent doctors that were recorded by Parliamentary committees. James Jackson was a surgeon and man-midwife imprisoned in King's Bench from around January 1787, and he remained there in May 1791 when he was called to give evidence.[72] John Palfreyman was a surgeon apothecary imprisoned in Ilchester gaol from October 1816 to April 1817, and he gave evidence to a Commons enquiry of 1821.[73] Both men practised medicine within their respective gaols and, while they took very different views of the facilities on offer in each prison, there were points of similarity between the two accounts.

Jackson and Palfreyman were both called upon to treat their fellow prisoners, especially at night or if no other assistance could be obtained. Both supplied medical assistance, drugs, and some nursing to their imprisoned patients, as both described feeding patients when they were incapable of supporting themselves. This generated income, if in different ways for the two men: Jackson was paid by some of his fellow prisoners, while Palfreyman was given a gratuity paid by the county at the time of his release.[74] Evidently imprisonment did not necessarily signal a temporary suspension of medical practice, and nor did it prove a decisive barrier to earning.

An important difference between the two accounts stems from the different treatment allegedly given to Jackson and Palfreyman respectively by their gaolers. Jackson endured a number of abrasive exchanges with the prison's Marshal and Deputy Marshals. On one occasion he recommended that two people who were ill should not be kept in the same room, only to be asked tartly if he would therefore take one of them into his own room. He confessed 'I found myself much hurt at so unjust a request.' His actions and letters on behalf of other prisoners also inspired angry exchanges. In contrast, Palfreyman was seemingly given the run of the institution, being allowed to move freely between the debtors' and felons' wards and to collect supplies for the benefit of sick prisoners from the gaoler's own residence. This positive cast to Palfreyman's experience must be read with extreme caution, though, since Ilchester was the gaol where Henry Hunt was held after Peterloo and was the subject of close investigation arising from alleged deaths in the gaol after Palfreyman's discharge.[75]

Prison surgeons, holding a salaried position rather than being coincidentally present as prisoners themselves, have been described as 'among the less visible of the unreformed prison's officers'.[76] In 1800–02 around 23 percent of prisons lacked a paid surgeon.[77] Therefore, in the early years of the nineteenth century, indebted practitioners might inadvertently become an important addition to their prison's resources. The advantages of having a medical man incarcerated with the other debtors diminished as the recruitment of official prison surgeons gathered pace in the 1820s and 1830s and prison infirmaries became a familiar part of the institutional provision.[78] By 1833, the majority of gaols had secured a medical man for a fixed annual payment, usually of between £20 and £120 *per annum*.[79] This means that the more regulated prison environment of the Victorian era might have signalled a diminution of status for the indebted practitioner, if his services as the man on the spot were increasingly ignored in favour of the man with the contract. Occupational overcrowding had arguably reached inside prison walls.

The sheer numbers of medical men who suffered either bankruptcy or insolvency can obviously be put together, but the view they would offer of the composite risk of exposure to legal process would be misleading. Regrettably, private arrangements or 'compositions' reached by medical debtors in negotiation with their creditors are largely an unknown quantity. Medical compositions and liquidations can be counted from the 1860s to set against totals for medical bankrupts and insolvents, but the facility for composition existed in law from 1825 and earlier in practice, so it is difficult to put these later figures into context.[80] Also the extensive use of compositions in the 1860s was spurred by the 1861 Act, so totals for that decade cannot be regarded as in any respect representative (Figure 1.3).[81]

Clearly these numbers must be seen as adding to the total risk of financial failure by practitioners, since compositions represented a

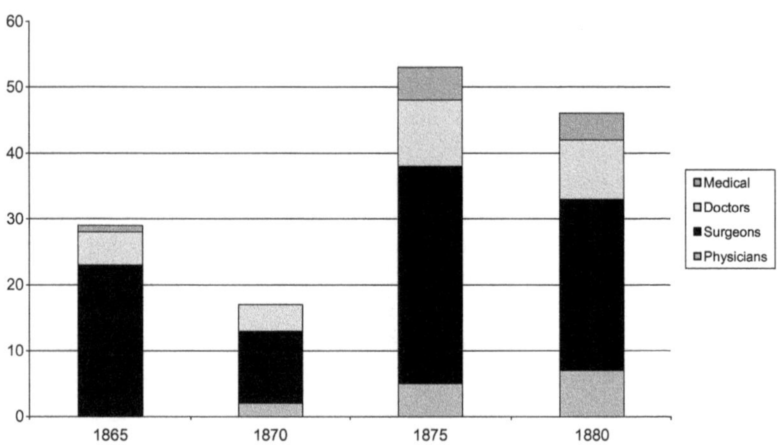

Figure 1.3 Numbers of medical compositions and liquidations

further way by which debt was externally managed, but the characteristics of this sort of strategy and its impact on medical men cannot be unfolded. There are no equivalents of the case files surviving for bankrupts, nor were there any concerted Parliamentary enquiries in this period into the phenomenon of composition. The names of these men can, though, be added to the lists for bankrupts and insolvents to augment our understanding of the risk of exposure to more than one type of process.

Recurrent indebtedness and prospects for recovery

A small cohort of medical men betrayed their vulnerability to financial problems by their repeated suffering of bankruptcy, insolvency, or the need to reach a composition with creditors. At least sixty-one men can be identified as either imprisoned on two or more separate occasions, or being declared bankrupt more than once, or by their escaping one form of penalty – such as composition – only by incurring another. These instances of failure have been located via the comparison of names found by searching the *Gazette* at five-yearly intervals 1780–1890 and for every year 1815–35. Therefore, the scope for identifying repeated failures has been constrained by the search methodology and its reduced efficiency towards the end of the period. Just seven of these repeats occur entirely after 1860, and three of them relate to men who strove to reach a composition immediately before their creditors chose to subject them to bankruptcy instead. Consequently, the occurrence of multiple processes against individual medical men was almost certainly higher.

It is remotely possible that these sixty-one examples overstate the risk of repeated failure in these years if they identify men with common first and surnames, or if the two apparent insolvencies/bankruptcies/compositions relate to fathers and sons respectively. The latter would be particularly difficult to detect if financial failure spanned two generations of practitioners who worked in the same location. There is no viable way to determine conclusively whether the Henry Edwards who became bankrupt in 1829, mentioned previously as the victim of a fraudulent business partner, was the same Henry Edwards whose bankruptcy was dated December 1840. He is included in this list of men with multiple financial crises because there is no systematic strategy for including some men but omitting others solely on the grounds of their surname. The chances of this sort of inflation are reduced by the fact that most men do not have exceptionally common surnames, and by the presence of middle names for twenty-one of the men (which would seem to constrain the scope for fathers and sons to be wrongly conflated).

Men in this cohort were most likely to undergo either repeated insolvency or one period of insolvency and one of bankruptcy, and this is unsurprising since insolvencies outnumbered bankruptcies each year, in some years by more than two to one.[82] Charles Henry Bamber suffered two insolvencies, and we can be confident that this was not merely one protracted legal proceeding or a period of unbroken imprisonment because he spent some time between his petitions abroad.[83] Bamber apparently qualified as a Licentiate of the Society of Apothecaries in 1822 and a Member of the Royal College of Surgeons in 1823, but his subsequent career in Plymouth was plainly not a success. He was subjected to legal process, submitted a petition to the Court for the Relief of Insolvent Debtors, and his case was heard in July 1831.[84] Later in the decade he went briefly to Australia, registering with the New South Wales medical board in July 1839, but he left precipitately for England the following month.[85] His financial affairs were again parlous, and November 1840 saw him petitioning the court once more, this time specifically from the gaol of St Thomas the Apostle in Exeter.[86]

One or two instances of insolvency followed by bankruptcy were causally connected, where a man was imprisoned for debt but quickly found a way to undergo bankruptcy instead and so obtain his liberty. This may have happened in unknown numbers of additional cases, where imprisonment was curtailed by the rapid onset of bankruptcy proceedings (in other words, in so short a space of time that the imprisoned man did not become visible in the *London Gazette* as petitioning the Court for Insolvent Debtors). The handful of examples found in the *Gazette* and cited here are of necessity confined to men legally entitled to petition for release from gaol by the passage of time. This was the case for John McNab Ballenden, of Sedgley in Staffordshire, who petitioned from Stafford gaol in September 1840 but had obtained a fiat in bankruptcy by November of the same year. Ballenden was an Orcadian, about twenty-seven years old in 1840 and recently married, patently suffering a rocky start to professional life. His career was not permanently blighted, however; he went on to become an MD and to oversee a household replete with both children and servants, all while remaining in Sedgley.[87]

It was more usual for a gap of some years to exist between different forms of financial failure, as there was for George John Richard James Dickinson. The surgeon, apothecary, and man-midwife of Ealing was awarded a fiat in bankruptcy on 23 May 1834 and his creditors were given notice that he would be awarded his certificate of discharge in November of the same year.[88] Dickinson's financial troubles were not over, however, as February 1840 saw him petitioning for relief from the debtor's prison for London and Middlesex.

It was much less common for men to suffer two bankruptcies. Under a fifth of repeaters fell into this category; but Henry Frederic Holt, for example, underwent one commission of bankruptcy on 23 October 1823 and (owing to a change in terminology) one fiat of bankruptcy on 13 January 1834.[89] Holt was probably around forty years old at the time of his first failure and fifty-one at his second, demonstrating that financial hardship was not just the lot of the youthful practitioner embarking on professional life.[90]

As these examples suggest, it was evidently possible to avoid permanent ruin following one or even two episodes of financial crisis. Recovery of a livelihood and of professional standing was achievable and achieved, although they were unlikely to become rich. Estate valuations in the probate index reveal just seven men, which is suggestive in itself of the career penalties of either bankruptcy or insolvency, and five of those found were valued between £20 and £300 only. Wealth following bankruptcy was improbable, but not absolutely impossible. If surgeon Henry Fuller was one person rather than three, then he was in the unusual position of living through two bankruptcies in 1821 and 1834 but nonetheless leaving an estate valued under £18,000 in 1866.[91]

More typical of this group was James Byron Bradley, for whom there is a probate valuation and an obituary. Obituaries would be a poor choice for the researcher looking for evidence of professional failure of any kind, so it is not surprising to read a placid and congratulatory summary of Bradley's life after he died in 1871. It would have been astonishing if his periods of insolvency in 1822 and 1834 had been cited in such an article.[92] What is more notable is the fact that he obtained both his MD from Paris and his LRCP in London between these two dates, and that he proceeded in the approximate decade 1835–45 to be appointed as the physician first to the Westminster General Dispensary and then to the South London Dispensary. Admission to the professional fold in the form of prestigious appointments, and even the 'good practice' which Bradley established at Buxton in the final twenty-five years of his life, did not guarantee riches, of course. When Bradley died his estate was valued at under £100.[93]

So if bankrupt and insolvent practitioners were not subsequently or permanently excluded from a medical career, how did men retrieve their finances and their working lives? Three viable support routes existed: family, professional peers, and community in the form of patients.[94] Prosperous parents, siblings or other relations might extend money to their medical sons and brothers to re-establish literal credit. Former and future patients might invest faith in men, particularly if medical reputations were given a boost by a successful case. Assistance from colleagues in the insolvent's immediate vicinity was likely to be complicated by marketplace competition, which was an inherent component in day-to-day dealings with neighbouring men. Even so, peer-to-peer support is the only possible recovery route with a related historical source base, in the form of evidence from the medical benevolent funds.

Medical benevolent funds

Medical funds designed to benefit practitioners, rather than charities for the sick poor, have their origins in the late eighteenth century.[95] The earliest such charity was probably the Essex and Hertfordshire Benevolent Society, based in Colchester from 1786, and it was soon followed by other regional examples.[96] Initially these charities were directed towards the dependents of practitioners rather than the men themselves, as in the Society for Relief of Widows and Orphans of Medical Men established 1788, and in operation they were more akin to friendly societies rather than to the subscription charities beloved of eighteenth-century philanthropists. The funds were happy to receive subscriptions or donations from people other than practitioners, but the benefits were designed only for the families of men who had maintained their subscriptions, rather than for the families of anyone in need. Payments were not proportioned to the subscriptions, however; as an address by the Essex and Hertfordshire society made clear, 'if it had been formed upon the general plan of Annuity Societies, the benefits might have fallen in many cases to widows and children not in want of assistance; and in others, relief could not have been proportioned to the degree of real distress, which is the object of this society'.[97] This move towards occupationally targeted charity was an understandable manifestation of professionalising practitioners' desire to promote a public face of financial disinterestedness. Not only did they refrain from forcing their poorest patients to pay fees, but also they extended support to the poor families of their peers.

The first fund with a national scope was the Medical Benevolent Fund instituted in 1836 by the Provincial Medical and Surgical Association, the predecessor body to the British Medical Association.[98] This fund was more expansive in its reach, because from the outset it was designed to assist medical men as well as their dependents, and was available to families and practitioners who were not members of the parent Association.[99] There was a condition that beneficiaries 'must be free of idleness, extravagance and evil habits of any kind', terminology associated with charities for the poor since the sixteenth century but even so a jarring reminder that all applicants for charity, whether incipient professionals or not, could expect to have their behaviour scrutinised.[100] Importantly, such a clause did offer the fund's managers the prospect of refusing an application on grounds other than insufficient funds. It was a problematic clause for bankrupt or insolvent practitioners to address, though, because it implied that acute financial need was not sufficient justification for assistance; they would be required to plead innocence in the matter of their 'failure'.

The relationship between the Medical Benevolent Fund and its male beneficiaries was potentially quite awkward, not least for the male applicants' sense of themselves. It was one thing to contemplate family members being relieved after one's death, and quite another to have to ask for help oneself from one's professional peers. The tenets of Victorian masculinity were of course constantly shifting, but at no point from 1836 onwards was it an acceptable middle-class masculine trait to be needy, or to ask for help.[101]

Yet the availability of money for men, in addition to widows or orphans, makes the Medical Benevolent Fund of particular interest and relevance to the consideration of medical hardship. How much money was devoted to the relief of medical men, and what proportion of annual expenditure went to practitioners rather than widows or orphans? What sorts of hardship among men were regarded favourably, and were there types of request that were rejected? Was the fund a viable resource for bankrupt and insolvent practitioners, or was it reserved for other forms of distress?

The annual reports of the Fund supply details about total expenditure, the sums devoted to one-off payments and the annual cost of funding annuities. Money was tight in the early years, so that the Fund was only able to disburse a very few, modest sums totalling under £100 per annum, but receipts rose quickly from the 1850s and by the 1880s the Fund was accustomed to give totals in excess of £3,000 a year. In terms of one-off payments, male practitioners were quite prominent among beneficiaries in the 1850s, but their number remained relatively constant so that, against a backdrop of increasing availability of money, their significance declined sharply. By the 1880s, less than 15 percent of grants were made to men each year (Figure 1.4).

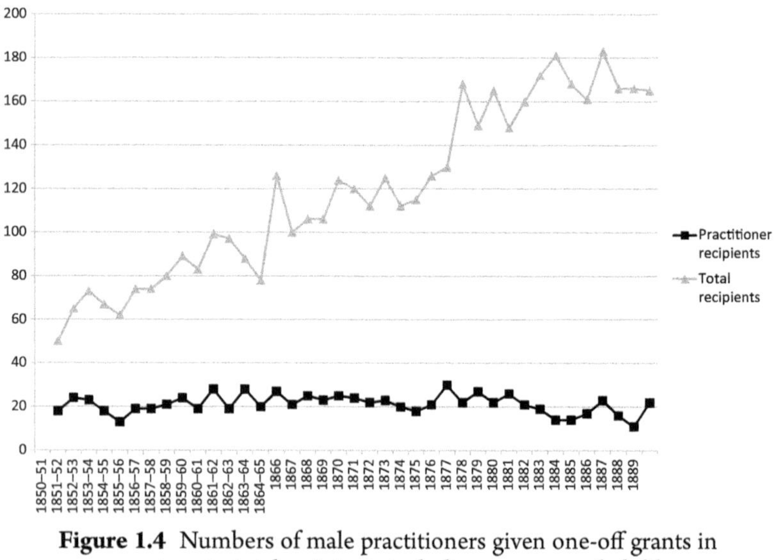

Figure 1.4 Numbers of male practitioners given one-off grants in comparison to total recipients including women and children

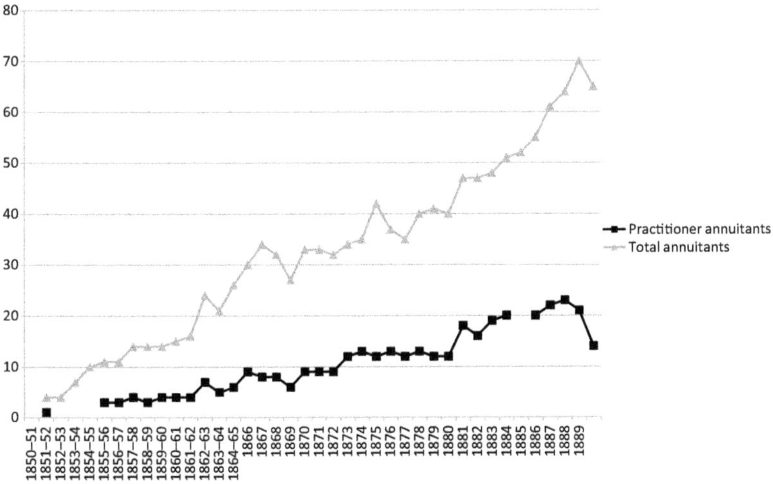

Figure 1.5 Numbers of male practitioners given annuities in comparison to total annuities including those given to women and children

Men were more strongly represented among annuity recipients in as much as their numbers kept rising across the second half of the century, if not at the same rate as their female counterparts. This meant that by the 1880s men usually occupied between 30 and 40 percent of the annuity places (Figure 1.5).

The decisions made by the Fund's committee in the case of named applicants was scrutinised in four sample years – 1851, 1861, 1871, and 1881 – in order that family and other circumstances surrounding men's applications for help could be amplified by reference to their census entry. In the cases of male applicants, old age, infirmity, illness or disability was reliably cited as justification for relief. Practitioners who were insane, and therefore required payments for their treatment in asylums, formed a small, notable subset of male beneficiaries.[102] The numbers of dependents in a practitioner's family, or their children's disabilities, were also prominent in the minutes. If hardship was ongoing but there were no annuity places available, individuals might be given multiple grants of £5 or £10. Larger sums and moral endorsement was available wherever an applicant had already had sums raised on their behalf by colleagues, patients, family, and other supporters. The

Fund favoured match-funding privately raised money at £15 or £25 per grant. This tendency to recognise and reward evidence of social connection was not new, since charities like the Gloucestershire Prison Charity Committee had behaved in exactly the same way in the late eighteenth century.[103] Not all applicants were successful, though, as meetings frequently noted that an applicant's case was not judged 'proper' or 'meriting relief', and the reasons behind negative judgements are not elucidated.

Reference to the men's census entries gives sporadic insight into their household structures and domestic facilities. Unfortunately, less than half of all male beneficiaries could be confidently located in a census of the same year, so no complete or systematic breakdown of men with spouses, children, dependents, servants or other employees is feasible. It is certain, though, that these men's domestic status ran the gamut from being institutional inmates to their retention of an independent home as the heads of households. In addition to two men in lunatic asylums, MS was the patient and residential inmate of a London workhouse infirmary. In contrast YS lived with his wife, two sons, and one servant.

Insolvency and bankruptcy were not in themselves an explicitly high priority for the Fund, since the minutes barely alluded to such legal confirmations of hardship in their deliberations. The only notable exception to this silence is the case of TS, a bankrupt who also happened to have served for many years as an honorary treasurer to a provincial branch of the British Medical Association. The size of his family was also adduced to strengthen his case for support. He was voted £20, to be disbursed in weekly sums of fifteen shillings.[104] Presumably this grant was in addition to any money for maintenance allowed by the bankruptcy process, and was not declared to the man's creditors (so could not be raided to augment dividends).

A sample comparison of the names of men given assistance by the Fund with the men who were named as either bankrupt or insolvent in 1861 reveals that the silence in the minutes was indeed a reflection of the Fund's relieving policy rather than a coincidental omission.[105] No men appeared in both lists and very few appeared as applicants to the Fund in a year that was not chronologically coincident with subjection to the law of debt. Of course, the chronological disjunction between the bulk of the bankruptcy and insolvency data (clustering before

1860) and the energetic actions of the Fund (from the mid 1850s onwards) militated against the identification of significant crossover. Ideally it would be possible to compare the names of all men assisted in the nineteenth century with bankrupts and insolvents in all years, for the simple reason that a financial crisis did not necessarily generate an application for relief in the same calendar year. Research on this scale was not possible, and perhaps inadvisable given the strong suggestion from the minutes that bankruptcy and insolvency were little noticed, but a chance find among the Fund's applicants in the early 1870s opened a window on to the life-cycle nature of professional hardship and poverty. AY was a practitioner in the south-east of England whose home town did not change from the time of his first entry in the *London Gazette* until his death. He was among the men who suffered repeated financial hardship, undergoing both insolvency and bankruptcy in the 1820s when aged in his thirties. The same decade saw the birth of his triplets, which event probably doubled his household dependents and magnified his outgoings at one stroke. His subsequent financial recovery is implied by the 1841 census, when he probably employed three household servants, and may have been predicated somewhat on his medical publishing; he authored two works in the years immediately after his bankruptcy. The General Medical Council registered him in the 1860s, but he encountered hardship again in old age. He applied to the Medical Benevolent Fund for grants and was given one-off payments of £10–15. He was then elected to an annuity, which he retained until his death in the mid 1870s.[106] Thus, AY's partial biography goes some way to confirm that applicants to the Fund may have suffered bankruptcy or insolvency, but at a distance of years or decades from their appearance in the minutes.

It is not surprising that philanthropic support from colleagues would concentrate on domestic, personal or bodily misfortune rather than on the direct consequences of legal prosecution for debt. Both generalised charitable motivations and the sometimes covert competition of the medical marketplace militated against this sort of focus for medical benevolent funds. This leaves open the question of how men did return to solvency, medical practice, and their career identity. Families and former patients presumably offered some men the support they needed, albeit their collective impact is unquantifiable. A final possibility remains: medical qualifications and occupational labels carried enough inherent value to re-establish a man's credit, both literally and figuratively, without the need for financial reinvestment.

Conclusion

Financial turbulence, hardship, and associated legal processes were a reality for a minority of all practitioners, and a recurrent one for the unfortunate few. Nonetheless, the risk of exposure to insolvency or bankruptcy rose noticeably in the 1820s and so was most acute in the period when the rhetoric of overcrowding emerged prominently among the profession. This is hardly a shock, but it is the first time that the calculations have been made. The experience of insolvent men must remain largely opaque, but bankruptcy case files offer a view of the difficulties that beset the profession, particularly in the 1820s and 1830s.

Repeated encounters with one or other process are evidence of a career shot through with financial uncertainty, but even for these men 'failure' was not a permanent blight on either their working lives or their social standing. Recovery from a financial crisis and the restoration of prosperity based on medicine was a viable ambition, even where men remained in the same locality where their former 'failure' was well known. The strategies and components of recovery must still be guessed, however, since they did not include the one official source of support open to practitioners from 1836 in the form of the Medical Benevolent Fund.

What elaborations are possible, then, in our understanding of the nineteenth-century medical marketplace? First, spending by medical practices and households could remain high long after incomes fell, or after a shortfall between earnings and outgoings should have become apparent. A costly performance of status was permitted to outrun resource. The confidence inspired by medicine as an occupation and by evidence of consumption seems to have encouraged both practitioners and their creditors to continue their business uninterrupted. In this way, undue or blind optimism made a discernible contribution to the scale of the problem; legal action only arose when medical debt had become so large as to be unavoidable. Second, the constrained nature of professional self-promotion encouraged the development of alternative measures to compete with colleagues or protect a practice. It should come as no surprise if some of those measures were covert or aggressive, only coming to light alongside public exposure of other problems such as debt. The most obvious way to challenge a competitor was to entice private patients away from them, as Hunter attempted with Steight in 1811. This was a palpable concern in the medical press, but there were other less obvious ways to undermine a local colleague, such as inscribing territoriality into partnership contracts – as Steight had demanded of Hunter in his turn. This phenomenon of covert competition is reinforced in later chapters, most prominently in Chapter 3 concerning allegations of neglect and Chapter 6 in relation to practitioner suicide. Third, the practical impact of financial failure was frequently outweighed by forces impelling recovery. This suggests that the social investment in practitioners by their patients, creditors, and others, perhaps by those keen to see medical men as respectable middle-class professionals regardless of messy details like individuals' debt, meant that confidence was rapidly reasserted. Arguably, medical solvency enjoyed a privileged reputation even in the first half of the nineteenth century when it was most challenged.

This chapter has analysed what might be considered the most obvious indication of career turbulence in any occupation: the inability to make a financial living. In the case of medical men this appears to have been, for many, a temporary material disruption to a professional career. Disappointment or uncertainty are much more difficult to pin down and perhaps, given the emphasis above on the potency of confidence, were sentiments that were highly likely to be suppressed in the nineteenth century. This renders any expressions of dissatisfaction with discrete medical career pathways of particular interest. Therefore, the next chapter turns to disappointment as a relative rather than absolute marker of turbulence.

Notes

1 S. Marriner, 'English bankruptcy records and statistics before 1850', *English Historical Review* 33 (1980), pp. 351–66, on pp. 352–6.

2 V.M. Lester, *Victorian Insolvency. Bankruptcy, Imprisonment for Debt, and Company Winding-up in Nineteenth-Century England* (Oxford: Clarendon Press, 1995), pp. 1–3.

3 Lester, *Victorian Insolvency*, pp. 88–93.

4 D.M. Evans, *Facts, Failures, and Frauds: Revelations Financial Mercantile Criminal* (Groombridge: London, 1859); T.L. Alborn, 'The moral of the failed bank: professional plots in the Victorian money market', *Victorian Studies* 38:2 (1995), pp. 199–226.

5 S. Collini, 'The idea of "character" in Victorian political thought', *Transactions of the Royal Historical Society* 35 (1985), pp. 29–50, on p. 40.

6 H. Goodman, '"Madness and Masculinity": Male Patients in London Asylums and Victorian Culture', in T. Knowles and S. Trowbridge (eds), *Insanity and the Lunatic Asylum in the Nineteenth Century* (London: Pickering and Chatto, 2015), pp. 149–65, for 'money mania'.

7 For random processes, see Lester, *Victorian Insolvency*, pp. 278–9.

8 J. Rule, *Albion's People: English Society 1714–1815* (London: Longman, 1992), p. 65; M.J. Peterson, *The Medical Profession in Mid-Victorian London* (Berkeley: University of California Press, 1978), pp. 91, 215, 222–4.

9 Lester, *Victorian Insolvency*, p. 3

10 Another way was through the Medical Directories published from 1845; A. Crowther and M. Dupree, *Medical Lives in the Age of Surgical Revolution* (Cambridge: Cambridge University Press, 2007), pp. 125, 176.

11 It is likely that even more commissions were initially sealed but never 'opened' and gazetted; Lester, *Victorian Insolvency*, pp. 73–5.

12 From 30 April 2013 the Discovery catalogue became the only way to search the archive's holdings; www.nationalarchives.gov.uk/news/834.htm viewed 3 December 2013.

13 Lester, *Victorian Insolvency*, pp. 21, 61–2, 73.

14 Satisfaction required the agreement of four-fifths of creditors, by number and by the value of the money owed to them; Lester, *Victorian Insolvency*, p. 18.

15 Collectively, the bad debts may have been the root cause of the medical bankruptcy, just as they could be in non-medical cases; Lester, *Victorian Insolvency*, p. 215.

16 P.H. Haagen, 'Eighteenth-century English Society and the Debt Law', in S. Cohen and A. Scull (eds), *Social Control and the State* (Oxford: M. Robertson, 1983), pp. 222–47, on p. 235. Lester, *Victorian Insolvency*, p. 103 for a short list of relevant eighteenth-century Acts.

17 Lester, *Victorian Insolvency*, pp. 95, 106–16.

18 Lester, *Victorian Insolvency*, pp. 15–16. Doctors were not of course alone in their ambiguous relation to trading status. Multiple cases of bankruptcy became caught up in the problematic definition of a 'trader', before and during the period of this study of doctors; see also I.P.H. Duffy, *Bankruptcy and Insolvency in London during the Industrial Revolution* (New York: Garland, 1985), pp. 18–23, 56–7.

19 Duffy, *Bankruptcy*, p. 22. For surgeons as 'doubtful' traders, see Parliamentary Papers (P.P.) *Report of the Commissioners for Inquiring into Bankruptcy and Insolvency* (1840), p. viii.
20 Duffy, *Bankruptcy*, p. 52.
21 J.G.L. Burnby, *A Study of the English Apothecary from 1660 to 1760* (Medical History supplement number 3, 1983), pp. 110–11.
22 M. Finn, *The Character of Credit. Personal Debt in English Culture, 1740–1914* (Cambridge: Cambridge University Press: 2003), p. 150.
23 Medical bankruptcy in the late eighteenth and early nineteenth centuries took place under an Act of 1732, which consolidated previous legislation in this area.
24 Lester, *Victorian Insolvency*, pp. 79–80.
25 Lester, *Victorian Insolvency*, p. 2
26 Lester, *Victorian Insolvency*, pp. 113–15. An Act of 1842 also enabled a debtor to petition the bankruptcy court to examine their assets and so protect the debtor from imprisonment.
27 Lester, *Victorian Insolvency*, p. 61
28 Lester, *Victorian Insolvency*, p. 117
29 Lester, *Victorian Insolvency*.
30 'Are Medical Practitioners "Traders"?', *British Medical Journal* 14 June 1888, p. 105.
31 The case was known as *Hance v. Harding*, decided by Baron Huddleston without a jury in December 1887.
32 P.P. *Fourth, Fifth, Sixth, Seventh and Eighth reports by the Board of Trade under section 131 of the Bankruptcy Act, 1883* (1887–1891), p. 50, p. 49, p. 51, p. 41, and p. 44 respectively. For the higher proportional risk to other professions, see A. Digby, *Making a Medical Living. Doctors and Patients in the English market for Medicine, 1720–1911* (Cambridge: Cambridge University Press, 1994), p. 166.
33 'Bankruptcy Analysis', *The Standard* 11 February 1830, p. 3.
34 Society for the Diffusion of Useful Knowledge, *Companion to the Almanac and Year Book of General Information for 1834* (London: Society for the Diffusion of Useful Knowledge, 1833) and subsequent editions.
35 References given in full at Table 1.3.
36 A. Digby, *The Evolution of British General Practice, 1850–1948* (Oxford: Oxford University Press, 1999), pp. 97, 124.
37 Lester, *Victorian Insolvency*, p. 261.
38 Lester, *Victorian Insolvency*, pp. 266–70.
39 Lester, *Victorian Insolvency*, pp. 273–80, 300–1.
40 'Progress of Temperance', *Liverpool Mercury* 10 January 1845, p 6.
41 Lester, *Victorian Insolvency*, p. 244.

42 I. Loudon, *Medical Care and the General Practitioner 1750–1850* (Oxford: Clarendon Press, 1986), pp. 214–23.
43 Fewer than 100 case files per year survive before 1811, and the total number rises little higher than 100 until 1826; Duffy, *Bankruptcy*, p. 369.
44 Marriner, 'English Bankruptcy Records', p. 361.
45 Lester, *Victorian Insolvency*, p. 303.
46 National Archives (N.A.), B3/3128.
47 N.A., B3/938.
48 Digby, *Evolution*, pp. 108–9 for the relatively late appreciation by practitioners of the significance of bad debt.
49 P.P. *Report from the Select Committee on the Bankrupt Laws* (1817), p. 42.
50 N.A., B 9/1.
51 N.A., B 9/3.
52 Lester, *Victorian Insolvency*, pp. 251–2; see also random factors such as illness and the small scale of businesses, pp. 278–9.
53 N.A., B 3/1630.
54 N.A., B 3/1962.
55 N.A., B 9/140.
56 N.A., B 9/3.
57 P.P. *Report from the Select Committee on Medical Education* (1834).
58 N.A., B 3/4813Q; emphasis is Sleigh's. He may also have been an early victim of the opposition to specialisation, see Peterson, *Medical Profession*, p. 272.
59 [Untitled] *London Gazette* 22 October 1852, p. 2775.
60 N.A., B 3/4488. John Steight's case file is dated 1815, but from internal evidence it is plain that the bankruptcy occurred in 1811.
61 The potential presence of such contractual clauses is mentioned without elaboration in Peterson, *Medical Profession*, p. 118; see also the dispute between Henry Hase and John Dakeyne discussed in Chapter 3.
62 Digby, *Medical Living*, p. 108 and *passim*.
63 This was the sort of 'patient-pinching' that, 100 years later, attracted firm professional penalties; see Digby, *Evolution*, p. 103.
64 Duffy, *Bankruptcy*, p. 372.
65 For example, the 1861 census gives 15,297 medical men while the same year saw thirty-nine medical insolvencies; this gives one insolvency for every 392 men.
66 This includes thirty-five men who were held in either King's Bench or, after 1842, the same place then known as Queen's Bench.
67 Finn, *Character of Credit*, pp. 115, 118.
68 P.P. *An account of the names, trades, and description, of the several persons, who have applied to be discharged under the acts of Parliament of the 53rd and*

54th *years of His Present Majesty's reign, "for the relief of insolvent debtors in England"* (1814–15).

69 This was the average for twenty-two of the men, omitting one man whose debt was clearly anomalous at £10,365, and one other man who was mad at the time of discharge (so his total debt could not be ascribed).

70 Duffy, *Bankruptcy*, p. 57.

71 P.P. *Returns of the names of Commissioners and Officers employed in the Court for the Relief of Insolvent Debtors in England, rules and orders, and other matters relating to the said Court* (1822), pp. 16–119.

72 P.P. *Report for the Committee appointed to enquire into the practice and effects of imprisonment for debt* (1792), pp. 60–2.

73 P.P. *Appendix to a report of the commissions appointed to inquire into the state of Ilchester Gaol* (1822), pp. 240–7.

74 Palfreyman was being rewarded for extraordinary rather than routine services, because he assisted the prison surgeon Dr Woodford in an epidemic of typhus fever. P.M. Higgins, *Punish or Treat? Medical care in English prisons 1770–1850* (Oxford: Trafford, 2007), pp. 76–7.

75 I. Burney, *Bodies of Evidence. Medicine and the Politics of the English Inquest 1830–1926* (Baltimore: Johns Hopkins University Press, 2000), pp. 31–3.

76 Finn, *Character of Credit*, p. 137.

77 Finn, *Character of Credit*, p. 137.

78 Higgins, *Punish or Treat?*, pp. 51–6.

79 P.P. *Return to an address to His Majesty, dated 2 May 1833; – for, return of the establishment of officers and servants employed in each county gaol and house of correction in England and Wales; specifying the number and description of such officers and servants, the salaries and emoluments of each, and by whom such officers and servants are respectively appointed.* (1833) Lower payments typically did not include the cost of medicines, while larger stipends were usually intended to be inclusive.

80 Duffy, *Bankruptcy*, p. 337.

81 Duffy, *Bankruptcy*, p. 340.

82 P.P. *Return of the Bankrupts and Insolvent Debtors in each Year between 1801 and 1819, and 1820 and 1846 inclusive* (1847–48).

83 His difficulties may have emanated from one period of acute financial difficulty, since relief from imprisonment did not wipe out debt in the same manner as a bankruptcy certificate, and since a second creditor from the same period in Bamber's life might seek the satisfaction of his arrest and imprisonment much later than the first one had done. Even if this were the case, the two legal processes against Bamber must still have been separate.

84 'The Court for Relief of Insolvent Debtors', *London Gazette* 5 July 1831, p. 1358.
85 www.medicalpioneers.com Australian Medical Pioneers Index, viewed 17 September 2012.
86 'Court for Relief of Insolvent Debtors', *London Gazette* 27 November 1840, p. 2840.
87 N.A., RG 11/2868/107. Ballenden's prosperity did not insulate him from other forms of career turbulence, though, because he suffered an allegation of medical negligence in an obstetric case at the height of his career; see Chapter 3.
88 [Untitled] *London Gazette* 23 September 1834, p. 1730 and [untitled] *ibid.*, 28 November 1834, p. 2184.
89 [Untitled] *London Gazette* 1 June 1824, p. 899, and [untitled] *ibid.*, 6 May 1834 p. 824.
90 www.ancestry.co.uk gives the birth of a Henry Frederic Holt on 12 September 1783 in Hornsey, Middlesex; viewed 13 July 2011.
91 National Probate Calendar 1858–1966, viewed via www.ancestry.co.uk on 25 May 2012.
92 'Obituary', *British Medical Journal* 1 April 1871, p. 356.
93 National Probate Calendar 1858–1966, viewed via Ancestry.co.uk on 12 June 2011.
94 For general reference to support from families, see Digby, *Making a Medical Living*, p. 159.
95 In addition to various funds outlined in the following, the 1850s saw the foundation of a Medical Benevolent College, to provide schooling for the children of practitioners and almshouses for men and their widows. This charity is not considered here, because its practical impact on adult men was minimal; only one man was resident at the time of the 1861 census for example. For further details, see M.A. Salmon, *Epsom College 1855–1980. The First 125 Years* (The College: Oxford, 1980) and A. Scadding, *Benevolence and Excellence. 150 Years of the Royal Medical Foundation of Epsom College* ([Epsom?]: The College, 2004).
96 A.B. Shaw, 'Two centuries of medical benevolence: the Norfolk and Norwich Benevolent Medical Society, 1786–1986', *British Medical Journal* 292 (1986), pp. 1066–7.
97 *A State of the Charity for the Relief of Widows and Orphans of Medical Men, in Essex and Hertfordshire* (Bocking: [The Charity?], 1794).
98 Other national bodies took much longer to develop. The Medical Sickness Annuity and Life Assurance Society was not founded until 1884; see G.J. Knapman, *Care for the Caring. Medical Sickness Annuity and Life Assurance Society Limited, 1884–1984* (London: Henry Melland, 1984).

99 E.M. Little, *History of the British Medical Association 1832–1932* (London: British Medical Association, 1932), pp. 254–5.

100 R.M. Handfield Jones, *A History of the Royal Medical Benevolent Fund* (London: The Fund, 1962), p. 9.

101 See my own discussion of the implications of poverty for masculinity: A. Tomkins, 'Labouring on a Bed of Sickness: The Material and Rhetorical Deployment of Ill-health in Male Pauper Letters', in A. Gestrich, E. Hurren, and S. King (eds), *Poverty and Sickness in Modern Europe* (London: Continuum, 2012), pp. 51–68.

102 This cohort included men found for Chapter 5. Insanity provided a justification for the support of men by provincial societies, too. Mr Headley of Folkingham was supported in the Lincoln Asylum by the Lincolnshire Medical Benevolent Society from 1836 until his death in 1864, one of only eight men assisted by the society up to 1890; see Lincolnshire Archives, LMBS 3/1 Lincolnshire Medical Benevolent Society account book 1823–67.

103 Finn, *Character of Credit*, p. 164.

104 Royal Medical Benevolent Fund Archive (R.M.B.F.) MIN/COM/4, minute book 1869–77.

105 1861 was chosen as the optimum year for this comparison because insolvency remained in operation, and the efficacy of digital searching probably remained high, while the Fund's scale of operation had risen from its fairly modest start in 1850.

106 R.M.B.F. MIN/COM/4, minute book 1869–77. This intermittent biography is generated by reference to the *London Gazette*, the 1841 census (which gives the composition of AY's household including his triplets), editions of the *Medical Directory*, the GMC *Register*, and death registration records, but in order to comply with the Fund's requirement of anonymity for recipients, specific references and pages cannot be given here.

2

Thwarted ambition and disappointing careers? Narratives of the Indian Medical Service

Those not able to find a remunerative position in Britain might forestall bankruptcy or other forms of severe career disruption by seeking service overseas. The British Empire opened up a variety of locations and roles to men willing to travel, but India offered more posts and potentially higher rewards than other options. Appointment to the Indian Medical Service (IMS) has been construed as instrumental in making individual fortunes or reputations, and in advancing medical professionalisation *per se*.[1] In contrast to the literature, however, this chapter shifts the perspective by considering the conflicts inherent in Indian service for men participating in a reforming, professionalising career. It does not merely repeat the claims of Terrence Johnson that salaried service inhibited the development of a specifically professional culture, but unpicks in detail the tensions between individual ambition, Company conditions, professionalising impulses, and the emotional range of medical masculinity.[2] The chapter argues that a posting to India might at first represent a decisive check to energetic medical ambition, and that while men might become reconciled to colonial living and enthusiastic about their lifestyle in India, they often did so in the face of palpable and unanticipated disadvantages. It examines narratives from men in IMS service to reveal the same concerns that troubled their medical counterparts in Britain around professional opportunity, patronage, income, expenditure, and promotion. It also analyses the reported emotional states of the men concerned, and their own attempts to chart their contentment or dissatisfaction with their professional choices and personal lives. The survey concludes that India provided an alternative forum for the display of medical competition rather than any scope for its meaningful reduction. In the process, it taps into a refrain of disappointment at odds with assumptions of opportunity.

Medical employment in the East India Company

Practitioners intent on working abroad could consider service with the army, the navy, on merchant, emigrant, or convict ships, or with the East India Company (EIC).[3] Terms of service before first entitlement to leave varied, but all offered the scope to earn a stock of money wherewith to buy into private practice on return to Britain, or even the chance to make a fortune by either dutiful or enterprising means.[4] Not all men took this path, as many completed their careers within their chosen service or died before their term was out, but return home was frequently the intended goal whether before or after effective retirement.[5] These options were particularly attractive for men with limited access to personal patronage, and for whom a notionally reliable salary was more attractive than the uncertainties of private practice.[6] The inherent requirement to travel was also a potential benefit, if not universally regarded as such.

The obverse of opportunity was distaste, as there were many reasons to find salaried service unpalatable. The danger and discomfort of absence from home and exposure to risk took many forms. Death from either violent conflict or disease was a distinct possibility, and the inconveniences of life on campaign or at sea were manifold.[7] There were also gradations between the services such that, for example, in the early nineteenth century the standing of practitioners in the army was generally higher than that of their naval colleagues, and an Indian posting might have been more attractive than either.[8] That said, exposure to one service might predispose practitioners in its favour, or bring to light disadvantages with their own or other services which were not obvious at first appointment. India was notably unattractive for those who had left the army medical service, partly because entry to the EIC disqualified former army doctors from half pay – they had no continued need of an army pension if they were once again in a salaried post – but also given other considerations including assumptions around climactic vulnerability. Only 2 of the 293 army practitioners studied by Ackroyd et al. who were recruited during the French wars 1793–1815 and died after leaving the service did so in India, a proportion attributed loosely to the climate of the sub-continent and the rhetoric surrounding tropical medical service as injurious to health.[9]

The IMS originated in the early seventeenth century as an adjunct to the military and trading ambitions of the EIC. By 1780, the service was of necessity a component in increasingly colonialist British intentions, and was organised under the three presidencies of Bengal, Madras, and Bombay. The total number of practitioners in the service in 1785 stood at 234, and for most of the nineteenth century the total fell between 600 and 800 men.[10] Therefore, appointments in the service offered a great many placements for practitioners, alleviating the professional overcrowding experienced in Britain. Perhaps as a result of both the background of recruits and their increasing numbers, 'the social and professional standing of medical officers in India appears not to have been very high, and certainly before 1857 they were often looked down upon by the European civilian and military elite'.[11]

Men concerned with their reputational status, and particularly any who considered it tied to prospects for medical reform, would have been given pause by the terms of IMS service. The Company effectively disrupted any moves by medical men towards professional disinterest by introducing a specialised, internal medical market. Open self-promotion in Britain was becoming increasingly unacceptable and, as Chapter 1 suggests, was being channelled into private strategies; in India, medical men were to some extent returned to an earlier era, in which personal patronage and canvassing for support were essential to advancement. This is not what might have been expected from a system which ostensibly prized seniority above all other considerations. Practitioners were promoted from assistant surgeon to full surgeon, in turn, solely on the basis of their place in the recruitment 'list' and not on performance or skill. This system would appear to obviate the need for any personal exertion, but in practice technical promotion was not the only route to higher incomes and advantageous postings. Active military service yielded higher daily allowances at the cost of personal comfort, but the really prized roles involved work with European civilians in attractive locations. Securing one of these jobs (after the requisite term of two years of service with the army) required high-status Company or Indian Government contacts, assiduous cultivation of social capital, and luck. The blatant self-promotion required in this context generated responses among medical men from disappointed surprise to bitter resentment.[12]

An appointment in India was equally disruptive for practitioners' sense of their identities as men. East India Company service has been linked with Victorian definitions of colonial masculinity, but medical masculinity was no less significant, and arguably was quite conflicted in the early-to-mid nineteenth century. The problem for practitioners before the mid 1850s was that they performed a version of medical masculinity that was valorised only later in the century. Their surrender of personal preferences in deference to duty, their self-reliance and physical exertion in the face of untamed nature and uncivilised humanity, were what contributed to later Victorian determinants of ideal masculinity.[13] In the earlier period, however, the social dividends of this performance were less obvious, not least because the 1830s to the 1850s comprised 'the heyday of masculine domesticity ... Middle-class men did not imagine that they were ever likely to be called to a life of adventure.'[14] At the same time, attempts to co-opt military metaphors and invest practitioners with heroic martial courage took time to become plausible beyond the confines of the medical press.[15]

Aside from trends in hegemonic manliness, there were at all times men who did not experience or express an 'undifferentiated proclivity for domination', whether over women or colonial subjects; not all men were content to assume a practical role in the civilising mission or wider political imperial project.[16] In the twentieth century, practitioners acquired the social cachet of those in authority able to explain disease and offer the reassurance of comprehension and alleviation.[17] This authority was arguably part and parcel of the rising status of medicine that eventually trumped the uncertainties of colonial masculinity. But the benefits of professional status partly derived from imperial service were yet to be realised for men in post before the mid 1850s.[18] Just as power was not necessarily granted to colonisers, so it was not necessarily taken, or taken willingly.[19]

It is also entirely possible that the struggles of individual medical men anticipated the diagnoses of neurasthenia or tropical neurasthenia which so marked the early twentieth-century and interwar periods.[20] They were certainly at risk of the same forms of alienation, deriving from separation from family, shortage of cash, monotony of activity, weariness of waiting for promotion, and irritation from the climate, flora, and fauna of the sub-continent; 'an alien environment that combined bodily discomfort with cultural disorientation made many of them susceptible to fear and depression'.[21] Across the nineteenth century these symptoms were collectively badged 'ennui' and recognised as highly dangerous or fatal, but the fact that medical practitioners were among those who defined the malaise did not insulate them from it.[22] Moreover, the evolution of British ambitions in India across the first half of the nineteenth century, combined with an ongoing or increasing sense of political and military fragility, meant that this was a critical period for the formation of 'white prestige' that so influenced later nineteenth- and twentieth-century colonial episodes in both Asia and Africa. Practitioners were emphatically representatives of British authority, holding 'dominance without hegemony – an autocracy that ruled without consent', responsible for forging and then upholding the characteristics of difference.[23] Many who did not recognisably suffer from ennui might nonetheless be beset with the unfocused anxiety that arose from the formulation of difference and separation, ignorance and uncertainty; the features of this anxiety specifically for the medical subalterns of the British state have not so far been heeded, since even in the historiography of professionalisation it has been 'enthusiasm that has been allowed to dominate [colonialist] narratives'.[24]

Consequently, this discussion comments tangentially on the robustness, or otherwise, of imperial networks. It is a well-established feature of recent histories of empire that the British, overtly and coincidentally, laid down worldwide networks that were not merely literal, using ports, ships and cargoes, but also discursive via newspapers, letters, and telegraphy.[25] This was, however, a gradual and cumulative process that could not rely on speedy or precise transmission of intangibles like professional values. For the men and careers featured in the forthcoming text, connections were just as likely to be attenuated or severed as they were to be forged.[26]

Therefore this chapter considers the men recruited to the IMS up to the end of 1854, both to align with a period of particular stress for medical (and colonial) masculinity but also to acknowledge the disjunctions between embarking on service before and after the mid 1850s. From 1855 to 1872 the terms of service changed so drastically, owing to conditions within India and developments beyond it, that service was transformed for the final third of the nineteenth century.

This began with reforms specific to the medical service, including the introduction of competitive entry examinations in 1855, meaning that recruits no longer needed to exert any influence to gain an appointment. This innovation was quickly succeeded by new warrants of service (in 1859 and 1864), moratoria on recruitment (1861–65, and again 1870–72), and the requirement to serve a year of training at Netley after 1863.[27] The imperial shock of the 'mutiny' in 1857 and the imposition of crown rule from 1858 made a significant difference to the mindset of later recruits, if rather less impact on the day-to-day experience of practising medicine in India.[28] From the 1850s, developments in communications and transport of all kinds, starting with the introduction of the electric telegraph, road improvements, and railway building, and capped by the opening of the Suez Canal in 1869, made a significant difference to the time it took to transport men, materials, and correspondence within India and between the sub-continent and Britain.[29] The disjunctions that these changes caused in the outlook of IMS recruits mean that narratives from men recruited before 1855 will be distinct from late-century equivalents. They are also fruitful for an examination of professional disadvantage.

There are three routes into this topic. The first is through an analysis of the aggregate practitioner experience that may be gleaned from Crawford's *Roll of the Indian Medical Service*. This work lists the outlines of men's working lives, including the dates of their qualifications, recruitment, promotions, and deaths. As such it can be used to test the probability of IMS employees reaching first and subsequent promotions, and to chart their propensity to die in Britain or India. The second strategy is to review the notice given to conditions of Indian medical service in the lay and medical press. How far was professional opportunity in India explicitly puffed or denigrated? The third opportunity is offered by the letters, diaries, and memoirs written by men during or after their service in India. The writers of letters and journals were able to reflect at length on their reactions to their working lives and coincidentally provide significant evidence of disappointment, frustration, and regret. The following discussion focuses on ten extended narratives that punctuate the period 1798 to 1867. The majority of these practitioners took service in the Bengal presidency; only one opted for Bombay and one for Madras. Six of the narratives came from men all recruited between 1823 and 1830 during the years when financial prosecutions at home were reaching an early peak, but if any of them hoped to avoid acute financial problems they were misled.[30] This was the same generation of men who saw a reduction in their salaries following government retrenchments in 1828 and who in all likelihood suffered to some extent from the failure of the great agency houses in India, concentrated in the years 1830–33 (Table 2.1).[31]

Five men's accounts survive as manuscript, typescript or microfilmed resources in the British Library. Two are only accessible as published memoirs, and therefore are stripped of a layer of candour; letters written for circulation among families have an unguarded immediacy and a level of detail that is typically missing from versions edited for publication, and this certainly seems to be the case with

Table 2.1 Indian Medical Service narratives

Name	Vital dates	Date of IMS admission	Dates of narrative
Robert Cumberland (b. Leicestershire, d. Devon)	1804–76	1828 (Bengal)	1828–54
William Dicken (b. Devon, d. Sialkot)	1804–61	1829 (Bengal)	1829–30
Thomas Ginders (b. Staffordshire, d. at sea)	1805–44	1830 (Bengal)	1829
Francis Maxwell (b. Glasgow, d. at sea)	1774–1805	1797 (Bengal)	1798–1805
Thomas Powell (b. Trinidad, d. Herefordshire)	1801/2–86	1823 (Madras)	1827–30
Edward Raleigh (b. Hampshire, d. Middlesex)	1802–65	1826 (Bengal)	1826–27
George Spilsbury (b. London, d. Calcutta)	1786–1857	1811 (Bengal)	1811–24
Henry Spry (b. Cornwall, d. Calcutta)	1804–42	1827 (Bengal)	1827–42
John Sylvester (b. Oxfordshire, d. London)	1830–1903	1853 (Bombay)	1853–67
Gurney Turner (b. Norfolk, d. Puri)	1813–48	1839 (Bengal)	1839–42

the memoirs of both Robert Cumberland and Thomas Powell.[32] These accounts are rather less well adapted to the purposes of this chapter, not least because both men were 'writing of hardship retrospectively … from a position of surety and strength'.[33] One man wrote both a diary and a memoir, permitting some comparison between the attitudes displayed across the two genres, while another two have both published works and unpublished letters to their names.[34] Possibly most unusual are the letters written by Thomas Ginders, by virtue of their combination of length, detail, and coverage of a period not usually witnessed in letters (namely the months before and during recruitment, giving insight into the precise workings of pre-appointment patronage).[35]

Naturally, not all of these men were uniformly or predominantly negative in their accounts. Gurney Turner was particularly upbeat and was aware of his own strategy for optimism, writing in his last surviving letter 'I find no use in grumbling; so follow my old plan of laughing at everything.'[36] Turner was matched for most of the time by Henry Spry, who enthused to his parents 'who can feel but delighted at going to such a place!'.[37] Furthermore his exuberance seemed undiminished throughout his journey and his early years of service; 'I have never regretted coming to India. Private practice ever appeared to me so forbidding.'[38] George Spilsbury, among others, found compensations in his Indian lifestyle. He was largely content with his chosen professional pathway, and thought that embarking on medical practice in Britain 'a serious matter indeed' running the risk of 'a most fagging life of it'.[39]

At the same time, this chapter is not designed to revive an outmoded view of Indian service written without the benefit of Edward Said's *Orientalism* and his analysis of the 'othering' of imperial subjects.[40] It will not repeat anachronistic rhetorics of tropical climactic difference, or more recent histories about ideas of racial superiority that developed in tandem with those of epidemiological vulnerability.[41] Nor will it explore the same ground as Margot Finn in surveying the intersection between public health, private life, and the home.[42] It will only touch coincidentally on the quotidian practice of medicine in a colonial context, and not at all on its contribution to new knowledge about military or tropical medicine. Instead, the chapter concludes, along with a growing body of research that complicates Said, that India was not decisively 'other' in terms of pursuing a medical career. Rather it exacerbated some features of British professional medicine, and sloughed off others.

Arguably the writers' perspectives were potentially conditioned by their family and geographical backgrounds. Early recruitment to the IMS was traditionally noted as drawing heavily on graduates of Irish and Scottish universities, those already regarded as at a disadvantage in the Metropolitan employment market.[43] The majority of these ten narrators were English (one Scottish, none Irish) and this might have had a negative influence on their reportage of contentment or otherwise. If the IMS in the late eighteenth and early nineteenth centuries was regarded as a reliable route into medicine for British practitioners beyond England and Wales, the downside to this reputation might have been a sense of disgruntlement among English men who were persuaded to take the same career route. Against this, though, is the fact that the one Scottish writer was not notably happier or more resigned than his English counterparts.

Furthermore, all of the narratives were written by men who were unmarried, never married, or (in the case of Cumberland, Powell and Turner) only married beyond the remit of their account of India.[44] Taking a wife was regarded as a matter of keen debate in advance of first sailing to India and then throughout one's service.[45] Since marriage was regarded as a decisive comfort, it was not one secured by these men (although it did provide them with material for extended reflection).[46] Ginders tried to engineer a marriage to a female acquaintance at the outset of his career, partly in order to benefit from the lady's supposed dowry.[47] Spilsbury wrote jocularly and over some years about the risk of being 'caught' but never married.[48] Even so, the narrative writers' uniformly single state, and their total silence about sexual relations beyond marriage, does not render them unrepresentative. Many men felt they could not afford to marry during the terms of their Indian postings and very few indeed felt at liberty to discuss sexual encounters frankly in narrative sources.[49]

Narrators' responses to IMS service undoubtedly changed over time, if only given alterations to British economic ambitions and achievements in India – Bayly described EIC rule as 'a dismal failure long before the Great Rebellion' – and fluctuations in experience dictated by periods of military suppression (ongoing, but particularly up to 1820) or outright war (as in Burma 1824–26 and Afghanistan 1839–42).[50]

Cultural change was not necessarily more moderate, witnessing the diminishing acceptability of absorbing Indian culture and lifestyle, growing pessimism about the acclimatisation of the British to the Indian climate, and the rising presence of both Christian missionaries and British women in India.[51] It is important to acknowledge that these developments will have modified the context in which men's lives and careers played out. Nonetheless, what is striking about these narratives is the propensity for familiar refrains to be detected across approximately three generations of IMS recruits in terms of dissatisfactions arising from Indian service.

Experience of service from Crawford's *Roll*

Practitioners should have been wary of opting for practice in India, since their prospects for promotion and even survival were highly uncertain. Around half of all recruits to service surveyed at decadal intervals between 1780 and 1850 could expect to die in India or another location in Asia covered by IMS service, and the next largest cohort was those whose place of death is unknown.[52] The chances of dying in Britain rather than abroad were slim, although this did improve from the first to the second halves of the period. This means that the death rate among IMS officers was almost certainly much higher than those among European soldiers in India. The men listed in Crawford's *Roll* have only a place of death recorded, not a cause, and *may* actively have chosen to remain in India after their term of Company service, particularly those recruited in the period 1780–1810. On the other side of the scales it is important to allow for the deaths of men 'elsewhere', which include men who died at sea on the way to or from service. The difference between the two cohorts is stark: only 3.8 percent to 6.9 percent of all European soldiers died of disease 1803–54 (Figures 2.1 and 2.2).[53]

The protracted interim between appointment and first promotion, and the slender chances of a second or subsequent promotion, exacerbated the practitioner's long-suffering lot.[54] Before 1805, men who survived typically waited six to eight years before being promoted from assistant to full surgeon, but after that year the delay was often doubled to twelve or sixteen years, and this fact at least was not lost on contemporaries.[55] Experiences varied a little across the presidencies, but on the whole they tracked one another. Indian service was not marked by swift

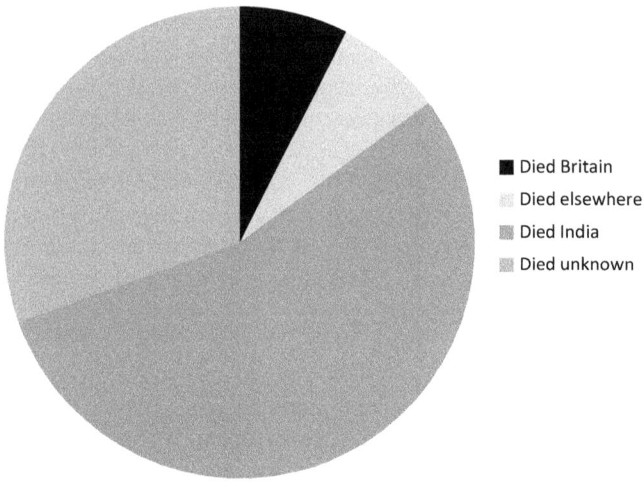

Figure 2.1 Place of death for IMS men recruited 1780, 1790, 1800, and 1810

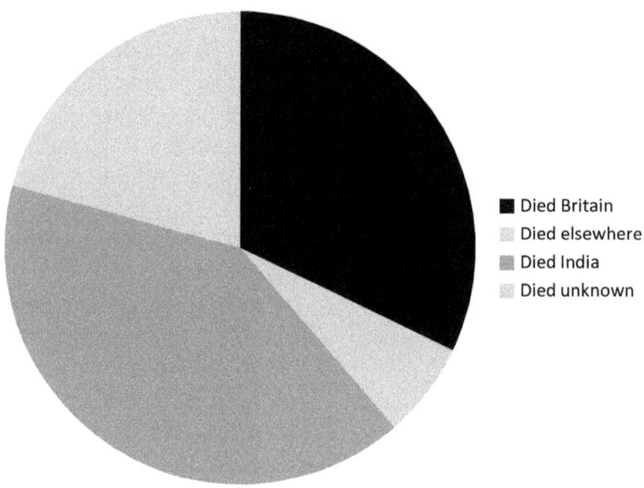

Figure 2.2 Place of death for IMS men recruited 1820, 1830, 1840, and 1850

advancement, or indeed any advancement. Given the high mortality rate among IMS officers, it should come as no surprise that a significant proportion of men did not secure any promotion at all. Nonetheless it is still startling that among all recruits reviewed at five-yearly intervals, the proportion not promoted was never less than 30 percent and frequently up to 60 percent. This means that while all men were eligible for promotion from the time of appointment, the realisation of promotion was out of reach for around half of all IMS recruits (Figures 2.3 and 2.4).

These figures bear comparison with the length of time men could expect to await promotion when they had joined the army or navy medical services. Medical men with the army who were recruited before 1810 were likely to be promoted from assistant to surgeon within five years, 'almost certainly within eight', but those who joined in the last years of the wars with France might have to wait ten or twenty years.[56]

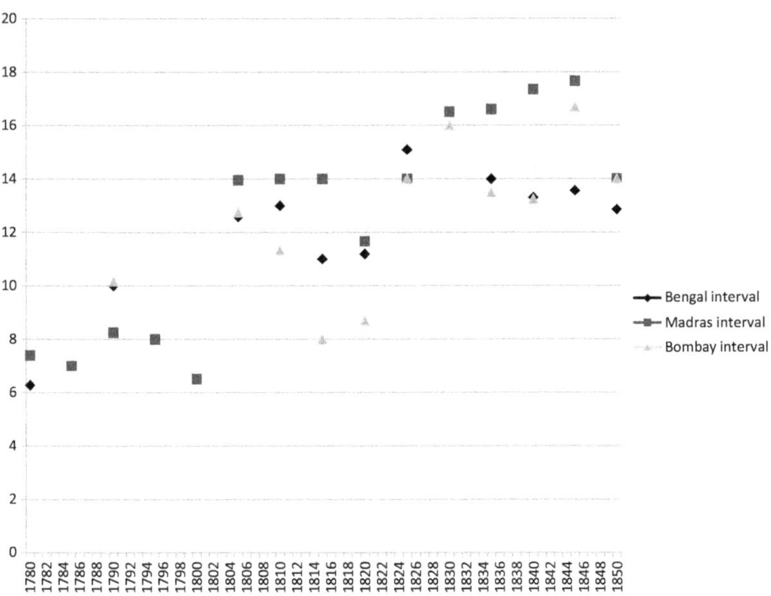

Figure 2.3 Interval in years awaiting first promotion

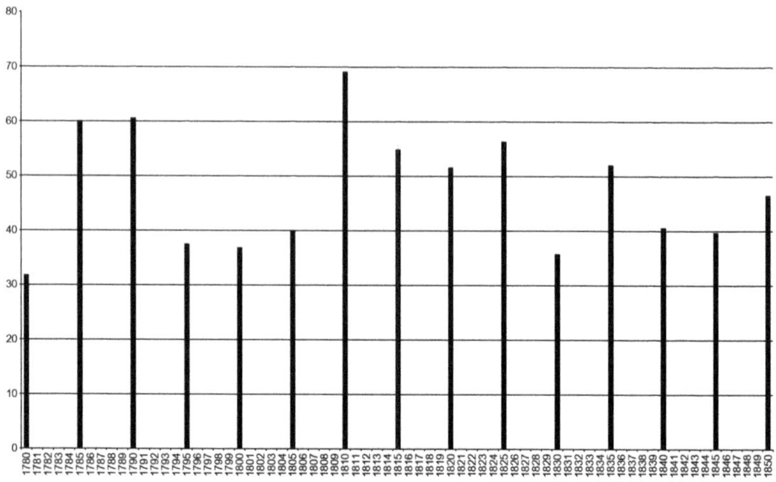

Figure 2.4 Percentage of IMS recruits securing no promotion before death or departure from service, all presidencies, 1780–1850

By these criteria, though, naval surgeons were best placed in the late eighteenth and early nineteenth centuries, since they could expect promotion from assistant to full surgeon in three years.[57]

The data for recruitment, promotion, and mortality suggest that, while men might have approached their Indian posting in a spirit of optimism, their career opportunities were no better and probably worse than those of their opposite numbers in the army and navy. Furthermore, no other salaried military service inherently dictated that successive years must be spent in a distant location overseas. Some army surgeons, for example, never left Britain and Ireland, while navy men might expect intermittent if unpredictable sailings home.[58] The high likelihood of dying abroad without benefit of status or salary enhancements was anecdotally confirmed at the time (albeit based on flawed assumptions about climactic risk).[59] It would be entirely understandable, then, if men had weighed their prospects of success and failure in India and concluded that it was a risky choice fraught with daunting and dispiriting challenges.

The IMS in the British press

Working conditions for IMS recruits received relatively little attention in both the medical and lay press before the mid 1850s, but where they were noticed they were criticised both for low pay and for the time lapse before promotion. This pattern of attention matched that for military medicine (both army and navy), which only became a focus in the *British Medical Journal* (*BMJ*), for example, in the second half of the nineteenth century.[60] Earlier attention to poor or dangerous conditions of overseas service was to some extent actively suppressed, as when George Guthrie squashed information concerning service during the Sikh wars of the 1840s, allegedly for fear of public alarm.[61] Mismanagement in military medicine was not blamed on individual doctors but on structural problems with the army's medical department, in marked contrast to the blame of individuals under the Poor Law.[62]

Public exposure of the assistant surgeons' lot in India relied on individual voices raised only sporadically. A clear intervention came when *The Lancet* reprinted a letter originally published in the *Bengal Hurkaru* in 1831. 'W.A.' drew attention to the discrepancies between remuneration for IMS officers and the army medical staff, to the disadvantage of men in India whether during service, on furlough or after retirement. Only three IMS officers with these initials were serving in 1831, two of whom had been appointed in 1829 (and so were the first cohort to be appointed after the reduction in allowances imposed 1828).[63] Nonetheless silence was largely resumed until the matter of IMS representation was taken up in a forceful editorial in *The Lancet* in 1842. Responding to an article in the *Bombay Monthly Times*, and in keeping with its brief to decry entrenched interests and ambivalence, the journal argued (with a degree of hypocrisy) 'not one of the many wealthy and old men whom the Indian medical service has sent home, has had the good feeling, or knowledge enough of the subject, to bring the condition of his brethren, whom he had left behind, to public notice'.[64] Four years later a petition was devised for signatures within the Bengal medical service, and published in full, but in an awkward attempt at disinterest it mingled protests about promotion and pay with appeals to the Court of Directors' desire for military efficiency.[65]

Conscious recognition of the role of medical practitioners in the British imperial project in India, and of the role of India in ambitions for medical reform, were just as likely to satirise the iniquities of medical organisation (the presidency medical Boards) or to regret the experiences of individual *senior* surgeons.[66] In reviewing the career of Sir James Annesley, the author of *Sketches of the Most Prevalent Diseases of India* (compulsory reading for new assistant surgeons), *The Lancet* deplored the fact that Annesley had been obliged to request public recognition and then only received a 'beggerly … trumpery' knighthood for his pains: 'He received from the hands of his sovereign the honorary distinction frequently bestowed upon respectable tradesmen, and such as was once actually awarded by a Lord Lieutenant of Ireland to his butler!!'[67]

This piecemeal approach to raising awareness was not, of course, solely the result of the apathy of retirees to the experience of new recruits to the IMS. It was also a function of the disunity of the profession. In addition to the ongoing presence on the British scene of covertly competitive medical practice, officers in India also suffered the neglect of their peers by being at a substantial geographical distance, compounded by few channels for legitimised expression of discontent. Local publications, such as the *Calcutta Gazette,* or even the more professionally specific journals that existed in the first half of the nineteenth century, such as the *Transactions* of the Medical and Physical Societies of Calcutta and Bombay, could not perform the same function for practitioners in India as rousing *Lancet* editorials could do for their English counterparts. The impediments to the circulation of property illustrated by Margot Finn were matched in the circulation of ideas: the months it might take to see oneself in print probably inhibited men already in India from approaching the British medical press.[68] Little wonder then, if protests about the terms of Indian service remained in non-official communications and if British practitioners were slow to rally to the cause.

Indian service in letters, journals, and memoirs

Narrative accounts of Indian service display less evidence of extreme aversion than might be expected from the slow rates of promotion, the risk of dying in service, and the paucity of alternatives for expressing discontent. Even so, resistance to a career in India, and unhappiness with its terms and conditions, were evident at the pressure points of recruitment, departure from Britain, arrival in India, and when confronted by the realities of life on the sub-continent.

An Indian post might be more difficult to obtain than a parallel position in either the army or navy, but that does not mean it was always regarded with enthusiasm. Recruitment might equally be marked by reticence, and this is seen in an unusual body of letters that illustrate both the technical workings of patronage and the emotional anticipation of service in India. Thomas Ginders was the son of a Staffordshire land agent who was a pupil of Sir Charles Bell and qualified as both MRCS and LSA in 1829.[69] He envisaged a medical career in London and was supported at first by his father (financially) and his older brother John (with whom he eventually shared lodgings).[70] Unfortunately, Ginders' ambitions far exceeded both his father's funds and the leverage which might feasibly be exerted on his behalf by his father's employer, Earl Talbot. In most cases the relationship between 'real patrons' and medical students or the newly qualified can only be guessed.[71] Ackroyd et al. posit the roles taken by immediate and extended family, or of a local grandee from a man's place of birth, in providing patronage to army medicine.[72] Thomas Ginders had a powerful advocate in his father's employer, and what is more the latter was willing to play an explicitly instrumental and even coercive role in Ginders' placement.

The twenty-four letters Ginders wrote to his father over the course of 1829 illustrate a man in transition from inflated optimism about the reach of Talbot's influence to exasperation at his father's hesitancy in accessing that influence, and ultimately resentment at the prospect of service in India. In February, his father tried to use Talbot to influence the appointment of a surgeon to the naval hospital ship 'Grampus', presumably at Thomas's direction.[73] This was a hopelessly ambitious project for a recently qualified surgeon aged twenty-four. In the 1840s a young surgeon could expect appointment as assistant surgeon at age thirty-one, while full rank for surgeons came at a median age of forty-one.[74] Similarly, Ginders was also probably overreaching himself when, in April, he aimed for a post as surgeon in the army with the Guards.[75] Of 389 first regimental postings for surgeons in the early nineteenth century, only eleven were in the Guards.[76] Ginders was told with brutal honesty by a contact in the army that most men's patronage was already promised elsewhere, prompting him to upbraid his father 'You are leaving me to struggle my way [to] preferment entirely alone. How am I to proceed? From the number of applications & the indefatigable exertion of each applicant and his friends I feel that the pursuit is useless without your assistance … unless you will come forward with the same spirit as my opponents.'[77]

The first reference to service in the East India Company emerged in July 1829, an option that Thomas described as 'security against the worst'.[78] He was clearly averse to the idea from the start, and modified his ambitions to try to secure an English career by any means, but once broached the project took on a life of its own and by November 1829 John Ginders was openly assuming that Thomas would go to India.[79] Thomas himself tried to play for time, telling his father 'we must act very cautiously … I shudder at the idea of £800 or even 2 thirds of that sum going to establish me in a land where those alone who endear life are wanting.'[80] He was clearly trying to play on his father's concerns about financial outlay in order to deflect the risk of work overseas. Yet this was one posting where Earl Talbot's influence could be decisive, and in due course Ginders' application to the East India Company was forwarded with Talbot's nomination. Thomas possibly saw working for the Company as a last resort. He continued to explore any other available avenue for employment, including applying for the post of district surgeon with the new Metropolitan Police Force, but without success.

This inexorable movement towards appointment met with a final burst of resistance. Thomas dug his heels in, complaining of ill health.[81] He refused to take passage for India until, in June 1830, Earl Talbot himself stepped in. Ginders' patron strongly advised 'the expediency of young men not setting up in opposition to the authorities under which they may be placed'.[82] Ginders bowed to his fate and eventually sailed for India in autumn 1830.[83]

Departure from Britain was a wrench, and there are numerous unsurprising examples of men's regret or distress at this point.[84] Partings from family and friends were compounded by the knowledge that it was typically nine or ten years before men earned their first furlough, or longer if they wished to return home without debts. There were also trials to be faced on board ship, in terms of both physical and social comfort. Gurney Turner sailed from India in 1839, and wrote forty-nine letters to his parents, siblings, and friends up to November 1842. In the first dated letter of the collection he told his sister Ellen that he did not realise the moment when he saw England for the last time which 'saved me a heartache', but that thereafter the sight of homeward ships gave him a pang not relieved by the presence of other travellers: 'My fellow passengers are not the set I should have selected.'[85]

Most characteristic, perhaps, were the men who endured something like depression throughout the journey to India, maintained to the point of arrival.[86] William Dicken was one year older than Thomas Ginders, and sailed for India exactly one year earlier. His journal depicts a man not reconciled to his posting until some time after his arrival in Calcutta. While sailing southwards from Madeira he reflected 'Two years ago this very day I was … as happy as I ever was and *more so* perhaps than I shall ever be again … If any person had then told me that instead of my now being … in dear old England I should be thousands of miles from it, I would not have believed them.'[87] On his birthday he wrote 'God grant the ensuing year may be propitious, its commencement presents but a gloomy prospect to me', a view that was not improved by intelligence from the sub-continent.[88] Governor General William Bentinck's reforms of administration and expenditure were starting to take effect, and included a reduction in remuneration for practitioners. An 'Indian newspaper' came to Dicken's hands anticipating the resignation of able medical officers, reporting 'for he must indeed be possessed of a most glowing enthusiasm and an utter contempt for self interest who can bury his talents and industry in a situation where obscurity, poverty and neglect, spread all their miseries before him' (an opinion that Dicken thought not exaggerated).[89] Even the prospect of the long journey's end did not bring any immediate respite: 'Every person looks forward with much greater pleasure at landing than I do, but this is not to be wondered at, for I am the only one on board that has not some relation or friend at least in India.'[90]

There was also the risk of a point of low ebb on first arrival.[91] Dicken judged himself most downcast at the time of sailing up river into Calcutta: 'I have never felt so miserable since I left England as I do tonight … It seems hard to have left home and all that is near and dear to me for the paltry sum of £180 or 90 pr ann. Everybody save myself seems happy, all have their friends coming off to welcome and take them on shore.'[92] Nonetheless, Dicken was quickly absorbed by a hectic social life, such that by the following February he seemed entirely at ease with life in India and contemplated sending for one or two of his sisters.[93] In general terms, Dicken's experience echoed that of Francis Maxwell a generation earlier: 'I am afraid I put you into low spirits by those [earliest] letters painting my situation in so deplorable a light; but from my late letters you will view my situation in a much more satisfactory light.'[94]

There were others not entirely reconciled to their lot despite the passage of time and the potentially attractive features of the colonial lifestyle. A generation after Dicken's recruitment, John Sylvester's diary, in distinct contrast to his published memoirs, paints a picture of a man chafing pretty constantly against the nature of Indian service. His published recollections depict a man keenly engaged in military service and regretting his absence from the Crimea, whereas his diary is introspective and gloomy. He regretted his expenses, his boredom, and his indigestion.[95] He reflected 'Eight years ago I had set sail from Southampton a long time it seems too … I think the Punjab a wretched country.'[96] Sylvester's editor recognised in him 'a certain sadness [common to] all those who have started off in life full of ambition, only to realise that, after years of striving, they have not risen to the hoped-for heights.'[97] Thomas Powell, the son of an army major and born on campaign, 'arrived in India with a very strong predilection for it', but reflected towards the end of his years of service 'India does not prove to be quite the El Dorado which I anticipated, and although there are many advantages arising from a service here, yet to my mind they do not compensate for the very serious loss of years, and those, moreover, the very best years of life, incurred by such service. It is not living but existing here.'[98] Fellow memoirist Robert Cumberland expressed himself bluntly even in print: after twenty-nine years abroad, he warned 'my advice to any one who can get a living in England is, to stay there and be thankful.'[99]

A major source of professional concern and discouragement was the continuing importance of personal connection and influence. Patronage for places was just as instrumental in India as it had been at the point of application in Britain.[100] In this, Indian service was no different to army service, where a relative lack of influence retarded the pattern and speed of promotion among men from Scotland and Ireland.[101] Once in India patronage was necessary to secure income beyond one's bare salary, typically by being accepted for work on military campaign or holding a military staff appointment. Gurney Turner was initially one of the most successful of the narrators, since he used his family connections assiduously to shift his duties and increase his salary well in advance of literal promotion.[102] But Turner was not representative. Typically narrative-writers were not so much dismayed by the ongoing significance of 'interest', but were notably downcast at its failure in their cases. Francis Maxwell, a graduate of Glasgow University and the youngest son of a Scottish landed family, maintained considerable and increasingly sarcastic commentary on the patronage that had been promised but which failed to materialise. He had hoped for great things from his family's connection with 'the Great Garthland', William MacDowall of Garthland, Lord Lieutenant of Renfrewshire, Scottish MP and heir to a commercial empire.[103] Two years after arriving in India, Maxwell told his father 'Your friend Garthland has behaved damned shabbily in regard to the letters he so frequently promised.'[104] Without some assistance, Maxwell recognised the limitations of his future in the service: 'I may jog on as the great body of the Medical Men here do on a bare livelihood, and at the end of 20 or 25 years find myself as poor or perhaps poorer than I am at present.'[105]

The majority of narratives speak to men's disappointment in securing preferment rather than reporting successful instances of patronage conferred. What was more, the process of garnering patronage could stick in the throat, even when supporting letters of introduction were forthcoming. Thomas Powell resented both the mechanism for deploying letters and their small likelihood of success: 'There are few things which I more detest than delivering letters of introduction; they are little better than soup-tickets, unless they are from direct influences, and to parties having actual power to serve.'[106] Of the three letters in his possession, he burned one unused, and a second he sent via servants rather than delivering himself (a sure way to earn the neglect rather than the support of the recipient). The final letter he took in person on the grounds that it was from a member of parliament to their cousin who was a person of genuine substance and influence in India. The ensuing contact was amiable but rendered politically useless by the recipient's death shortly afterwards. There was also distaste among writers for the white lies that such pleas for support extracted from their objects. Gurney Turner, when told via letter that a contact could not help him, observed wryly 'I know too well the power of a Brigadier Gen[era]l to believe that' but went on 'Never mind! My turn must come some day.'[107] It never did.[108]

Under terms of service imposed in 1788, medical officers had to perform at least two years military service before they could be eligible for civilian posts, and this favourable state might take rather longer to achieve.[109] The most prolonged consideration of deploying personal connections to advantage while suffering repeated disappointments is offered by George Spilsbury. He was the son of a goldsmith and the younger brother of Edgar Spilsbury who settled in Walsall as a surgeon and apothecary in 1818.[110] George Spilsbury wrote extensively to Edgar, his sister-in-law Emma, and his nieces and nephews, one of whom followed him to India (in the army rather than the IMS). Spilsbury confirmed 'Interest rules here as well as at home.'[111] He charted the actions of his supporters to secure him a more remunerative posting from 1813 to 1822, when he finally transferred to a lucrative civil appointment. This involved writing letters to people he had never met, soliciting letters of support from those who knew him or knew of him, and paying attention to the posts likely to fall vacant. The summit of his ambition as an assistant surgeon in military service was to be transferred to the Champaran Light Infantry in northern Bihar. Spilsbury first aspired to the job in December 1818, and after six months of hearing nothing found that he had been 'cut out' of the post by a man with better interest than himself.[112] A year later he heard that the same posting was likely to fall vacant again and put every effort into snaring it. This entailed mobilising an army adjutant called Thomson, the latter's Commandant called Hay, and calling in favours with Superintending Surgeon and Medical Board member John Gillman (who visited Colonel Nicol and Colonel Casement on his behalf).[113] This had no effect; but nothing daunted, Spilsbury tried again two years later when he felt he had never been so near his goal. Once more his prospects 'all vanished in smoke' when it went to a candidate favoured by Lady Hastings (strongly supposed to guide the patronage of her husband, the Governor General).[114] Ironically, his eventual good fortune came unsolicited, from an entirely unsuspected source.[115]

The issue of interest was a hot potato for the British in early nineteenth-century India. On the one hand it seemed always to carry the day against merit, but on the other even those like Spilsbury who suffered in a system that seemed stacked against them were to some extent willing participants. In 1817, on failing to get yet another place, Spilsbury admitted that it had gone to the nephew of a commanding officer but that, in the same position, he would have used his own interest to the same effect.[116] In terms of colonial activity and governance, 'The expansion and cultivation of useful connections ... was a business taken seriously and pursued avidly by all involved.'[117] Even so the conflicts inherent in the patronage system beyond medicine came publicly to the fore in 1821 when James Buckingham, the founder and editor of the *Calcutta Journal*, published a letter from 'Sam Sobersides' (actually Lieutenant Colonel William Robinson of the 24th Foot). In a satire on Calcutta society, Sobersides/Robinson made a fairly mild allegation, that 'If no wrongs are to be redressed, or suggested improvements listened to, except those which go through secretaries and public officers to government, none will be redressed or listened to but those whom they favour.'[118]

The response was draconian. Buckingham was threatened with expulsion from the country unless he revealed the identity of Sobersides, and on doing so Robinson was court-martialled (although quickly found not guilty).[119] This came three years after Governor General Lord Hastings had renounced his own powers of censorship over the Indian press. The workings of patronage were an oppressive open secret, and no one who was recruited or functioned under the system was willing to have its terms openly surveyed or renegotiated. Little wonder if professionalising medical men suffered a confusion of loyalties in Indian service when faced with such an entrenched, anti-meritocratic, but sporadically advantageous, system of advancement.

Promotion from assistant surgeon to surgeon was a question of serving one's time, and was awarded in strict order of appointment to men who survived or were not invalided. On the one occasion when *The Lancet* appears to have noticed this reliance on 'MERE SENIORITY', it deplored the inability to reward merit out of turn, and the propensity to reward nothing more than remaining alive.[120] But the relationship of this process to medical reform and professionalisation was much more complicated than Wakley envisaged as a result of the continuing influence of competitive practice. Longevity as a mechanism for advancement obviated the spirit of medical competition in theory. In practice, the premiums and penalties of a patronage system in advance of promotion meant that men were anything but relaxed about their medical competitors. Maxwell and others tracked their position in the medical list and thus their proximity to promotion to full surgeon: 'There are still upwards of sixty assistant surgeons on the list above me, so I cannot expect promotion for a number of years.'[121] The Company's method of ranking candidates for promotion required individual men to pay attention to the numbers of deaths and resignations among their technical seniors, plus any propensity of the Company to increase military, and therefore medical, recruitment.[122] In 1842 Turner was cataloguing those above and below him in the queue in a manner that demanded an awkward attention to morbidity. He noted two of his seniors who had been murdered by Afghans as giving him a 'lift' towards his surgeoncy.[123]

An eagle eye on the promotion lists could also raise a dilemma for practitioners. George Spilsbury served at Cawnpore under a Surgeon Cooke, probably William Cooke who had received his first promotion in 1797.[124] Cooke was ill for a number of months in 1813 meaning that Spilsbury's workload suffered: 'This old man is a sad clog upon me … a sad old servile superannuated wretch.'[125] Spilsbury took the view that Cooke would never be well again, and with hindsight it is clear that Cooke was very ill, dying on the boat home in 1815. But Spilsbury could not see his way to treating Cooke medically: 'He frequently asks my opinion & I invariably decline, nor will I ever prescribe for him as sh[oul]d anything happen to him, I being next to succeed to the allowance the world with its usual charity might hint at me being his doctor', and his fervent hope was to 'get rid of him soon by promotion.'[126]

The years before promotion hung heavy on men's hands. John Sylvester, during his ninth year of service, eagerly anticipated his elevation: 'they say the [post-mutiny] Amalgamation will be shortly out and I shall be a surgeon.'[127] He waited nearly four years more before his promotion was confirmed, and in his case even good news carried a sting since 'I treat all our people to Champagne tonight – a horrid waste of money which might have been better spent but these institutions cannot be avoided.'[128]

Medical finances underpinned men's concerns about advancement and promotion. In addition to the optional drains on income from drink, smoking, and gambling, there were hidden costs of service.[129] Uniform, equipment, transport, subscriptions to charities, mess obligations, and the salaries of any personal servants might all have to be procured from one's pay. In 1800, Francis Maxwell had bought two camels (at 50 guineas the pair) and employed at least fourteen servants.

This was not a token of lavish living but a testament to the practical difficulties of living on the road. Maxwell was accompanying three Bengal volunteer battalions on a march heading north from Seringapatam.[130] Thomas Powell's nine servants in the peacetime 1820s cost him 59 rupees a month, or 17 percent of his income.[131] Additional problems of cash-flow arose from the practice of being paid in arrears. Henry Spry relished all aspects of his Indian appointment at first, other than the Company practice of paying two months in arrears, necessitating short-term loans.[132] Similarly, George Spilsbury started his life in India in debt, 'landing without a rupee in my pocket' in 1811; he hoped to be out of debt by 1815 or 1816 but was nonetheless 'as poor as I was 4 years ago' in early 1819.[133] By September 1820 he had repaid around 4,430 rupees of his debt to his agent, commenting 'it is confounded uphill work paying off a few thousands for the compound interest at 12 percent works up a sum in no time'.[134] Even after securing a lucrative posting he found himself 'always, not exactly distressed for money, but a hamperish sort of feeling'.[135]

Saving out of one's salary was a 'herculean effort' but easier while on the raised allowances owed for military service; Maxwell was still able to save 50 guineas a month even when his savings were reduced, and during three years in India saved 'fifteen hundred pounds sterling'.[136] Reflecting on the higher remittances he secured on campaign, Maxwell observed that 'several of my Brother Doctors have been biting their fingers, and expressing their regret that they had not volunteered'.[137] At all times assistant surgeons were at risk of ceding money to their medical superiors. Maxwell found himself in much less favourable circumstances when he reached Berhampore in August 1800. As one of the 'great stations of the army' the hospital at Berhampore employed a HeadSurgeon who drew all of the allowances for the military companies stationed there 'so that the surgeons and assistant surgeons of regiments have not the least emolument from their Corps while remaining at this place'.[138] At the same time, if military forces divided then allowances were also rendered fractional: Spilsbury thought himself 'not a very lucky fellow' when his battalion divided for thirteen months, halving his allowances, reunited for a single month, and then were separated again.[139]

The experience of embarking on service in debt and then striving for solvency probably became worse in the first half of the nineteenth century, as the occasional chance of quick profits that occupied public consciousness in the eighteenth century diminished.[140] Certainly the Company came to restrict opportunities for emolument beyond salaried service and bound its medical employees not to accept corrupt presents, or engage in any business other than their profession.[141] An inability to make money was compounded at intervals by losses beyond practitioners' control, as in the failure of the Indian agencies from 1827 to the mid 1830s. Henry Spry lost money in one of the later failures, writing home in 1833

> I have dropt nearly £400 in that rascally Agency House – I was so far lucky as to get about an equal sum out of the fire just 48 hours before they failed ... It is distressing to see old men grey in the Service looking forward to taking their leave of this hot country and spending the few remaining days of their life in their Native country now for ever exiled.

The only financial advantage of residence in India was that it was allegedly quite difficult to be prosecuted for debt. Spilsbury assured his brother 'you must be deep in the mire indeed in this country to be dunned & arresting a man is only done to the incorrigible.'[142] Nonetheless insolvencies were incurred in India and reported in the *London Gazette*, including two men in 1830 (one of whom was in gaol in Calcutta).[143]

The anxieties occasioned by money were intimately tied to men's ambitions, but not necessarily with their careers foremost in their minds: saving was the route back to Britain. Thomas Powell estimated 'Ninety men out of every hundred who go to India resolve to return to England as soon as ever they can, after having realised a certain contingency ... The contingency, however, so fondly looked to but rarely arrives.'[144] The goal might be a particular level of promotion or balance of credit, but Powell thought that reaching it was complicated by the individual's willingness to admit that they had done so, and that delay resulted in probable death in service. His own intention had been to raise 'one vernacular plebeian thousand pounds', in which he was disappointed since it remained hypothetical.[145]

Men's broader emotional responses to their careers, their social lives, and their Indian context were therefore conflicted. Pleasurable excitement was unusual, and perhaps part of the reason for infrequent treatments in narratives was the difficulty of admitting pleasure to one's correspondents. Francis Maxwell would have been hard pressed to describe the sensuality of Nautch dancing in a letter to his father, writing instead 'it is impossible to describe them – they are such a jumble of stuff and nonsense'.[146] Game-hunting was an option, but this too could prove a disappointment. Thomas Powell had been predisposed in favour of India on the basis of hunting with leopards rather than hounds. He had imagined hunting 'mounted on "my Arab steed", a pack of leopards in full cry' but was confronted instead with a single leopard which failed to bring down any deer; Powell recalled 'I was no longer guilty even of a momentary infidelity to my "first love" – *fox-hunting*.'[147] Boredom was a perennial problem: 'the transactions of one day are very similar to those of the previous one ... there is very little variety to be met with. By going 20 miles you see almost all that is to be seen.'[148] For George Spilsbury, too, 'one day now is every day and no alteration' which risked resulting in a damaging absence of either intellectual or physical impetus.[149] Opportunities to study unfamiliar aspects of medicine, botany or geology, for example, find only muted expression in letters and diaries and might have taken time and energy to evolve in a context when energy, at least, was often in short supply.[150] In the 1820s Henry Spry elaborated 'I can hardly conceive a place where a man is thrown more on his own resources than at a military station in India and thus it is true for want of something to engage the mind individuals so often fall into the indolent & lethargic state for which they are oftentimes too unjustly stigmatised.'[151]

Men suffered isolation in both literal and figurative terms, since their distance from home and meaningful family ties was exacerbated by the attenuated exchange of correspondence. Traditionally this was construed in wholly negative terms: 'the long silence began, slowly dissolving all connection, unless interrupted by a sudden unexpected, exhilarating and providential return'.[152] Margot Finn has since suggested that letters were used to tie absent family members to their British families.[153] Nonetheless the intermittency of letters, dependent on secure shipping and overland transfers of mail, as well as family commitment to the maintenance of communication, caused upset for assistant surgeons. Francis Maxwell complained 'I certainly expected letters from my Brothers, and confess I feel myself rather hurt at their apparent neglect. How easy might it be for them to find a spare moment for them to write me a few lines, for tho' it contained no news, the merely receiving anything in their hand writing would be pleasant.'[154] Replies to specific questions could take years, given the uncertainties of delivery (particularly when on campaign) and the variable time lapse inherent in different postal routes. Maxwell sailed from southern England in May 1797, and in August 1799 was anticipating the arrival of letters containing responses to those he wrote on first arrival in India: he commented 'A whole year has this day elapsed since I have had any accounts from home.'[155] He later asked for duplicates of his father's letters to be sent by multiple routes 'particularly at such a time as the present, when I am anxious to learn of the health of my brother'.[156] Maxwell himself catalogued seventeen letters that he wrote between 2 June 1799 and 22 March 1800 to his father, brothers, and friends.[157] A decade later George Spilsbury could record in January 1813 that he had as yet received no replies to his own letters of December 1811, and a year later had gone several months without any correspondence from his brother's family.[158] He received one letter that took two years to arrive.[159] Later in his career he wrote to his sister-in-law 'you say you do not hear from me so often – I am aware you do not & I am not sure that not hearing from you so often is not an indirect cause'.[160] Piqued reticence stayed people's hands on both sides of correspondence.

Company doctors could also suffer isolation from their peers *in situ*. Social interaction with friends and acquaintances made in India was valued, and Thomas Powell thought the British more hospitable abroad than at home, but socialising was problematic on the grounds that preferences could not always be observed, either by lack of control over postings or by reason of cost.[161] George Spilsbury feared the loss of his social skills, albeit in other terms, when he regretted 'without a being to care for one or express more than the ordinary civilities of life, all the social duties in me may expire for want of fuel to keep them alive'.[162] His closest friendships were interrupted by professional movement, as in his contact with Major John Greenstreet's family.[163] When he lost the domestic company of Charles Chesney, eventually a Captain in the Bengal Artillery, he admitted 'there is no other fellow here I w[oul]d chuse to live with at present'.[164] Leaving Cawnpore he was once more obliged to make the sort of social effort likely to establish a sustaining friendship: 'this is all to be done over again'.[165] Spilsbury was also aware of the risk of social debts being financially unaffordable. After nine years in India he wrote 'I am now living as economically as I can without actually hermitizing'.[166]

Friendships as seen through the lenses of letters and memoirs were socially restricted. Few if any men alluded to any significant relationships beyond immediate professional and British acquaintances. Spilsbury occasionally moved in Anglo-Indian circles, but while some men employed teachers to enable them to learn native languages there was no hint of friendships with Indian people. Therefore the potentially diverse social landscape, available to practitioners and others such as missionaries in the late nineteenth century, was not apparently accessed in this earlier period.[167]

Against friendship, IMS officers also had to set the risk of enmities. George Spilsbury was much troubled in his early career by friction with a fellow assistant surgeon to Bengal, Peter Fair, who had been appointed ahead of Spilsbury in 1808. Fair initially agreed to cover the necessary medical work while Spilsbury went on a hunting trip in early 1813, but then asked their Colonel to forbid the leave. Colonel Grace recognised that Fair was trying to 'throw the odium of refusal on me'; he gave Fair a dressing-down for his 'duplicity' with the result that Fair was 'cut by almost all the officers'.[168] Spilsbury was clearly agitated by the dispute, so that when Fair approached him by letter asking for the same friendly relations they had previously enjoyed, Spilsbury snubbed him.[169] Another early source of tension lay with Adam Burt, Head Surgeon next in line for appointment to the Medical Board: 'I wish he w[oul]d get the step and take himself off from this.'[170] Spilsbury was socially slighted by Burt, but this was not the most disruptive run in with a medical or military senior.[171] The following year he was embroiled in another public falling out, this time with Lieutenant General Watson. This arose from a disagreement over Spilsbury's alleged neglect of Watson (who Spilsbury thought a hypochondriac), and Watson's attempt to demand treatment as a right which Spilsbury regarded as 'an outrage on my feelings': for the sake of Watson's daughter 'I have agreed to take no further notice provided the Medical Board take none & to overlook the lies & injustice contained in his letters'.[172]

The most sobering apprehension that lay behind most men's writings was the awareness of their own mortality, even if they were not well informed about the literal probability of dying in service. The risk of death in India informed every expression of love for families back home, and every projection of future meetings. But was an Indian grave a symbol of 'failure, disappointment, abandonment'?[173] The IMS narrators made no direct judgements on their own deaths beyond those implicit in fervently expressed hopes of returning home, and their fates give a fair representation of IMS destinies. Thomas Powell said of miscellaneous British people dying in India (rather than exclusively of himself) 'for him no ancestral vault will be opened, no natal sod be turned; and those, perhaps, who love him best, will have to shed *ex post facto* tears.'[174] Hopes of retrospective weeping may have been misplaced. Of the ten narrators, four died in India, four in Britain, and two at sea. Death at sea was arguably the worst outcome of all, being both quite likely and conferring no place of burial and no focal point for friends and family in either India or Britain. Francis Maxwell suffered this fate without surviving commentary from his family, but Thomas Ginders provides a final and fuller example. He remained in India for fourteen years without furlough, despite being eligible after ten years of service, a career which might be read in either positive or negative terms: either like Dicken and Maxwell he became acclimatised to life in India and did not seek leave, was too indebted to leave, or he felt so alienated from his family by the circumstances of his recruitment to the service that, once in India, he resisted leaving it.[175] He was involved in military service, and was mentioned in dispatches in 1841.[176] At length he fell ill and boarded a ship to return to England, but died two or three days out from Calcutta.[177] When the news reached his father the paternal reaction was decidedly muted. Jeremiah Ginders retrospectively recorded in his diary for 28 March 1844 the day that his son Thomas was said to have died, 'the account seems rather mistirious [sic].'[178] Contrast this restraint with the entry one year earlier, when in October 1843 'My poor Dear son Jeremiah died at Hilderstone Windmill Inn on Friday the 20th Inst 2pm. Ellen his widow went on Sunday evening to see him before he was moved from the place.'[179] The death of his eldest son made him ill, while Thomas's death seems to have made him curious. This disparity was the somewhat inevitable conclusion to Thomas's fourteen-year absence from home, and confirmation of the impact of the 'long silence'.

Conclusion

Medical service in India comprised a measure of professional opportunity, but men's reactions to both the prospect and the reality were freighted with ambivalence. Some were bullish about their career from the outset when they might have had good reason to be apprehensive, while others expressed reservations and more in their writings and actions. The majority could expect death in service or in transit, with restricted prospects for social and financial advancement, and narrators generally came to realise the limitations of an Indian posting. Optimism and opportunity were at least balanced, if not outweighed, by regret and stifled ambition. Awkward though it may be to admit, 'Coercive imperial hegemony' applied to subalterns among the colonisers as well as among the colonised, and despite their notional position above the groups studied by Fischer-Tiné, assistant surgeons of the IMS can still be counted here.[180] Consideration of white subalternity is not new in the context of colonial histories, but it has not previously been applied to medical professionalisation and its discontents.[181]

A good deal of conflict arose from the need for heavy reliance on pre-reform modes of behaviour, and adherence to them even in the face of their failure. The necessity for aggressive deployment of interest, involving unequivocal commitment to semi-public displays of self-interest, sat very uneasily with a professionalising group who in other contexts were being deterred from advertising for patients and were encouraged to be circumspect in their dealings with other practitioners. Medical competition was not removed by the receipt of EIC earnings, but rather channelled in ways that quickly became entrenched and were not open to disruption until merit, rather than seniority, came to govern admission, advancement, and promotion. Given the emphasis on covert competition in Britain, one might assume that this made life easier for surgeons in India, since they enjoyed *de facto* permission to engage in some jostling for position. The result, though, was a process that was equally or more likely to induce resentment than it was to secure advancement, forcing participants on both sides (supplicant practitioners and their potential patrons) into false protests of allegiance or impotence.

It is also clear that medical masculinity could not entirely take refuge in early forms of colonial masculinity. The occasional spot of game-hunting aside, there was little scope for advantageous display of physical courage or hardihood. Life on march was merely a relentless and expensive slog, and boredom is a more reliable theme in practitioner narratives than either physical prowess or intellectual stimulation. There was occasional hope for greater emotional engagement when friendships developed into substitute family groupings, but these were rendered highly unstable by disruptive postings, furloughs, and early deaths. Communications and sympathies with birth families wore literally paper thin and, unless men could afford to replace them with marital families on the spot, the outlet for their affections relied largely on hope.

One remote compensation for undergoing the trials of Indian service was the relative improbability of being exposed in public as professionally inadequate. IMS officers guilty of everything from conduct unbecoming to a gentleman through to murder might be tried by court martial, but Crawford's history of the Service makes it clear that very few men were found guilty and cashiered or discharged as a result; just twenty-nine men were implicated in these judgements throughout the entire period 1600–1913.[182] In contrast, men who remained in England were exposed to public censure and criminal conviction much more regularly from the 1830s onwards as a result of the mutually reinforcing results of newspaper reporting and expressions of grievance with the poor law. Neglect of patients or medical incompetence received notice, scrutiny, and negotiated judgement from within the profession and without.

Notes

1 D.M. Haynes, 'Victorian Imperialism in the Making of the British Medical Profession: An Argument', in D. Ghosh and D.K. Kennedy (eds), *Decentring Empire: Britain, India, and the Transcolonial World* (Hyderabad: Orient Longman, 2006), pp. 130–56.

2 T. Johnson, 'Imperialism and the Professions: Notes on the Development of Professional Occupations in Britain's Colonies and the New States', in P. Halmos (ed.), *Professionalisation and Social Change* (Keele: The Sociological Review monograph 20, 1973), pp. 281–309, on p. 281.

3 M.J. Peterson, *The Medical Profession in Mid-Victorian London* (Berkeley: University of California Press, 1978), pp. 124–6. The IMS can boast a magisterial, two-volume history written in the early twentieth century, see D.G. Crawford, *A History of the Indian Medical Service 1600–1913* (Calcutta: Thacker, Spink & Co., 1914).

4 These opportunities were apparently most fruitful in the earliest part of the period covered here; G. Marshall, *East Indian Fortunes. The British in Bengal in the Eighteenth Century* (Oxford: Clarendon Press, 1976), p. 234. For a medical example, see Alexander Gray in D.G. Crawford, *A History*

of the Indian Medical Service 1600–1913 (Calcutta: Thacker, Spink & Co., 1914) volume 2, p. 77. The nabob controversy, and in all likelihood the phenomenon, was in decline by the end of the eighteenth century; T. Nechtman, *Nabobs: Empire and Identity in Eighteenth-Century Britain* (Cambridge: Cambridge University Press, 2010), conclusion.

5 This remained the case in the final third of the nineteenth century; M.A. Crowther and M.W. Dupree, *Medical Lives in the Age of Surgical Revolution* (Cambridge: Cambridge University Press, 2007), p. 319.

6 M.J. Cardwell, 'Royal Navy Surgeons, 1793–1815: A Collective Biography', in D.B. Haycock and S. Archer (eds), *Health and Medicine at Sea 1700–1900* (Woodbridge: Boydell Press, 2009), pp. 38–62, on p. 54.

7 Cardwell, 'Royal Navy Surgeons', pp. 57–8.

8 M. Lincoln, 'Medical Profession and Representations of the Navy', in G.L. Hudson (ed.), *British Military and Naval Medicine 1600–1830* (Amsterdam: Rodopi, 2007), pp. 201–6, on p. 202; L. Rosner, *Medical Education in the Age of Improvement* (Edinburgh: Edinburgh University Press, 1991), p. 20. The same ranking was observed in the mid century; A.M. Annand (ed.), *Cavalry Surgeon. The Recollections of John Henry Sylvester* (London: Macmillan, 1971), p. 29.

9 M. Ackroyd, L. Brockliss, M. Moss, K. Retford, and J. Stevenson, *Advancing with the Army: Medicine, the Professions, and Social Mobility in the British Isles 1790–1850* (Oxford: Oxford University Press, 2006), p. 227.

10 Crawford, *History of the Indian Medical Service*, pp. 197–221.

11 D. Arnold, *Science, Technology and Medicine in Colonial India. New Cambridge History of India* (Cambridge: Cambridge University Press, 2004), p. 61.

12 For advancement in either military or civilian service, see Crawford, *History of the Indian Medical Service*, volume one chapter 16.

13 J.M. MacKenzie, 'The Imperial Pioneer and Hunter and the British Masculine Stereotype in late Victorian and Edwardian Times', in J.A. Mangan and J. Walvin (eds), *Manliness and Morality: Middle-class Masculinity in Britain and America, 1800–1940* (Manchester: Manchester University Press, 1987), pp. 176–98.

14 J. Tosh, *A Man's Place: Masculinity and the Middle-class Home in Victorian England* (New Haven: Yale University Press, 1999), pp. 6–7.

15 M. Brown, '"Like a Devoted Army": medicine, heroic masculinity, and the military paradigm in Victorian Britain', *Journal of British Studies* 49:3 (2010), pp. 592–622.

16 M. Roper and J. Tosh, 'Introduction', in M. Roper and J. Tosh (eds) *Manful Assertions; Masculinities in Britain since 1800* (London: Routledge, 1991), pp. 1–24, on pp. 9, 14.

17 D.K. Kennedy, 'Diagnosing the Colonial Dilemma: Tropical Neurasthenia and the Alienated Briton', in D. Ghosh and D.K. Kennedy (eds), *Decentring Empire: Britain, India, and the Transcolonial World* (Hyderabad: Orient Longman, 2006), pp. 157–81, on p. 178.
18 Haynes, 'Victorian Imperialism', on p. 131.
19 D. Ghosh and D.K. Kennedy, 'Introduction', in D. Ghosh and D.K. Kennedy (eds), *Decentring Empire: Britain, India, and the Transcolonial World* (Hyderabad: Orient Longman, 2006), pp. 1–15, on p. 5.
20 M. Jackson, *The Age of Stress: Science and the Search for Stability* (Oxford: Oxford University Press, 2013), p. 25 and *passim*; Kennedy, 'Diagnosing the Colonial Dilemma'.
21 Kennedy, 'Diagnosing the Colonial Dilemma', p. 158.
22 Kennedy, 'Diagnosing the Colonial Dilemma', p. 164–5.
23 R. Guha, 'Not at home in Empire', *Critical Inquiry* 23:3 (1997), pp. 482–93, on p. 485.
24 Guha, 'Not at home in Empire', p. 487.
25 A. Lester, *Imperial Networks. Creating Identities in Nineteenth-century South Africa and Britain* (London: Routledge, 2001), p. 6.
26 Z. Laidlaw, *Colonial Connections 1815–45. Patronage, the Information Revolution and Colonial Government* (Manchester: Manchester University Press, 2005), chapter two; M. Finn, '"Frictions" d'empire: les réseaux de circulation des successions et des patrimoines dans la Bombay coloniale des années 1780', *Annales* 65:5 (2010), pp. 1175–204.
27 Crawford, *History of the Indian Medical Service*, volume one pp. 524–6.
28 Lester, *Imperial Networks*, pp. 161–2 for the cultural shock occasioned by the mutiny.
29 C.A. Bayly, *Indian Society and the Making of the British Empire. The New Cambridge History of India* (Cambridge: Cambridge University Press, 1988), p. 133.
30 See Chapter 1.
31 'The failures in India', *Asiatic Journal* 16 n.s. (1834), pp. 85–91.
32 [R. Cumberland] *Stray Leaves from the Diary of an Indian Officer* (London: Whitfield, Green & Son, 1865) substitutes all surnames with pseudonyms; Powell's diary was published anonymously in sixteen instalments in the *Asiatic Journal and Monthly Register* between 1 May 1841 and 1 June 1843, and is more sporadic in its attempts at anonymity. Both comprise edited versions of contemporary journals.
33 W. Jackson, *Madness and Marginality. The Lives of Kenya's White Insane* (Manchester: Manchester University Press, 2013), p. 31.
34 For the diarist, see Annand, *Cavalry Surgeon*; British Library (B.L.) Mss Eur C 241/2, diary of John Sylvester. For the correspondents see [G.

Turner] *First Impressions, or, a day in India. A letter from an Assistant Surgeon, lately arrived in Calcutta* (Yarmouth: Charles Sloman, 1841) compared with B.L. Mss Eur D 692 letters of Gurney Turner 1839–42, and H.H. Spry, *Modern India: with illustrations of the resources and capabilities of Hindustan* (London: Whittaker and Co., 1837) compared with B.L., IOR PHOTO Eur 308 letters of Henry Harpur Spry. Spry's book is more a miscellany of information interleaved with personal experience than a memoir proper.

35 For all parts of Thomas Ginders' narrative, see Staffordshire Record Office (S.R.O.), D 240/E(I)/4/18/4, correspondence of Jeremiah Ginders.

36 B.L. Mss Eur D 692, letter from Gurney Turner at Ferosepor to his parents 23 November 1842.

37 B.L., IOR PHOTO Eur 308, letter of Henry Harpur Spry in London to his parents 7–21 March 1827.

38 B.L., IOR PHOTO Eur 308, letter of Henry Harpur Spry at Saugor to his brother Edward 1 July 1833.

39 B.L. Mss Eur D 909, letters from George Spilsbury at Cawnpore to his brother Edgar 9 August 1817 and from Nursingpore 25 September 1819.

40 E.W. Said, *Orientalism: Western Conceptions of the Orient* (London: Routledge, 1978).

41 M. Harrison, '"The Tender Frame of Man": disease, climate, and racial difference in India and the West Indies, 1760–1860', *Bulletin of the History of Medicine* 70:1 (1996), pp. 68–93.

42 'East India Company at Home 1757–1857', http://blogs.ucl.ac.uk/eicah/home/ viewed 23 October 2015; M. Finn, 'The Private Life of Public Health: East India Company Surgeons, Medicine, and the Domestic Sphere, c. 1800–1857', unpublished paper supplied personally.

43 T. Devine, *Scotland's Empire. The Origins of the Global Diaspora* (London: Penguin, 2003), p. 251.

44 For Cumberland's marriage of 1847, see his entry in the Australian Medical Pioneers Index viewed 19 September 2012, www.medicalpioneers.com; for Turner's marriage of 1844, see B.L. India Office Family History Search viewed 24 July 2015, www.bl.uk/catalogues/iofhs.shtml; for Powell's marriage of 1835, see A.D. Powell, 'The Powell family of Castleton, Priory Wood, and Dorstone, Herefordshire', *Radnorshire Society Transactions* 38 (1968), pp. 54–60, on p. 57. Only chapters XXVI–XXX of Cumberland's narrative concern time spent in India with his wife.

45 J. McCosh, *Medical Advice to the Indian Stranger* (London: Wm. H. Allen & Co., 1841), pp. 25–6 (in chapter 23 entitled 'Equipment').

46 Marriage was later recommended as the best defence against neurasthenia, but was rarely an option for the new recruit pre-1857; Kennedy, 'Diagnosing the Colonial Dilemma', p. 169.

47 S.R.O. D 240/E(I)/4/18/4 letter of Thomas Ginders in London to his father 11 December 1829. This is ironic, given that wives and families were regarded as a ruinous drain on income by men once they had arrived in India.
48 Finn, 'Private Life of Public Health'.
49 William Hickey was unusual in discussing his heterosexual physical relationships even in retrospect; P. Quennell (ed.), *Memoirs of William Hickey* (London: Purnell Book Services, [1975]), p. xiii.
50 Bayly, *Indian Society*, p. 106.
51 Bayly, *Indian Society*, pp. 106, 115; M. Harrison, *Climates and Constitutions. Health, Race, Environment and British Imperialism in India 1600–1850* (Oxford: Oxford University Press, 1999), pp. 111–12; M. Macmillan, *Women of the Raj* (New York: Thames and Hudson, 1988).
52 Data is taken from D.G. Crawford, *Roll of the Indian Medical Service 1615–1930* (London: W. Thacker, 1930).
53 D. Arnold, *Colonising the Body. State Medicine and Epidemic Disease in Nineteenth-Century India* (Berkeley: University of California Press, 1993), p. 69.
54 In this they were not alone; H.V. Bowen, *The Business of Empire: The East India Company and Imperial Britain, 1756–1833* (Cambridge: Cambridge University Press, 2006), p. 142 for slow advancement in the home service.
55 'The Indian Medical Service', *The Lancet*, 48:1214 (1846), pp. 623–4.
56 Ackroyd et al., *Advancing with the Army*, pp. 173–4.
57 Cardwell, 'Royal Navy Surgeons', p. 55.
58 Ackroyd et al., *Advancing with the Army*, p. 165.
59 Harrison, '"The Tender Frame of Man"', pp. 68–93.
60 P.W.J. Bartrip, *Mirror of Medicine: A History of the BMJ* (London: British Medical Journal, 1990), p. 47.
61 Bartrip, *Mirror of Medicine*, p. 48.
62 See Chapter 3.
63 'Medical Service of India', *The Lancet* 16:420 (1831), pp. 783–5. The two most likely authors were therefore either William Andrew (Bengal presidency) or Willoughby Arding (Bombay presidency).
64 [Untitled] *The Lancet* 39:997 (1842), pp. 69–70.
65 'The Indian Medical Service', *The Lancet* 48:1214 (1846), pp. 623–4.
66 [Untitled] *The Lancet* 39:1017 (1843), pp. 798–9; 'Insubordination at the Bengal Medical Board', *ibid.* 39:1019 (1843), pp. 873–4; 'The Medical Department of the Indian Army', *ibid.* 53:1339 (1849), pp. 463–4.
67 [Untitled] *The Lancet* 51:1275 (1848), p. 160.
68 Finn, '"Frictions" d'empire'.

69 A. Tomkins, 'Fragility and resilience in a middle-class family: Jeremiah Ginders (1777–1845) and his kin', *Staffordshire Studies* 13 (2001), pp. 79–108, on pp. 91–4.
70 S.R.O. D 240/E(I)/4/18/4 letter from John Ginders to his father 14 November 1829.
71 Ackroyd et al., *Advancing with the Army*, p. 337.
72 Ackroyd et al., *Advancing with the Army*, pp. 147–51.
73 S.R.O. D 240/E(I)/4/18/4 letter from Jeremiah Ginders to Earl Talbot 17 February 1829.
74 Peterson, *Medical Profession*, p. 161.
75 S.R.O. D 240/E(I)/4/18/4 letter from John Ginders in London to his father 23 April 1829.
76 Ackroyd et al., *Advancing with the Army*, p. 156.
77 S.R.O. D 240/E(I)/4/18/4 letter of Thomas Ginders in London to his father 23 May 1829.
78 S.R.O. D 240/E(I)/4/18/4 letter of Thomas Ginders in London to his father 19 July 1829; Thomas Ginders in London to his father 24 July 1829.
79 S.R.O. D 240/E(I)/4/18/4 letter of Thomas Ginders in London to his father 6 May 1829 (expressing reluctance to become a Licentiate of the Society of Apothecaries); S.R.O. D 240/E(I)/4/18/4 letter of John Ginders in London to his father undated but early November 1829 (describing Thomas's determination to secure the Apothecary's qualification); S.R.O. D 240/E(I)/4/18/4 letter of John Ginders in London to his father 14 November 1829 (referring to Thomas's appointment in the East India Company).
80 S.R.O. D 240/E(I)/4/18/4 letters of Thomas Ginders in London to his father 18 November 1829 and 3 December 1829.
81 S.R.O. D 240/E(I)/4/18/4 letter of Thomas Ginders in London to his father 23 December 1829.
82 S.R.O. D 240/E(I)/4/18/22 letter of Earl Talbot to Jeremiah Ginders June 1830.
83 'Passengers to India', *Asiatic Journal and Monthly Register* 10 (1830), p. 120.
84 J. Wallace, *A Voyage to India* (London: T. and G. Underwood, 1824), pp. 4–5; Wallace was surgeon on the 'Lonach' and possibly the former appointee to the Bombay service who deserted in 1803; see Crawford, *Roll*, p. 495.
85 B.L. Mss Eur D 692, letter from Gurney Turner to his sister Ellen apparently posted in Calcutta and spanning dates December 1839 to June 1840.
86 Lengthy sea voyages have been accounted a risk to mental health in other contexts; A. McCarthy, 'Migration and Madness in New Zealand's Asylums, 1863–1910', in A. McCarthy and C. Coleborne (eds), *Migration,*

Ethnicity, and Mental Health. International Perspectives, 1840–2010 (London: Routledge, 2012) pp. 55–72, on pp. 63–5.

87 B.L. Mss Eur C 366/1 typescript journal of a voyage to India, p. 48, entry for 1 September 1829.

88 B.L. Mss Eur C 366/1 typescript journal of a voyage to India, p. 60, entry for 30 September 1829.

89 B.L. Mss Eur C 366/1 typescript journal of a voyage to India, p. 78, entry for 29 October 1829.

90 B.L. Mss Eur C 366/1 typescript journal of a voyage to India, p. 67, entry for 8 October 1829.

91 In addition to Dicken, see also Sylvester's reluctance in Annand, *Cavalry Surgeon*, p. 34.

92 B.L. Mss Eur C 366/1 typescript journal of a voyage to India, p. 86, entry for 9 November 1829.

93 B.L. Mss Eur C 366/1 typescript journal of a voyage to India, pp. 88–106, entries for 12 November 1829 to 1 February 1830.

94 B.L. Mss Eur C 101 transcript p. 10, letter from Francis Maxwell on the banks of the Toombuddra river to his father 13 August 1799.

95 Annand, *Cavalry Surgeon*, p. 312.

96 B.L. Mss Eur C 241/2, diary entries of 5 December 1861 and 17 February 1862.

97 Annand, *Cavalry Surgeon*, p. 317.

98 Powell, 'The Powell family of Castleton'; 'Diary of an Assistant Surgeon No. II', *Asiatic Journal and Monthly Register* 138 (1841), p. 101; 'Diary of an Assistant Surgeon No. XIII', *ibid.* 157 (1843), p. 50. Ironically he had claimed otherwise earlier in his career when stationed at Arni; 'Diary of an Assistant Surgeon No. VII', *ibid.* 146 (1842), p. 69.

99 Cumberland, *Stray Leaves*, p. 294.

100 See, for example, Bowen, *Business of Empire*, p. 141 for role of connections in securing clerical and posts at East India House.

101 Ackroyd et al., *Advancing with the Army*, pp. 155, 170, 174–6, 180, 200–8.

102 Finn, 'Private Life of Public Health'.

103 T.M. Devine, 'Glasgow Colonial Merchants and Land, 1770–1815', in J.T. Ward and R.G. Wilson (eds), *Land and Industry. The Landed Estate and the Industrial Revolution* (Newton Abbot: David & Charles, 1971), pp. 203–65.

104 B.L. Mss Eur C 101 transcript p. 8, letter from Francis Maxwell near Seringapatam to his father 2 June 1799.

105 B.L. Mss Eur C 101 transcript p. 6, letter from Francis Maxwell in Calcutta to his father 23 October 1798.

106 'Diary of an Assistant Surgeon No. II', *Asiatic Journal and Monthly Register* 138 (1841), p. 103.
107 B.L. Mss Eur D 692, letter from Gurney Turner at Dinapore to his brother Dawson 29 May 1841.
108 Turner died before his first promotion: Crawford, *Roll*, p. 115.
109 Crowther and Dupree, *Medical Lives*, p. 303.
110 B.L. Mss Eur D 909, letter from George Spilsbury at Cawnpore to his brother Edgar 28 May 1819.
111 B.L. Mss Eur D 909, letter from George Spilsbury at Cawnpore to his brother Edgar 26 March 1813
112 B.L. Mss Eur D 909, letters from George Spilsbury at Camp Heerapore, Camp Gurrawarrah and Cawnpore respectively to his brother Edgar 8 December 1818, 7 January 1819 and 28 May 1819; the job was given to either John or Robert Tytler, brothers from Scotland.
113 B.L. Mss Eur D 909, letter from George Spilsbury at Nursingpore to his brother Edgar 30 August 1820.
114 B.L. Mss Eur D 909, letters from George Spilsbury at Bhopalpore to his brother Edgar 23 April 1822, 1 July 1822 and 31 October 1822.
115 He became the surgeon for the Governor of Saugor on the recommendation of Charles Molony, the Governor's political agent; B.L. Mss Eur D 909, letter from George Spilsbury at Bhopalpore to his brother Edgar 31 October 1822.
116 B.L. Mss Eur D 909, letter from George Spilsbury on the banks of the Sinde to his brother Edgar 20 December 1817.
117 Laidlaw, *Colonial Connections*, p. 16.
118 Quoted in 'Practical view of the liberty of the press in India', *Oriental Herald* 19 (1828), p. 278.
119 Covered rather obliquely in the British press but accurately in B.L. Mss Eur D 909, letter from George Spilsbury at Bhopalpore to his brother Edgar 28 November 1822. See for example [untitled] *The Times* 19 April 1822, p. 2.
120 [Untitled] *The Lancet* 39:997 (1842), p. 70.
121 B.L. Mss Eur C 101 transcript p. 39, letter from Francis Maxwell in Calcutta to his brother John 11 March 1802.
122 B.L. Mss Eur C 101 transcript p. 15, letter from Francis Maxwell in camp near Ellore to his father 22 March 1800; B.L. Mss Eur D 909, letter from George Spilsbury at Jubbulpore to his brother Edgar 13 September 1823.
123 B.L. Mss Eur D 692 letter from Gurney Turner at Ferozepore to his parents 23 November 1842.
124 Crawford, *Roll*, p. 33.
125 B.L. Mss Eur D 909, letters from George Spilsbury at Cawnpore to his brother Edgar 25 October 1813 and at Allahabad 30 January 1814.

126 B.L. Mss Eur D 909, letter from George Spilsbury at Cawnpore to his brother Edgar 24 November 1813.

127 B.L. Mss Eur C 241/2, diary entry of 27 January 1862.

128 B.L. Mss Eur C 241/2, diary entry of 20 December 1865.

129 As there were in military service; Ackroyd, *Advancing with the Army,* p. 209.

130 B.L. Mss Eur C 101 transcript p. 13, letter from Francis Maxwell in camp near Madras to his brother William 3 February 1800; transcript p. 14 letter from Francis Maxwell in camp near Ellore to his father 22 March 1800.

131 'Diary of an Assistant Surgeon No. VII', *Asiatic Journal and Monthly Register* 146 (1842), pp. 71–2.

132 B.L., IOR PHOTO Eur 308, letter of Henry Harpur Spry at Dum Dum to his brother Edward 30 December 1827.

133 B.L. Mss Eur D 909, letters from George Spilsbury at Allahabad to his brother Edgar 30 January 1814 and at Camp Gurrawarrah 7 January 1819.

134 B.L. Mss Eur D 909, letter from George Spilsbury at Nursingpoor to his brother Edgar 25 November 1820.

135 B.L. Mss Eur D 909, letter from George Spilsbury at Jubbulpore to his brother Edgar 13 September 1823.

136 Ackroyd et al., *Advancing with the Army,* p. 211; B.L. Mss Eur C 101 transcript p. 14, letter from Francis Maxwell in camp near Ellore to his father 22 March 1800; transcript p. 16, letter from Francis Maxwell in camp at Rajahmundry to his father 15 May 1800.

137 B.L. Mss Eur C 101 transcript p. 22, letter from Francis Maxwell in Berhampore to his brother William 13 August 1800.

138 B.L. Mss Eur C 101 transcript p. 22, letter from Francis Maxwell in Berhampore to his brother William 13 August 1800.

139 B.L. Mss Eur D 909, letter from George Spilsbury at Camp Gurrawarra to Richard Stileman 15 January 1819.

140 Nechtman, *Nabobs,* conclusion; 'Diary of an Assistant Surgeon No. III', *Asiatic Journal and Monthly Register* 138 (1841), p. 196.

141 B.L. Mss Eur E 382 papers of John Colvin, covenant of 15 January 1823.

142 B.L. Mss Eur D 909, letter from George Spilsbury at Jubbulpore to his brother Edgar 13 September 1823.

143 [Untitled] *London Gazette* 17 August 1830, p. 1762 for William Wright Hewett and [untitled] *ibid.* 10 August 1830, p. 1715 for Henry Francis Hough.

144 'Diary of an Assistant Surgeon No. XV', *Asiatic Journal and Monthly Register* 1 n.s. (1843), p. 89.

145 'Diary of an Assistant Surgeon No. XV', *Asiatic Journal and Monthly Register* 1 n.s. (1843), p. 90.

146 B.L. Mss Eur C 101 transcript p. 4, letter from Francis Maxwell to his father undated.
147 'Diary of an Assistant Surgeon No. IV', *Asiatic Journal and Monthly Register* 141 (1841), pp. 15–16.
148 B.L. Mss Eur C 101 transcript p. 15, letter from Francis Maxwell in camp near Ellore to his father 22 March 1800 and transcript p. 23, letter from Francis Maxwell in Berhampore to his father 17 August 1800.
149 B.L. Mss Eur D 909, letter from George Spilsbury at Cawnpore to his brother Edgar 25 October 1813; see also 'Diary of an Assistant Surgeon No. XIII', *Asiatic Journal and Monthly Register* 157 (1843), p. 50.
150 George Spilsbury eventually developed an active interest in geology and palaeontology; see for example his contribution of fossils to the Asiatic Society of Bengal, commemorated posthumously in *Proceedings of the Asiatic Society of Bengal* (J. Thomas, Baptist Mission Press: 1859), pp. 85–6.
151 B.L., IOR PHOTO Eur 308, letter of Henry Harpur Spry at Dum Dum to his brother Edward 15 March 1828.
152 J.M. Bourne, *Patronage and Society in Nineteenth-Century England* (London: Edward Arnold, 1986), p. 99.
153 See perhaps most obviously Spilsbury, filled with 'poignant and strategic reminders to the sender and recipients of their vital family ties'; Finn, 'Private Life of Public Health'.
154 B.L. Mss Eur C 101 transcript p. 5, letter from Francis Maxwell in Calcutta to his father 23 October 1798. George Spilsbury also liked to see his sister-in-law's handwriting, see B.L. Mss Eur D 909, letter from George Spilsbury at Dinapore to his brother Edgar July 1814.
155 B.L. Mss Eur C 101 transcript p. 10 letter from Francis Maxwell on the banks of the Toombuddra river to his father 13 August 1799.
156 B.L. Mss Eur C 101 transcript p. 15, letter from Francis Maxwell in camp near Ellore to his father 22 March 1800.
157 B.L. Mss Eur C 101 transcript pp. 15–16, letter from Francis Maxwell in camp near Ellore to his father 22 March 1800.
158 B.L. Mss Eur D 909, letters from George Spilsbury near Cawnpore to his brother Edgar 1 January 1813 and from Allahabad 30 January 1814.
159 B.L. Mss Eur D909, letter from George Spilsbury at Dinapore to his brother Edgar October 1814.
160 B.L. Mss Eur D 909, letter from George Spilsbury at Nursingpoor to his sister-in-law Emma 15 July 1820.
161 'Diary of an Assistant Surgeon No. VI', *Asiatic Journal and Monthly Register* 144 (1841), pp. 217–18; Cumberland, *Stray Leaves*, p. 239.
162 B.L. Mss Eur D 909, letter from George Spilsbury at Allahabad to his brother Edgar 27 February 1813.

163 Finn, 'Private Life of Public Health'.
164 B.L. India Office Family History Search, viewed 24 July 2015, www.bl.uk/catalogues/iofhs.shtml, for Charles Cornwallis Chesney 1791–1830; B.L. Mss Eur D 909, letter from George Spilsbury at Cawnpore to his brother Edgar 25 October 1813.
165 B.L. Mss Eur D 909, letter from George Spilsbury at Allahabad to his brother Edgar 30 January 1814.
166 B.L. Mss Eur D 909, letter from George Spilsbury at Nursingpoor to his sister-in-law Emma 15 July 1820.
167 I am indebted to Hilary Ingram for this point.
168 B.L. Mss Eur D 909, letter from George Spilsbury at Cawnpore to his brother Edgar 26 March 1813.
169 B.L. Mss Eur D 909, letter from George Spilsbury at Cawnpore to his brother Edgar 18 May 1813.
170 B.L. Mss Eur D 909, letter from George Spilsbury at Cawnpore to his brother Edgar 9 August 1813.
171 B.L. Mss Eur D 909, letter from George Spilsbury at Cawnpore to his brother Edgar 25 October 1813.
172 B.L. Mss Eur D 909, letter from George Spilsbury at Dinapore to his brother Edgar July 1814 and copy letters by Lt. Gen. Watson to George Spilsbury 2 July 1814, from George Spilsbury to Lt. Gen. Watson 3 July 1814, and from George Spilsbury to Mrs C. Morgan [Watson's daughter] July 1814.
173 T.L. Broughton, 'The Bengal Obituary: reading and writing Calcutta graves in the mid nineteenth century', *Journal of Victorian Culture* 15:1 (2010), pp. 39–59, on p. 57.
174 'Diary of an Assistant Surgeon No. V', *Asiatic Journal and Monthly Register* 142 (1841), p. 90.
175 For the rules governing Ginders' furlough, see *East India Register and Directory* (London: J. Mathison et al., 1831), p. xxi.
176 Crawford, *Roll*, p. 102.
177 S.R.O. 6850, diaries of Jeremiah Ginders, entry for 4 July 1844.
178 S.R.O. 6850, diaries of Jeremiah Ginders, entry for 28–29 March 1844.
179 S.R.O. 6850, diaries of Jeremiah Ginders, entry for October 1843.
180 Finn, 'Private Life of Public Health'; H. Fischer-Tiné, *Low and Licentious Europeans. Race, Class and 'White Subalternity' in Colonial India* (Hyderabad: Orient BlackSwan, 2009).
181 A. Nandy, *The Intimate Enemy. Loss and Recovery of Self under Colonialism* (Delhi: Oxford University Press India, 2009), pp. 30–48.
182 Crawford, *Indian Medical Service* II, p. 221.

3

Accident or on purpose? Neglect, incompetence, and unintentional killing

Allegations of neglect or incompetence provided an evolving medical profession with a structured set of opportunities to set out the boundaries of acceptable practice. Complaints might come from patients and their relations, from within the profession, or from figures in authority including the police, coroners, and poor-law guardians. Reproach from any one of these sources might result in a newspaper article, and so supply a platform for commentary by doctors and others about regular versus unqualified practice, or offer targets for advice or criticism. Reports of neglect collectively comprised a public schooling in professional morality, and the most typical legal venue for charges to be made against practitioners in public was the inquest. Therefore, this is the first of three chapters that will take newspaper reporting of inquests and criminal trials as a central source, and will necessarily examine claims of neglect or incompetence that typically emerged in relation to a patient's death.[1]

Inquests in late eighteenth- and nineteenth-century England were designed to investigate categories of 'unnatural' death and determine a cause. A coroner, elected to the post, would receive information about deaths, call the inquest and summon the jury. Juries comprised at least twelve men, and no property qualification was imposed. The coroner and jury collectively viewed the body and heard evidence from witnesses, but the jury alone was responsible for determining the verdict. Juries enjoyed considerable independence in the way that they questioned witnesses, and in the manner of their verdict being recorded. It was permissible for juries to add a commentary or 'rider' to their verdicts, to gloss their intent or to add notes of praise or condemnation about individuals or organisations associated with the death. For this and other reasons inquests were regarded by some as a valuable instance of a participatory political tribunal, with the power to monitor and comment upon the actions of those in authority.[2]

The status of both inquests and their verdicts was not legally secure, however. Inquests were not subject to the same rules of evidence that developed in other courts.[3] This meant that there were many more inquest verdicts of manslaughter and murder, for example, than there were criminal prosecutions for the same events. As a result, a number of practitioners were castigated by inquest juries and committed for trial in a higher court only to see their cases thrown out as unsupported.

The importance of the inquest for the medical profession and for the professionalisation process has so far been characterised in terms of the struggle between practitioners and lawyers in elections to coronial office, with particular focus on Thomas Wakley (both in terms of his election campaigns in Middlesex and his use of *The Lancet* to supply ongoing commentary on the fulfilment of coroners' duties).[4] But doctors might fill roles other than that of medical or legal expert. The idea that the inquest might in some cases offer revelations of practitioner wrong-doing leading to a prosecution, as in this chapter and the next, was theoretically repugnant to the emerging profession and likely to induce the kind of 'studied neglect ... to minimise direct engagement lest it should seem to lend credibility to outrageous calumny' which met charges of human vivisection.[5] But silence might be equally unsatisfactory. Practitioners upbraided by juries or coroners could not make statements in their own defence after the verdict, and were not permitted to lodge appeals against jury riders.[6]

Practitioners' presence at inquests, as witnesses or the target of blame, offer another window onto the nineteenth-century medical marketplace. Men under duress in the glare of juries' attention were less likely to preserve their commitment to disinterest, and even expressions of self-defence could be construed as self-interest or denigration of rivals. In at least some cases of neglect and manslaughter, it is possible to detect a fairly complicated agenda at work within the profession, to marginalise a certain type of practice or deprecate forms of medical behaviour. The dangers of 'quackery', however construed, were easier to identify and publicise when confronted by a corpse, and Michael Brown has charted the use of inquests to attack the credentials of James Morison's hygeiaism.[7] At the same time, negative publicity, whether intentionally or coincidentally addressed to competitors, could backfire given the broader tastes and judgement of the lay public, and qualified men were not insulated from exposure by the same means.[8]

Any middle-class man might be challenged, reprobated or prosecuted as a result of inquest proceedings, but the risks for medical men were occupationally inflected in ways that queried their claims to manly probity. Death was an event which practitioners were supposed to postpone, so an inquest was at the very least evidence of inadequate or thwarted medical science, even where no blame was in question. Yet blame was frequently a possibility, and while an honest admission of error and regret might express masculine courage and a willingness to face consequences, this was not a prominent characteristic of medical evidence as outlined later in the chapter. More usual was the dismissal of blame, an angry or wearied rebuttal of charges, or wilful evasion of responsibility. The stakes were highest where the death was that of an unborn infant or its mother (or both) in cases of suspected abortion. Aborting a foetus was always a clandestine activity, and one historically associated with women. One of the charges levelled against female midwives *en masse* was their alleged propensity to conduct abortion.[9] This potentially rendered the involvement of qualified practitioners in abortion an underhand, feminised failing and, where the child was allegedly their own, implied gross betrayal of disinterested and professional masculinity.

This chapter will consider charges against practitioners that entailed their neglect, incompetence or questionable practice which occasioned a threat to patients' lives, and which were usually given public notice at the inquests on patients' bodies. As such it will cover allegations of unplanned or unintentional crimes against the body where the victim was a patient who died. The reaction to medical men in these contexts constituted at best commiseration with misfortune but at worst a condemnation of wilful harm to others in the pursuit of self-interest. As such, an examination of these cases opens opportunities to witness the profession being schooled in acceptable practice, both by professional peers and by the public.

Medical involvement in neglect, manslaughter, and abortion was sought using a combination of searches for terms that were explicit (such as 'abortion') or in more euphemistic references (such as

Table 3.1 Hits found for neglect, manslaughter, and nineteenth-century synonyms among keywords, 1800–90

	Physician	Surgeon	Doctor	Medical	Total
Neglect	0	31	11	75	117
Manslaughter	1	56	34	29	120
Abuse	0	0	1	5	6
Complaint	0	1	1	14	16
Disgraceful	0	3	5	6	14
Allegations	0	5	8	20	33
Negligence	0	7	2	6	15

Table 3.2 Hits found for abortion, serious or extraordinary charges among all words using a proximity measure of ten, 1800–90

	Physician	Surgeon	Doctor	Medical	Total
'serious charge against a'	32	363	177	297	869
'extraordinary charge against a'	7	29	12	41	89
Abortion	7	139	37	162	345

'complaint against a' practitioner). These searches involved use of one of the British Library Newspaper databases' filtering functions, here meaning either proximity searches or searches of headlines and subtitles rather than articles' full text (Tables 3.1, 3.2, and Figure 3.1).

All hits were checked manually to determine discrete cases where practitioners were publicly charged with neglecting patients, committing manslaughter or attempting/performing abortion. This involved some tidying of the data, chiefly to sort men technically accused of murder under *de facto* manslaughter or abortion headings. As a result, 193 men were found to have been accused of neglect broadly defined, fifty-nine of manslaughter, and seventy-three of abortion. Cases were spread unevenly over the period, as none arose before 1820 and the majority were concentrated in the thirty years in 1860–89.

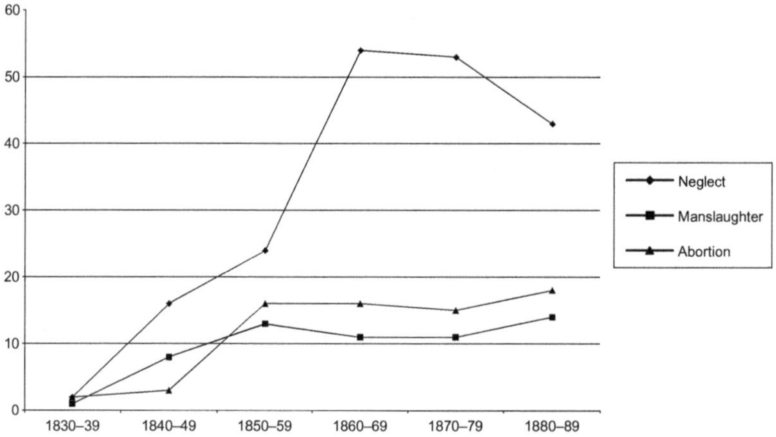

Figure 3.1 Reported neglect, manslaughter, and abortion cases, 1830–89

Neglect

Charges of neglect could arise when paying patients thought that medical attendants fell short of their expected duties. Patient survival was not necessarily essential to satisfactory performance, but practitioner attention, advice, prescription, and the conduct of surgical and other procedures might all be assumed to be included in the range of services to be supplied. Practitioners could be sued for damages by a private patient after inappropriate treatment, as when colliery doctor Motherwell Duggan and his unqualified assistant T.C. Hoffman were prosecuted for their treatment of a broken leg and were jointly fined £45 plus costs, and such cases were not new in the nineteenth century.[10] The majority of neglect claims, though, derived from men's medical service with the New Poor Law as a district or workhouse medical officer: two-thirds of the 193 reports of neglect arose in this context. Poor-law medical officers were retained for an annual fee and were expected to treat all paupers sent by the union under the contract. Union authorisation of treatment in emergencies could also be signified in a 'relieving order', issued by non-medical union officers, and therefore a complicated web of expectation and disappointment could occur. Poor-law guardians might feel that practitioners evaded the terms of their contract by failing to attend pauper patients, but paupers could also question the care they received and raise a complaint. At the same time, medical men could perceive the number of relieving orders sent to them as punitive, and might bridle under the necessity of obeying a relieving officer they regarded as an inferior (in both social and professional terms).[11] In this way, union medical officers were obliged to consider three different sorts of task-master: the guardians, the relieving officers, and the paupers themselves.

At the same time, practitioners suffered drastic conflicts of interest when they entered into a poor-law contract. Such contracts rarely yielded medical men any surplus income, because unions drove hard bargains with an overstocked profession, but they did at least allow their holders to drive out competitors for public office.[12] Once signed, poor-law contracts typically imposed a very high workload across a dispersed geographical area, rendering the treating or even visiting of all pauper patients impossible. Non-attendance was routinely compounded by falsified claims of attendance, or incompetent treatment where qualified men delegated their poor-law duties to assistants at variable stages of medical education.[13] Added to this, there was space for a significant mismatch between the cases that lay relieving officers were prepared to recognise as legitimate medical emergencies and the cases that professional medical judgement might prioritise. A rare union might try to determine whether medical officers were permitted to decide whether a case was a proper one for relief, but most did not.[14] This meant that doctors might be blamed for failing to attend a pauper with a relieving order whose medical state was moderate, but not be reimbursed for attending a patient in a more parlous state of health for whom no relieving order had been issued.[15] Finally, where practitioners were required to choose whether to attend a pauper or a private paying patient, their financial self-interest might win out over clinical imperative. Private patients could be given itemised bills, whereas poor-law contracts typically required practitioners to offer attendance, services, and medicines to paupers for the contracted sum.[16] Pauper patients undoubtedly died as a result of this structural double bind, as Kim Price has recently shown so clearly, but systemic faults were not recognised in the Victorian period.[17] Instead individuals were blamed, and medical officers were particularly vulnerable to lofty judgements from guardians and poor-law inspectors. At least one inspector assumed that compensation must be adequate or no one would accept the posts, so when neglect cases arose the accused men were asked why they had not given up the contract if the workload was so unmanageable.[18]

This means that the bulk of neglect allegations did not spring from a simple disparity between patient expectation and practitioner performance. Instead they derived from power struggles within the poor law, in disputes with both discrete unions and the central authority (successively the Poor Law Commission, the Poor Law Board, and the Local Government Board). Kim Price argues that both local and central officials remained intent on opposing higher positions for medical officers throughout the period.[19] 'Neglect' was used as a tool, but more effectively by those outside the profession than as a means to school medical peers from within.

Nonetheless, a small minority of neglect accusations emanated from other doctors, because the poor law served as a very effective driver of intra-professional infighting. This began in the immediate aftermath of the 1834 Act with the use of competitive tendering for posts. Unions asked practitioners to bid for the medical work in a district or workhouse, and were pressured by both ratepayers and the policy intentions of the Commissioners to accept the lowest offer.[20] Little wonder that tendering was fiercely resisted by practitioners in theory and pandered to in practice, as it forced into the open the sentiments that evolving medical ethics preferred to be hidden. At least one contemporary observer thought it created jealousy, when more probably it brought existing or latent rivalries to the fore. It set local colleagues against one another and pitched established men against interlopers, particularly the career-young.[21]

To some extent, tendering constituted a rude intrusion upon men otherwise intent on covert competition, although emergent professional bodies were not necessarily so coy as to deny that competition existed. In 1836, the Provincial Medical and Surgical Association openly referenced 'the wretched spirit of rivalry, speculation, underbidding, and jobbing, which unfortunately are but too frequently found among medical men.'[22] It was also little wonder if those outside the profession (and not intent on buttressing medical statuses) initially took exception to bruised medical pride. It was in the interests of the Poor Law Commission to draw medical competition into the open, and so in the early days of the poor law the Commissioners wilfully closed their eyes to the way that tendering might undermine medical professional ambitions. Instead, they disingenuously remarked that guardians had never been required to accept the lowest tender.[23] Medical pressure meant that tendering was technically edged out from poor-law recruitment between the General Medical Order of 1842 and successive central directives to 1859, but throughout the nineteenth century unions found other ways to use professional competition to fill posts.[24] At the same time, attempts from within the profession to encourage practitioners to act collectively as poor-law employees largely failed.[25] This was partly a function of the imbalance of power in practitioners' relationships with relieving officers, guardians, and central authorities, but it was also underpinned by private adherence to competitive practice.

The number of men potentially drawn into charges of neglect or worse as a consequence of poor-law work was very high, given that thousands of practitioners were filling medical-officer posts at any one time. There were over 2,000 by the early 1840s, and numbers rose gradually over the century to nearer 5,000 by 1906.[26] Therefore the extent to which any man was liable to exposure in the newspapers was, by this set of searches, very slight. Less than 0.2 percent of such men per year were identified in this way. The strategy of searching only among keywords has probably taken its toll on the yield of successful hits on cases of medical neglect, but it is questionable by how much. Sam Shave has pointed to the difference between private tragedies and public scandals in the context of the New Poor Law, given the capacity for transformation of one into the other; print media has a role in the process, both in the transition and the consolidation of 'scandal'.[27] What is notable is that full-scale poor-law scandals reported exhaustively and nationally were few. If scandal develops from 'exposure followed by disapproval' it is perhaps surprising that it did not happen more often, but then even the Victorian reading public could suffer from something akin to scandal fatigue.[28] The appetite for exposure of medical men as incompetent, immoral or criminal had definite limits, as can be shown most decisively in the next chapter. Therefore it is likely the stories found here are only a reliable minimum of allegations, and may be some way distant from a full list of potential hits, yet still represent some core characteristics of medical conflicts over competence.

The pattern of cases loosely confirms Price's contention that allegations of neglect did not decline across the century, but is less demonstrative of an atmosphere of heightened neglect in the wake of the 'crusade' against outdoor relief of 1869 onwards.[29] As with Price's surveys, allegations of neglect could be used for administrative purposes, enabling unions to rid themselves of practitioners – including those who asked for salary increases, or who failed to observe union protocols in reducing expenditure on medical relief, or for a wide range of other reasons.[30] Complaints often arose from non-attendance, or improper issue of death certificates when practitioners had not attended pauper patients when they were alive. Non-attendance is a difficult fault to parse, given that the reasons could feasibly range from being grossly indefensible to being amply justified: as human beings, practitioners were occasionally in need of welfare themselves. Therefore the following discussion draws illustration from cases of 'failure' to attend but is also concerned with the features of active neglect, where men attended but were still found wanting.

One of the most notable features in extended reportage of neglect was the propensity of articles to include apparently verbatim quotes from doctors. Practitioners' irritation spilled over in verbal exchanges with paupers, relieving officers, guardians, and others and was reported in ways that almost always implied reproach of the practitioner. These expressions ranged from dismissive, belittling of patient concerns, through to frustration and anger. Elijah Barker told Alfred Pemberton 'It was all gammon' that Pemberton's wife was in labour (when she was on the point of giving birth), whereas William Marshall asked Joseph Blewett's wife 'Well, what are you frightened about now?' as Blewett himself lay dying.[31] Joseph Massingham must have known full well that he was misrepresenting the scope for obstetric complications when he told Anne Ferry, daughter of his patient, 'Fiddle de dee, nonsense; if your mother was put to bed yesterday it can't be said that she will die today.'[32] His optimism proved entirely unjustified as Mrs Ferry died two hours later. Practitioners sometimes protested that they had not spoken unkindly or rudely, but on other occasions their anger was undeniable. In 1855, Alexander Marshall told Patrick Savage's father 'I do not give a d— for you or your son', and while he did express sorrow after the boy's death, he also tried to manipulate Mr Savage into forestalling an inquest.[33] James Harrison went further in 1879 when told that Francis

Cook was dead: he snapped at Cook's wife Caroline, who later charged him with neglect, 'It's a good job he's dead; he ought to have been dead six months ago.'[34]

Often there was no third-party witness to doctors' words and actions, whether in poor-law cases or not, and rarely an auditor whose own interest was not bound up with either the patient or the medical man himself. That said, an assiduous inquiry could reveal manipulation of the evidence. When questioned about the death of Elizabeth Fletcher in childbirth, surgeon George Smith denied having said 'Go to h— for a doctor' and protested 'my word is as good, at least' as that of Fletcher's husband. Unfortunately for Smith, an independent witness had heard him use exactly that objectionable form of words. The coroner recorded that Smith had 'outraged all respect for yourself and the profession by adding cruelty to inhumanity. I confess I envy not your feelings.'[35]

Practitioners were possibly driven from hurtful words to wilful harm on occasion, actions representing the reverse of the gratuitous treatment which allegedly benefited so many of the poor.[36] In 1877, a Dr Jones of Cardiff attended a domestic violence case: Elizabeth Moore had been stabbed twice in the arm by her husband Robert, and Jones's assistant sewed up the two wounds and bandaged her. Moore argued that Jones then demanded immediate payment of five shillings. Moore had no money with her in Jones's surgery but offered to return home and fetch some. Moore claimed 'He replied that I must pay then, or he would take my bandage off and open my wounds again, for he was not going to attend me for nothing.'[37] Attempts by Moore and her friend Martha Costa to raise the money came to naught, so Jones cut the stitches on the largest wound and covered it with sticking plaster. In retrospect there was no denial that stitches had been cut. The dispute was over the meaning of the removal: was it an act of spite in response to a patient's failure to pay, or was it a medical procedure to remove overly-tight stitches? If Moore and Costa were reporting events accurately, then Jones was guilty of avarice, cruelty or both, but the press and the courts both heard the voices of the two poor women and found them wanting. When the case was brought before the Cardiff police court, the prosecutrix was unrepresented, whereas the defence was conducted by a Mr Vachell who called as his chief witness Jones's own assistant. The defence also marshalled the support of numerous practitioners in the town, willing to testify that cutting stitches shortly after they had been put in was a perfectly legitimate medical decision. Finally it cast aspersions on the reliability of Elizabeth Moore, and implied without proof that the women lived together in a disorderly house. Unsurprisingly the women's accusations were dismissed.

The solidarity of middle-class professionals when under attack from without varied somewhat, as the words of the coroner to George Smith cited previously suggest, but relationships between practitioners and incumbent coroners were generally very respectful. Elizabeth Hurren has shown that coroners 'needed to build alliances amongst the medical fraternity' to perform their office with efficiency and authority.[38] Unfortunately, this sometimes allowed practitioners leeway to the detriment of coronial justice. In another case from 1877, Robert Seely or Ceely was questioned about his treatment of a labourer's wife. Sarah Ann Bowers had recently given birth but suffered with pains in the head and bowels, so was given a draught, medicine, and a blister by Seely. She died the following day, whereupon her husband Henry Bowers claimed that Seely had requested the return of his medicine bottle. Furthermore, Seely allegedly told Bowers 'If the police ask you any questions you need not say much – say a few words in a rough way.'[39] This might have raised justifiable questions about Seely's conduct of the case; but far from questioning Bowers' treatment, the coroner Maurice Carter invited Seely to perform the post mortem. This procedural irregularity prompted the foreman of the inquest jury to suggest that coroners should seek post mortem reports from independent members of the medical profession, but the coroner was not persuaded. He took the view that to adopt the suggestion 'would be to cast a slur on the whole medical profession'. In other words, rather than imply that any practitioner might feasibly be guilty of misconduct, the coroner would rather risk allowing a man of imperfect probity to cover his own tracks. Carter's standing as a solicitor, the very occupation that competed with medicine for coronial office and usually succeeded, reinforces the sense of mutual protection among middle-class professionals when under scrutiny.[40]

Coroners' circumspection was not matched by boards of guardians, who were not necessarily or predominantly fellow professional men; instead boards tended to treat their doctors authoritatively.[41] It was a familiar refrain among guardians' comments that the poor had as much entitlement to attendance as the rich, drawing attention to practitioners' division of time between paupers and their list of private patients.[42] This had the effect of identifying practitioners' self-interest in their assiduous care of paying clients. Some unions achieved particular prominence in newspaper reports for their criticism of multiple medical men, suggesting a culture of complaint or ongoing friction between medical officers *per se* and guardians (rather than individual clashes of personality and professional practice, evident where one man was subject to more than one complaint). Portsea Union in Hampshire was unusual among the authorities implicated in the 193 neglect cases, because it raised specific concerns of patient neglect about four separate doctors in the ten years 1864 to 1874, and concerns of a different kind about three additional medical men in the same period.[43] Aside from indicating a general willingness to challenge medical authority, however, there is no other pattern to these complaints discernible from the press, and it is notable that in Portsea the complaints fell both before and after the start of the 'crusade' against relief. This suggests that the crusade did not give rise to an increase in complaints in this location in the way that Price and Hurren might have expected.

Justifications by doctors themselves were heard less frequently and forcefully, or were subtly undermined by implications of self-interest (as where they observed the extent of their workload in relation to the remuneration for poor-law work). They might also anticipate a tart rebuke in editorial commentary. Augustus Packman told the Sheffield guardians in 1875 that he 'thought it time a guardian was appointed for the medical officers as well as for the paupers', part of a defence against the neglect of a dying child that the *Sheffield and Rotherham Independent* regarded as 'ill-judged and ill-timed'.[44] Similarly guardians' defence of their medical officers, where it occurred, was muted and frequently equivocal. Hilary Hill was acknowledged by the guardians of the Worcester Union to be overworked by his poor-law duties in 1869, but they also observed that he had accepted contracts with two different unions at the same time.[45]

As a number of the quoted examples suggest, obstetric cases were invested with particular significance: 20 percent of charges of neglect were associated with attendance or non-attendance at a birth (and obstetrics emerge even more prominently in the manslaughter cases detailed later in the chapter). Childbirth offered the grim risk of losing two patients at once. While it was important for the general practitioner in gaining access to a household, attending childbirth was also a less well-regarded area of medicine among trained practitioners. This meant that obstetric treatment attracted acute patient scrutiny at the same time as offering considerable trouble and little status to practitioners, and it was quite possible for a medical man simply to walk away from a problematic birth. A Mr Howell, when faced with a malpresentation in 1844, left when the child was half born despite the entreaties of a woman attending the mother.[46] John Ballenden left Mary Edwards in labour when her child was presenting crosswise because he judged that there was nothing to be done; Edwards was later delivered by another practitioner using chloroform.[47] Yet the role of medical status could also work against patients in another way: wherever a doctor insisted on his own authority and overrode other voices and opinions (particularly those of midwives). In 1876, Mr Watson claimed that Caroline Ashman had miscarried, and when Ashman protested that she was still pregnant he told her to 'hold her tongue'. The midwife Mrs Paske held a different, more accurate, opinion of Ashman's condition, but did not want to deny Watson's authority directly; she was said to have commented 'I know better than that; let him have his way; do not contradict, that won't do.'[48]

Obstetric cases highlight intermittent practitioner ambivalence for their work and can bring into sharp relief the structural problems for patients with professionalising medicine. Where did responsibility lie, particularly when cases fell on the borders of or beyond the poor law? A lack of clarity on this point gave rise to several examples of patient neglect arising from non-attendance. For instance, three Exeter men were retrospectively attacked for their serial failure to attend Caroline Bray.[49] In July 1862, Bray was seven months pregnant when she fell into a fit and her mother Priscilla Stoneman went in search of a doctor. She first tried surgeon William Hunt, who told her that he would not attend as it was not his case, but that she should secure the parish doctor (even when Stoneman offered to pay him). Returning home to see her daughter and ensure she would be attended by a female friend, Stoneman set out again for the house of Arthur Cumming (who she knew as a practitioner attached to the Exeter dispensary). Cumming echoed Hunt and insisted she find the appropriate parish doctor, as he was a Union medical officer, but for a different district of Exeter.[50] Stoneman duly sought out John Perkins, the relevant poor-law medical officer, at his house but despite ringing the bell and waiting she was not answered. She returned home to her daughter but set out again two hours later, and again failed to persuade Hunt to attend. A second trip to Perkins' house yielded some medicine and advice, plus a request to be told how Bray fared. Stoneman waited three hours and sent a messenger to Perkins' house asking for his immediate attendance, but in the event he only arrived after a further five-hour wait (and two hours after Bray had died). The distress occasioned by Stoneman's fruitless search for medical attention was compounded by Perkins' willingness to issue a death certificate for a patient he had not seen when alive. The coroner took Hunt, Cumming, and Perkins to task for both unkindness and procedural irregularity, and the jury followed suit with a rider of disapprobation.

A willingness to eschew responsibility in cases of childbirth was not at all unusual, and Priscilla Stoneman's dashes around central Exeter were not uncommon.[51] The most extraordinary example of the reluctance of practitioners being matched by the tenacity of a woman's relations occurred in Newcastle upon Tyne.[52] Jane Chambers had a ticket for Newcastle's lying-in hospital for her final pregnancy in 1865, which entitled her to a choice of midwife and delivery in her own home. When she went into labour in late January her midwife arrived as planned, but in the face of a transverse presentation the midwife recommended seeking medical assistance. First Jane's sister-in-law Isabella Chambers and later her husband Thomas Chambers set out to secure it. Their first thought was to call at the hospital for advice, but when the designated hospital doctor Charles Gibson refused to attend, the pair took multiple recommendations from others (including some from among the non-attending doctors themselves, and from the midwife's daughter). Between 7.30pm and midnight, they visited the houses of eight different practitioners scattered across the city, all of whom were either away from home or refused to attend on the grounds that they had patients of their own, did not go out on such cases, or had just got into a warm bath. The inquest jury found the most culpable to be Charles Gibson, the surgeon responsible for attending women in the St Peter's district on behalf of the lying-in hospital for that month. He had refused to come because he was 'waiting on a lady'. Dr James Lownds' assistant John Tait Mackey who finally attended, moments after Jane Chambers died, took the view that in all probability her life could have been saved if a medical man had been present earlier.

The Chambers' family tragedy illustrates a number of points about the shortfalls that might be revealed between an assumption of professional dignity and a growing expectation of public duty. Gibson was happy to have his name associated with the lying-in hospital, but was not prepared to allow public office to cut across his own sense of appropriate professional action; he decided to stay with 'the lady' (who presumably was not dying and whose case was not flagged in the press as urgent) rather than attend a birth. Since Gibson, the man with explicit responsibility for the lying-in hospital, relinquished his duties so readily there is less surprise in the unwillingness of other doctors to interfere. In contrast to Gibson, the Chambers case was not within their normal remit. Even so, the number and the justifications for refusals by other practitioners to attend Jane Chambers could clearly be the source of generalised reproach in retrospect. Finally it is significant that the man who did ultimately deliver Jane Chambers' dead infant in the middle of the night was a twenty-three-year-old assistant.[53] Established men could refuse a commission where assistants were not at such liberty to pick and choose.

Patient neglect occurring when practitioners avoided uncongenial work is matched by claims of neglect as men competed to secure attractive and lucrative practices. The reformed poor law might be used as a vehicle for open competition, if with geographical variations, but the newspaper cases extend the limited and dismissive evidence of early historians about medical competition, and can augment even Price's recent and thorough analysis of neglect.[54] This was because a charge of neglect could be mobilised to achieve competition on apparently selfless grounds, because it could be couched as in the interests of guardians, paupers, and ratepayers. The aim might be simply to denigrate a rival, as seems likely in the case of Arthur Steele. He had treated pauper Ellen Ashworth for syphilis, and her subsequent death was attributed to his actions. Steele was quick to identify Dr Gee, the workhouse medical officer, as the source of the complaint.[55]

Friction between two or more appointed poor-law medical officers was not common. Strife between a man in post and a man aspiring to salaried work was more characteristic. Wherever one man took a post to keep another out, unsuccessful candidates for poor-law work might reliably await their chance to point the finger at their colleague for non-completion of duties (which, given the pressure of overwhelming workloads, was almost certain to follow). Conflict might be intergenerational, but it was certainly hot between the established and the career-young.[56] Henry Hase had obtained both his Licence from the Royal College of Surgeons in Edinburgh and his Licence from the Society of Apothecaries in London in 1834.[57] He took up practice in Worksop and appointed John Deakin or Dakeyne as his assistant in 1850 on payment of £40 a year plus board and lodging. The two were less than a decade apart in age, and probably held identical qualifications.[58] Hase tried to impose an exclusivity contract on Deakin to protect his own private practice, much in the same way as had been tried by John Steight in relation to his assistant Richard Hunter in 1807.[59] The document was drawn up by local solicitor John Whall, who also happened to be the Clerk to the Worksop guardians.[60] The deed required Deakin to avoid practising as a surgeon and apothecary on his own account within ten miles of Worksop for seven years after ceasing to work for Hase, on pain of a £2,000 penalty if he should do so. Unfortunately for Hase this understanding was not decisively converted to a contractual arrangement. Deakin gave his notice to leave in late 1851, and a verbal dispute arose over whether Deakin had ever been offered formal partnership in the practice, but in any event Deakin set up for himself in Worksop and Hase failed to secure an injunction restricting him.[61] This was all preliminary to charges of neglect.

In November 1852, Deakin arranged some sort of compact with disgruntled patients among Hase's pauper clientele.[62] According to Deakin he was approached by the pauper John Salmon who complained of neglect by Hase, and he later protested 'the course I have taken has been forced upon me'.[63] It is also possible that Deakin subtly encouraged or solicited complaints from Salmon and others. In either case, discussions between Deakin and Salmon gave rise to two letters complaining about Hase, both written by Deakin but one purporting to come from Salmon and one written in disguised handwriting allegedly from a ratepayer. The Poor Law Board was content to ignore an anonymous letter, but acted decisively when John Deakin wrote again as himself, making additional specific allegations and enclosing affidavits from six paupers willing to testify to Hase's neglect. Hase's shortcomings included multiple failures to attend promptly, sending an unqualified female midwife to attend a labour, and using harsh and abusive language to sick or dying paupers. A Poor Law Board inquiry was duly held before the Worksop guardians in January 1853, where Deakin freely admitted to writing at first in 'a disguised style' because he was 'afraid it would prejudice the case by giving it an appearance of professional antagonism'.[64] The appearance was all too evident to the Worksop inquiry, but both men's professional reputations suffered as the evidence unfolded. Hase was found to be the victim of a 'disgraceful conspiracy' but also did not deny using abusive words to pauper Thomas Simpson, and admitted prescribing Simpson (among other poor patients) medicine with a disagreeable nauseating effect to prevent his coming to his surgery again 'because he was tired of seeing him'.[65] This rather undermined the testimonials offered protesting Hase's kindness to the poor. Yet the inquiry also threw out claims about Deakin in addition to his having manipulated the pauper witnesses, to the effect that he had been forcibly ejected from his post at the Birmingham lying-in hospital. Deakin was not prepared to accept this quietly and secured testimonials of his own from his former colleagues at Birmingham. Deakin concluded triumphantly and with no apparent sense of irony that 'the appetite for defamation has missed the prey of which it thought itself so secure'.[66]

This level of public animosity between two men who were equally well qualified was precisely the sort of conflict that professionalising medicine was hoping to avoid, and unsurprisingly the medical press seems to have given no notice to the dispute.[67] If this case is in any way indicative of the tensions that might simmer behind the façade of even a minority of poor-law appointments, the failure of Joseph Rogers and his predecessors to establish an association to defend medical officers becomes more comprehensible. Intra-professional allegiances were simply too weak to counteract the pressing sense of self-interest that motivated both exclusivity contracts and poor-law competition.[68]

Unfortunately for reformers, attempting to penalise the non-registered practitioner was not a sure way to boost professional standing either, as the public was quite as sensitive to the value of the open market for medicine as the profession was to its drawbacks. For example, one doctor made particular efforts to demonise the unqualified and instead secured public opprobrium for qualified men. In 1884 an inquest was held on the body of Edward Watson who had died of smallpox after being attended by William Thompson, an American practitioner not on the GMC *Register*. The *Northern Echo* reported that Dr

Henry Franklin Parsons had instructed that the coroner be informed whenever a death occurred after treatment from an unregistered man. Parsons was a sanitary campaigner and Local Government Board Inspector who had published a Report in January of the same year claiming that 23 percent of deaths in Spennymoor were among people treated by unqualified men.[69] At the inquest, Thompson was quite eager to offer evidence (and taste the medicine he had prescribed) in order to scotch claims that he had poisoned Watson.[70] The jury exonerated Thompson from blame, but this was not enough to satisfy public feeling which ran high in Thompson's favour. Two days, later over 2,000 people attended an 'indignation meeting' organised by the town's Secularist Society. It comprised a procession including the fourteen members of the Whitworth Brass Band and a flag reading 'Our motto is freedom of physic'.[71] The gathering voted unanimously in favour of the motion 'We condemn the medical men of the town for the officious and vexatious interference with the rights and liberties of the people by causing an inquest to be held simply through professional jealousy and spite towards the unregistered practitioners'. Far from convincing the public to accept the authority of orthodox practitioners, Parsons' campaign had at least the short-term effect of hardening opposition to the dominance of registered professionalism.

Manslaughter

Egregious cases of neglect and incompetence gave rise to charges of manslaughter by inquest juries, which were taken up by the police or others and could result in the criminal prosecution of a practitioner.[72] The historiography of manslaughter as a discrete phenomenon is relatively slim, given the propensity among historians of crime to conflate manslaughter and murder as homicide. That conflation is not appropriate when dealing with a group of people who routinely exposed themselves to charges of manslaughter by the simple fact of professional involvement with patients who subsequently die.[73]

Medical manslaughter in the nineteenth century arose in two ways: either the practitioner neglected to act, and by withholding treatment caused or hastened a patient's death, or they acted incompetently and fatally undermined the patient's hopes for recovery. Either might constitute medical error in a modern sense, although in the twenty-first century the establishment of clinical protocols means that cases span a different divide. In the present day the desire to apportion blame for patient death typically sees allegations claiming either that practitioners have transgressed agreed rules of conduct, or have made an unconscious error in carrying out approved actions.

Keyword searches of the British Library Newspapers database yielded fifty-nine names of men accused of manslaughter by the action of coroners' courts or subjected to criminal trial.[74] The cases span 1830 to 1890, with only two cases falling before 1840. Unlike other searches, this set of cases can be compared with those found by Jennie Hubbard (using a more flexible set of search criteria).[75] She found forty instances of manslaughter in the same period, but only twenty of her hits coincided with the fifty-nine examined here. A varied methodology was notably more successful in identifying cases before 1840 (where she achieved five hits to my one). The fifty-nine hits are not coterminous either with instances of medical manslaughter found by Ferner and McDowell, whose searches for nineteenth-century cases were conducted across the digital archives of *The Times*, *The Scotsman*, and *The Lancet* and whose keywords excluded my terms 'physician' and 'medical' but included 'anaesthetist', 'assizes', 'criminal court', and 'verdict'. Nonetheless the rate of hits across both methodologies was very similar (0.8 hits per year by Ferner and McDowell 1790–2005, 0.6 hits per year here), where Ferner and McDowell's research was weighted in favour of hits after 1890 owing to the inclusion of additional resources for searching twentieth-century publications.[76] In both methodologies, there were never more than four cases in any one calendar year before 1890.

A slight majority of accusations, both here and in the Ferner and McDowell data, arose in relation to obstetric cases. Childbirth was an occasion of notable bodily risk, and the deaths of mothers and infants were particularly difficult to accept.[77] In contrast, deaths from administration of anaesthesia were not prominent in generating accusations of manslaughter from incompetence; despite heightened concern about inhalation anaesthetics by the last quarter of the century, no cases at all arise from these keyword searches.[78] Fifteen men, or a quarter of those accused, were found guilty following a criminal trial, and convictions were distributed evenly between men found on the GMC *Register* and those not found. Sentences ranged from two days in solitary confinement for killing a man during a bar-room brawl (a rare case not involving a patient), to eighteen months for a Hampshire surgeon whose offence was judged in 1857 to be insufficiently bad to warrant transportation, but the majority of practitioners received between one and six months in prison (three with hard labour).

A notable disparity between the neglect cases and those which were amplified into manslaughter charges was the relative absence of the poor law in the latter. It was rare for a man's status as a district or workhouse officer to impinge on the description of criminal transactions, which suggests that while guardians of the poor were quite ready to pursue claims of general neglect, they were much more wary of legal charges (whether ideologically or on the grounds of cost). This is not to say that poor-law medical officers enjoyed a clean slate before allegations of crime. James Stephenson was a medical officer for Stepney Union and was named at two inquests in 1856. The inquiry into the death of Henrietta Sheehan in August concluded that Stephenson was not guilty of manslaughter 'this time', but the coroner remarked on his long record of inhuman treatment towards paupers and recommended that he resign – Stephenson was only twenty-nine years old, so he had clearly made a potent impression despite being career-young.[79] In fact this was the third reprimand he faced from the same coroner, and he was suspended from office. Nonetheless he was reinstated on the advice of the Poor Law Board, to considerable public disquiet. A condemnatory handbill was drawn up for distribution, and was in the press in October of the same year when Stephenson was called to a further inquest.[80] He had failed to attend Elizabeth Malding, and the jury insisted on a rider of public censure for Stephenson's punctilious insistence on his legal right to await a relieving order.[81] Aside from the hits on Stephenson found here, he was criticised during at least two further inquests, in 1857 and 1861, before his career as Union surgeon was over.[82] But Stephenson was anomalous. This level and frequency of public reproach bordering on active prosecution was unusual among poor-law doctors.

Thirty of the men accused (including Stephenson) were qualified, so constituting half of all alleged manslaughterers, but three-fifths of all men whose cases occurred after 1850 (as obviously it was impossible for men who died before 1858 ever to have sought registration). The unqualified, and those committed to alternative therapies, offered a valuable opportunity for medical critique of men who claimed medical authority but whose false claims imperilled their patients. At the same time, too much obvious self-interest on the part of the profession might prove unacceptable to the courts and ultimately counterproductive. For example, medical student and homoeopath Charles Pearce was prosecuted in 1849 for having starved his own brother to death when treating him for cholera, but the profession's loud, self-interested opposition to homoeopathy as 'humbug and quackery' was all too evident to the judge; the charge was dismissed as an attempt to attack homoeopathic methods *per se*.[83]

The real problem with using manslaughter charges as a vehicle for professional chastisement was the scope for misdirection, risking either unjustified criticism or undue leniency. For example, *The Lancet* proved quick to judge Dennis Cronin, acquitted in the courts of manslaughter, because he held his MD from Geissen; the implication was that Cronin had purchased his degree rather than earned it, and was recklessly prescribing 'foreign poisons'.[84] Nonetheless Cronin's qualifications were sufficiently robust to admit him to the medical *Register* eleven years later.[85] Conversely, John Griffith was only a nineteen-year-old surgeon's assistant, charged with the death of Ellen Jones and her infant by reason of violent use of instruments. The apportionment of blame fell between Griffith and his qualified employer called Roberts, but the case against Roberts was dropped. In a highly unusual outcome, Griffith was found guilty of manslaughter but with a rider from the jury that he was not guilty of culpable negligence and he walked free. The *British Medical Journal* (*BMJ*) followed this verdict with an article which neatly glossed the finer details of the outcome and instead referred to both Griffith and Roberts as straightforwardly acquitted. It went on to observe of the 'precocious young obstetrician' that he 'had to bear the punishment of a criminal trial, with all its attendant anxiety, and we have no wish to add to this penalty by any censure of ours'.[86] This was despite the fact that Griffith had been guilty of inflicting grotesque injury on his patient.

Obstetric tragedies occasioned a discrete subset of cases where practitioners were accused of killing their female patients by violent instrumental intervention in deliveries. Eighteen accusations or prosecutions followed this pattern and give fairly unequivocal evidence of actual bodily harm. It was either the case that practitioners' knowledge of anatomy was so sketchy as to prompt entirely inappropriate uses of forceps or other implements, or that men's capacities were drastically undermined by alcohol (as was the case for at least six men). The five most grotesque cases involved women whose delivery of either an infant or the afterbirth encouraged men to use instruments such that the patient's small intestines became exposed or partially removed.

John Griffith represents one of the worst of these cases, yet the medical press went out of its way to extenuate his actions. The same article in the *BMJ* which expressed gladness at his acquittal set out the evidence of the post mortem in clinical terms: 'the uterus was detached from the vagina, and a laceration into the peritoneal cavity effected. It seems probable that intestine prolapsed through this laceration, and that young Griffith cut sixteen or eighteen inches of it away.'[87] Griffith's incompetence was both unquestioned and exonerated.

Practitioners were much less likely to stand trial for manslaughter than they were to suffer charges of neglect, and the extraordinary nature of the trials invited both the profession and the public to make exemplars of doctors (positive or negative). The determination to judge men in the press, as well as in the courtroom, gave rise to hasty, divergent or equivocal pointers for medical behaviour. In the cases of both Cronin and Griffith the medical press proved too quick to judge and so reached inappropriate or even grossly inequitable conclusions. Reactions to the prosecution of abortion, though, inspired even clearer divisions between professional and lay opinion.

Abortion

In abortion cases, the death of an unborn infant was a prerequisite of successful practice. Yet abortions that killed women accidentally rather than intentionally were very different in motive and intent to other forms of bodily injury. They were usually on some level requested by a female patient, albeit that the women concerned might have felt compelled to seek such a dangerous solution to unwanted pregnancy.[88] In this sense, practitioners were simply enacting a form of violence that was effectually imposed by social mores rather than one emanating from their own impulses. Similarly, while women might suffer drastic injury or death as a consequence of abortion, and maternal mortality was almost certainly raised by deaths from post-abortion sepsis, this was neither the medical attendants' design nor a calculable phenomenon.[89] There were circumstances where women's acquiescence and practitioners' disinterest were complicated, specifically if a medical man attempted to abort his own illegitimate child. In this scenario, coercion of female patients and injurious medical practice were both possible and plausible, but even here public responses were more likely to confirm concern for mothers than for infants. Intentional killing of extant individuals was always deplored by contemporaries, whereas the abortion of foetuses that had never achieved the status of live birth was not universally condemned by Victorian lay opinion as constituting murderous intent.[90] Therefore abortion has a more equivocal place on the spectrum of 'harm'.[91]

It held a very important place, though, in the rising status of orthodox medicine. English abortion law altered very substantially over the nineteenth century, and legal change has been explained by Keown partly on the basis of practitioner power. Up to 1803 there was little legal restraint on the termination of pregnancy before 'quickening', typically associated with the start of the second trimester. This was for both ideological and practical reasons: life was not thought to exist before the onset of discernible foetal movement, and in any case proving pregnancy before it became externally evident via quickening was all but impossible.[92] Termination of pregnancy could be prosecuted across the eighteenth century, however, if this was the intent of the woman and/or of the practitioner carrying it out.[93]

Lord Ellenborough's Act of 1803 clarified the law pertaining to crimes against the person, of which abortion was one among many, and prohibited the procuring of miscarriage in women who were not yet 'quick'.[94] It was passed in the notable absence of public demand but partly as a result of elite medical deprecation of the popular significance attached to quickening. Orthodox medical men towards the end of the eighteenth century had also drawn attention to the disparity of legal treatment issued to women who escaped prosecution for abortion, compared with women liable for execution following infanticide. Furthermore, theoretical interventions by practitioners against abortion can be seen as part of the growing trend in the first decade of the 1800s to find new ways to oppose irregular practice of any kind.[95] Therefore the Act of 1803 both confirmed the influence of learned medical authority and offered to augment the status of regular practice still further.

This offer was realised in the recognition given to medical opinion by refinements to the law of abortion in 1828, 1837, and 1861. The importance of quickening was erased in law by the Act of 1837 in acknowledgement of the views of male obstetricians as expressive of their desire to diminish the traditional authority of female knowledge.[96] The Act of 1861 got around the potential difficulties of proving pregnancy by confirming that a pregnancy was not a requirement for a conviction, and extended the law's field of action by explicitly including the pregnant woman herself and anyone who knowingly supplied her with abortifacient drugs or instruments as equally culpable. These clauses sprang from the desire for legal consolidation, and from a concern for maternal and foetal health; but medical professionals were clearly not disinterested in the drift of these provisions, given the additional scope they offered to curtail and punish untrained, part-time, sometimes female, practice.[97]

Professional interest arguably trumped human concern, given the contradictions evident in the official medical arguments. On the one hand, it was routinely asserted that attempts to abort typically ended in the death of the mother as well as the termination of the pregnancy.[98] On the other, there were loud claims in the medical press that the rate of abortion was high and increasing across the late 1840s and early 1850s. This is impossible to verify, but should surely have given rise to obvious deaths among prospective mothers. It was much more difficult to conceal an adult body than it was to secure treatment secretly.[99] Yet the same strain of medical protest simultaneously alleged that 'for one case that comes to light probably a dozen are effectually concealed'.[100] In polemic terms, practitioners were having their cake and eating it.

Abortion certainly touched one of the most sensitive points for a medical man, the relationship between his skill and his income. The dilemma faced by all practitioners and which fostered covert competition among regulars, to secure patients and income while appearing above material concerns, intensified attitudes to abortion. Here was a lucrative medical procedure for which there was substantial and possibly growing demand, but which was forbidden by the tenets of nineteenth-century medical opinion and training except under the most compelling therapeutic circumstances. Since abortion could feasibly be carried out by people otherwise untrained in medicine, it offered an easy target for professional critique at the same time that it supplied a divided medical body with an issue on which it could unite.[101] Quackery was hard to define but abortion was not, so influential medical deprecation of abortion deprived competitors of custom without reducing the market for other medical procedures. Attacks on abortion had the additional benefit of reminding trained men of their duty to circumspection when recruiting patients. Abortionists advertised what was clearly a commercial undertaking, so high-profile expressions of revulsion at canvassing for medical business carried a sub-textual warning against any form of medical advertising by men who considered themselves regular. Finally, abortion allowed medical commentators to set down another of the century's markers of what constituted a professional man: he was someone who did not abort for any but the most pressing and defensible reasons.[102] *The Lancet* argued in 1861 that 'the high sense of honour pervading the legitimate ranks of the profession, as well as the ordinary rules of morality, effectually prevent, *of course*, all pandering upon the part of medical practitioners, either to the depraved sentiments of the higher classes, or to the criminal desires of the lower ranks' (italics mine).[103] For all of these reasons, abortion was quite useful to professionalising medicine.

In contrast, tighter statutory control of abortion, and vocal opposition to the practice by medical leaders, was not very helpful to patients who continued to be faced with unwanted pregnancies and to seek solutions in spite of the rhetoric surrounding the danger to women's health. For Knight, 'Women themselves regarded abortion with tolerance, and saw it as an inevitable part of everyday working-class life, only to be regretted if it failed or resulted in ill-health or death', and it seems likely that the only class-based difference between women's attitudes arose where higher incomes facilitated a wider range of methods for fertility control.[104] Middle- and upper-class families could afford to take a long-term view and employed a range of contraceptive strategies, whereas working-class families – and particularly households with adults in industrial employment – had income- and gender-based rationales for preferring abortion. McLaren makes a persuasive case that 'knowledge of abortive techniques was widespread in factory districts and spreading' owing to movements of employees, procedures conducted by surgeons, and advertisements by quacks.[105] As a result, social practice diverged quite substantially from the law at all periods, in that contraceptive and abortifacient knowledge was relatively widespread, and social opinion changed obliquely if at all in response to legal redefinitions.[106] Furthermore a traditional adherence among women to the idea that they were entitled to restore regular menstruation dovetailed neatly with a historic medical emphasis on the dangers of menstrual blood being withheld.[107]

Therefore, scrutiny of prosecutions for procuring abortion which did involve a medical practitioner of some description needs to consider three perspectives: first, how did the public react to men tried for procuring abortion? The active involvement of pregnant women in seeking out people willing to conduct abortions, and the implication that they found abortion and its attendant risks the lesser of two evils (materially and morally), suggest that prosecutions might not meet with popular approval. This proved the case in the 1910s when the conviction for manslaughter and striking off of Henry Jelley, in all probability a qualified supplier of abortions in Hackney, was protested by thousands of former patients; this chapter shows that Jelley's was not an isolated or pioneering example.[108] Second, to what extent were trained practitioners apparently involved in meeting the demand for abortion? This can only be determined with accuracy after 1859 and the publication of the first Register of the General Medical Council, but earlier cases sometimes feature men's claims to hold a Licence from the Society of Apothecaries, or to be members of one of the two Royal Colleges.[109] Third, how often did either trained or untrained men seek to abort their own child? Practitioners' sexual partners had readier access than others to abortion as a *post-hoc* contraceptive strategy, but by the same token were more vulnerable to coercion by fathers who regarded themselves as able to attempt a termination. Can anything be learned of women's reactions to suggest whether abortions were mutually desired or a form of assault?

In common with other chapters in this book, practitioners accused and tried for abortion were sought in nineteenth-century newspapers and were identified by a variety of keywords. The phrase 'procuring abortion' was frequently used alongside other forms of formal charge, such that men were technically tried for infanticide, manslaughter or murder, or where abortion was the crime implied by the evidence but not explicitly labelled. Therefore the cases reserved for treatment here were gleaned from multiple keyword searches and later coded as *de facto* trials for failed, botched or discoverable abortion. Collectively, searches yielded seventy-three allegations of abortion against practitioners across the years 1827 to 1890, where only seven cases arose before 1850. Thereafter a remarkably steady fifteen to eighteen allegations arose in each decade. Most cases were one-off occurrences where the practitioner named was not implicated in successive terminations (albeit some men were identified in newspapers as repeat offenders), but two 'medical men' were actively prosecuted more than once. The Pascoe family of Cornwall suffered prosecutions over two generations, suggesting that between them father and son had longstanding reputations for offering abortion.[110]

Among the sixty-five men named between 1850 and 1889, twenty-six – or over a third – were listed at some time on the medical *Register* (either in the years before the charge or, in the case of men prosecuted in the early 1850s, after the first publication of the *Register*). Of this subset of men accused, seven were found guilty and served prison sentences, while two others committed suicide before or during trial.

Neither of the two men prosecuted more than once appeared on the medical *Register*. Nonetheless they were both described in newspaper reports as surgeons or accoucheurs, and both were prosecuted twice during the 1860s. They are part of a pattern which emerges across prosecutions in this chapter and the next, pointing to this decade as one of heightened concern about medical practice and professionalisation. The public reception of accusations against them is contradictory but not incomprehensible, given the two men's different settings and clienteles. John Daubeny Hind worked in Stroud and had probably offered terminations in collaboration with his wife, Ann, for at least seven years before he was first accused of manslaughter in 1860.[111] He was initially convicted and sentenced to six years penal servitude, but imposition of the sentence was delayed by a question of law and in the event the judgment was reversed.[112] He was tried again for the murder of Sarah Gough in 1862 and was acquitted, even though the second trial took place in the context of strong local feeling against Hind. The day of Gough's interment witnessed 'a popular "demonstration", almost amounting to a riot' in front of Hind's house which encouraged the police to execute the warrant for Hind's arrest immediately, rather than wait for the next day as originally planned. Hind and his wife were extracted from the back of the house, whereafter the crowd broke in and demolished the furniture and contents. Reporting implied that the state of Gough's body after death, presenting a 'horrid spectacle', contributed to the level of local animosity against Hind.[113] Up to this point, Hind and his wife claimed to have offered a valued service; as Ann Hind said at the Gloucester assizes 'We can't help these things; we don't go to these girls – they come to us.'[114] In this case it is not clear that acquittal resulted in a resumption of practice, or at least not by John Hind in person; he was around seventy-eight years old in 1862, was admitted to the Gloucestershire asylum in 1865, and died of old age in 1866.[115]

In contrast, popular feeling was strong in the defence of Alfred Thomas Heap, who was clearly a serial abortionist in Manchester.[116] Public responses to Heap align with McLaren's depiction of women in industrial Lancashire as having recourse to abortion as a normative and valuable contraceptive strategy. Heap was found not guilty in 1867 after being tried for the murder of Phoebe Lock. His acquittal was greeted with strong approval in the form of courtroom applause.[117] He was found guilty when tried for a second time the following year on a charge of procuring abortion, and was sentenced to five years penal servitude – without the reaction of the court being recorded.[118] But neither Heap nor the courts were finished. On discharge from prison, Heap returned to his former practice in Manchester, such that he was prosecuted a third time in 1875 again on a charge of murder and again with the enjoyment of considerable local support. On conviction the jury recommended him to mercy, and the imposition of a death sentence prompted widespread dismay. Jury members were alleged to have said they would have found Heap guilty of manslaughter only if they had thought that conviction would lead to the death penalty, and a petition was sent to the Home Secretary asking for his release.[119] Heap's eventual execution was marked outside the prison (in Liverpool rather than Manchester) by only a small crowd, but the prison chaplain was apparently so distressed by Heap's death that he experienced difficulty in completing the usual prayers.[120] Moreover, in Manchester itself feeling was strong in Heap's favour. The execution on 19 April was greeted with 'great indignation' and a large crowd threatened violence to the mother of the dead woman.[121] The reactions to Heap and Hind suggest that there was tacit appreciation or lively popular sympathy for men who offered abortion, and an anxiety to retain access to abortionists that could become quite strident in industrial areas, so long as practitioners' efforts did not comprise outright butchery.

The medical press naturally took a different view. Hind's case was either ignored or was reported tersely and without commentary.[122] *The Lancet* used the occasion of Heap's execution to reproach the lay press for being too ready to identify a quack as a surgeon, but otherwise remained silent on all of his cases.[123] The *Medical Times and Gazette* was marginally more expansive, and hoped that Heap's example would result in 'restraining those wretches who traffic in crime of the same kind', so sending a clear signal to practitioners who might have contemplated performing abortions on demand.[124] The wretches in question might not have been solely presumed men, but there is an implication here for male readers that abortionists expressed a degraded form of masculinity, despicable and shameless, engaged in lucrative trafficking that should have been antithetical to the professional male.

Nonetheless, trained men were not uniformly deterred by either the prosecution of irregulars or warnings from within the profession, since a quarter of qualified defendants were found guilty. The numbers are small, only seven men in total, but they indicate that professionalising rhetorics were sometimes unheard, or superseded by the realities of maintaining a medical practice. They are also suggestive of a larger, if indeterminable, group who conducted abortions unprosecuted. The seven qualified medical convicts were sentenced to terms of penal servitude ranging from five to fifteen years, and unsurprisingly could attract stinging reproach from the Bench. Robert Charles Moon was given a longer sentence than his co-defendant the chemist Henry Charles Darley because, as a qualified man, he was 'a member of an honourable profession ... whose conduct, therefore, was all the more criminal'.[125]

The cases of Thomas Millerchip and Francis Hammond illustrate the potential link between marginal practice, financial difficulty, and the appeal of abortion. Both men were declared bankrupt in the years before they were convicted.[126] Furthermore, Millerchip had already two criminal convictions to his name, having been found guilty of manslaughter in 1879 and of deserting his wife and children in 1881 (for which he received two separate terms of penal servitude).[127] Hammond, meanwhile, suffered one failed partnership before bankruptcy and another four years later.[128] Medical reactions to Millerchip are particularly interesting because in 1879 his cause was taken up energetically by his peers. He was convicted at the Warwickshire Assizes of the manslaughter of a child, George Bastock, and sentenced to four months with hard labour. The verdict was based solely on his failure to attend while holding the appointment of medical officer in number two district of the Coventry Union, rather than on any active maltreatment. He was only twenty-eight years old, and it was not entirely clear that he had received all of the requests for attendance, since an unspecified number had been handed to his wife (with whom he was not on good terms).[129] As a poor-law medical officer who had suffered a harsh sentence for manslaughter and subsequent bankruptcy, he attracted a petition recommending leniency signed by 276 of his fellow practitioners, the support of Joseph Rogers, and a fund was gathered on his behalf.[130] A conviction for abortion, however, was a transgression that could not be countenanced, and no extenuating factors or profession-wide protests were raised. Instead he was struck off the medical *Register*, and his name was only mentioned twice more in the *BMJ* (and only then as an offender or recidivist).[131]

At least six qualified men including Hammond, and eleven men overall, were charged with having aborted their own illegitimate child. The voices of the parturient women in these cases are typically absent, not least because they died following the abortion in two instances, and perhaps predictably there is evidence for both female collusion and male coercion. Hammond's victim, Ellen Saunders, had been living with him as though married, and had gone by the name of Mrs Hammond. He had performed an instrumental abortion on her in February or March 1879 apparently with her consent, but when she fell pregnant again in May 1879 she was reluctant to undergo the same ordeal on account of the pain she had suffered at the first operation. Hammond seems to have carried out a second instrumental abortion without consent; Saunders complained of her treatment to a female friend, who reported Hammond to the police.[132] A very different story arises from the case of the unqualified Thomas Hunter who was charged with newborn child murder in 1865. Hunter was found guilty only of concealing a birth, for which he was given two months with hard labour, and his fellow defendant (Isabella Shannon, the mother of his child) was acquitted.[133] On being discharged from prison, Hunter immediately married Shannon and they had at least a further seven children.[134] While Shannon's own voice is never heard, she might presumably have escaped Hunter's companionship during his imprisonment if she had been fearful or angry about his treatment of her. Instead she married him immediately and remained living with him in all the subsequent censuses up to Hunter's death in 1910.

Aborting one's own child or performing an abortion on a lover could be at once a desirable goal and highly distressing, or tragic if the woman suffered or died as a result. John Price performed an abortion on his fiancée Ellen Blucke in 1889, and three months later she was removed to a lunatic asylum. When confronted by Ellen's brother, Price admitted his part in events and claimed that 'his first impulse was to go to the surgery and take a big dose of poison.'[135] While Price went on to fulfil a long career in medicine, at least two other men found they could not live with the consequences of effectively killing the women they loved and committed suicide.[136] Clement Carnell was considered guilty of Elizabeth Freshfield's murder from lacerations at the inquest on her body, despite the fact that there was no evidence he had used instruments on her; his suicide was taken as an admission of guilt.[137] John Powell left the dead body of Louisa Thomas in his consulting room and immediately wrote an account of his complicity in a letter to a friend; 'She was in the family way, but not by me. She begged me to procure abortion, and I have tried to do so … I loved her dearly … I cannot live.'[138] He threw himself under a train, and was thought guilty of murder by the inquest on Thomas.

This analysis suggests that there are two very distinct accounts of abortion in the second half of the nineteenth century, one associated with the rhetoric of professionalising medicine and a much more pragmatic and domestic one concerning women's or couples' attempts to manage their fertility. Leading qualified men were loud in their deprecation of the practice, but this should not disguise the fact that many women probably sought and obtained abortion without inviting their own deaths, and a range of men (qualified and unqualified) met the demand.

Conclusion

In cases of neglect under the poor law, structural conditions 'allowed the perception of responsibility towards the pauper to be passed about between officials like the proverbial hot brick', but this was also permitted by emergent medical ethics that were driven by uncertainty and competition as much as disinterest.[139] To some extent it was a weakness in the emergent professional persona that enabled aggression and finger-pointing on the part of the poor-law authorities. At the same time, the poor law offered practitioners the scope for charges of neglect against each other, which veiled self-interest in public spirit wherever treatment of a pauper, or a failure to serve the guardians adequately, could be cited. Misdemeanour under the poor law did not tend to offer the opportunity to levy manslaughter allegations, though, since these tended to cluster around deaths among obstetric patients and spanned a wider section of the social spectrum.

Neither charges of neglect nor manslaughter proved useful for schooling the incipient profession, whereas abortion charges were much more suitable for giving unequivocal signals to struggling doctors about the importance of professional (and by implication manly) probity. Nonetheless, the pressures of the medical market meant that these messages were not always heeded. A significant proportion of even the visible abortion trade was conducted by fully-qualified men, at least a proportion of whom were motivated by money. A desire to remain solvent won out against allegiance to professional strictures or sub-textual appeals to masculine disinterest.

Charges of neglect, manslaughter, and abortion collectively illustrate the risks and frustrations associated with rising expectations both inside and beyond the profession. These expectations are best detected in the frequency of quotes from practitioners driven to exasperation and then reported verbatim; the implication of such reporting practice is that readers were being invited to agree that all such expressions were inappropriate or reprehensible.

Even so, public reaction to practitioner prosecution ran the gamut from sentimental support for doctors to violent opposition. The reaction to Heap in Manchester is particularly telling, since it points to a deep disparity between patient and marketplace requirements, for reliable access to efficient abortion, and professional discourse, which severely deprecated the termination of pregnancy. It is perhaps ironic that this divergence seems less pronounced in the case of allegations of sexual assault and murder, covered in the next chapter. Professional and lay popular opinion seem to have been closer together, if not entirely coincident, in these latter types of felony.

Notes

1 See also Chapters 4 and 6.

2 I.A. Burney, *Bodies of Evidence. Medicine and the Politics of the English Inquest 1830–1926* (Baltimore and London: Johns Hopkins University Press, 2000), pp. 4–6.

3 Burney, *Bodies of Evidence*, p. 6.

4 Burney, *Bodies of Evidence*, chapter 2; P. Fisher, 'The Politics of Sudden Death: The Office and Role of the Coroner in England and Wales, 1726–1888' unpublished PhD thesis (Leicester University, 2007), chapter 4. *The Lancet*'s commitment to Wakley's campaign outlived him; Fisher, 'Sudden Death', p. 98.

5 Burney, *Bodies of Evidence*, p. 149.

6 They could, however, turn to the press. See, for example, the protest by Thomas Rolph following the inquest on Mary Berry; 'Correspondence', *Hampshire Advertiser* 14 November 1857, p. 5.

7 M. Brown, 'Medicine, Quackery and the Free Market: The "War" against Morison's Pills and the Construction of the Medical Profession, c. 1830–c. 1850', in M. Jenner and P. Wallis (eds), *Medicine and the Market in England and its Colonies, c. 1450–c. 1850* (Basingstoke: Palgrave Macmillan, 2007).

8 K. Price, *Medical Negligence in Victorian Britain. The Crisis of Care under the English Poor Law, c.1834–1900* (London: Bloomsbury, 2015), p. 21.

9 J. Donnison, *Midwives and Medical Men. A History of Inter-Professional Rivalries and Women's Rights* (New York: Schocken Books, 1977), p. 34.

10 'Action for Negligence Against Medical Men', *Northern Echo* 10 May 1884, p. 4; C. Crawford, 'Patients' rights and the law of contract in eighteenth-century England', *Social History of Medicine* 13:3 (2000), pp. 381–410 on pp. 401–8.

11 See, for example, Cornelius Fitzpatrick's outburst against 'medical orders with a vengeance' and Leonard Goddard's resentment at being instructed by a relieving officer who was a brushmaker by trade; 'West Derby Board of Guardians', *Liverpool Mercury* 19 December 1856, p. 8; 'Alleged negligence of a medical officer', *Lloyd's Weekly Newspaper* 20 December 1863, p. 12.

12 M.W. Flinn, 'Medical Services under the New Poor Law', in D. Fraser (ed.), *The New Poor Law in the Nineteenth Century* (London: Macmillan, 1976), pp. 45–66, on p. 50.

13 J.M.T. Ford, 'John Gorham 1814–1899. Victorian Medicine in Tonbridge' unpublished PhD thesis (Exeter, 2009), pp. 169–81; Price, *Medical Negligence*, pp. 168–9.

14 D. Brown, 'Negligence and Neglect: The Sick Poor and Poor Law Medical Services, 1837–71' unpublished MA dissertation (Birkbeck, 2009), p. 14.

15 Price, *Medical Negligence*, pp. 163–4.
16 There might be exceptions for specialist services such as midwifery; Flinn, 'Medical Services', p. 50.
17 Price, *Medical Negligence*, p. 13.
18 R.G. Hodgkinson, *The Origins of the National Health Service. The Medical Services of the New Poor Law, 1834–1871* (Berkeley: University of California Press, 1967), p. 395.
19 Price, *Medical Negligence*, p. 23.
20 Hodgkinson, *Origins*, p. 73.
21 Hodgkinson, *Origins*, p. 76; see also p. 139 for career-young. I. Loudon, *Medical Care and the General Practitioner 1750–1850* (Oxford: Clarendon Press, 1986), pp. 245–6.
22 Hodgkinson, *Origins*, p. 142 quoting Report of the PMSA read at a meeting in Manchester, July 1836.
23 Second Annual Report (1836) quoted Hodgkinson, *Origins*, p. 74.
24 Price, *Medical Negligence*, p. 29.
25 Price, *Medical Negligence*, chapters two and three.
26 Flinn, 'Medical Services', p. 49; M.A. Crowther, *The Workhouse System 1834–1929 – the History of an English Social Institution* (Athens: University of Georgia Press, 1981), p. 136.
27 S. Shave, '"Immediate Death or a Life of Torture are the Consequences of the System": the Bridgwater Union Scandal and Policy Change', in J. Reinarz and L. Schwarz (eds), *Medicine and the Workhouse* (Rochester: Rochester University Press, 2013), pp. 164–91, on pp. 165–6.
28 I. Butler and M. Drakeford, *Scandal, Social Policy and Social Welfare* (Bristol: Policy Press, 2005), pp. 223, 232.
29 Price, *Medical Negligence*, pp. 95, 176.
30 Price, *Medical Negligence*, p. 91–2, 110. See, for example, Henry Carter in 1870, accused of spending three times as much as other Union doctors; 'Portsea Island Board of Guardians', *Hampshire Telegraph* 9 April 1870, pp. 6–7.
31 'The alleged neglect of a Union surgeon', *Sheffield and Rotherham Independent* 3 May 1867, p. 4; 'Alleged neglect by a Union Medical Officer in Dean Forest', *Western Mail* 22 June 1874, p. 8.
32 'Disgraceful conduct of a parish doctor', *Daily News* 8 January 1867, p. 6.
33 'Alleged neglect by the dispensary surgeon of Birkenhead', *Liverpool Mercury* 26 January 1855, p. 9.
34 'Alleged neglect by a Sheffield surgeon', *Sheffield and Rotherham Independent* 23 May 1879, p. 3.
35 'Serious charge against a surgeon', *Hampshire Advertiser and Salisbury Guardian* 5 July 1851, p. 3.

36 Loudon, *Medical Care,* p. 242 citing a source from 1844 about the free treatment of thousands in the vicinity of Newark alone. A. Digby, *Making a Medical Living. Doctors and Patients in the English Market for Medicine, 1720–1911* (Cambridge: Cambridge University Press, 1994), pp. 249–53.
37 'The allegations against a Cardiff surgeon', *Western Mail* 20 February 1877, p. 3.
38 E.T. Hurren, 'Remaking the medico-legal scene: a social history of the late-Victorian coroner in Oxford', *Journal of the Social History of Medicine* 65:2 (2009), pp. 207–52, on p. 251.
39 'Extraordinary allegations against a doctor in Dean forest', *Western Mail* 29 January 1877, p. 5.
40 *Commercial Directory and Gazetteer of Gloucestershire* (Nottingham: Morris & Co., 1876). The latitude granted to Seely was echoed in other inquests; see, for example, the attendance of Edwin Wykes at the inquest on Sarah Ann Gibbs, 'Complaint against a medical man', *Birmingham Daily Post* 4 November 1890, p. 7.
41 Ford, 'John Gorham', pp. 182–3.
42 See, among others, the case of Joseph Poppleton, reproached by the Bradford guardians in 1850; 'Charge of Neglect Against a Medical Officer', *Bradford Observer* 21 November 1850, p. 6.
43 The latter three cases were therefore in addition to the 193 men involved in 'neglect' previously tabulated.
44 'The Charges against Workhouse Officials', *Sheffield and Rotherham Independent* 13 February 1875, p. 6.
45 'Complaint Against a Medical Officer', *Berrow's Worcester Journal* 20 November 1869, p. 6; 'Worcester Board of Guardians', *Berrow's Worcester Journal* 18 December 1869, p. 6.
46 'Neglect of a Medical Assistant', *The Standard* 2 November 1844, p. 4.
47 'Serious Charges against a Parish Medical Officer at Gornal Wood', *Birmingham Daily Post* 20 April 1877, p. 5.
48 'Local Government Board Inquiry at the Thingoe Union. Charges of Neglect on the Part of a Parish Surgeon', *Bury and Norwich Post* 23 May 1876, p. 6.
49 'Alleged Medical Neglect', *Trewman's Exeter Flying Post* supplement 30 July 1862, p. 1.
50 N.A. MH 9/6.
51 For similar cases, see 'Domestic Intelligence', *Lancaster Gazette* 1 March 1851, p. 3, and Price, *Medical Negligence,* pp. 154–5.
52 'Death from Alleged Medical Neglect', *Newcastle Courant* 3 February 1865, p. 2.
53 N.A. RG 10/5018/22 for the personal details of James Tait Mackay.

54 For open competition, see Loudon, *Medical Care,* pp. 239–40; for geographical variation, see Digby *Medical Living* pp. 119–20; Hodgkinson, *Origins,* pp. 419–48; Price, *Medical Negligence,* throughout.
55 'Alleged negligence of a medical officer', *Liverpool Mercury* 1 August 1848, p. 4.
56 Hodgkinson, *Origins,* pp. 340–1.
57 General Medical Council, *The Medical Register* (London: General Medical Council, 1859), p. 135. I am grateful to Jennie Hubbard for her insight into this case.
58 N.A. HO 107/2212/13. The date of Deakin's qualifications is not specified in the census of 1851, and he died in 1858, before a possible listing in the first medical *Register.*
59 See Chapter 1.
60 N.A., MH 9/19; MH 12/9553, Poor Law Board annotations on a letter sent by Whall, dated 2 December 1852.
61 'Hase v. Dakeyne', *Morning Post* 23 April 1852, p 7.
62 N.A., MH 12/9553.
63 N.A., MH 12/9553, letter from John Deakin/Dakeyne to the Poor Law Board 15 December 1852.
64 'Charge against a Medical Officer', *Sheffield and Rotherham Independent* 15 January 1853, p. 7.
65 'Charge of Neglect against a Medical Officer', *Sheffield and Rotherham Independent* 22 January 1853, p. 3.
66 'Worksop Investigation', *Sheffield and Rotherham Independent* 29 January 1853, p. 6.
67 In this instance, electronic searches of both the *British Medical Journal* and *The Lancet* revealed no hits.
68 See also the case of William McHugh, who thought himself the victim of his former employer Mr Carnes; 'Assize Intelligence', *Morning Chronicle* 8 March 1859, p. 8. I am grateful to Jennie Hubbard for initial information on McHugh.
69 H. Franklin Parsons, *Report to the Local Government Board on the sanitary condition of the Spennymoor urban district, in reference to the prevalence therein of fever and other infectious diseases* (London: Eyre and Spottiswoode, 1884).
70 'Smallpox at Spennymoor. Grave Allegations against a Medical Man', *Northern Echo* 10 June 1884, p. 4.
71 'When Doctors Differ. An "Indignation" Meeting at Spennymoor', *North-Eastern Daily Gazette* 13 June 1884, p. 4.
72 The analysis of manslaughter in this section includes two anomalous cases of murder (i.e. where the victim was a patient but the formal charge was not given as manslaughter).

73 The only published research to explore the specific phenomenon of historic manslaughter charges against doctors occurs in the medical press by clinicians; R.E. Ferner and S.E. McDowell, 'Doctors charged with manslaughter in the course of medical practice, 1795–2005: a literature review', *Journal of the Royal Society of Medicine* 99 (2006), pp. 309–14. J. Hubbard, '"The outraged public required a scapegoat and the Guardians threw them the doctor!" District Medical Officers of the New Poor Law and Charges of Neglect in Cases of Childbirth in England, 1834–1900' (unpublished MRes dissertation, Keele University, 2013) covers charges associated with obstetric deaths in poor-law cases but is not confined to technical allegations of manslaughter.

74 This list includes a handful of cases where practitioners were suspected of manslaughter but inquest verdicts fell short of finding them responsible for a death.

75 Hubbard, '"The outraged public"'.

76 For example, Ferner and McDowell found the case of a Dr Raeburn in 1831 missing from my own data; Ferner and McDowell, 'Doctors', pp. 309–10.

77 The prominence of obstetric cases among accusations of malpractice has proved resistant to change; R. Johanson et al., 'Has the medicalisation of childbirth gone too far', *British Medical Journal* 13 April 2002, pp. 892–985, on p. 893.

78 Burney, *Bodies of Evidence*, p. 138.

79 'Accidents and Occurrences', *The Examiner* 16 August 1856, p. 524.

80 'The Stepney Union – More Neglect of Pauper Patients', *Morning Chronicle* 27 October 1856, p. 7.

81 'Alleged Neglect of a Medical Officer at Stepney', *Morning Chronicle* 28 October 1856, p. 7.

82 'Frightful Starvation at Ratcliff', *Lloyd's Weekly Newspaper* 17 May 1857, p. 7; 'The Suicides in Mile-End Workhouse', *Lloyd's Weekly Newspaper* 7 April 1861, p. 9.

83 'Death from Starvation under Homoeopathic Treatment', *Morning Chronicle* 10 October 1849, p. 5 and 'Central Criminal Court', *Daily News* 29 October 1849, p. 6. For protests by orthodox practitioners against homoeopathy, see P. Nicholls, 'Homoeopathy in Britain after the mid-Nineteenth Century', in M. Saks (ed.), *Alternative Medicine in Britain* (Oxford: Clarendon Press, 1992), pp. 77–89, on pp. 78–81.

84 [Untitled] *The Lancet* 49:1233 (1847), pp. 415–18.

85 General Medical Council, *The Medical Register* (London: General Medical Council, 1859), p. 71.

86 'Trial for Manslaughter in Midwifery Practice', *British Medical Journal* 9 April 1870, p. 365.

87 'Trial for Manslaughter in Midwifery Practice', p. 365.
88 The exceptions to this general rule were the occasional prosecutions of men seeking to abort their own offspring without mothers' consent.
89 Post-partum sepsis of all kinds, whether from abortion or other causes, were counted together until the twentieth century; I. Loudon, 'Some International Features of Maternal Mortality, 1880–1950', in V. Fildes, L. Marks, and H. Marland (eds), *Women and Children First. International Maternal and Infant Welfare 1870–1945* (London: Routledge, 1992), p. 11.
90 This is implied throughout A. McLaren, '"Not a stranger: a doctor": Medical Men and Sexual matters in the Late Nineteenth Century', in R. Porter and M. Teich (eds), *Sexual Knowledge, Sexual Science. The History of Attitudes to Sexuality* (Cambridge: Cambridge University Press, 1994).
91 Ferner and McDowell also omitted abortion cases from their consideration of manslaughter; Ferner and McDowell, 'Doctors', p. 309.
92 J. Keown, *Abortion, Doctors and the Law. Some Aspects of the Legal Regulation of Abortion in England from 1803 to 1982* (Cambridge: Cambridge University Press, 1988), p. 3.
93 Keown, *Abortion*, pp. 8–11.
94 43 Geo.3 c.58.
95 Keown, *Abortion*, pp. 12, 23–4.
96 A. McLaren, *Reproductive Rituals; the Perception of Fertility in England from the Sixteenth to the Nineteenth century* (London: Methuen, 1984), pp. 138–44.
97 Keown, *Abortion*, p. 40; M.L. Arnot, 'Infant death, child care and the state: the baby-farming scandal and the first infant life protection legislation of 1872', *Continuity and Change* 9:2 (1994), pp. 271–311, on p. 284.
98 There is no way to confirm or rule out this allegation, but the fatality rate from abortion in England in the 1930s stood at only 3–5 percent; I. Loudon, *Death in Childbirth. An International Study of Maternal Care and Maternal Mortality 1800–1950* (Oxford: Clarendon, 1992), p. 114.
99 Numbers of homicides are probably closer to 'real' numbers of events than for other crimes; C. Emsley, *Crime and Society in England 1750–1900* (London: Longman, 1987), p. 41.
100 Taylor quoted in Keown, *Abortion*, p. 43.
101 MacLaren, *Reproductive Rituals*, p. 137.
102 MacLaren, '"Not a stranger: a doctor"', p. 270.
103 *Lancet* quoted in Keown, *Abortion*, p. 46.
104 P. Knight, 'Women and abortion in Victorian and Edwardian England', *History Workshop Journal* 4 (1977) pp. 57–69 on p. 65.

105 A. McLaren, 'Women's work and regulation of family size: the question of abortion in the nineteenth century', *History Workshop Journal* 4 (1977), pp. 70–81, on p. 72.
106 MacLaren, *Reproductive Rituals*, p. 107.
107 H. King, *The Disease of Virgins. Green Sickness, Chlorosis and the Problems of Puberty* (Abingdon: Routledge, 2004), p. 70; many options existed to prompt menstruation, see list in MacLaren, *Reproductive Rituals* p. 103.
108 A. Tanner, 'The threepenny doctor: Henry Percy Jelley of Hackney', *Journal of Medical Biography* 10:1 (2002), pp. 28–39, on p. 36.
109 Research on 1930s America estimated that around half of illegal abortions were carried out by (qualified) physicians; Taussig *Abortion* (1936) quoted in Loudon, *Death in Childbirth* p. 127.
110 'Cornwall Lent Assizes', *Royal Cornwall Gazette* 2 April 1852, p. 2; N.A., PCOM 3/49/5291; 'Assize Intelligence', *Reynolds's Newspaper* 9 November 1879, p. 6; N.A. RG 9/1561/19.
111 See, for example, an account of the trial in 'Law and Police', *Wrexham and Denbighshire Advertiser* 7 April 1860, p. 2.
112 'John Daubeny Hind', *Bristol Mercury* 5 May 1860, p. 8.
113 See among other reports 'An "Accoucheur" and his Wife Committed for Murder. Riotous Proceedings', *Nottinghamshire Guardian* 28 February 1862, p. 7, reprinting material from the *Bristol Daily Post*.
114 'Gloucester Spring Assize', *Bristol Mercury* 5 April 1862, p. 8.
115 Gloucestershire Archives HO 22/60/1 Gloucester county lunatic asylum admission and discharge book 1863–83, patient number 4417; death certificate dated 25 July 1866.
116 He was allegedly frequently reproached for abortionist practice; [untitled] *The Royal Cornwall Gazette, Falmouth Packet and General Advertiser* 21 February 1867, p. 5. For an initial treatment of Heap, see H. Wallis, '"Trust not the physician" Interpersonal Violence in an Age of Medical Reform', unpublished MRes dissertation, Keele University (2011), pp. 44–6.
117 For an extended discussion of the role of courtroom applause, see Chapter four.
118 'Manchester Summer Assizes', *Manchester Times* 8 August 1868, p. 3.
119 These features of the case were widely reported, but see for example [untitled] *Nottinghamshire Guardian* 23 April 1875, p. 6.
120 *Ibid.* p. 4.
121 'Execution at Liverpool', *Bradford Observer* 20 April 1875, p. 4.
122 'Medical Trials', *The Lancet* 79:2015 (1862), p. 394. The trial was not noticed in the *British Medical Journal*.
123 'Abortion-Producers', *The Lancet*, 105:2693 (1875), p. 521.

124 Reprinted in 'The Condemned Criminal in Kirkdale Gaol', *Liverpool Mercury* 12 April 1875, p. 6.
125 'The Brighton Abortion Cases', *Reynolds's Newspaper* 21 July 1878, p. 6.
126 For Millerchip, see *London Gazette* 13 June 1879, p. 3946 and 'Warwickshire Assizes', *Birmingham Daily Post* 1 August 1885, p. 8; for Hammond see *London Gazette* 20 November 1866, p. 6288 and 'Serious Charge Against a Physician', *Lancaster Gazette and General Advertiser* 27 September 1879, p. 3.
127 'Summary of this Morning's News', *Pall Mall Gazette* 21 February 1879, p. 5; 'Latest News', *Liverpool Mercury* 19 December 1881, p. 5.
128 *London Gazette* 14 September 1866, p. 5043; *London Gazette* 26 August 1870, p. 3973.
129 N.A., MH 12/13388.
130 'The Case of Mr Millerchip', *British Medical Journal* 22 March 1879, p. 453, and 'The Millerchip Fund', *British Medical Journal* 30 August 1879, p. 353.
131 His removal from the *Register* was reported in the *British Medical Journal* 25 March 1905, p. 695 at the time of Millerchip's second conviction for abortion. In the period 1859–90, seven men were struck off the General Medical *Register* for artificially procuring miscarriage or abortion; R.G. Smith, *Medical Discipline. The Professional Conduct Jurisdiction of the General Medical Council, 1858–1990* (Oxford: Clarendon Press, 1994), pp. 238–44.
132 'Serious Charge against a Physician', *Lancaster Gazette and General Advertiser* 27 September 1879, p. 3.
133 'Northumberland Assizes', *Newcastle Courant* 21 July 1865, p. 3.
134 'Births Deaths Marriages and Obituaries', *Newcastle Courant* 29 September 1865, p. 8; N.A. RG 12/4241/5.
135 'Serious Charge against a Surgeon', *Reynolds's Newspaper* 1 December 1889, p. 2; see Chapter 6 for the prevalence of self-poisoning among medical suicides.
136 'Deaths', *The Times* 4 September 1944, p. 1; 'Obituary', *British Medical Journal* 23 September 1944, p. 419.
137 'The Balls Pond Tragedy', *The Morning Chronicle* 18 August 1859, p. 7.
138 'Extraordinary Case of Murder by a Medical Man', *Bristol Mercury* 31 October 1868, p. 3.
139 Price, *Medical Negligence*, p. 154.

4

Crimes against the body: causing harm

The proverbial Hippocratic injunction that medical practitioners must 'do no harm' makes accusations against doctors of crimes against the body particularly problematic. Violence should be completely antithetical to the medical identity, but violent behaviour is a common human reaction to multiple forms of motive or threat. It is also a prominent feature of 'news', however construed at whatever period. This chapter focuses on the occurrence and reporting of violent crime by medical men, specifically serious sexual assault and murder, where the latter includes all cases of suspected intentional, malicious killing rather than instances of incompetent treatment.[1] It argues that physical injury inflicted by medical men was likely to be penalised lightly by Victorian courts and exonerated by their peers unless, or until, the apparent evidence of gross wrong-doing became so blatant that wholesale condemnation was unavoidable. As the chapter demonstrates, this was never decisively the case in relation to sexual violence, but could apply in relation to murder or suspected murder. In some of these latter instances practitioners could be marked down as irredeemable by the press or popular feeling, even when they had secured a trial acquittal or when no trial took place.

Courts were presented with an immediate and complex dilemma when they were asked to contemplate guilty verdicts for men of inherently 'respectable' character by dint of their birth, profession or other status.[2] This may have encouraged some juries, and even justices, to believe that such men were effectively incapable of acts of premeditated violence.[3] There is certainly evidence pointing to juries' propensity to find in favour of those defendants with the highest conformity to respectability.[4]

Medical practitioners might arguably have faced a parallel dilemma when making decisions about their own deportment, because professionalism might contradict or be undermined by the imperatives (or at least the permitted scope) of masculinity. In the eighteenth century, violence had been regarded as a natural component of masculine behaviour. Aggressive conduct might be regrettable, damaging or criminal but certainly did not threaten, and could only enhance, masculine identities as an alleged consequence of male strength and virility. At that time, it has been argued, an accusation of rape did not challenge the accused's status as a man.[5] The first half of the nineteenth century witnessed a change in the rejection of numerous forms of personal violence.[6] This did not mean that it 'moved' indoors, since the active witnessing of wife-beating, for example, had already become noticeably differentiated by class and economic status: witnesses among neighbours in poor quality, overcrowded accommodation were matched by servants, friends, and relations in more prosperous settings.[7] There was no 'veil of silence', no matter what the context.[8] It is debatable, however, whether greater scrutiny of, and sanctions for, male violence, even after the Act for the Better Prevention of Aggravated Assaults on Women and Children of 1853, made a significant difference to the place of violence in masculine identity. Reportage of domestic violence in the 1850s reproached its occurrence while simultaneously offering factors in mitigation, such as husbands' alcohol consumption or wives' allegedly unfeminine demeanour; these contradictory responses served to reinforce the normative status of male violence.[9] Carolyn Conley has argued that 'While it was the duty of a respectable man to refrain from abusing [his] power, sexual aggression was perceived as normal, healthy, and inevitable.'[10] This assumption is now being problematised in that the centrality of violence to masculinity in the mid Victorian period was 'losing its traditional commonsensical quality'; but were the two properties decisively dissociated?[11] Foyster argues that it is a mistake to assume that rising complaints about male violence in marriage, for example, necessarily represented changing ideas about the place of violence for masculinity.[12] The augmented opportunity to prosecute domestic violence after 1853 was not reliably pursued, and more generally the relationship between masculinity and bodily capacity was maintained or enhanced over the century.[13] Body and sex, says John Tosh, encompassed the most prestigious aspects of manliness, and physicality was given a new boost by the 1870s in the increasing prominence given to organised sport.[14]

The expression of masculinity through extreme physicality and violence was notionally constrained by the status of the man concerned. Civilised restraint became explicitly associated with middle-class culture, where male identity was deemed to emanate from occupation, marriage, and fatherhood instead of physical prowess.[15] There were two problems with this association, however, one ideological and one practical. First, the validity of domestic masculinity was always jeopardised by a fear of emasculation that had to be countered in cultural discourse, perhaps by casting certain varieties of violence as themselves civilising in military or other contexts.[16]

Second, even after both physical and verbal violence to wives was decisively labelled degrading to a gentleman, middle-class men continued to act violently.[17] The focus by contemporaries on domestic violence assumed that perpetrators were typically working class, but this was not universally the case. Middle- and upper-class men who were accused of violent crime may have been partially shielded by 'the fixing of the "respectable" gaze on the working-class murderer, rapist, or abusive husband' but a mediated gaze alone could not entirely occlude the presence of middle-class and elite defendants in court.[18] Similarly, divorce petitions reveal that upper-class men were just as likely to threaten, injure, wound or force sexual intercourse on their wives as were their lower-class counterparts. Middle-class and professional men were perhaps marginally less likely than either upper- or lower-class contemporaries to engage in traditional, aggressive modes of masculinity, but violence in the form of sexual cruelty, for example, could emanate from a failed imposition of middle-class domestic ideology.[19] For practitioners, there was an acute contradiction in giving rein to a violent persona, because it implied the presence of competing impulses within an ostensibly unitary masculine identity; was the healer capable of inflicting harm, and under what circumstances might the transition from healer to aggressor occur? Was it allowable for this transition to take place on a man's own doorstep?

News of violent crime had been widely reported throughout the eighteenth-century metropolitan and provincial press, but in the second half of the nineteenth century it became a staple of reporting. As more column inches were devoted to violent crimes to meet readers' fascination, coverage was extended from the higher courts, such as assize and quarter-sessions sittings, to include the lower magistrates' and police courts.[20] Different publications may have been motivated to various extents by the desire to inform, to deter the commission of such crime by recounting trials and punishments, or to boost sales via sensational copy. The detail of what might be included under each of these headings was constrained, though, by what was acceptable to papers' readership. The net result was probably a continuation of the 'kaleidoscope of different and often contradictory messages' that King identified in the late eighteenth- and early nineteenth-century London newspapers, albeit with inflections of sentiment for specific cases.[21] Historians of the newspaper press continue to question the extent to which the process of reporting crime affected, or was affected by, the social context.[22] Similarly, there are debates around whether newspapers were more significant in reflecting or shaping attitudes given the potential for divergence between, for example, the incidence of crime and the perception of crime.[23] At issue here is the relationship between the portrayal of specifically medical defendants and the expectations placed on practitioners by both reporters and the reading public.

It is likely that there was 'a high degree of homogeneity' in general crime reporting in the nineteenth century up to the mid 1880s.[24] Stories might be treated with more or less attention to detail, in emotive or dispassionate language, but the same cases were covered in daily, weekly, evening, and Sunday newspapers.[25] This element of uniformity arose from the pervasive involvement of legal professionals in providing articles about crime to newspapers across the political and social spectrum. This was the case from the late 1830s onwards as newspaper coverage of violent crimes supplied specialist legal commentary for the reading public at the same time as it provided a welcome source of additional income to early-career barristers.[26] Lawyers were apparently trying to address the low regard in which the public held the legal profession and coincidentally boosting the legal accuracy of newspaper accounts.[27] This authorial trend had the effect of diverting attention from the scenes of punishment towards the conduct of criminal trials in the courtroom. It also meant that one of the historic learned professions was making explicit use of the press to consolidate its credentials as modernising and respectable. Medical practitioners did not have the same access to self-fashioning in the lay press, although the emergence of medical journals provided in-house media for debating matters of collective concern.[28] Class-based allegiance might have encouraged lawyer-reporters, as fellow professionals who shared many of the same social and occupational goals as medical men, to frame their narratives favourably for practitioners. Before reports even reached the press, there was arguably a 'concerted effort on the part of the law courts to construct a more positive public image of the male professional'.[29]

As this closing of ranks implies, prosecution for felonious violence reveals the outer limits of medical competitive behaviour. Rivals might have used the forum of an inquest to make sly allegations about one another to gain market advantage, but the threat of a criminal prosecution amplified the value of intra-professional allegiance. Practitioners could almost always call on stout defence by their professional fellows, and unequivocal congratulation on acquittal (even in the face of decidedly equivocal evidence). The only exceptions to this rule occurred where men were convicted of multiple killings, when it was in the interests of the collective profession to repudiate the offender as grossly anomalous.

Serious sexual assault

The recent history of rape has concentrated on the experience of female plaintiffs and the role of character assessments in undermining their evidence in court to secure acquittals of accused men.[30] Attention is now turning to the rapist, his dichotomous characterisation as either 'everyman-rapist' or monster, and the contingent meaning of rape for men in different eras or locations.[31] In the context of this book, it is essential to consider the treatment of practitioners who were placed in the dock for acts of sexual violence, but not to exonerate men's actions or conversely to condemn them in retrospect. It is rather an attempt to see how allegations of serious sexual assault against medical men functioned to amend the expectations of medical professionals, both among aspiring practitioners themselves and among their collective patients, the latter assumed here to be substantially coterminous with the newspaper-reading public. This seems particularly important given the repeated propensity of doctors to be construed as sexual predators.[32] Fear of the practitioner arising from use of anaesthetics, and later following the passage of the Contagious Diseases Acts, is considered below.

The characters available for the participants in a trial for sexual assault have been loosely categorised as victim, attacker, police, parents, and doctor.[33] In the following cases, the doctor has been forcibly removed from his customary role of providing evidence about the physical consequences of an assault and cast as the alleged criminal. This suggests he would be regarded from outside the profession as 'particularly transgressive', in other words monstrous in diverging so drastically from an implied role as a healer and protector of bodily health who should, by virtue of the calling, exercise more than usual self-control.[34] It might be assumed that the period up to the late 1880s also fostered a growing awareness that practitioners might inhabit a new and very negative role, that of the maniac surgeon, which was then accepted and assimilated quickly in the light of the 'Jack the Ripper' murders and the theories surrounding potential perpetrators.[35] How far were these stereotypes visible in reportage of trials involving medical defendants?

The view from inside the profession was rather different, because practitioners believed that they were particularly prone to false allegations of sexual misconduct upon female patients.[36] This sort of claim turned a *prima facie* opportunity to commit crime into an occasion of defence for specifically medical men, and represented an updated and medicalised version of the blackmail myth in relation to rape. Contemporary wisdom of the eighteenth and nineteenth centuries held that rape could not be committed on able-bodied women unless they were drunk or their natural strength was otherwise depleted.[37] Simpson has argued convincingly that there was no endemic risk in the eighteenth century of men being falsely accused of rape by women intent on financial gain.[38] Nonetheless, persistent fears of malicious accusations and blackmail were given an additional twist for medical men. It was thought that the combination of relatively free access to patient bodies, and a lack of due caution in conducting close physical examination, exposed practitioners to drastic misinterpretation or false prosecution. In obstetric and gynaecological cases in particular the risks for both patients and practitioners were supposedly heightened by the necessity for intimate examination.[39] Practitioners' vulnerability, and the challenges they faced in proving their innocence, were lamented in both the lay and medical press. At the same time, the scope for clearing one's name via a civil suit for perjury was thought to be highly problematic.[40] So what evidence is there of financial motive among the alleged victims of practitioners, and did men seek to defend themselves with subsequent prosecutions for perjury?

The risk of exposure to opportunistic and false allegations of sexual crime was thought by contemporary medical men to be exacerbated by the development of chemical anaesthesia. Anaesthetics were increasingly demanded by patients in the 1850s and 1860s and practitioners felt that this rendered them even more vulnerable to the fantasies of their female patients.[41] Sexual fantasy was quickly flagged as an apparently common side-effect of anaesthetic application on women, whereby thoughts that might be submerged in the conscious mind quickly came to the fore when inhibitions were chemically removed. So what proportion of allegations against practitioners featured the application of anaesthetics?

Notions of the practitioner as sexual predator were given a further boost from the 1860s in the enforcement of the Contagious Diseases Acts, and in the repeal campaign they inspired. The Acts permitted the forcible vaginal examination of suspected prostitutes with a speculum, a procedure that opponent of the Acts, Josephine Butler, termed instrumental rape.[42] Medical supporters of the Acts were thought to be satisfying the 'medical lust of handling and dominating women'.[43] Disgust and horror were directed by repeal campaigners towards practitioners who were allegedly guilty of both tyranny and self-interest, by recommending a prurient intervention for which they must be paid.[44] Doctors were placing themselves in the path of sexual (and financial) temptation and simultaneously jeopardising their patients. The sexual risk inherent in both medical practice and medical consultation was consequently prominent in the public imagination, and makes the study of sexual crime in the 1850s, 1860s, and 1870s particularly pertinent.

Rape, indecent assault, criminal assault, and felonious assault were all terms used in contemporary reporting to reference serious sexual crime. Some of these terms, plus some even more euphemistic language, were clearly designed to desexualise descriptions of the attacks. Other ambiguous terms included 'unnamed offence', which was used in cases of probable sodomy. Not all sex crime amounted to rape, and terms employed in the press represented a variety of possible attacks and behaviours, ranging from unambiguous rape to unwanted forms of touch that were much less invasive. Even so, the likelihood of prosecuting men on lesser charges than the ones initially levelled against them means that, in practice, very similar cases were brought under different headings, depending on the influence of the magistracy and other factors.[45] Judicial procedures around both charging and trial conduct in sexual assault cases have been described as highly irregular, both in the eighteenth century and in the decades 1859–80.[46] Naturally, the manipulation of due process had consequences for defendants, usually in terms of lighter sentences. Rape could technically incur life imprisonment, although more typically it attracted sentences of up to five years. Up to two years imprisonment was more usual for convictions of indecent assault.

Therefore all cases featuring in the British Library Newspapers database ascribed to indecent, criminal or felonious assaults, in addition to rapes, are included here when they occurred in relation to a defendant who was described as a physician, surgeon, doctor or medical man (Table 4.1).[47]

Searches for violent crime revealed that the portmanteau claims of a 'serious charge against' or an 'extraordinary charge against' a practitioner were common ways to describe charges of all descriptions. Allegations did not inevitably lead to a formal criminal trial, but reporting could nonetheless be quite detailed. Indeed, the information available

Table 4.1 Hits found for allegations of serious sexual assault by practitioners using a proximity measure of ten, 1800–90

	Physician	Surgeon	Doctor	Medical	Total
rape	3	119	51	97	270
raping	0	2	1	0	3
criminal assault	1	37	6	11	55
criminally assaulting	0	6	3	2	11
indecent assault	2	43	14	33	92
indecently assaulting	2	28	8	17	55
felonious assault	3	11	2	13	29
feloniously assaulting	0	11	2	6	19
'serious charge against a'	32	363	177	297	869
'extraordinary charge against a'	7	29	12	41	89

in the press was occasionally relatively fulsome until the time of a trial, when proceedings might be deemed unfit for publication and suppressed. The proliferation of print journalism from the 1830s onwards, however, meant that the consensus about the definition of 'unfit' began to break down. Different publications took very different views on what was suitable for public consumption, and the sensationalism which marked some titles from the 1870s onwards was fuelled by a mixture of explicit and cloaked reporting combined with a sense that stories with a sexual frisson sold papers.

It quickly became clear that very few medical cases related to years before 1841. Just five allegations were revealed, all of which were either untried or resulted in not guilty verdicts, and this is entirely unsurprising in context. Before this date the prosecution of the specific felony of rape and the propensity of juries to convict were both decidedly muted by the threat of the death penalty being imposed for guilty verdicts, whereas the removal of capital punishment for rape in 1841 meant that cases were more readily pursued.[48] Therefore, this study of sexual assault is concentrated on the half century following the abolition of capital sentencing, when there were ninety-two recovered instances of practitioners who were accused (with or without progressing to trial). The vast majority of the alleged victims were female, as only three cases were concerned with allegations of indecent assault on men or boys.

Clearly, medical men accused of such crimes represent a very tiny proportion of all practitioners, since just ninety-two claims made against them represented fewer than two per year discoverable by these means. Of these men, twenty were never tried, and of the remaining seventy-two just twenty-seven were convicted.[49] This means that the conviction rate for practitioners tried for any serious sexual offence was 37 percent, a rate very similar to the 40 percent found by Conley for all specifically rape trials in Kent.[50] This means, though, that medical practitioners on average fared rather worse than the 'respectable' defendants of Kent, because the latter group were likely to be tried for lesser offences than rape (and so not be counted among rape defendants).[51] The numbers of convictions were so small, and their distribution so chronologically diffuse, that it is unlikely they made a significant difference to public perceptions of medical professional conduct *per se*. Certainly no difference is discernible from the reports of individual cases. However, what is notable is the difference between reactions to doctors convicted of serious sexual assault and those convicted of murder (surveyed later).

Furthermore, most of the cases revealed by these searches are concerned with 'indoor' attacks involving people who were already known to each other as patients, relatives, acquaintances, or servants, rather than 'outdoor' assaults on strangers, which is significant for conviction rates. Interior locations were typically given as practitioners' surgeries or patients' homes. The venue for a number of alleged medical assaults is unclear, but more than two-thirds definitely constituted 'indoor' cases and it is possible that just five cases concerned 'outdoor' attacks. This puts assaults said to involve practitioners substantially at variance with the types of case likely to result in a conviction; in Kent 1859–80, 70 percent or more of guilty verdicts arose in relation to assaults committed outside or beyond the home, where the victim and the alleged aggressor were otherwise unknown to each other.[52]

The combined force of these comparisons, of practitioners accused of a variety of sexual crimes with all rape defendants in Kent, indicates that medical defendants were more likely than other respectable, middle-class men to be found guilty of serious sexual crime. They suffered a comparable conviction rate with all Kentish rape defendants, despite their middle-class standing and despite the overwhelming majority of incidents involving practitioners that were said to have occurred 'indoors'. Therefore the contemporary, rumoured vulnerability of medical men to successful prosecution in sexual assault cases is somewhat borne out, albeit that all of the individuals found guilty in this cohort may still have been genuinely guilty.

This occurred despite the judicial irregularities that arose in some of the cases tried, deriving from some blatantly preferential treatment accorded to practitioners. The trial of George Saunders in 1867 for rape on Mrs Elizabeth Harrison was brought to a premature conclusion when the prosecuting counsel surrendered his brief; he would not ask the Bench to credit the information of his client against the word of a medical practitioner of unblemished reputation.[53] Conversely, the trial of William Rowe or Roe at the Old Bailey for indecent assault was stopped by the jury in 1889 when they decided they did not need to hear any more in order to reach a verdict of not guilty.[54] The willingness to mitigate even unequivocal sexual assault is emphasised in a case of 1875. Robert Brown, a doctor and magistrate, was tried by the

Middlesex sessions for felonious assault on servant Louisa Masters.[55] He was found guilty of a misdemeanour only, and was sentenced to two months imprisonment without hard labour. This is a fairly typical account of a serious allegation being commuted to something carrying less severe punishment – except that Robert Brown was not the defendant's real name. He was permitted to be tried under a pseudonym, on the grounds that he did not wish his 'friends' – presumably the expansive definition of friends as family members, colleagues, neighbours, and patients – to apprehend the full details of the case. The presiding magistrate announced that he would not inquire into the true identity of Robert Brown, but would deal with him as he stood before him.[56] What we cannot know is whether this anonymity was conferred because 'Brown' was a doctor, because he was a magistrate, or because the combined force of both roles rendered this prosecution particularly embarrassing for the medical and legal professions.

In a similar vein, guilty practitioners were rarely singled out for particular condemnation as monsters, and this was apparently never the case after the early 1850s.[57] The medical defendant in sexual assault cases through 1840–90 was therefore in the 'everyman' mould, unremarkable except in their lenient treatment by the courts. This was at least partly because typical features of 'monstrous' attack, such as disparity between the ages of defendants and victims, additional physical violence, or aggravating factors such as gang rape, were rarely cited in medical cases.[58] But the everyman medical defendant was not necessarily excused on the grounds of 'normal' male lust either, since reports did not try to explain away medical assaults as a feature of practitioners' sexualised masculinity. Instead, doctors relied on different forms of contextual extenuation.

To this end, defences were mounted in a variety of ways beyond simple denials that any attack had taken place. These included pleas for clemency on the basis of practitioners' youth or previous good character.[59] One enterprising legal team defending a man accused of multiple counts of felonious assault admitted that their client's behaviour had been 'most disgraceful and immoral', but urged the jury to concentrate on the technical definition of felony and not allow their abhorrence of the defendant's general conduct to dictate their verdict. The tactic meant that the practitioner was found not guilty in relation to the first case, but ultimately found guilty of another and sentenced to transportation for life.[60]

Conley has argued that a guilty verdict in rape trials was of much less significance in undermining male respectability than was a sentence involving hard labour.[61]

In the case of practitioners found guilty, even hard labour did not condemn men to social exclusion, because where they enjoyed previously good relationships with patients and colleagues they could mobilise significant support. Arguably, medical men were increasingly insulated by their profession from long-term disadvantage from an allegation or even conviction of sexual assault. Two cases serve to illustrate this point neatly. In 1871 Frederick Morris of Swindon was convicted of attacking the servant of a former patient, and was sentenced to six months hard labour as a result.[62] By this date, the register of the General Medical Council was a well-established feature of medical professional life, and in light of his conviction the Council agreed to remove Morris's name from the register. Yet pleas were made on Morris's behalf by his medical colleagues that his name should be kept on the *Register*, and these were heeded.[63] A man might be convicted by a jury of his peers, but the GMC was reserving the right of final judgement on his fate as a medical professional.

An even more polarised case arose in 1884. David Bradley of Derbyshire was accused of raping the daughter-in-law of a patient, in an incident which Bradley attributed to the woman's falling victim to an epileptic fit. The jury acquitted him of rape but convicted him instead of attempted rape, exemplifying Conley's contention that 'lesser charges were used when "respectable" men were accused of rape and the evidence was too serious for the case to be dismissed altogether'.[64] The case was described by the presiding judge to be as bad as it could possibly be and the maximum sentence of two years imprisonment with hard labour was imposed.[65] The judge defended his explicit severity on the grounds that, given their advantages in life and education, 'gentlemen' should be held to higher standards and therefore suffer higher penalties for crime.[66] Bradley's case should have been hopeless, but it was entirely retrieved by his medical colleagues. The profession united behind Bradley, although whether wholly from a belief in his innocence or complicated by outrage at the judge's particularism is not certain. A petition carrying over 160 signatures of fellow practitioners was prepared for submission to the Home Secretary, calling for a reconsideration of the verdict on the grounds that epileptic seizures were liable to inspire erotic delusions.[67] This endeavour was supported by a memorial signed by 2,000 people from among Bradley's patients and neighbours near Chesterfield.[68] The conviction was duly overturned, but matters did not end there. The profession went on to raise a fund of 400 guineas to compensate Bradley for his sufferings, and arranged a presentation event to mark his formal return to the medical fold.[69]

As Bradley's example suggests, the fate of the men accused in the months and years after allegations had been made reinforces the sense that social recovery and reintegration were quite usual. A small subset emigrated within a decade after the accusation of sexual assault and pursued their medical career overseas, presumably to benefit from the relative anonymity conferred by removal; but given the global mobility of the profession (discussed at more length in chapter three) they might have done this anyway. At least half of all the men remained living in Britain, and while some did move away from the address they gave at the time they were accused, the removal was not always immediately after the accusation (and so might have been prompted by some other motive).

Frederick Morris and David Bradley both re-established their practices in England (albeit not in the immediate locality of their former residence). Morris relocated to Wellingborough Northamptonshire where he lived with his wife of twenty-three years and his three children, including one son born after his criminal conviction. The family remained in the same town with two or three servants until at least 1911 (when Morris would have been aged around eighty-one).[70] His term in prison for a sexual offence did not end either his marriage or his career. Bradley's experience was similar, although he did not travel such distances in his attempt to re-enter medical life. By 1887 he and his wife Elizabeth had relocated to Hebden Bridge in Yorkshire, around 70 miles north of his former home in Chesterfield.[71] The couple remained there for about a decade, then moved again to Blackburn in Lancashire where they remained until Bradley's death in 1914.[72]

Resumption of medical practice was eminently possible even when a practitioner was found guilty and remained living in, or returned to, their address at the time of the incident. James Field did not go anywhere at all after being accused of criminal assault in his home town of Bradford in 1856. He had targeted his own seventeen-year-old housemaid Sarah Jane Quinn and had repeatedly climbed into her bed while she was asleep until the fourth such occasion when he 'achieved his purpose'. There seemed little doubt about his actions, but nonetheless he was convicted of the lesser offence of aggravated assault for which he was fined £20. The result of the trial was received with 'suppressed approbation' from his friends, who immediately paid his fine.[73] In this context it is less surprising that he felt no social pressure to relocate. He remained in Bradford continuously until at least 1881.[74]

Practitioners were plainly capable of recovering, personally and professionally, following conviction for serious sexual assault. This suggests that wider public attitudes towards practitioners convicted for sexual crime were relatively forgiving and conciliatory. Yet this does not mean that there was never a reputational price to be paid. It is not obvious that medical men would have borne such charges with insouciance – the energetic defence of David Bradley speaks to an anxious concern about the potential stigma of a conviction – nor that they could have restored their standing following all forms of sexual violence. Wife-beating was perhaps even more likely than rape to inspire shame and ostracism, but the searches for sexual crime revealed just one man accused of indecent assault against his wife (aggravated by his apparently keeping a disorderly house). Medical perpetrators of domestic violence, like Foyster's exemplar James Veitch, are better sought in separation cases than in newspaper reports of prosecutions.[75]

Returning to the profession's perspective on serious sexual assault, what validity was there in fears about false, mercenary accusations, or in the vulnerability of practitioners from obstetric or anaesthetic patients? The belief that financial motives underlay accusations of sexual assault is not justified by these cases. Ten assaults definitely featured the potential for financial restitution, but money was just as likely to be offered by medical defendants to settle the case out of court as it was to be requested by plaintiffs. Counterclaims by defendants that their erstwhile accusers had been guilty of perjury were also very few; there were only two clear instances among medical defendants, both in the late 1860s.[76] This might appear a very minor detail, but the timing of these prosecutions for perjury is potentially significant (and will be mentioned again later).

Practitioners were rather more justified in being wary of obstetric and anaesthetic patients. Twenty-one cases arose when an assault was alleged to have occurred under one or both of these circumstances; some apparently involved the application of a speculum which in context might well have violated women's expectations of a suitable medical examination.[77] Richard Freeman was presumably either excessively unguarded or aggressively exploitative with his female patients, because he was twice accused of assaulting women under anaesthetic in 1867 and 1870 respectively.[78] He was found not guilty on both occasions. The medical press repeatedly notified practitioners of the potential legal significance of administering anaesthesia to female patients without any witnesses to testify to their probity while the patient was sedated.[79] The wisdom of due caution was eventually recognised by juries too; Charles Gamble was acquitted of attempted rape in 1876 but the jury did convict him of 'great indiscretion' in not having a third party present.[80]

One case against a practitioner encompassed both elements of anaesthesia and the prospect of financial motive, and dominated the news in the final months of 1865.[81] It also exemplified a further, unexpected, element of medical trials for sexual crime, namely courtroom applause for practitioners who were acquitted. Robert Hunter was an American who travelled to Britain in order to promote his supposed cure for tuberculosis.[82] While in London he also practised general medicine, and his patients included Annie Merrick. Hunter was accused by Merrick of anaesthetising her by inhalation and then raping her. After this consultation, Merrick returned home but did not tell anyone about the attack for two weeks. In this way, Merrick unfortunately undermined her chances of legal success from the start. Juries were much less likely to give credence to women's accounts if they had not sought to inform someone of their injury as soon as possible after the event. Eventually Annie Merrick told her husband and brother, who launched their own violent attack on Hunter. These events resulted in two criminal trials, one of Hunter for rape and one of Merrick's male relations for assault.[83] At Hunter's trial it emerged that Merrick's husband had suffered bankruptcy, and the public was thereby encouraged to perceive a financial motive behind the rape allegation. Hunter was acquitted to forceful expressions of congratulation both within the profession and beyond it, including loud cheers in court when the verdict was announced.

Hunter was not alone in being literally clapped and cheered from court; practitioners found not guilty were quite likely to receive this response. In some ways the incidence of applause represents the most intriguing pattern to emerge from these medical trials for sexual assault. Of the thirty-five medical defendants acquitted, thirteen were explicitly reported to have been applauded in court, meaning that 38 percent of all acquittals featured this immediate signal of approval. What is more, eleven of these cases occurred in the years 1861–74.[84] The 'era' of applause therefore coincided with the chronology of the two counter-prosecutions of plaintiffs for perjury mentioned above. Cheering might take place in magistrates' courts, at assizes or at the Old Bailey. What meanings might be ascribed to such displays of feeling?

The courtroom audience – aside from the judge, jury, legal counsel, and witnesses – could comprise members of the public in the gallery, press reporters, and court officers. The public gallery might be empty, or be packed with relatives, friends, neighbours, colleagues or indeed enemies of the defendant and the victim. It is not clear in any of these cases who among the assembled participants in the court process applauded. It was sometimes reported that the applause was hastily silenced, but again not by whom. Depiction of the courtroom as a theatre of sorts has a long history; 'entertainment was part of the complex matrix of meanings generated by the court'.[85] Crowd participation in trial processes and outcomes was apparently a common feature of eighteenth-century criminal prosecution.[86] Lemmings has argued that from the early nineteenth century, with the rise of the modern criminal trial as a dialogue between the counsels for the prosecution and defence, 'lay voices in the courtroom were progressively silenced'.[87] Godfrey's work in contrast suggests that Victorian and Edwardian magistrates' courts at least continued to exhibit outbursts of expression from audiences, which were only diminished by the withdrawal of the public from the whole process in the mid twentieth century.[88] There is, of course, the scope for some intermediate level of involvement that fell short of noisy intervention but also of complete silence, that might have encompassed whispering, pointing, murmuring or drawing breath.

Historically courtroom crowds had favoured mercy, so outbreaks of applause by nineteenth-century counterparts may plausibly have constituted a continuation of community endorsement for defendants who were given the benefit of the doubt. At the same time it may provide a clear instance of a transgressive practice being co-opted by a mainstream social group to serve its own purpose. A potentially disruptive or threatening behaviour is hereby appropriated for non-typical ends that met a need within the profession but also without.[89] Audible approbation of a 'not guilty' verdict in repeated cases of specifically medical trials suggests that some strong collective feeling of satisfaction was being expressed about the public assertion of medical innocence. Furthermore, if Lemmings is right to suggest that the participatory element of the courtroom proceedings was partly relocated to the press, the reporting of applause served to amplify and reinforce sentiments which, contrary to the prevailing trend, were still expressed *in situ*.[90] People were arguably very glad to see medical men removed from the role of attacker, perhaps because of how they were being assigned this role in debates around anaesthesia and the Contagious Diseases Acts.

This could be the case even where sex had definitely occurred. In 1870, for instance, William Clendinnen, a surgeon of Cheswardine in Shropshire, stood trial for the rape of Margaret Turnbull who was described as a young woman 'of limited intellect'.[91] The judge concluded that intercourse had certainly taken place, but was not clear whether this qualified as rape because there was no evidence that Turnbull had put up any resistance. He reflected that perhaps this could not be expected given the intellectual status of the alleged victim, but even so Clendinnen was acquitted and treated to considerable applause from the crowded court.

It is possible that the function and perception of applause on the occasion of doctors' acquittals was not static, and I want to suggest one way to construe the apparent appearance and then disappearance of the phenomenon. In the 1860s, applause was a way to defend the medical persona against the reallocation of their role from expert witness to attacker in a decade when medical status was still quite friable. This could have pertained irrespective of whether the applause derived mainly from courtroom personnel, fellow practitioners or from the lay public. As mentioned in the introductory chapter to this book, applause may also have recognised a new or newly ascendant form of manly identity because it coincided with a drive seen in literary sources to utilise 'a spectacle of failed masculinity only to assert a new kind of gendered authority'.[92] This took the form of generically professional competence, in this case played out in the exoneration and endorsement of *medical* men. Disinterest and control were on trial, and acquittal represented their restoration. Evidence of sexual activity, as in the case of Clendinnen, could still form a cognate part of the story since it could be construed as a form of control over women's bodies. Applause was increasingly at odds, however, with a specifically medical professional demeanour that, becoming more stable, should have exhibited calm assurance and the confidence of rectitude. A profession that is more confident of its status does not require the reassurance of such applause, and a public secure in its admiration of medical professionals does not see the need to congratulate the visible maintenance of the *status quo*. Therefore the decline of applause in cases of medical acquittal, whether it was real or merely the function of reporting omissions, potentially signals that the meaning of applause was shifting from relief at restoring a practitioner to his proper position of respectability, to an unseemly admission of there having been any risk of guilt.

The two instances of counter-prosecution for perjury can also fit this thesis. They too might be expressive of a desire to shore up medical reputations at a particularly sensitive moment in the professionalising process, not just via acquittals but also with public assertions that 'victims' were maliciously motivated. But the need for such defensive action could be disputed as needlessly overstated even in the 1860s. For example when surgeon Other (sic) Berry brought a charge of perjury against his former accuser Cecilia Jones, his solicitor asked the presiding magistrate for an expression of his opinion that there had been no foundation for the charge of criminal assault against Berry. The magistrate refused, on the grounds that 'to say so much as that would … be an insult to Dr Berry'.[93] Berry's innocence literally went without saying.

Other chapters in this book have indicated the potential for covert competition in the medical marketplace. The examples of practitioners prosecuted for sexual assault point to the limits of competitive behaviour. A public criminal charge of this type represented such a decided affront from outside of the profession that other forms of division were set aside. Individual men were even unabashed in their admission of having closed ranks. In the prosecution of William Haywood in 1862, for example, medical evidence was presented about the physical injuries borne by the prosecutrix Alice Sheldon; however, one of the three practitioners who examined Sheldon said under cross-examination that he had been 'trapped' into giving evidence, and that if he had known who the defendant was 'he would not have been in the case for the world'.[94] What is more, medical defendants' innocence was never questioned in the medical press, but rather their financial and social sufferings were compensated generally and specifically. David Bradley was by no means alone in receiving an honorarium.[95]

The analysis of these accusations of serious sexual assault against medical practitioners illustrates that they were perhaps more likely than other middle-class professionals to be found guilty of sexual violence. Their occupational duty to conduct intimate examination, operate on patients with instruments, and to do so while patients were insensible or unconscious, all contributed to ambiguity and doubt when doctors were accused. Sector fears about the risks of obstetric and anaesthetic practice were partially justified (although whether on the grounds that they invited malicious prosecutions, or because they supplied opportunities to assault, is not clear). These heightened risks were mitigated, however, by the response of both professional colleagues and the public to allegations of sexual crime. Arguably the prospect that practitioners might appear in court as the accused rather than as an expert witness was so disturbing to Victorian sensibilities that great efforts were made to ameliorate the consequences of accusation, trial, and even conviction. This amelioration took place in the judicial irregularities which saw men tried for lesser crimes (a benefit also on offer to other 'respectable' defendants), applause for acquittals (which may have been a distinctive feature of exclusively medical trials), and re-establishment in practice with support from colleagues after punishment had been completed. There has long been anecdotal evidence of the medical profession closing ranks in relation to insults from without; what is more surprising is the clear evidence here of collaboration by the wider public in this endeavour, and the extent of its success.[96]

Murder

The historiography of murder has been multivalent in a way that the equivalent literature on sexual assault has not. Murder is the epitome of violent crime and so is the zenith (or nadir) of studies of interpersonal violence in the past. It is also a focus for the histories of policing and detection, capital punishment, legal change, popular entertainment, literary motif, and the relationship of news to crime. Furthermore, medical murder has been at the forefront of this pervasive topic since the mid nineteenth century owing to the pre-eminence of one case. William Palmer, the Rugeley poisoner, was a surgeon whose horse-racing and gambling debts encouraged him to view family members as disposable forms of investment. His *modus operandi* was to insure the lives of close relatives and then benefit from their early deaths, although it only required one conviction for murder (as it happens arising from the death of fellow gambler John Parsons Cook) to ensure his execution. Palmer's trial broke new ground in a number of ways. The unprecedented feeling against him in his native Staffordshire meant that the law had to be altered to allow for his trial to be held at the Old Bailey rather than at the Stafford Assizes. Palmer's trial for murder now constitutes the lengthiest transcript of any case on the Old Bailey Online website, and the proceedings had longstanding consequences for forensic medicine, toxicology, and the relationship of the newspaper press to murder.[97] The result was a hanging that attracted an estimated crowd of 50,000 people, but no sense of closure on the deaths of Palmer's friends and relations, owing to his persistent refusal to confess.

Palmer became the grisly template for poisoners who followed him, by exemplifying a type of activity and justifying a pre-existing set of fears; 'the speed and intensity with which Palmer became codified as the archetypal modern poisoner suggests that this was a discourse in search of a referent, with Palmer serving not so much as the ordinary cause of these concerns than as the perfect channel for their articulation.'[98] He also came to embody a certain type of doctor, rare but very dangerous, who used his medical knowledge to murderous effect. Palmer was followed less than a decade later by Edward Pritchard, a Glasgow practitioner who was executed for poisoning his wife and mother-in-law, and the two names were commonly linked into the 1890s.[99] By the end of the nineteenth century they had been joined by George Lamson and Thomas Cream, both medical poisoners who were convicted and hanged. These four men were the exceptions who proved the rule of medical probity, although some newspapers paused to wonder how many medical murderers escaped detection by dint of their training and skill. The medical and lay press both alluded, in the wake of Pritchard's discovery, to 'the difficulty of believing, and of diagnosing, such a horrible act of criminality … especially as being committed by a brother medical man.'[100] A combination of sophisticated

Table 4.2 Hits found for allegations of murder by practitioners using a proximity measure of ten, 1800–90

	Physician	Surgeon	Doctor	Medical	Total
murder	33	69	87	50	239
'serious charge against a'	32	363	177	297	869
'extraordinary charge against a'	7	29	12	41	89

concealment and professional etiquette arguably militated against medical murderers being recognised at all.

In the period up to 1890, the number of practitioners who can be identified as suspected and tried for murder (where death did not arise as a consequence of patient treatment) were certainly few in comparison to men accused of serious sexual assault (Table 4.2).[101]

When charges of murder arising from abortion or varieties of treatment were stripped out, the searches yielded very few cases where a practitioner was thought to have killed, or attempted to kill, a person who was not also their effective patient. Excluding Palmer as an extraordinary case, there were only twelve clear instances of alleged intentional killing and six of attempted murder (all dated after 1840). Six of the eighteen examples were concerned with poison, and the remainder with violence using weapons or strangulation. It is tempting to conclude that the propensity to prosecute medical men for killing was all but entirely satisfied by cases brought against procurers of abortion or those who botched their obstetric cases, considered in Chapter 3.[102] Alternatively, given the state of forensic knowledge, medical training offered practitioners opportunities to conceal homicide successfully, particularly when the victim was not also their patient.

The relationship of the defendant to the victims followed a pattern familiar to murder allegations *per se* in that many people were known to or related to each other, but this trend was exacerbated in the perpetration of medical violence. Nine practitioners' wives or lovers were attacked so seriously that it was initially treated as murder or attempted murder, and other relations, including parents-in-law, accounted for a further six people. This meant that 70 percent of victims were related to practitioners. A further six were either policemen or neighbours, servants or strangers. This breakdown can be compared with the findings for all homicides and attempts reported in *The Times* between 1850 and 1860.[103] Among all killing reported in this way, a rather lower 37–42 percent of victims were spouses or other family members.

The verdicts and their consequences for the eighteen practitioners imply that juries did not automatically find medical men guilty of murder. Indeed, after Palmer's execution no other medical murderers were found guilty and hanged in England until Lamson in 1882, and these comprised the only two executions of practitioners in the whole period 1840–90.[104] Aside from Lamson, the seventeen additional cases resulted in three men being untried, three acquittals, six defendants admitted to Bethlem or Broadmoor as insane, and five men found guilty but sometimes for a lesser crime.[105] Two of the men found guilty were initially sentenced to hang, but one was reprieved and the other pardoned.[106] The willingness to mitigate and exonerate violent crime on the part of practitioners, particularly where none were associated with the moral shock inherent in abortion cases, is strongly reminiscent of the treatment of men under charges of serious sexual assault. This was despite the examples of Palmer and Pritchard, and could even pertain when a man's name had already been linked with these infamous antecedents. Charles Sprague had the misfortune to be tried for the attempted murder of his wife, servant, and parents-in-law in July 1865, the same month that Pritchard was tried and executed in Glasgow. This chronological coincidence, among other points of equivalence between the cases, was widely reported.[107] Sprague was alleged to have poisoned a rabbit and beef pie with atropine, a poison definitely in his possession at the time. The defence would have hinged on his apparent lack of access to the pie or ingredients and in his alleged victims' unanimous belief in his innocence, but in the event a defence was not required. The case broke down when the judge and prosecution counsel agreed that there was no case to answer, so the jury acquitted Sprague without hearing the evidence in his favour.[108]

This does not mean that the example set by Palmer had little or no impact. Eight of the eighteen cases were publicly aired or tried in the decade after 1856. Palmer's notoriety meant that suspicion was heightened, even if the appetite for punishment was diminishing. Also, public feeling in relation to practitioners had possibly reached a form of crisis with the case of Palmer, but the origins of that crisis can be found rather earlier. Two examples of suspected medical murder fill out the context of the reaction to Palmer. One case from 1844, which has been all but forgotten until now, provides the missing precursor to Palmer. The other from 1866 demonstrates the opportunistic nature of criticism levelled at practitioners, both from without and within the profession. Both examples also bring to the fore the way that ambivalent or negative reporting in the medical press could frame apparent instances of medical murder as truly exceptional. Palmer's case might have pointed up the desirability of professional solidarity in the face of public scrutiny, but this lesson could also be set aside to yield collective benefits.[109]

Additionally, both cases were drawn from the minority of allegations against practitioners founded on a presumption of poisoning. Poison had traditionally been characterised as the murder technique that was most to be expected from women or people of the lower classes. By the mid nineteenth century, suspicions of poisoning were shifting onto the middle-class, well-educated criminal whose intentions and guilt might be concealed behind a 'veil of prudish propriety'.[110] Secrecy and the upholding of respectability demanded that violent impulses be expressed only in planned episodes rather than physical wounding or struggles. In the case of medical men, there is a further way to understand the use of poison as a means of inflicting harm. Surgeons in particular might be somewhat accustomed to cutting human bodies for therapeutic purposes, even where the body in question made vocal protest. But the inculcation of a medical identity via training and practice might well have inhibited forethought of inflicting immediate damage on a still-living, wholly non-compliant body. Poison, in contrast, allowed intentional killing to be practised in a way that deviated very little from practitioners' usual activities, and given the number of poisons in the medical pharmacopoeia, perpetrating murder might be a matter of mere dosage. This is not to imply that the two cases below concerned practitioners who were emphatically guilty; rather it is a claim that medical masculinity, when contemplating violence, might well have been drawn to quasi-therapeutic means as consonant with a professional identity in a way that immediate interpersonal assault was not.

Courtroom acquittal and popular condemnation: James Cockburn Belaney

The case of James Cockburn Belaney arguably went some way to create the discourse later satisfied by Palmer as referent.[111] Belaney was charged in 1844 with the murder of his wife Rachel by poisoning. The couple lived in North Sunderland but had been visiting London, so the trial was held at the Old Bailey. Belaney's case resulted in acquittal, but his reputation among his former patients and neighbours was irretrievably lost, and his life was repeatedly threatened when he returned home. He probably left England or changed his name, since the practitioner James Belaney disappears permanently from the public record after 1846.

The events of 8 June 1844 were not much in dispute, but the verdict hung on the meanings that could be attached to Belaney's actions. He had allegedly been in the habit of self-dosing with prussic acid, a dangerous but sufficiently common phenomenon among the medical profession at this time.[112] His bottle of the poison broke, so he decanted the remainder of the liquid into a tumbler and left it while he went to find an alternative vessel. In the interim he was distracted from his purpose and began writing letters, so that the poison was left unattended in his bedroom and the tumbler may well have appeared to be empty. Belaney's wife then added Epsom salts and water to the glass, drank the resulting mixture, and died within twenty minutes.

Belaney was later criticised for failing to apply the proper remedies for a victim of prussic-acid poisoning, and of displaying a cool and purposefully deceptive demeanour in the letters he wrote to family and friends on the day of his wife's death. He was also suspected of having mixed the Epsom salts himself. In his favour, the trial supplied a plausible case for Rachel Belaney's death being a tragic accident, perhaps occasioned by Belaney's gross negligence but not arising from a malicious and planned attempt to kill. Furthermore, the prosecution failed to supply a motive for murder, since to all appearances the marriage had been very happy and Belaney secured few or no gains from his widowerhood. He already enjoyed full and unqualified control of the lime works in North Sunderland that his wife had inherited on the death of his mother-in-law, and there is no evidence that he exercised later a legal entitlement to remarry.[113]

Three factors worked to foment public fury in the face of Belaney's legal exoneration. First, Rachel had been much loved in North Sunderland. She was a notable local beauty, allegedly known as the 'Rose of the North.'[114] Second, the lay press was quick to endorse Belaney's apprehension and prosecution as a poisoner, and united in their deprecation of the trial verdict. The *Examiner* castigated the jury's credulous faith in respectable men who were akin to themselves in status, and this analysis was reprinted in the provincial press.[115] More sinister, it was claimed in some reports that the jury were united in believing Belaney guilty but unwilling to see him hanged.[116] Third, in-trial reporting of Belaney's dilatory and inappropriate treatment of his wife was contrasted with his assiduity in assembling his own legal defence. The evidence of his correspondence written immediately after the death seemed to confirm that he was primarily occupied with securing evidence of his own reputable character and dismissing his wife's demise as arising from hereditary heart disease; grief at the loss of his spouse and his own part in her poisoning seemed a secondary concern.[117]

The people of North Sunderland therefore enacted their own form of punishment. When Belaney returned home he was first stoned *en route* to his house and then burned in effigy in a poplar demonstration allegedly involving hundreds of people.[118] A week later, three effigies were paraded outside Belaney's house (representing Belaney himself, one of his defence witnesses, and the devil). Unwisely, Belaney fired a pistol into the crowd, whereupon the participants attacked his residence and forced him to flee. Then on 18 September 1844 his house was set alight. The household sought assistance from the constable at nearby Seahouses, but tellingly the constable refused. Help was found at North Sunderland itself but the house burned to the ground and news of Belaney's escape from the conflagration was received in the locality with some disappointment.[119] Driven from home in this way, Belaney left the district with his brother and solicitor, narrowly evaded being lynched on the road to Alnwick, travelled to Newcastle on Tyne, and promptly disappeared.[120] He later sought damages for the destruction of his house and was awarded £110 but it is not clear that he ever returned. After his wife's death, Belaney had planned to remove to Scotland, but later was said to have fled to France.[121]

In stark contrast to the public response, the leading medical journals were largely silent on Belaney's case. The *Provincial Medical and Surgical*

Journal appears never to have printed his name in the period 1844–46, although it did publish a number of letters and articles in 1844 and onwards about the effects of poisoning with prussic acid.[122] *The Lancet* refrained from any editorial comment, but did publish a short series of letters (again concerned with prussic acid but this time mentioning Belaney by name) between May and July 1845. The *Medical Gazette* was therefore unusual in making an outspoken intervention on the side of the prosecution. This journal assumed the case to be one of gross neglect rather than murder, but still asserted with unusual vigour 'our blood boils as we write, to think that a human being was thus cruelly left to perish – that life was allowed by the husband slowly to ebb away when the means of saving his wife were readily at hand'.[123]

Given the timing of the prosecution, it is probable that Belaney's case was mobilised by the *Gazette* in the interests of medical reform. The 1840s was a decade that saw multiple drives towards reform so this uncharacteristic article could be construed as a continuation of the case for change.[124] The circumstances surrounding Rachel Belaney's death were set down as 'another instance of a man practising medicine without adequate education', so putting Belaney himself outside of the orthodox medical fold and placing him in the company of the untrained and irresponsible.[125] Yet there is good reason to suppose this was an attempt to make political capital rather than comprising a statement of fair comment. Belaney probably served an apprenticeship and then attended Edinburgh's medical school where examination success admitted him to practice.[126] The *Gazette*'s design was apparently to press for reform under the guise of urging the public to seek well-trained medical men in order to avoid 'such events' in future.

James Belaney's prosecution established a precedent for medical poisoning to be suspected and punished without the usual rules of evidence being applied because punishment was imposed by the people not the state. As such it supplied an object lesson to both the medical profession and the wider public, illustrating what could happen if a suspected medical murderer was allowed to walk free. The medical press might reasonably (if tacitly) have drawn some significant conclusions. Condemnation of a medical colleague who was still alive risked contributing to that colleague's public denunciation without securing any medico-political gains. Circumspection until and beyond the point of a guilty verdict was advisable. In the criminal courts and the lay press medical poisoning might not be technically established but this did not mean that exoneration was possible, which makes the readiness to convict Palmer and others in the light of uncertain toxicology analyses more comprehensible.

Reputational ruin without trial by jury: the alleged murders by Alfred William Warder

The case of James Belany demonstrates that an acquittal in the 1840s was not necessarily sufficient to reassure a sceptical public that had already become convinced of a practitioner's guilt. Alfred Warder's treatment by public opinion and the press in 1866 confirms in addition that the absence of a trial by jury was no protection against condemnation. Warder was suspected of having murdered his third wife Ellen by poisoning, and during one of the adjournments of her inquest he took his own life with prussic acid.[127] Thereafter the deaths of his first two wives were re-evaluated during Ellen's inquest, and he was posthumously convicted by public opinion of having murdered all three women. His suicide was read as an admission of guilt for multiple murders rather than in any other way (as, for example, an expression of grief). The fact that Warder's private life came before the public less than twelve months after the trial and execution of Edward Pritchard for the murder of a wife was explicitly a factor in the negative response to Warder. He was readily labelled 'this second Pritchard'.[128] It is also likely that his wilful absence from the prosecution process, by dint of his suicide, gave the public freer rein than it would otherwise have had to denigrate him absolutely. Moreover, Warder's palpable ambition, evident in both his medical and social aspirations, gave rise to much retrospective suspicion among his former colleagues that was mobilised to undermine even further his possible claims to exoneration. As with the allegations of serious sexual assault or murder considered above, the question here is not whether Warder was guilty or innocent. Instead the interest in his case arises from the way it functioned in negotiating the definition of medical professionalism between practitioners and the public.

Alfred Warder was the younger son of a Portsea innkeeper, so he had no family connections in medicine to promote his career.[129] Instead he was entirely self-dependent and achieved early recognition. He had his first letter to *The Lancet* published in 1836 aged nineteen, and thereafter became a reasonably regular correspondent.[130] He secured formal qualifications in 1839 and 1840, and became notable for his support of the proposed Medical Protection Society, to address the grievances of doctors who worked for poor-law unions.[131] He had a vested interest in the project as the medical officer of the Chelsea workhouse from at least 1841.[132] In the 1850s he briefly held a post at the School of Anatomy and Medicine in Grosvenor Place where he lectured on medical jurisprudence.[133]

Warder's personal life seemed equally successful. In 1844 he married Alicia Gunning, the daughter of Joseph Gunning the secretary and solicitor of St George's Hospital.[134] The Gunnings were an illustrious medical family; therefore Warder had managed to secure by marriage what he lacked from his birth family, access to a prestigious medical dynasty and the opportunities that such connections offered.[135] Alfred and Alicia had four children up to 1851.[136]

Problems first arose within his private practice, and these probably had consequences for his domestic security. Warder entered into at least three partnerships in the 1850s, the third of which ended when Warder apparently tried to obtain financial restitution from his partner, James Stilwell. Warder made a spirited case, but public feeling and the law united behind Stilwell.[137] In the aftermath of this public humiliation Warder wrote no more letters to *The Lancet*, and separated from his wife. By 1861 he was living in Devonshire with his children, rather ominously describing himself inaccurately as a widower.[138] There was a form of domiciliary reunion in 1862 or early 1863 when Alicia rejoined Warder and her children, but this arrangement was short-lived because Alicia died on 15 January 1863. The cause of her death was given variously as abscess of the ovary, fatty degeneration of the heart, or unknown causes after suffering for one hour (all written on one certificate).[139] The death was reported in the local press, though, so Warder had not attempted to maintain the illusion that he had been a widower throughout.[140]

The family returned to London and Warder became immediately caught up in a Chancery suit. Alicia had left a fortune in a settlement made before her marriage but this money could not be inherited directly by her husband. Instead it was held in trust until her four children became adults, which Warder challenged.[141] It is possible that the dissolution of the partnership with Stilwell and the subsequent public opprobrium directed at Warder in 1857 may have deterred or prevented him from again practising medicine in the capital, which would have meant he badly needed an income from an alternative source.

In late December 1864, Warder married Jane Anne de Valerie, the daughter of a Scottish naval Commander and the widow of a French cuirassier, in the presence of selected witnesses including Jane's friend Ellen Branwell.[142] Warder did not inform any of his own friends about his marriage; he excluded the Gunnings and his Derbyshire solicitor from information about the match, and in the event there was little time to learn of it.[143] Jane Anne, known as Annie, was dead within seven months; whereupon Ellen Branwell was quickly persuaded to become the third Mrs Warder.[144] Like Alicia Gunning before her she was a woman of some fortune with medical relations, this time including a brother who was a doctor in Brighton.[145] She was also third cousin to the Brönte sisters.[146] Ellen fell ill shortly after her marriage, and was later reported to have said 'It is but the one thought of my life that this is the same illness as poor Annie died of.'[147]

The Warders took lodgings in Brighton in May 1866, and as Ellen's health deteriorated Alfred became both her practitioner and her sole attendant. She had no servant of her own and furthermore 'she could not endure him [ie Alfred] to leave her for a moment … she preferred her husband to do everything for her'.[148] He dosed her with aconitine for pain in her abdomen. This was a recognised treatment, but was typically delivered in doses of up to five drops while Warder administered it twenty drops at a time.[149] Ellen Warder died on 1 July 1866, less than twelve months after her predecessor, and Alfred committed suicide ten days later.[150]

The final decade of Warder's life therefore saw him acting in ways that raise concerns about his financial probity, his acquisitiveness, petty deceptions in personal dealings, and the sincerity of his relations with his wives. He was assumed to have been motivated throughout by financial gain, evidenced by the assurance policy on Annie's life and by Ellen's fortune.[151] The inquest jury charged with determining Ellen's cause of death spent little time deliberating, and found that Ellen had been murdered by aconite and that Alfred had killed himself to avoid prosecution. Even so, none of his behaviour in life proved that Alfred was a murderer, and none of the investigations made after his death confirmed it either. A portion of Ellen's digestive system was sent to

Alfred Swaine Taylor, the London toxicologist whose professional analyses were often employed in cases of suspected poisoning, but Taylor's reports were inconclusive because no aconite was detected in Ellen Warder's remains.[152]

The lay and medical press were largely united in damning Warder. One or two muted voices in the medical press urged caution: the *British Medical Journal* challenged the conclusions of the inquest, claiming 'the unqualified verdict of the jury was scarcely warranted by the facts', but on the whole reporting around the events in Brighton was clear that Warder had been guilty and had feloniously evaded justice.[153] Medical colleagues also used Warder's demise and supposed guilt to rehash aspects of his career in a way that put even more distance between him and his innocent colleagues. For example, his tenure at the Grosvenor School as a lecturer was very short, and after his death one anonymous practitioner protested 'although Warder did … try to hold the Forensic chair, he was an utter failure, and simply showed that he really knew nothing of the subject'; if he was a successful poisoner in practice, he had not been a very good theorist.[154] Similarly, his name was linked with the earlier medical murderer William Palmer, when it was claimed that Warder had given evidence defending Palmer at his trial. This allegation was much repeated but was almost certainly apocryphal.[155]

Warder was either very unfortunate, or guilty of gross overconfidence (as a practitioner, or as a killer). It is possible that he married three women who all died at relatively young ages from rather similar complaints, potentially accelerated by inappropriate treatment. If this was the case he would almost certainly have suffered a measure of legitimate grief at the same time that he was coming under suspicion for up to three murders. In this context, an act of suicide becomes the recognisable expression of misery, despair, and the permanent surrender of a medical identity. Other doctors killed themselves from grief at their failure to cure their loved ones without the additional aggravation of being suspected of murder.[156] There is circumstantial evidence that at least one of Warder's children did not denigrate his memory (and so presumably did not suspect him of murdering Alicia). Alfred junior spent time in Germany, married a local woman, and had at least three children, one of whom he named Alfred William Ludwig Warder.[157]

Conversely, if Warder poisoned Ellen (and, if Ellen's unwitting testimony is to be believed, Annie as well) he must have thought himself invulnerable. He seems to have relied on the same treatment/poison at least twice if not three times, and did not wait even a year after his second and third marriages before administering life-threatening dosages. He positively courted detection when he took his third wife to Brighton and so returned her to the scrutiny of her practitioner-brother Robert.

Warder's informal but largely undisputed condemnation in 1866, therefore, suggests two things. First the suspected fragility of the medical profession in the 1860s, which was partially detected in the rise and fall of applause for acquittals of medical defendants in cases of sexual violence, can also be read into the willingness to cast Warder as guilty by practitioners and public alike. Second, a polarised view of medicine as a profession worthy of patient trust, but that was subject to occasional infiltration by the wicked, served everyone's purposes. For fellow professionals, Warder was personally lost to their number because he was dead, and this meant his reputation could be debased with relative safety to draw fire away from other forms of medical wrong-doing or evidence of incomplete/unsatisfactory professionalisation. For the newspaper-reading public, he provided an easy choice of target, his case coming so soon after that of Pritchard. Unfocused uncertainty or discontent with medical practice found a convenient outlet. Warder was drawn as irredeemably evil, and because his example was apparently so stark (and without the need to hear troubling evidence in a criminal trial that might destabilise the surety of his guilt) he appeared to confirm that other practitioners were moral, dutiful professionals by contrast. As one report put it 'We are far from saying one word against a profession which bears the very highest character, merely because it has contained two sheep of such a black dye as Pritchard and Warder.'[158] Once again both medical men and the lay public had a vested interest in maintaining unambiguous ideas about the rectitude of the vast majority of practitioners. In the case of sexual crime, this involved some rather difficult or awkward processes (such as repeated judicial irregularity) to sustain a uniform impression of technical medical innocence or exoneration. In a case of alleged murder and suicide, it was more convenient to manipulate Warder's story to become a variety of negative exemplar, the 'bad apple' who leaves 'the barrel itself ... intact.'[159]

Conclusion

Criminal trials of practitioners for serious sexual assault or murder illustrate the limits of competitive behaviours, but also the desirability of identifying rare individuals as exceptional and irredeemable scapegoats. A public allegation of rape spurred one response only among medical men, unequivocal defence of the accused man irrespective of the circumstances surrounding the assault. Any personal animosity or generalised resentment of competitors was subsumed by the more pressing professional project of countering the feasibility of doctor as sexual predator. Lay reporting, courtroom applause, and the re-establishment of medical careers following a trial for sexual assault extended this defence to the non-medical public, despite an official, statutory diminution in the acceptance of personal violence. The emerging professional medical identity was utterly incompatible with the perpetration of sexual violence, and therefore the prosecution of this violence was distorted to the benefit of medical defendants. The result was not so much a veil of silence as one of extenuation and approval.

Wilful public rejection of practitioners' sexual crime does not rule out the possibility that medical men experienced a measure of professionally inflected criminal opportunity. Chapters 1 and 3 have already discussed the ways in which the medical marketplace forced men into covertly competitive behaviours to secure some advantage over their colleagues. The evidence of this chapter also raises the prospect of medical masculinity being channelled into covert violence, specifically sexual violence. The professionalising rhetoric emphasised the risk to medical men of false accusations of sexual wrong-doing given their privileged access to women's bodies, but perhaps some among the ninety-two cases here point to another, more uncomfortable possibility that patient fears were justified; intimate examination and the spread of chemical anaesthesia also offered the concomitant risk of opportunistic, indoor attack. In the twentieth century, rape which occurred between a victim and attacker who knew each other tended to occur where the acquaintance was slight, and where both were 'in a vulnerable setting by mutual consent'.[160] Debates around criminality may dispute the relative significance attributable to low self-control (and other personality characteristics), motivation, and opportunity, but the presence of opportunity remains a key component in understandings of crime.[161] Intimate medical examination arguably offered a viable pathway to wrong-doing for a small minority of Victorian medical men, perhaps enhanced from the mid century onwards by increasing use of the speculum. Lacking other studies of occupational patterns among defendants in rape cases, this can be no more than a suggestion.

More decisively, the evidence in relation to cases of medical crimes against the body has identified the 1860s as a precarious decade for the medical profession. The executions of Palmer and Pritchard either side of the Medical Registration Act of 1858 were a sobering reminder both within and outside of medicine of the potential for aberrant men to make deadly use of their medical training. Arguably, this gave an added urgency to the defence of medical authority and probity in the 1860s, for the purpose of reassuring the public that confidence in practitioners was very substantially well placed. The willingness of the profession to join popular condemnations, chiefly represented here by Warder, gave a measure of reassurance that the profession was not an entirely closed shop and would act against its own members if need be.

At the same time, there is no denying that the pressures of medical practice drove some men to desperation, expressed in ways that harmed only themselves. If Warder did commit suicide from motives other than guilt he was not alone, as the ample evidence in Chapter 6 attests, but less extreme behaviours are also visible in the evidence of medical admissions to Victorian asylums. Hospital admissions have the additional advantage of being supported by case note narratives providing the background to medical insanity. Therefore the next chapter investigates medical mental health, and continues the account of men convicted of serious crime but incarcerated as criminal lunatics.

Notes

1 Murder excludes deaths occasioned by duelling, where their reading as violence is complicated by victims' willful, if coerced, involvement.

2 J. Rowbotham and K. Stevenson, 'Causing a Sensation: Media and Legal Representations of Bad Behaviour', in J. Rowbotham and K. Stevenson (eds), *Behaving Badly. Social Panic and Moral Outrage – Victorian and Modern Parallels* (Ashgate: Aldershot, 2003), pp. 31–46, on p. 33.

3 S. D'Cruze, *Crimes of Outrage. Sex, Violence and Victorian Working Women* (London: University College of London Press, 1998), p. 164; C.A.

Conley, *The Unwritten Law. Criminal Justice in Victorian Kent* (Oxford University Press: Oxford, 1991), p. 84.

4 K. Stevenson, '"Most Intimate Violations": Contextualising the Crime of Rape', in A-M. Kilday and D. Nash (eds), *Histories of Crime. Britain 1600–2000* (Basingstoke: Palgrave Macmillan, 2010), pp. 80–99, on p. 91; S. Felton and S. Hipkin, '"Trenching the ground of medical men": criminality, respectability and justice in the "West Malling Poisoning Case". 1882–1883', *Archaeologia Cantiana* 133 (2013), pp. 167–84, on pp. 179–80.

5 A.E. Simpson, 'The "Blackmail Myth" and the prosecution of rape and its attempt in 18th century London: the creation of a legal tradition', *Journal of Criminal Law and Criminology*, 77 (1986), pp. 101–50, on p. 123.

6 R. Shoemaker, 'Male honour and the decline of public violence in eighteenth-century London', *Social History* 26:2 (2001), pp. 190–208; J. Carter Wood, *Violence and Crime in Nineteenth-century England. The Shadow of our Refinement* (London and New York: Routledge, 2004), pp. 29–30.

7 J. Bailey, '"I dye [sic] by Inches": locating wife beating in the concept of a privatization of marriage and violence in eighteenth-century England', *Social History* 31:3 (2006), pp. 273–94, on pp. 283–4; E. Foyster, *Marital Violence. An English Family History, 1660–1857* (Cambridge: Cambridge University Press, 2005), chapter 4.

8 E. Foyster, 'Creating a veil of silence? Politeness and marital violence in the English household', *Transactions of the Royal Historical Society* 12 (2002), pp. 395–415.

9 J. Rowbotham, K. Stevenson, and S. Pegg, *Crime News in Modern Britain. Press Reporting and Responsibility, 1820–2010* (Basingstoke: Palgrave Macmillan, 2013), pp. 34–8.

10 Conley, *The Unwritten Law*, p. 91.

11 M. Weiner, 'Domesticity: A Legal Discipline for Men?', in M. Hewitt (ed.), *An Age of Equipoise? Reassessing Mid-Victorian Britain* (Aldershot: Ashgate, 2000), pp. 153–67, on p. 158.

12 Foyster, *Marital Violence*, p. 63.

13 Foyster, *Marital Violence*, p. 220.

14 J. Tosh, *A Man's Place. Masculinity and the Middle-Class Home in Victorian England* (New Haven: Yale University Press, 1999), pp. 112, 188.

15 Carter Wood, *Violence and Crime*, p. 31; M.J. Weiner, 'The Victorian Criminalisation of Men', in P. Spierenburg (ed.), *Men and Violence. Gender, Honor, and Rituals in Modern Europe and America* (Columbus Ohio: Ohio State University Press, 1998), pp. 197–212, on p. 201.

16 Carter Wood, *Violence and Crime*, p. 45.

17 Foyster, *Marital Violence*, pp. 79, 81.
18 D'Cruze, *Crimes of Outrage*, p. 180.
19 A.J. Hammerton, *Cruelty and Companionship. Conflict in Nineteenth-Century Married Life* (London: Routledge, 1992), pp. 107–8.
20 Rowbotham et al., *Crime News*, p. 22.
21 P. King, 'Newspaper reporting and attitudes to crime and justice in late-eighteenth and early-nineteenth-century London', *Continuity and Change* 22:1 (2007), pp. 73–112, on p. 73.
22 Rowbotham et al., *Crime News*, p. 7.
23 C.A. Casey, 'Common misperceptions: the press and Victorian views of crime', *Journal of Interdisciplinary History* 41:3 (2011), pp. 367–91.
24 Rowbotham et al., *Crime News*, pp. 12, 60, 66.
25 Rowbotham et al., *Crime News*, p. 51.
26 Rowbotham et al., *Crime News*, p. 42.
27 Rowbotham et al., *Crime News*, pp. 20–3.
28 J. Loudon and I. Loudon, 'Medicine, Politics and the Medical Periodical 1800–50', in S. Lock and R. Porter (eds), *Medical Journals and Medical Knowledge: Historical Essays* (Routledge: London, 1992), pp. 49–69. Practitioners might enhance their income by writing, but not generally crime reporting; for medically-trained contributors to *Punch*, see C.L. Horrocks, 'Proselytising Public Health Reform in Punch 1841–1858' unpublished PhD thesis (Liverpool John Moores University, 2009), p. 15.
29 P.J. Reiter, 'Doctors, detectives, and the professional idea: The Trial of Thomas Neill Cream and the mastery of Sherlock Holmes', *College Literature* 35:3 (2008), pp. 57–96, on p. 71.
30 A. Clark, *Women's Silence Men's Violence: Sexual Assault in England, 1770–1845* (London: Pandora, 1987); D'Cruze, *Crimes of Outrage*, chapter 7; E. Snell, 'Trials in Print: Narratives of Rape Trials in the Proceedings of the Old Bailey', in D. Lemmings (ed.), *Crime, Courtrooms and the Public Sphere in Britain, 1700–1850* (Ashgate: Farnham, 2012), pp. 23–42.
31 G. Walker, 'Everyman or a monster? The rapist in early-modern England, c. 1600–1750', *History Workshop Journal* 76:1 (2013), pp. 3–31.
32 This phenomenon has a long history; see R. Porter, 'A Touch of Danger: The Man-Midwife as Sexual Predator', G.S. Rousseau and R. Porter (eds), *Sexual Underworlds of the Enlightenment* (Manchester: Manchester University Press, 1987), pp. 206–33.
33 D'Cruze, *Crimes of Outrage*, p. 149.
34 D'Cruze, *Crimes of Outrage*, p. 181.
35 J. Walkowitz, 'Jack the Ripper and the myth of male violence', *Feminist Studies* 8 (1982), pp. 643–74, on p. 556.

36 L. Jackson, *Child Sexual Abuse in Victorian England* (London: Routledge, 2000), pp. 81–2.
37 M. Anne Crowther, 'Forensic Medicine and Medical Ethics in Nineteenth-century Britain', in R. Baker (ed.), *The Codification of Medical Morality* (Dordrecht: Kluwer Academic Publishers, 1995), pp. 173–89, on p. 187.
38 Simpson, 'The "Blackmail Myth"', pp. 113–14.
39 R. Porter, 'Rape – Does it Have a Historical Meaning?', in R. Porter and S. Tomaselli (eds), *Rape. An Historical and Cultural Enquiry* (Oxford: Basil Blackwell, 1986), pp. 216–36, on p. 233.
40 For example, see 'Perils of Practice', *British Medical Journal* 1 June 1889, p. 1257 and 'An Unfounded Charge Against a Medical Man', *British Medical Journal* 28 May 1887, p. 1176.
41 D'Cruze, *Crimes of Outrage*, p. 145; J. Bourke, *Rape. A History from 1860 to the Present Day* (London: Virago, 2007), pp. 58–61.
42 J. Walkowitz, *Prostitution and Victorian Society. Women, Class, and the State.* (Cambridge: Cambridge University Press, 1980), p. 101.
43 J.J. Garth Wilkinson, *The Forcible Introspection of the Women for the Army and Navy by the Oligarchy Considered Physically* (London: F. Pitman, 1870), p. 15.
44 P. McHugh, *Prostitution and Victorian Social Reform* (London: Croom Helm, 1980), p. 249.
45 C. Conley, 'Rape and justice in Victorian England', *Victorian Studies* 29 (1986), pp. 519–36, on p. 521.
46 Simpson, 'The "Blackmail Myth"', p. 122; Conley, 'Rape and justice', pp. 523, 536.
47 The British Library Newspapers database was searched on 28 May 2013 and subsequently.
48 Stevenson, '"Most Intimate Violations"', p. 82.
49 Not guilty verdicts were found in thirty-five cases; the result of ten accusations is unknown.
50 Conley, 'Rape and justice', p. 521.
51 Conley, 'Rape and justice', p. 523.
52 Conley, 'Rape and justice', p. 525.
53 'Extraordinary Charge of Rape', *Derby Mercury* 10 April 1867, p. 6. Saunders was congratulated on his acquittal with a purse of 120 guineas, collected by the inhabitants of Chigwell; [Untitled] *British Medical Journal* 1 June 1867, p. 647.
54 'Alleged Indecent Assault – an Unfounded Charge', *Reynolds's Newspaper* 12 May 1889, p. 8.
55 'A Magistrate Convicted on a Serious Charge', *York Herald* 23 January 1875, p. 7.

56 There were other isolated instances of defendants being permitted to plead under an assumed name, including other medical men; see, for instance, 'A Medical Student Committed for an Assault', *Illustrated Police News* 22 October 1870, p. 3.
57 'Charges of Indecent Assault Against a Medical Man', *Liverpool Mercury* 16 January 1849, p. 4; 'A Beast', *Reynolds's Newspaper* 31 October 1852, p. 11.
58 Walker, 'Everyman or a Monster', pp. 18–23.
59 'Charge of Rape', *Morning Chronicle* 22 September 1843, p. 4; 'Alleged Indecency by a Surgeon', *Reynolds's Newspaper* 11 May 1873, p. 4 and 'The Charge Against A Surgeon', *Lloyd's Weekly Newspaper* 16 October 1864, p. 4.
60 'Central Criminal Court', *Daily News* 10 April 1851, p. 7; the defendant was not ultimately transported, see NA, PCOM 3/22/2221.
61 Conley, 'Rape and justice', p. 529.
62 'Serious Charge against a Medical Man', *York Herald* 25 February 1871, p. 11.
63 'Restoration of a Name to the Register', *British Medical Journal* 5 April 1873, p. 376.
64 Conley, *The Unwritten Law*, p. 83.
65 'A Medical Man Sentenced to Imprisonment', *Dundee Courier and Argus* 5 November 1884, p. 3.
66 'The Attempted Outrage by a Surgeon', *Sheffield and Rotherham Independent* 5 November 1884, p. 3.
67 'The Case of Dr David Bradley', *British Medical Journal* 21 February 1885, p. 403.
68 'The Case of Dr Bradley', *British Medical Journal* 8 August 1885, pp. 272–3.
69 'The Case of Dr Bradley', *Derby Mercury* 16 December 1885, p. 5.
70 N.A. RG 11/1571/160, RG 12/1212/13, RG 13/1442/12 and RG 14/8521/475.
71 General Medical Council, *The Medical Register* (London: General Medical Council, 1887), p. 185.
72 N.A. RG 12/3543/30; death certificate of 7 November 1914.
73 'Conviction of a Medical Man for a Criminal Assault', *Leeds Mercury* 20 December 1856, p. 2.
74 The *General Medical Register*'s successive editions place him in Bradford in the 1850s, 1860s, and 1870s; N.A. RG 11/4437/129.
75 Foyster, *Marital Violence*, p. 1 and *passim*, 66–7. See the case of Theodore Poncia, 1884.
76 Namely, Alexander Moseley in 1866 and Other Windsor Berry in 1869.
77 'The Speculum: Criminal Charge against a Physician', *British Medical Journal* 27 May 1853, p. 275; O. Moscucci, *The Science of Woman.*

Gynaecology and Gender in England 1800–1929 (Cambridge: Cambridge University Press, 1990), pp. 123–6.

78 'Serious Charge Against a Medical Man', *Reynolds's Newspaper* 14 July 1867, p. 1; 'Serious Charge Against and Committal of a Surgeon', *The Standard* 4 June 1870, p. 6.

79 For example, see 'Conviction of a Dentist for Violating a Patient While Under the Influence of Ether Inhalation', *British Medical Journal* 11 May 1855 p. 439, and 'Some Phenomena of Anaesthesia by Protoxide of Nitrogen', *ibid.*, 23 January 1869, p. 67.

80 'Alleged Attempted Rape at Elland', *York Herald* 3 August 1876, p. 7.

81 There were over ninety articles in the London and provincial press concerning this case in November and December 1865.

82 Hunter's case was a *cause celèbre* in more ways than one; *The Great Libel Case. Dr Hunter versus Pall Mall Gazette* (C. Mitchell and Co: London, 1867).

83 'Trial of Doctor Hunter for Rape', *Reynolds's Newspaper* 26 November 1865, p. 5; 'The Assault on Dr Hunter', *ibid.*, 24 December 1865 p. 3.

84 Ten other instances of practitioners acquitted of violent crime occasioned applause that was reported in the press, three in relation to manslaughter and seven following prosecution for abortion. These were more disbursed, covering 1843–88, but saw four instances falling in the same period as the majority of applauded medical defendants in sexual assault cases, 1861–74.

85 D'Cruze, *Crimes of Outrage*, p. 137.

86 P. King, *Crime, Justice, and Discretion in England 1740–1820* (Oxford University Press: Oxford, 2000), pp. 252–7.

87 D. Lemmings, 'Introduction: Criminal Courts, Lawyers and the Public Sphere', in D. Lemmings (ed.), *Crime, Courtrooms and the Public Sphere in Britain, 1700–1850* (Ashgate: Farnham, 2012), pp. 1–22, on p. 3.

88 B. Godfrey, 'Sentencing, Theatre, Audience and Communication: The Victorian and Edwardian Magistrates' Courts and their Message', in B. Garnier (ed.), *Le Temoins devant la Justice* (Rennes: University of Rennes Press, 2003), pp. 161–71.

89 M. Presdee, *Cultural Criminology and the Carnival of Crime* (Routledge: London, 2000), p. 38.

90 Lemmings, 'Introduction', p. 4.

91 'A Surgeon Charged with Rape', *Birmingham Daily Post* 24 March 1870, p. 7.

92 M. Sullivan, 'Spectacular failures: Thomas Hopley, Wilkie Collins, and the Reconstruction of Victorian Masculinity', in M. Hewitt (ed.), *An Age of Equipoise? Reassessing Mid-Victorian Britain* (Ashgate: Aldershot, 2000), pp. 84–108, on p. 85.

93 [Untitled] *Pall Mall Gazette* 10 May 1869, p. 7.
94 'Charge of Criminal Assault Against A Surgeon At Oldbury', *Birmingham Daily Post* 17 April 1862, p. 3.
95 'Bower and Keates Indemnity Fund', *British Medical Journal* 18 August 1888, pp. 386–7.
96 Crowther, 'Forensic Medicine', p. 179.
97 'How to read an Old Bailey trial', www.oldbaileyonline.org/static/HowToReadTrial.jsp viewed on 13 November 2015; I. Burney, *Poison, Detection, and the Victorian Imagination* (Manchester: Manchester University Press, 2006).
98 Burney, *Poison*, p. 121.
99 C. Emsley, *Elements of Murder* (Oxford University Press: Oxford, 2005), pp. 229–32; Conan Doyle linked the two names in the Sherlock Holmes story 'The Speckled Band', first published in *Strand Magazine* (1892).
100 'The Pritchard Murder', *British Medical Journal* 22 July 1865, p. 63.
101 The British Library Newspapers database was searched on 28 May 2013 and subsequently.
102 The eighteen counts of murder and attempted murder exclude eleven instances of duelling that emerged from the newspapers between 1804 and 1838.
103 Figures for 1850 and 1860 have been extrapolated from C. Emsley, *Crime and Society in England, 1750–1900* (London: Longman, 1996), p. 43. All homicides include all cases of manslaughter as well as murder.
104 Pritchard was hanged in 1865 but in Scotland. Cream was tried and executed in 1892.
105 The experiences of men admitted to Bethlem or Broadmoor are considered in Chapter 5.
106 These were Thomas Smethurst tried in 1859 and William Burke tried in 1888. Smethurst is considered in Burney, *Poison*, pp. 163–8.
107 See for example [Untitled] *Pall Mall Gazette*, 26 July 1865, p. 9; 'Charge of Poisoning a Whole Family', *Bristol Mercury* 29 July 1865, p. 6.
108 [Untitled] *The Standard* 4 August 1865, p. 4. Sprague was also accused of rape in August 1865 but not prosecuted; 'Occasional Notes', *Pall Mall Gazette* 15 August 1865, p. 9.
109 Burney, *Poison*, pp. 157–8.
110 *The Leader* quoted in Burney, *Poison*, pp. 122–3.
111 For an initial treatment of Belaney, see H. Wallis, '"Trust not the Physician" Interpersonal Violence in an Age of Medical Reform', unpublished MRes dissertation, (Keele University, 2011), pp. 50–63.
112 See Chapter 6 for further discussion of self-dosing as a prelude to *de facto* suicide.

113 'The Alleged Murder by Prussic Acid at Stepney', *The Morning Post* 22 August 1844, p. 3.
114 *A Full Report of the Evidence Taken at the Thames Police Court, and the Coroner's Inquest, Before Mr. Baker, and a Respectable Jury at Stepney on 10 June 1844; on the alleged poisoning case, also, the trial of J.C. Belaney for the murder of his wife at the Central Criminal Court on August 21st & 22nd 1844; with all the letters and opinions of the public press* (Alnwick: G.Pike, 1844), where pagination is given in two sections, part one pp. 1–60 and part two pp. 1–23, in part two on pp. 14–15.
115 'Belany's Case', *Examiner* 31 August 1844, p. 1, reprinted for example in 'Belany's Case', *Hampshire Telegraph and Sussex Chronicle* 14 September 1844, p. 2.
116 *A Full Report*, part one, p. 59.
117 'Alleged Poisoning by Prussic Acid', *Bell's Life in London and Sporting Chronicle* 30 June 1844, p. 1.
118 'James Cockburn Belaney', *The Northern Star and Leeds General Advertiser* 7 September 1844, p. 5.
119 'James Cockburn Belaney', *Freeman's Journal and Daily Commercial Advertiser* 23 September 1844, p. 4; 'Spring Assizes', *Morning Post* 2 March 1846, p. 7; 'Before Mr Justice Patteson', *Newcastle Courant* 6 March 1846, p. 3.
120 'J.C. Belany', *John Bull* 28 September 1844, p. 609.
121 'Belaney', *The Leicester Chronicle: or, Commercial and Agricultural Adviser* 7 March 1846, p. 4; 'Before Mr Justice Patteson', *Newcastle Courant* 6 March 1846, p. 3.
122 'Fatal poisoning from fifteen or twenty drops of the essential oil of bitter almonds', *Provincial Medical and Surgical Journal* 11 September 1844, pp. 364–7. See also Chapter 6.
123 *Medical Gazette* reprinted in *A Full Report*, part two pp. 5–9.
124 I. Loudon, *Medical Care and the General Practitioner, 1750–1850* (Oxford: Oxford University Press, 1986) for example on pp. 282–96.
125 *Medical Gazette* reprinted in *A Full Report*, part two pp. 5–9.
126 'Mr James Cockburn Belaney', *Morning Post* 9 July 1844, p. 6.
127 This prevalence of this method of suicide among practitioners is discussed in Chapter 6.
128 'Murder on principle, murder from passion, and murder on no principle at all', *Cheshire Observer* 21 July 1866, p. 8.
129 Baptism of 21 December 1817, www.familysearch.org viewed on 20 February 2012; [Untitled] *London Gazette* 29 April 1806, p. 552 for the Warders as innkeepers.
130 [Untitled] *The Lancet* 26:676 (1836), p. 686.

131 General Medical Council, *The Medical Register* (London: General Medical Council, 1859), p. 312; 'Medical Protection Society', *The Lancet* 6 November 1847, p. 502.
132 Old Bailey Online reference t18411129–111, www.oldbaileyonline.org, viewed on 13 November 2015.
133 'Medical Education', *British Medical Journal* 30 September 1853, p. 363.
134 Marriage certificate of 30 April 1844.
135 C.J.H. Gunning and A. Warder, *Genealogy of the Gunning Family* (London: A. Prickett, 1907).
136 N.A. HO 107/1473/160.
137 *Post Office Directory* (1851), p. 509; N.A. C 15/350/W192; [Untitled] *London Gazette* 8 August 1854, p. 2444; 'Uxbridge Middlesex – Extraordinary Proceedings', *The Lancet* 69:1764 (1857), p. 646; 'Address to Mr Stilwell', *The Lancet* 69:1765 (1857), p. 658.
138 N.A. RG 9/1378/103.
139 Death certificate of 15 January 1863.
140 'Deaths', *Trewman's Exeter Flying Post* 28 January 1863, p. 5.
141 N.A. C 16/244/W255.
142 Marriage certificate of 29 December 1864; 'Marriages', *Glasgow Herald* 22 December 1854, p. 5; 'Deaths', *Caledonian Mercury* 22 March 1855, p. 3.
143 'The Suspicious Death of a Physician's Wife at Brighton', *Daily News* 14 July 1866, p. 3.
144 'The Suicide of Dr Warder at Brighton', *Liverpool Mercury* 14 July 1866, p. 5; Jane Anne's death is given as 22 July 1865 on her headstone in Caithness.
145 'Mysterious Death of a Lady & Suicide of Her Husband at Brighton', *Hampshire Telegraph and Sussex Chronicle* 14 July 1866, p. 3.
146 Ellen's grandfather Richard Branwell (1744–1812) was brother to the Brönte sisters' grandfather Thomas Branwell (1746–1808).
147 'The Suspicious Death of a Physician's Wife at Brighton', *Daily News* 14 July 1866, p. 3.
148 'Singular Death of a Lady at Brighton', *Daily News* 6 July 1866, p. 7.
149 [Untitled] *Glasgow Herald* 18 July 1866, p. 4.
150 Death certificates of 1 July and 10 July 1866.
151 'Murder on principle, murder from passion, and murder on no principle at all', *Cheshire Observer and Chester, Birkenhead, Crewe and North Wales Times* 21 July 1866, p. 8.
152 'The Suspicious Death of a Lady at Brighton', *Daily News* 17 July 1866, p. 9.
153 'The Brighton Tragedy', *British Medical Journal* 21 July 1866, p. 74.
154 [Untitled] *The Lancet* 88:2238 (1866), p. 77.

155 Old Bailey Online reference t18560514–490, www.oldbaileyonline.org viewed on 13 November 2015, where the transcript of Palmer's trial makes no mention of Warder.

156 See the case of Angus Cameron, treated in Chapter 5.

157 Baptism of Alfred William Ludwig Warder at Mannheim, Baden, 26 December 1879, www.familysearch.org viewed on 13 November 2015.

158 [Untitled] *Glasgow Herald* 18 July 1866, p. 4.

159 I. Butler and M. Drakeford, *Scandal, Social Policy and Social Welfare* 2nd edn (Bristol: Policy Press, 2005), p. 230.

160 M.R. Gottfredson and T. Hirschi, *A General Theory of Crime* (Stanford: Stanford University Press, 1990), p. 37.

161 H.G. Grasmick, C.R. Tittle, R.J. Bursik Jr., and B.J. Arneklev, 'Testing the core empirical implications of Gottfredson and Hirschi's General Theory of Crime', *Journal of Research in Crime and Delinquency* 30:1 (1993), pp. 5–29.

5

Mad doctors: lunacy and the asylum

Medical practitioners who were deemed by their nineteenth-century contemporaries to be suffering from severe mental-health problems frequently warranted an asylum admission.[1] The supposed causes of their complaints covered the same range as for non-medical patients, in that these were ascribed to contextual causes – such as overwork, domestic disharmony, financial troubles – and to physical or moral causes including opiate addiction, alcohol consumption, heredity, and masturbation.[2] However, medical patients were different to other asylum inmates in that they were the former (and in some cases future) colleagues of their keepers.

There is a good deal of anecdotal evidence that doctors who held roles caring for or treating the mad were particularly prone to suffer mental disturbance. In *Shattered Nerves*, Janet Oppenheim makes the point that medical officers of asylums were urged in 1860 to be careful of their own mental health, and alludes to instances of medical depression or neurasthenia more generally, but her claims are substantiated by contemporary allegations rather than by concrete examples, although examples can be found.[3] It has since emerged that fifteen medical practitioners were admitted to Ticehurst asylum in Sussex between 1845 and 1885, including Samuel Hill, the former superintendent of the North Riding asylum in Yorkshire, thought to be suffering from 'overpressure of duties'.[4] This shows that some doctors were sufficiently affluent to afford the Ticehurst fees, were desirous of the privacy it could offer, and could be former employees of the asylum sector. But this does not explain whether Ticehurst entirely accounted for the nation's doctors who suffered disruptions to their mental health, or whether (given the high fees there) these fifteen men were the tip of the iceberg.

If Oppenheim's general points are correct, then professional men in general may have been more prone to stress, breakdown, and even 'insanity' than either elite or working-class men, whether or not they were themselves doctors, or doctors of the mad.[5]

Even average levels of vulnerability to mental distress, however, are difficult to detect from the sources left directly by doctors. There were good reasons for medical men to be reticent about their mental ill-health in their public, and even private, writings. Micale has argued that between 1790 and 1860 there was medical denial that hysteria, for example, could be suffered by men. He sees this as part of a broader redefinition of masculinity, such that 'By the end of Victoria's reign, the spectrum of emotions deemed appropriate for adult men in Britain had greatly diminished, as the familiar historical image of stoical insensibility and the stiff upper lip emerged and hardened.'[6] Consequently, expressions of uncertainty, anxiety, fear or distress became increasingly problematic, and practitioners would have shared this restricted scope for manly expression with their middle-class peers.

Ever sharper definition of professionally appropriate qualities and behaviour should theoretically have rendered professional achievement more difficult at the same time that public tolerance towards doctors' mental breakdowns would arguably have been in decline. Did the fluid, but gradually more stringent, professional ideal have this effect of reducing public tolerance and/or raising expectations among medical men by widening the gap between the ideal and experience? This question can be investigated in part via an examination of unstable practitioners whose difficulties became subject to an institutional context and to systematic record-keeping.

It should not be surprising to find medical men as patients in establishments for the insane, particularly if Scull is right to argue that 'men who were active in business or the professions tended to be institutionalised more rapidly than their womenfolk' owing to the impact of their reduced earnings or their potential for violence.[7] Yet to see medical practitioners as the recipients rather than the providers of mental health care is also to run counter to the historiography of the asylum. Historians who would support the general outline of Foucault's 'great confinement' thesis have characterised doctors as among those responsible for defining, capturing, and incarcerating the insane. The rationales for admitting pauper patients to county asylums or workhouses have circled around the limitations of domestic care, the function of poor-law officers in determining the criteria for institutional admission, or whether the system constituted the wholesale consignment of 'inconvenient' people away from public view.[8] Movement of middling and elite patients into and out of private asylums was not dependent on local government policy but was similarly guided by household, family, community, and institutional definitions of unacceptable behaviours. The impulses which acted in admissions of middling, professional patients have not been surveyed discretely, but it is reasonable to suppose that shifting norms of professional identity may well have given rise to controversial cases; eccentricities of personal, professional or public demeanour might be understood as mental illness.

Analysis of the institutional destinations of 'insane' practitioners is complicated by the heterogeneous provision of private and public accommodation. Licensed houses run by private entrepreneurs were assumed to be most suited to the middle-class patient, but the capacity of county asylums and the demand for affordable places meant that asylums could offer and readily secure custom for different 'classes' of admission among paying patients, as Melling and Forsyth demonstrated at Exminster.[9] The routes by which doctors were admitted to one or more types of institutional care offer insights into the role of family members, fellow practitioners, and others in certifying, admitting, and cataloguing the case of a doctor deemed 'insane'. Consequently, patterns of admission speak to complicity or to conflicts within medicine in determining the boundaries of institutionalised 'madness'.

Considering aspects of asylum care demands some attention to the case notes generated by institutions. The potential and pitfalls of case note scrutiny have been surveyed for Gartnavel Royal Asylum in Glasgow, and the generalities observed there are broadly applicable to the case notes of English county asylums. In the Glasgow case notes there is a discernible difference between notes written for pauper or working-class patients and those from a more prosperous background or who had been well educated.[10] Additionally, I will argue that case notes could sometimes achieve a particular pitch of poignancy when the medical author (frequently the asylum superintendent) was annotating the case of a fellow medical man. The disparity between the career ambitions or achievements of a fellow practitioner and their some-time asylum residence, combined with empathy from their medical observers, could inspire unduly personal reflections amid the more routine chronicle of case developments.

At the same time, the training, professional experiences, and occupational stress undergone by medical patients could influence the specific forms of their paranoia, delusions or hallucinations. At the simplest level the habitual thoughts and preoccupations of an asylum patient followed them into the hospital, such that a person accustomed to think about medicines and cures continued to think about them but in less typical 'rational' ways. For some medical patients, though, it was the challenges of the medical market and the struggle to make their occupation pay that prompted a drastic decline in their mental health. Case-notes bear witness to the consequences of professional rivalry, and an occupational affinity between asylum doctors and their patients perhaps facilitated enhanced transcripts of patient testimony on such topics. The pressures of practice driven by market concerns, of jeopardised solvency, and the strain of supporting a professional identity all feature among case notes.

The experiences of medical men as patients need not be considered exclusively through the prism of institutional case notes, however. The same men can be tracked through censuses, vital registration, and other genealogical materials. What is more, the public identity of the former or even future practitioner can be traced in trade directories and newspapers. The capacity of men to resume professional life after a period of acknowledged mental disturbance, even if that episode was concealed from potential patients, was limited. Regained mental health did not necessarily permit a return to the rigours of professional life and, even if it did, the reputational damage or loss of confidence in a practitioner who had been absent might prove insuperable. Nonetheless participants in the nineteenth-century medical market did not enjoy perfect knowledge of that market; a man might resume practice in a different town, county or country without having to face down the potential stigma of being known as a former patient.

The research that follows provides a means to test the validity of these multiple assumptions and to set the numbers of doctors who were themselves diagnosed 'insane' into context. The chapter will begin by considering the permeability of different institutions to medical patients across England and Wales by a simple count of asylum patients whose former occupation was listed as medical in the census of 1881. This introductory survey provides a setting for a closer, detailed study of 165 practitioners who were admitted to one or more county, borough, private or criminal insane asylums up to 1890. The detailed study focuses on seventeen institutions including some of those presumed most likely to hold medical men by virtue of their offering private or charitable accommodation. How were admissions and the resulting cases of medical patients captured, and how far do they attribute incarceration to professional stress? How did asylum superintendents react to the prospect of their medical patients returning to professional endeavour, and was successful resumption of practice a reality for men who were discharged 'cured'? What happened when encounters between doctors on both sides of the treatment divide spilled over into the public domain? Is it possible to discern the reactions of the general public to evidence of practitioners' instability and weaknesses via press reporting?

Medical patients in English and Welsh asylums in 1881

The institutional options available for the care of the insane varied according to the fees that families could afford.[11] For those with little or no money to spare, there were the county 'pauper' asylums which charged patients to Poor Law Unions or levied modest fees for paying places. The range of fees was more diverse among the private licensed houses, which were frequently small-scale and potentially exclusive; Ticehurst asylum was undeniably elite and, depending on their wealth, residents might pay in excess of 1,000 guineas a year for the benefits of a place, but the majority of licensed houses commanded more moderate fees of up to £150 per patient per year.[12] The numbers of these establishments naturally fluctuated over the nineteenth century; there were eighty-six in 1819 (thirty-seven located in Middlesex) but only fifty-nine at the time of the 1881 census (that were noticeably more dispersed across the provinces).[13] It is quite likely that market pressures forced the consolidation of the private house 'market' in the face of increased supply from county asylums. In addition there were charity hospitals funded by endowment or subscription that accommodated greater numbers than the private houses but fewer than the county asylums; these could offer fee bursaries or exemptions. In this way, the variety of settings ranged from the domestic through to the large-scale asylums.[14]

Table 5.1 Medical patients in institutions for the insane in 1881

Institution	Number of medical patients
York Lunatic Asylum	7
St Andrew's Hospital Northampton	6
West Riding of Yorkshire Asylum, Ecclesfield	5
Carmarthen, Cardigan and Pembrokeshire Joint Counties Asylum	4
Broadmoor Criminal Lunatic Asylum	4
Middlesex County Asylum, Hanwell	3
St Luke's Hospital Middlesex	3
Bethlem Hospital	3
County or borough asylums accommodating one or two medical patients each	18
Charity lunatic hospitals accommodating one or two medical patients each	6
Private licensed houses accommodating one or two medical patients each	22

A snapshot of the choice of establishments made by medical patients and their families can be confirmed via the institutional listings within census returns (Table 5.1).

A comparison of the 137 asylums listed in appendix 'P' of the 35th annual report of the Commissioners in Lunacy with the contemporaneous 1881 census has located all but eight of the extant asylums. A survey of the inmates in each place identifies eighty-one medical men under confinement across forty-three establishments. Of the eighty-one men identified, sixty were physicians, surgeons or general practitioners, while twenty-one were medical students or assistants. No institution accommodated more than seven of these patients at any one time in 1881 and, as might be supposed given their greater capacities, the county asylums and charity hospitals tended to account for the highest numbers. The York asylum and St Andrew's at Northampton were the most popular destinations for medical patients, and both happened to be charitably rather than publicly funded. Even so, the presence of the Ecclesfield county asylum in Yorkshire in Table 5.1, among other county and some borough institutions, provides further confirmation that the 'pauper' lunatic asylums were not exclusively reserved for the impoverished but were also utilised by families of the middle-income 'insane'. This was despite the fact that over the second half of the nineteenth century private patients were increasingly likely to be removed from county asylums.[15] Medical patients were proportionately more likely to enter entirely private establishments, however, since a quarter of them were found in licensed houses (where licensed houses supplied only 9 percent of all male institutional places).[16] This data testifies to the demand for affordable, private or charity places for unstable members of the middle class, later expressed in the popularity of the Holloway sanatorium.[17]

The distribution of medical patients across individual institutions goes some way to conceal their geographical spread, which broadly conformed to the overall distribution of practitioners and medical students across England and Wales. Around a third of all practitioners and students were located in London or its constituent counties of Middlesex, Surrey, and Kent, as were just under a third of medical patients. Yorkshire and Lancashire also featured concentrations of resident doctors; the former is somewhat over-represented as the destination for medical patients, while the latter is under-represented. Numbers for other counties are rather too small for firm conclusions. Therefore geographical spread alone does not hint at regional or local foci of stress in the medical marketplace.

Medical patients in England

The admissions registers and case notes of eleven county asylums, one city institution, one private licensed house, three charitable hospitals, and Broadmoor asylum for the criminally insane, with locations ranging from Exeter in the south-west of England to the North Riding of Yorkshire in the north-east, have been analysed to learn the details of medical cases for all of the years when records survive up to 1890.[18] These hospitals were chosen for the quality of their records and their representation of different types of institution.[19] Twelve were founded as county or city pauper asylums. Cheshire, Devonshire, Gloucestershire, Leicestershire, Nottinghamshire, Staffordshire, and North Riding asylums were created under the auspices of the permissive legislation of 1808 (albeit that the North Riding hospital did not open until 1847). Birmingham,

Derbyshire, Lincolnshire, Warwickshire, and Worcestershire asylums were founded following the statutory requirement to make provision for the insane from 1845. Northamptonshire's St Andrew's Hospital was both a charitable foundation and the first *de facto* county asylum without conforming to either the 1808 or the 1845 Act.[20] A mixed-funding model incorporating charity was used in Nottingham, and the North Riding asylum took significant numbers of paying patients which helped to subsidise the costs of pauper patients; but the Lincoln, Wonford, York and Northampton hospitals were funded exclusively by charity and the latter was also explicitly designed to benefit the middle and upper classes, to spare them the ignominy of a pauper institution.[21] As a result of this policy, St Andrew's made a significant difference to the supply of places available to medical patients and accounted for 25 percent of all the medically related admissions in these asylums.[22] Only Barnwood House was run wholly as a private, entrepreneurial concern, and it too took a significant number of medical patients given the mere thirty-one years covered by sources.

The 171 admissions in Table 5.2 related to 165 individual medical men who experienced life in one of these asylums.[23] There are some distinctive features of practitioners' tenure as inpatients which mean that they tended to fit one of three models of institutional career. One was the short-lived stay prior to death. Around 20 percent of men were admitted and died within two years (although typically within a much shorter time). One example of this trajectory would be Henry Day, a surgeon admitted to the Leicestershire asylum in March 1859, who died on 7 May in the same year. He was in all likelihood suffering the final stages of tertiary syphilis, for which the cause of death was typically denoted 'general paralysis of the insane' or GPI (a diagnosis specifically cited in the case notes of six medical patients). The second model was a short- to mid-length stay of up to two years, when the patient was discharged relieved or cured, or transferred to an alternative setting; this was the experience of 33 percent of the men. Angus Cameron fitted this mould, since he stayed in the Warwickshire asylum for over seven months and on his discharge found his way back to medical practice in Somerset. The third model was of the long-stay resident, who remained in the same institution for two years or considerably longer before ultimately dying there, which was the case for 32 percent of the patient-doctors.[24] The patient who remained in hospital the longest was Peter

Table 5.2 Medical patients in institutions for the insane in selected English counties

Institution*	Physicians	Surgeons (+ medical practitioners)	Medical students (+ surgeons' apprentices)	Total
Barnwood House, Gloucestershire 1860–81	3	10	4 (+1)	18
Birmingham 1845–66	0	0	0	0
Broadmoor 1863–1890	1	5 (+1)	1	8
Cheshire 1845–90	0	1	1	2
Derbyshire 1851–90	0	2	0	2
Devonshire (later Exminster) 1845–90	0	2	0	2
Gloucestershire 1823–90	0	8	1	9
Leicestershire 1845–88	1	5	1	7
Lincoln (later The Lawn) 1845–90	0	8 (+3)	4	15
Lincolnshire (later St John's) 1852–77	0	4	0 (+1)	5
Northamptonshire 1838–90	10	20 (+3)	6	39
Nottinghamshire 1824–29	1	1	0	2
Staffordshire 1818–27, 1848–59, 1873–81, 1883–90	1	5 (+ 1)	1	8
Warwickshire 1852–90	2	0	0	2
Wonford House (formerly Bowhill House or St Thomas's Hospital) 1804–90	3	14(+1)	4	22
Worcestershire 1852–90	1	4	1	6
York 1846–89	1	8 (+1)	5	15
Yorkshire, North Riding 1847–90	0	3 (+5)	1	9
Total	24	115	32	171

* Different dates for each institution refer to the coverage of surviving admissions registers or case books.

Clements in Wonford House, residing there for over fifty-two years.[25] The remaining 15 percent of patients experienced an atypical stay, such as a long residence before transfer or discharge 'not improved'. This pattern means that if doctors did not die quickly after admission, or recover quite promptly and obtain discharge, they could expect a very protracted institutional stay. In this respect, the experience of medical patients was starkly at odds with those for patients of all occupations at the Buckinghamshire asylum, where half of patients went on to be discharged (most within twelve months of admission).[26] It is a profile which is consonant with modern understandings of medical psychiatric patients, however, who have been slow to seek formal help and generally neglectful of emotional problems.[27]

Medical patients were shunted between county asylums, private houses, and family care in exactly the same manner as their non-medical counterparts.[28] Sixty-eight, or 40 percent, of all medical patients were on record has having experience of another mental health setting (by the definitions of the day). At least nine were detained in gaols or workhouses prior to asylum admission (chiefly the Broadmoor patients), while a further six had been admitted to Bethlem.[29] Forty-one stayed in a private licensed house or a county asylum prior to their entry to one of the institutions under study. On departure, at least twenty-one were transferred from a county hospital to a different setting, ranging from a union workhouse to the Holloway Sanatorium. The most travelled of the doctors identified here was Paris Bradshawe, who by the age of thirty had already been admitted to five different establishments in the south-east of England, including Bethlem and a private house at Epsom.

The decision to conflate the experiences of patients in Broadmoor with those of other institutions might be regarded as idiosyncratic, given the criminality of that hospital's clientele. Victorian contemporaries certainly regarded it as a place apart, from which patients would never be released.[30] Yet, in practice, the experience Broadmoor offered to patients had more parallels with other asylums than with prisons. In common with other large establishments it ran a farm, and had other resources which fulfilled the dual function of employing patients and supplying the hospital's domestic needs.[31] Like private licensed houses, it encompassed different grades of accommodation to cater for people from prosperous families.[32] Patients did sometimes emerge prior to death: of all men admitted from 1863 who were not still resident in 1900, 9 percent had been discharged and 44 percent had been transferred to alternative institutions.[33] Broadmoor was more secure than was usual for county asylums, and staffing levels were typically higher, but it self-consciously styled itself in the 'asylum spirit'.[34] Men who were sent there may therefore have recognised little difference between an asylum *per se* and this new type of hospital for the criminally insane. There were probably many more differences between an elite private house, such as Ticehurst, and a poor borough asylum than there were between asylums in general and Broadmoor.

The admissions data elaborate on the geographical picture gleaned from the 1881 census, in that some practitioners were admitted to institutions specifically because they were not close to home. Privacy, with the scope to conceal the nature of a man's illness from his neighbours and patients, was presumably desirable if at all possible since it could limit reputational damage. John Hewitt, for instance, was admitted to the Staffordshire asylum in September 1888, at some distance from his home and practice in Manchester. He was discharged the following March 'in a perfect state of health both mentally and bodily', but when his illness recurred in July his family acted again on the same policy; by then living at Parkstone in Dorset, he was admitted to Wonford House in Devon.[35] This strategy is only evident for a small minority of medical patients, but echoes patterns of admissions of medical professionals elsewhere in Europe and in the twentieth century.[36] The pattern of admissions suggests, therefore, that privacy was a potential concern, but one usually trumped by the nearness of asylum provision to the doctor's home.

The professional background and experiences of medical men admitted to asylums cannot be characterised simply. They ranged very widely from the individual who was barely functional outside of the asylum to the high-profile professional exemplar. John Daniel was admitted to the Derbyshire asylum in June 1853 and may never have practised medicine. The 1851 census described him as 'M.R.C.S. London not practising' and his case notes elaborated 'his attainments are of the most meagre kind. Indeed it is difficult to believe than anyone with his peculiarly slender knowledge should have ever been enrolled as a Member of a scientific body.'[37] In contrast, Cornelius Suckling's qualifications were impeccable and the roster of his professional responsibilities was lengthy, including poor-law duties and teaching obstetrics at Queen's College Birmingham.[38] Similarly, there is no clear pattern of admissions among men who suffered or were anxious about financial failure. 'Money Mania' may have been a feature of professional stress, but it was not cited regularly in medical certificates, asylum admissions registers or subsequent case notes.[39] What is clear though is that, contrary to Oppenheim's claim, men who had made a career from the care of the insane were not prominent among the doctors admitted to asylums. Just three men fit this profile, even remotely. James Pownell ran a licensed house at Calne in Wiltshire before his conviction for murder and eventual transfer to Broadmoor, whereas Edwin Bishop possibly ran his own unlicensed institution for female patients at Culworth Hall near Banbury prior to admission at Northampton; Samuel Hine plausibly fell into this small group too, as a patient in Barnwood House briefly in 1869–70 but with an 'imbecile' boarder in his own home by 1881.[40] It was not treating the insane that rendered doctors mad, suggesting that the problem lay instead with the pursuit of medicine more generally.

Thirty-two of the men were medical students, predominantly aged in their late teens or early twenties. The aetiology of some disorders suggests that young males are notably vulnerable to the onset of mental illnesses. Men who would be diagnosed in the twenty-first century as schizophrenic or bipolar, for example, might in the nineteenth-century context have been subjected to asylum admission. What is more, in the modern era, medical students are recognised as unduly vulnerable to psychiatric morbidity.[41] A handful of these students were admitted explicitly for anxiety about study or overwork.[42] Therefore, medical students might be regarded as under-represented among these patients in purely numeric terms, but their relative absence is perhaps suggestive of the differential judgements being made about behaviours among qualified, as opposed to unqualified, practitioners. Wild, promiscuous or drunken exploits among medical students might be deprecated by their contemporaries but were not necessarily seen as evidence of mental aberration.[43] A riotous demeanour as a medical student might, however, be cited as a contributory cause to poor mental health in later life. John Young must have excelled himself to acquire a reputation as 'one of the most dissolute young men in London', but his 'years of indulgence in excessive drinking' were blamed for his eventual diagnosis of brain inflammation.[44]

The diverse career profiles and backgrounds of these medical patients support the idea that the strains of professional life were diffuse, because no specialism or geographical location proved unduly difficult. An obvious risk of stress for all men, though, lay in failing to recognise wrong-doing by others. One extraordinary case of 'insanity' emanated from the prosecution of William Palmer discussed briefly in Chapter 4, and so illustrates the potential for poisoning cases in general and Palmer's example in particular to have inspired pervasive and unexpected effects on individuals and the profession as a whole. William Gibson was admitted to the York Lunatic Asylum in May 1857, supposedly suffering from mania arising from losses in railway speculation.[45] At first sight, therefore, Gibson represented a rare example of a medical man for whom financial loss was a significant cause of mental ill health. His case notes tell a fuller and more poignant story. When Palmer first poisoned John Parsons Cook, the murder for which he was convicted, the two men were in Shrewsbury for the races. Gibson was working in Shrewsbury at the time, and was the practitioner who attended Cook in the first instance. The case notes report 'After Palmer's trial the whole affair appears to have continually preyed on his mind … He often talks about Palmer and Cook, saying that if he had been allowed to have his way, Cook would not have been permitted to go to Rugeley, because he knew that Palmer had poisoned him.'[46] Failure to avert a murder by a fellow medical man induced in Gibson unmanageable feelings of guilt. In this way, Palmer's conviction and that of other poisoners had as-yet untold implications for the story of English medical men.[47]

Gibson's example further suggests that the challenges of medicine *per se* may have been exacerbated somewhat by the personalities of the individuals who made it their occupation. In the twenty-first century, there is good reason to suppose that medical training and practice are undertaken by ambitious, competitive, and self-critical people who are not always well placed to deal with stress.[48] The detailed evidence of the case notes cannot support a retrospective allocation of personality type (which would perhaps be a more egregious error than even retrodiagnosis) but it certainly provides repeated allusion to the pressures of collaboration or competition between doctors and the potency of self-reproach.

Case notes, superintendents, and medical patients

The case notes compiled by asylum superintendents provide one way to assess the reactions of doctors to mental fragility among their peers. Case-notes for asylums were kept patchily from the 1820s and more reliably from 1845.[49] As with any other source, the reading of case notes must be cautious and critical, preferably augmented by sources speaking to the period before and after admission. Disparities can be exposed between different elements of the institutional collection, as between competing interpretations of information at admission, different understandings of mental illness by successive medical superintendents, or contradictions between warder testimony and patients' accounts. Andrews has argued convincingly that the case note element of a hospital archive will speak most reliably to the perceptions of the medical officers, and only tangentially or unevenly to the patient experience.[50]

The reactions of asylum superintendents to their medical patients were mixed. They never accused fellow practitioners of malingering, but might reflect rather sceptically on their suffering. At Barnwood House, Thomas Buchanan was described as a former hospital surgeon who had suffered with his nerves over many years, becoming agitated by professional difficulty or private perplexity. Yet his case notes mention in an aside 'in fact his position in life has been easy and prosperous and his professional career made less harrowing than that of the majority of practitioners'.[51] To be harrowed, then, was the norm.

Typically, superintendents' attitudes seem to have been regulated less by the former careers of their patients as by the perceived likelihood of their recovery. Where men were suffering from tertiary syphilis or where admission was swiftly followed by death there was little prospect of a relationship based on shared education and professional experience. A longer stay and a remission of symptoms, however, offered the opportunity for collaboration over treatment, exchanges of books and ideas, or a form of professional counselling. Charles Herbert was effectively permitted to prescribe for himself on at least one occasion after admission to the Northampton Asylum in September 1862.[52] Both Angus Cameron at the Warwickshire asylum in 1873 and John Hewitt at Staffordshire 1888–89 spoke to or wrote to their superintendents about their intention to return to practice.[53]

The most successful and concerted attempt to support a fellow practitioner among these examples was made by William Orange, superintendent of Broadmoor. Surgeon's assistant Charles Grimes was admitted to Broadmoor from Newgate following his trial for attempted murder in 1876. His routine use of alcohol and opiates was blamed for his developing a number of false beliefs, which ended in his shooting two policemen through the door of his lodgings.[54] Grimes spent nearly a year in Broadmoor 'without exhibiting a single sign of relapse, or indeed a single bad symptom' before writing to Orange formally to request his release into the custody of a relative.[55] Orange took up Grimes's case with enthusiasm and sought permission for his release from the Home Secretary. Whitehall was willing to countenance a release, but only on condition that Grimes was discharged to the care and at the cost of his brother – in New Zealand. Fortunately for Grimes, his brother was willing to assume this responsibility, sending £25 to defray the cost of a one-way passage to the Antipodes. This left Grimes with one further practical hurdle, to find a ship willing to accept him as a passenger. The shipping firm approached by Orange initially returned Grimes' fare money and refused to transport him on the grounds that he could not categorically be prevented from consuming alcohol while in transit.[56] Nonetheless, Orange was determined to defend Grimes, and wrote the following day to reiterate his confidence in his patient, adding 'I may remind you that a patient from this asylum named John Green went out to Canterbury under similar circumstances in one of your vessels in March 1870.'[57] The company relented and Grimes sailed for New Zealand in early October.[58]

In contrast, the most poignant and abortive attempt to restore a medical man to his mental faculties via shared medical knowledge was tried in Derbyshire by John Hitchman, a former student of John Conolly and in 1856 President of the Association of Medical Officers of Asylums and Hospitals for the insane.[59] Hitchman was the superintendent of the Derbyshire asylum for twenty-one years and so supervised the admission and ensuing patient career of Frederick Wright, a Derby surgeon who was transferred to the asylum from the town gaol.[60] Wright had exhibited erratic behaviour for some time, but things reached a head when he was bound over to keep the peace towards the other medical practitioners of the town. He believed that his fellow doctors were conspiring against him and became violent in consequence. He arrived at the Derbyshire asylum on 11 March 1856 and was still there at the time of Hitchman's retirement in February 1872.

Hitchman's case notes suggest that, from the first, he was compelled to manage Wright's violence towards his fellow patients. From the time of his admission to the early 1860s Wright is recorded as having successfully hit, kicked or knocked down a number of other inmates. Wright was able to talk sensibly, but the people around him were quickly incorporated into his world view (in other words, implicated in the supposed conspiracy against him) at which point he became a danger to them. In particular he considered that his good reputation was being maligned. He would approach strangers and expostulate 'Why have you traduced my professional character? What have you been saying respecting my midwifery practice?'[61] Hitchman perceived ample grounds for empathy with Wright as a fellow middle-class professional. In October 1858 he reflected

> It is a distressing case – because apart from these especial delusions – that is towards parties for whom he entertains no morbid dislike – he is amiable enough if they speak to him; and as an educated man he feels his detention among illiterate and rude paupers to be a cruel act; I consult his feelings as far as possible because I know that his brain is in a very unhealthy state. I give him his choice of Wards – but in each one, he soon discovers an Enemy – and becomes dangerous from this circumstance.[62]

Indeed, Wright was capable of such seeming rationality that Hitchman quickly became alerted to Wright's ability to smear the innocent. Wright would routinely make allegations against his keepers of 'a serious character', including the murder of patients who died. He did so 'with such plausibility, that it requires some investigation to elucidate their real nature' and as such might genuinely 'prove dangerous to the reputation of his attendants'.[63] This combination of the prospect of rational conversation and unpredictable aggression eventually took their toll on Hitchman, and by the February of 1860 he was beginning to realise that the amelioration of Wright's case may well be impossible. In a very personal outburst, quite uncharacteristic of generic case notes, Hitchman wrote

> Daily for more than four years – I have endeavoured by unremitting kindness – by unswerving good humour – by the daily offer of a change of room, of Ward, of scene – by the use of my Library – and every other

> possible expedient to gain his confidence – but in vain; and latterly he rarely addresses me, by any better term, than 'Scamp' or 'Rascal'.[64]

Their relationship broke down entirely in the early 1860s when Wright eventually became violent to Hitchman himself, by hitting him on the neck. Hitchman reacted to this so negatively that it seems he could no longer bring himself to interact with Wright at any level; Wright's case-notes cease on the day after the assault, and are not resumed until 1872 by Hitchman's successor.

Wright represents a well-documented example of practitioners whose delusions circled around conspiracy which could be expressive of professional jealousy or suspicions of wrong-doing by colleagues. The clarity of patient voices in such instances is always suspect, being muffled, mediated or silenced (in Wright's case) by their medical superintendents who feasibly had a vested interest in minimising allegations of genuine professional strife, even in private ledgers and case books. The stresses of the medical marketplace are most obviously evident in a handful of practitioners' concerns about irregular medicine, and specifically mesmerism. Doctors were not of course alone in developing elaborate ideas about the supposed power of mesmerism. Yet their profession was tangentially allied with practitioners of animal magnetism, mesmerism, and hypnotism, and as such some men clearly became fixated on this allegedly powerful but intangible force.[65] Mesmerism gave an additional fillip to the delusions of conspiracy since it allowed medical patients to construe their own situation as one of enforced subordination to the will of others. Evan Leyson, for example, was admitted to the Gloucestershire Asylum in 1855 convinced that he was under mesmeric influence, that people watched him with intent to do him injury, and that wires were placed across his bed for the purpose. He also attributed a suicide attempt to external instruction.[66]

Similarly, medical delusions of grandeur could mimic those of non-medical patients (in imagining possession of great wealth, inordinate power or royal title) but in selected cases took on a more exclusive occupational flavour. James Haslam in St Andrew's thought he had a cure for cholera in 1876, but more than one man believed that they had discovered a cure for all diseases.[67] William Tinney in Wonford House began his asylum career in 1850 boasting of his professional accomplishments, but had progressed by the time of his readmission in 1854 to a conviction that he could cure all diseases by breathing on the sick.[68] Conversely, practitioners might suffer crippling fear of professional incompetence or criminality. An apprehension of disgrace arising from professional malpractice haunted Francis Southam, admitted to St Andrew's asylum in 1874, and induced him to attempt suicide more than once.[69]

Hard evidence of occupational inadequacy close to home was particularly difficult for practitioners to bear. The death of a patient was regrettable, but the death of a patient who was also the doctor's own child might prove utterly insupportable. The repeated admissions of Frederick Warren to St Andrew's were attributed to the death of his daughter, and he was not alone.[70] Among devoted Victorian fathers the prospect of child death could be blamed for male insanity, and could even be seen to mitigate punishment for men whose acute anxiety inspired them to bring an end to tortuous uncertainty, namely by murdering their child themselves.[71] Medical training arguably added an extra impetus to feelings of despair and self-loathing when practitioners were unable to save their own children. In this way medical patients' mental distress was, like that of other men across the working and the middle class, linked to a loss of their sense of adult masculine identity.[72]

Patient voices and the press

The reactions of doctors themselves to their confinement, especially if they were adverse or negative, must largely be sought beyond case-notes since the official institutional transcript was unlikely to record them. There are occasional hints that patients perceived their admission with resentment. Herbert Williams at Gloucester initially refused to eat 'while in this Bastille', so invoking the standard nineteenth-century motif of oppression.[73] Francis Hudson was repeatedly admitted to the North Riding Asylum at his son's behest, and on the third occasion protested that he had been brought illegally and would sue.[74] Some professional patients also apprehended forces detrimental to their medical identity. Cornelius Suckling at Warwickshire tried to reason with his keepers on the grounds of lost income: 'he asked if he could not get out as he was losing £1000 a year by remaining here'.[75]

Yet a very negative response to asylum admission might plausibly be deemed rational (both from a modern and a contemporary perspective, given the Victorian preoccupation with potentially false asylum detentions), and one doctor took up this issue passionately as both a practitioner and a sometime patient. Francis Fox spent fourteen months in the Nottinghamshire asylum. He could not be identified via the asylum case books (which only survive for 1824–29) and so does not feature in Table 5.2. Instead, evidence of his experiences derives largely from his letters to the press.[76] Fox was a high-ranking member of the Derbyshire medical fraternity, as a physician who in the mid 1830s held an honorary appointment at the Derbyshire Infirmary. He hailed from an established local family; his father and namesake had also been a Derby doctor and two of his three brothers were also practitioners in the locality. Fox authored a number of articles for *The Lancet* and was noted for the interest he took in the working class.[77]

His reputation and standing underwent drastic revision, however, in 1836 when he started to make complaints about the conduct of the infirmary. His concerns were initially treated with the utmost care and inspired some enquiries about the treatment of both servants and patients in the Derbyshire Infirmary, but by the end of June the hospital's weekly board was beginning to react to Fox cautiously. Fox, for his part, mobilised the considerable following which he enjoyed among the working people of Derby to ensure their vocal support for his complaints. The infirmary board took drastic action and held a special general meeting on 2 August to propose the motion that Dr Fox be removed as a physician and governor, and his subscription be returned. The motion was carried by fifty-three votes to fourteen. There was then some debate at the infirmary about the legality of Fox's removal, in which Fox was publicly defended by his younger brother Douglas, but it was finally confirmed by a repeat vote in September.[78]

His public loss of face must have been difficult enough, but Fox's family were also about to move against him. Douglas seems to have become alarmed by Francis' behaviour, and eventually this concern gave rise to the latter's admission to the Nottinghamshire asylum in late autumn 1836. Fox's subsequent, detailed account of what occurred between the summer of 1836 and his release in December 1837 cannot be corroborated, but nonetheless he made a powerful, lucid, and very public statement of wrongful restraint. Fox wrote a series of over twenty letters and articles on the subject, published in *The Satirist* between November 1838 and December 1839, inspired by the publicity that autumn surrounding Richard Paternoster's false confinement in a private licensed asylum.[79] The choice of such a notorious mouthpiece may not have helped to agitate widespread support among the reading public. Indeed his revelations seem to have generated no interest for his case in the remainder of the lay press.[80] Yet, across his collected writings, Fox provides a coherent account of the controls placed on him at home and later his appalled reaction to the Nottinghamshire asylum. According to his recollection, on 10 August 1836 his brother Douglas suddenly began to treat him as though he were insane, specifically by locking him in a garret room and using bolts, bars, and handcuffs to ensure he remained in his room and strapped to his bed. Fox claims that his friends were not permitted to see him and that at least one 'keeper' employed by Douglas was turned away, from an unwillingness to impose such a drastic scheme of restraint. This treatment allegedly persisted for twelve days, whereupon Douglas is said to have sent Francis to Barrow on Trent for the restoration of his health in the hands of a 'keeper'. This arrangement persisted until 6 September when he was returned home and imprisoned once more. His amateur confinement only ended when he was conveyed to the asylum at Nottingham on 10 October by another younger brother, Archibald Fox.[81]

Francis recognised absolutely that his own angry responses were liable to be misinterpreted. He postulated

> ... if it be granted that it is within the range of possibility that I might have been in my senses all the time, I am fully convinced that every individual action can be shown to be consistent with a man of sound mind, having to deal with almost unheard of persecutions, misrepresentations, and barbarous cruelties! ... But when an individual is once stamped with even the name of lunatic, self-defence ceases to be defensible – every resistance is quoted as a proof of insanity.[82]

He went on to name and shame the doctors of Derby who authorised his incarceration by certificating his 'madness', but he reserved his most damning criticisms for the staff of the Nottinghamshire asylum, superintendent Andrew Blake and surgeon Thomas Powell. Blake he characterised as an army surgeon who obtained his post through patronage rather than ability. Powell was allegedly Blake's jackal, a failure in private practice 'who is better suited to certain occupations in the West Indies than to manage the delicate fabric of the mind'. These men were effectually unlimited in their actions, if Fox was right to describe the body of governors as unwilling to interfere 'from feelings of etiquette'.[83]

Fox's version of events is given some confirmation by a letter written in June 1839 by Andrew Blake to the Home Secretary Lord Russell.[84] Blake's stance is predictably defensive, but he did report that Fox's brother confined him at home until he became unduly violent and that Fox was discharged into the care of a brother in London (albeit disputing the circumstances of the release). Furthermore, some of the complaints that Fox had made against employees of the Derbyshire Infirmary, that had initiated the whole series of events, were eventually substantiated.[85] After the late 1830s Fox seems to have retained command of himself, living for some time in Derby and also in Charing Cross. He died at Camberwell in 1860 without obviously having been hospitalised again.[86]

Collectively, Fox's experiences are suggestive of the peculiarly vulnerable position of middle-class medical men once their mental health had been drawn into question. He was rapidly cast down in the opinion of his social and medical peers, such that in June he was seriously regarded as a physician and a man but by October he could be certified insane by his former colleagues (who were also, as Fox pointed out, his rivals for business). This is arguably an early demonstration of the high standards demanded of the personal and professional conduct of medical men. There was apparently insufficient room for eccentricity by Fox to be accommodated by his family or his acquaintances in Derby – he must either be treated as an equal or labelled as a madman. Ironically, his reputation was rehabilitated for posterity at the celebrations for the 60th anniversary of the opening of the Derbyshire Infirmary. At that safe distance of time, Francis was eulogised as among the men 'whose souls were centred in their profession, and against whom the tongue of slander could affix no stigma'.[87]

Fox's case was probably exacerbated by his feeling for, and influence among, the working class. Blake's letter to Lord Russell alleged that Fox had on one occasion assembled a crowd of thousands of Derby's ordinary citizens, an event which inspired the town to send for military reinforcements from the garrison at Nottingham. The event, if not the magnitude of the crowd, is confirmed by contemporary newspaper reports.[88] This raises the possibility that too much sympathy for the poor (especially if expressed in opposition to one's medical colleagues) could be construed as a form of mental aberration.[89]

Fox's decision to draw attention to his own asylum experiences was at odds with the reactions of most former patients and their family members. Practitioners and their families attempted to maintain a public face of sanity and competence even where this was a poor reflection of a person's perceived mental state. While there are no explicit explanations of this by families, the implications are clear: doctors would be stigmatised and their professional claims undermined if knowledge of their poor mental health became widely known. There was nothing to prevent the public maintenance of a professional presence while not actually capable of practice. Charles Beard was admitted to St Andrew's hospital in Northampton in 1886, was moved to an alternative asylum at the suggestion of the Lunacy Commissioners in 1889 'not improved', and he died at the Holloway Sanatorium in 1916.[90] Yet his family kept up his entries in the *Medical Register* throughout his terms as an asylum patient.[91] After he had effectively ceased to practice there was no reason for his repeated listing. Indeed, continued inclusion in the *Register*, and updating the entry, took a modicum of effort. But there was nothing to require the exclusion of a man by reason of illness. It was perhaps presumed that recovery was possible, and that any return to home life or even to work would benefit from continuous representation on the *Register*. Absence from the *Register* during life might also look as though a doctor had been subject to formal removal under the disciplinary processes of the General Medical Council, and so reflect poorly on his character, while continued presence might yield rewards for the maintenance of professional visibility. Even so, continued inclusion could also be construed as fairly misleading. Beard, for instance, was listed at home in Brighton for the 1887 *Register* (a year when he plainly spent the majority of his time at St Andrew's). His address was given as a private house in Shepherd's Bush throughout the 1890s and into the twentieth century (when it is highly questionable whether he was living at home continuously), but he or his family did not balk at giving his address as Virginia Water in 1915, presumably a concession to his admission to Holloway. At his death, *The Times* listed Charles' qualifications but made no allusion to illness.[92]

The reaction of the broader public to these medical admissions, among contemporaries who might be patients but never fellow practitioners, can only be recovered partially and by inference. After all, there was hardly any reason why one person's admission to a hospital would give rise to a newsworthy report, except in the most dramatic of circumstances. Consequently, discernible reactions arise only where a practitioner's illness was forced upon public notice, where asylum admission gave rise to immediate or eventual public consequences. The two physicians admitted to the Warwickshire asylum provide some of the only evidence available here. Cornelius Suckling (Figure 5.1) held a variety of official posts at the onset of his illness, among them the role of medical officer to the Birmingham Bluecoat School. Given Suckling's prolonged absence from home, he had to be replaced in his multiple official roles, but nowhere in the Birmingham press was his 'serious illness' given further elaboration.[93] Reportage surrounding the death of Angus Cameron is even more poignant. After his departure from the Warwick asylum, Cameron pursued a successful career in Bath, first by gaining a post at the Batheaston dispensary and later in private practice.

Figure 5.1 Cornelius Benson Suckling. Warwickshire Record Office 1664/637 Warwickshire asylum case book, 1898–1909

But his mental health obviously remained fragile because in 1878 he took hydrocyanic acid and successfully committed suicide. The inquest heard evidence from Cameron's brother, Alexander, who reported that Angus had been 'under restraint' following the death of his only two children. The jury found that he had acted during 'temporary insanity' – clearly a misnomer whatever the conventions in relation to suicide verdicts at this time.[94] Reports of the inquest beyond the local papers for Bristol suppressed the references to his period of mental illness. *The Times* went so far as to claim 'None of his friends had the slightest suspicion that his mind was affected.'[95] This admittedly slender evidence begins to suggest that wherever information about the jeopardised mental health of a practitioner was somewhat propelled into the public, the press did nothing to capitalise upon it and may have actively occluded the facts. Even if this is a fair inference, though, it remains unclear whether doctors' ill-health was shielded from motives of class cohesion or whether this sort of protection was specific to the medical profession.

Conclusion

A tiny proportion of medical practitioners experienced life as a patient in an asylum, but this group is significant because it represents some dimensions of the difficulties facing doctors in a period of professionalisation. There was scope for many more men to suffer than merely those who were hospitalised, and the experiences of the few exemplify the concerns and stresses of many more. This is particularly noteworthy because the case notes of medical patients dwell decisively on all aspects of professional life, from medical education to maintaining an established practice. Their stresses were not merely human, personal, domestic, and familial, but sharply occupational.

It is clear that these men were admitted to a range of institutions, but that assumptions about the preference for private licensed houses over charity hospitals or 'pauper' asylums can be confirmed. Doctors who treated the insane were no more at risk than their fellows of serious mental ill-health. Medical superintendents of asylums who found themselves responsible for the treatment of their former colleagues exhibited a fairly muted response to medical patients who were not likely to recover. Unusually, John Hitchman became significantly engaged with his patient Frederick Wright. The stormy and sudden ending to their shared experience is perhaps a testament to the challenges facing any arrangement other than a clear division between doctors and patients, no matter what their former occupations. Medical patients could, and sometimes did, express considerable aversion to their institutional surroundings, but only Francis Fox was so fortunate as to secure his release and then find a public outlet for his anger. The potential gravity of his account was dissipated, however, by the fact that his correspondence was supported by a satirical, lay publication rather than in any medical journal, and by his failure to capitalise on his experiences in the manner of Richard Paternoster.

Wright and Fox are the two most prominent examples of asylum admission under substantial external coercion (one was delivered from gaol, the other forcibly admitted by his brothers) and both men expressed vocal or violent resentment towards medical colleagues as complicit in their diagnosis and detention. The inter-personal competition that was an inherent feature of the medical marketplace was intensified in these two men's perceptions to assume an overwhelming character. It was not the specifics of their practice, but rather the pursuit of medicine *per se* that informed their obsessions.

The seeming evasion of public notice for Fox's story in the 1830s, and his ideological inclusion in the medical fold in Derby after his death, is echoed by the way the press avoided drawing undue attention to the instability or prior incarceration of the two physicians at Warwickshire in the 1870s. Practitioners themselves and their families may have been highly protective of their professional reputations, to the extent of maintaining representation on the *Medical Register* when most or all future prospect of practising medicine had disappeared, but the press and public were not necessarily seeking every opportunity to undermine them. Indeed they seem to have been similarly, if not equally, anxious to shield doctors from personal criticisms. The newspaper evidence relating to practitioners who were ill echoes the response of the press to allegations of serious sexual assault surveyed in Chapter 4, where acquittals were met with loud congratulations. If this is an accurate reflection of public attitudes, it would suggest that the process of rising status in medicine was promoted by failure, as well as by success. Success received plaudits, and failures (whether in criminal prosecution or, as here, the perceived failure to maintain sanity) encouraged complicity and silence, an absence of prurient inquiry, and a willingness consciously to gloss misfortune.

Notes

1 Portions of this chapter were first published as A.E. Tomkins, 'Mad doctors?: the significance of medical practitioners admitted as patients to the first English county asylums up to 1890', *History of Psychiatry* 23:4 (2012), pp. 437–53. I am grateful to the *History of Psychiatry* for permission to reprint them here.

2 Opiate addition was not reported as a priority cause of medical asylum admissions, although this may be a significant omission from the case notes; see T. Parssinen, *Secret Passions, Secret Remedies. Narcotic Drugs in British Society 1820–1930* (Manchester: Manchester University Press, 1983), pp. 83–4; J.V. Kragh, 'Women, Men and the Morphine Problem, 1870–1955', in T. Ortiz-Gómez and M.J. Santesmases (eds), *Gendered Drugs and Medicine. Historical and Socio-cultural Perspectives* (Farnham: Ashgate, 2014), pp. 177–98; M.F. a'Brook et al., 'Psychiatric illness in the medical profession', *British Journal of Psychiatry* 113 (1967), 1013.

3 J. Oppenheim, *Shattered Nerves. Doctors, Patients and Depression in Victorian England* (Oxford: Oxford University Press, 1991), pp. 153–4.

4 C. MacKenzie, *Psychiatry for the Rich. A History of Ticehurst Private Asylum, 1792–1917* (London: Routledge, 1992), pp. 130, 132, 153.

5 Stress was not a diagnostic criterion for asylum admissions until the early twentieth century; M. Jackson, *The Age of Stress. Science and the Search for Stability* (Oxford: Oxford University Press, 2013), p. 45.

6 M.S. Micale, *Hysterical Men. The Hidden History of Male Nervous Illness.* (Cambridge, Mass.: Harvard University Press, 2008), p. 57.

7 A. Scull, 'Museums of Madness revisited', in *The Insanity of Place/The Place of Insanity. Essays on the History of Psychiatry* (London: Routledge, 2006), pp. 63–84, on p. 79.

8 J. Walton, 'Casting Out and Bringing Back in Victorian England: Pauper Lunatics, 1840–70', in W. Bynum, R. Porter, and M. Shepherd (eds), *The Anatomy of Madness: Essays in the History of Psychiatry* (London: Tavistock, 1985), pp. 132–46.

9 J. Melling and B. Forsyth, *The Politics of Madness: The State, Insanity and Society in England, 1845–1914* (London: Routledge, 2006), p. 146.

10 J. Andrews, 'Case notes, case histories, and the patient's experience of insanity at Gartnavel Royal Asylum, Glasgow, in the nineteenth century', *Social History of Medicine* 11:2 (1998), pp. 255–81, on p. 266.

11 A. Shepherd, *Institutionalising the Insane in Nineteenth-Century England* (London: Pickering and Chatto, 2014) for a recent comparison of two contrasting Surrey institutions.
12 P.P. *Copy of the thirty third report of the Commissioners in Lunacy to the Lord Chancellor* (1879), p. 113.
13 P.P. *Return of the number of houses in each county… licensed for the reception of lunatics* (1819).
14 Scull, 'Museums of Madness revisited', pp. 80–1.
15 L.D. Smith, 'Social Class in the Lunatic Asylum', in O. Ashton, R. Fyson, and S. Roberts (eds), *The Duty of Discontent* (London: Mansell, 1995), pp. 142–66, on p. 162.
16 The total male occupancy of all licensed houses amounted to 2,031 filled places, in contrast to the 20,712 filled male places in rate-funded or charity asylums. This total of 22,743 places for male lunatics excludes places for males deemed 'idiots' or 'imbeciles' and therefore lacking former occupations.
17 A.C. Shepherd, 'Mental Health Care and Charity for the Middling Sort. Holloway Sanatorium 1885–1900', in A. Borsay and P. Shapley (eds) *Medicine, Charity and Mutual Aid. The Consumption of Health and Welfare in Britain, c. 1550–1950* (Aldershot: Ashgate, 2007), pp. 162–83.
18 This included the case of William Chesters Minor; see S. Winchester, *The Surgeon of Crowthorne* (London: Penguin, 1999).
19 Berkshire Record Office, D/H14 Broadmoor Hospital, D1/1/1/1–2 admissions registers 1863–1900; Birmingham City Library, 12/1, 12/2, 12/2a, Birmingham asylum case books 1845–50, 1850–55, 1855–66; Borthwick Institute, CLF 6/2/1/1–8 Clifton Hospital (formerly North Riding Asylum) male admissions registers 1847–96, BOO 6/1/33 Bootham Park Hospital (formerly York Lunatic Asylum) admissions forms and reception orders 1846–89, BOO 6/2/3/2–6 registries of admissions 1850–90; Cheshire Archives, ZHW/128–131, Chester asylum admissions registers 1845–90 (private patients), 1865–73, 1873–82, 1882–90; Derbyshire Record Office, D 1658/1/2–6, Derby asylum admissions registers 1853–61, 1861–67, 1872–77, 1877–84, 1884–90; Devon Record Office 3769A/H3/1–6 Exminster admissions registers 1845–91 and 3769A/H18/1–2 Exminster discharge registers 1868–95; Devon Record Office 3992F/H19 Wonford House register of patients admitted 1831–69, 3992F/H20/1–3 Wonford House registeries of admissions 1804–73, 3992F/H32/1–5 Wonford House case books 1873–99; Gloucestershire Archives HO22/63/3 Gloucestershire asylum admissions register 1880–86, HO22/63/37 Gloucestershire asylum admissions register for private patients 1845–1906, HO22/70/1–3, case books of

private and pauper patients 1823–28, 1828–37, 1837–41, D3725 box 127 Barnwood House admissions register 1881–90, D3725 box 134 admissions register 1860–81,; Leicestershire and Rutland Record Office DE 3533/185–95, Leicestershire and Rutland asylum case books 1845–48, 1848–52, 1852–56, 1856–58, 1858–61, 1861–65, 1865–68, 1868–70, 1870–73, 1873–77, 1877–80, DE 3533/217 Leicestershire and Rutland asylum charity case book 1839–88; Lincolnshire Archives, LAWN 2/6/1–2 Lincoln Asylum admission registers 1845–90 and HOSP/ST JOHNS/2/2/1–4 Lincolnshire Asylum admission registers 1852–77; St Andrew's Healthcare Archives Northampton R2–4, Northampton General Lunatic Asylum registers of admissions 1845–66, 1866–74, 1874–88, CL1 Northampton General Lunatic Asylum case book 1838–41; Nottinghamshire Archives SO/HO/1/9/1 Nottinghamshire asylum superintendent's case book 1824–29; Staffordshire Record Office D 4585/4 Staffordshire asylum register of admissions 1873–81, D 4585/6 Staffordshire asylum patients' case book 1818–27, D 5379/2/4 Staffordshire asylum male patients' case book 1848–59, D 4553 Staffordshire asylum male patients' case book 1883–94; Warwickshire Record Office CR 1664/416 Warwickshire asylum register of admissions 1876–94, CR 2379/1 Warwickshire asylum register of admissions 1852–75; Worcestershire Record Office B/A10127 Ref 499:9 Worcestershire asylum patient case books volumes 5, 6, 8, 10, 14, and 15 covering 1858–60, 1860–61, 1862–63, 1863–64, 1868–70, 1870–72, B/A 10371 Ref 499:9 Worcestershire asylum patients' case book volume 9 covering 1863–71, B/A 13237 Ref b599:4 Worcestershire asylum male patients' case book volume 18 covering 1873–82, Worcestershire asylum admissions register 1857–1906 with index of private patients. I am indebted to David Helm for information about medical patients in Barnwood House.

20 C. Smith, 'Parsimony, power, and prescriptive legislation: the politics of pauper lunacy in Northamptonshire, 1845–1876', *Bulletin of the History of Medicine* 81 (2007), pp. 359–85.

21 R. Ellis, 'The asylum, the poor law and the growth of county asylums in nineteenth-century Yorkshire', *Northern History* 45:2 (2008), pp. 279–93, on pp. 289–90; Staffordshire Record Office, D 25/A/G/1417, printed notice of the Northampton Asylum for the middle and upper classes, n.d. but after 1863.

22 St Andrew's remained prominent in a twentieth-century study into psychiatric illness in doctors; a'Brook et al., 'Psychiatric illness', p. 1013 in which 46 of 114 medical inpatients studied were treated at the Northampton hospital 1954–64.

23 Six men each attended two of the asylums in the cohort.

24 The length of stay by four men or 3 percent of the cohort could not be determined.
25 Devon Record Office 3992F/H15/1–5 Wonford House case books 1845–72, 3992F/H 32/1 Wonford House case book 1873–77.
26 D. Wright, 'The Discharge of Pauper Lunatics from County Asylums in mid-Victorian Britain. The Case of Buckinghamshire, 1853–1872', in J. Melling and B. Forsythe (eds), *Insanity, Institutions and Society, 1800–1914* (London: Routledge, 1999), pp. 93–112, on p. 108.
27 a'Brook et al., 'Psychiatric illness', p. 1013.
28 Ellis, 'The asylum', p. 285.
29 By the mid nineteenth century, Bethlem had shifted away from treating only paupers in order to cater for a more socially elevated clientele; C. Gale and R. Howard (eds), *Presumed Curable. An Illustrated Casebook of Victorian Psychiatric Patients in Bethlem Hospital* (Petersfield: Wrightson Biomedical Publishing, 2003), p. 5.
30 D.E.B. Weiner, '"This coy and secluded dwelling". Broadmoor Asylum for the Criminally Insane', in L. Topp, J.E. Moran, and J. Andrews (eds), *Madness, Architecture and the Built Environment. Psychiatric Spaces in Historical Context* (London: Routledge, 2007), pp. 131–48, on pp. 144–5.
31 Topp et al., *Madness, Architecture,* p. 140.
32 Topp et al., *Madness, Architecture,* p. 142.
33 J. Shepherd, '"One of the best fathers until he went out of his mind": paternal child-murder, 1864–1900', *Journal of Victorian Culture* 18:1 (2013), pp. 17–35, on p. 30.
34 L. Spurrier, 'The Broadmoor archive: a preliminary survey of the historic records of Broadmoor Hospital and their research potential', *Archives* 123 (2010), pp. 48–62, on pp. 50, 57.
35 Staffordshire Record Office, D 4553 Staffordshire County Asylum male case book 1883–94; Devon Record Office, 3992F/H/32/5 Wonford House male case book 1885–26.
36 Kragh, 'Women, Men and the Morphine Problem'; T.M. Hassan, S.O. Ahmed, A.S. White, and N. Galbraith, 'A postal survey of doctors' attitudes to becoming mentally ill', *Clinical Medicine* 9:4 (2009), pp. 327–32, on p. 329.
37 N. A., RG 9; Derbyshire Record Office, D 1658/11/1, Derbyshire asylum case book 1851–53.
38 *London and Provincial Medical Directory* (1875), p. 632.
39 H. Goodman, '"Madness and Masculinity": Male Patients in London Asylums and Victorian Culture', in T. Knowles and S. Trowbridge (eds), *Insanity and the Lunatic Asylum in the Nineteenth Century* (London: Pickering and Chatto, 2015), pp. 149–65, on pp. 154–8.

40 Berkshire Record Office, D2/2/1/230 Broadmoor Hospital case file of Dr James Pownall; P.P. *Copy of the ninth report of the Commissioners in Lunacy to the Lord Chancellor* (1855), p. 1; RG 10/1469/26; Gloucestershire Archives D3725 box 134 admissions register 1860–81; RG 11/2383/108.
41 J. Firth-Cozens, 'The Stresses of Medical Training', in R. Payne and J. Firth-Cozens (eds), *Stress in Health Professionals* (Chichester: John Wiley and Sons, 1987), pp. 3–22, on p. 5.
42 See also Chapter 6 for suicide among medical students.
43 K. Waddington, 'Mayhem and medical students: image, conduct, and control in the Victorian and Edwardian London teaching hospital', *Social History of Medicine* 15:1 (2002) pp. 45–64, on p. 48.
44 Leicester Record Office, DE 3533/185 Leicestershire and Rutland asylum patient casebook 1845–8.
45 Borthwick Institute, BOO 6/2/3/3 Bootham Park Hospital (formerly York Lunatic Asylum) registry of admissions 1855–59, patient number 428.
46 Borthwick Institute BOO6/1/12 Bootham Park Hospital reception orders 1857, William Gibson.
47 For example, see also the case of Charles Beard, discussed briefly later and unpacked fully in A. Tomkins 'Case Notes', in M. Jackson (ed.), *Routledge History of Disease* (London: Routledge, 2016); Beard was caught up in the case of Christiana Edmunds, the 'chocolate cream' poisoner.
48 Personal communications in 2011 from Dr Michael Peters of the BMA's 'Doctors for Doctors' unit and from Dr Mike Myers, global expert on physician suicide.
49 Andrews, 'Case Notes', p. 257.
50 Andrews, 'Case Notes', p. 265.
51 Gloucester Archives, D3725/box 136 male case book 1865–74, p. 288.
52 St Andrew's Healthcare Archives, CL 4 Northampton General Lunatic asylum case book, 211.
53 Warwickshire Record Office, CR 1664/623 Warwickshire asylum case book 1872–5, patient 2098; Staffordshire Record Office, D 4553, Stafford County Asylum male patients case book 1883–94, 280.
54 Old Bailey Online reference t18760529–400; www.oldbaileyonline.org viewed on 21 October 2010.
55 Berkshire Record Office, D/H14 D2/2/1 875/ 6 letter of 13 April 1877.
56 Berkshire Record Office, D/H14 D2/2/1 875/ 30 letter of 20 September 1877.
57 Berkshire Record Office, D/H14 D2/2/1 875/ 31 letter of 21 September 1877.

58 Berkshire Record Office, D/H14 D2/2/1 875/ 37–40 letters of 4–8 October 1877.
59 A. Scull, *The Most Solitary of Afflictions. Madness and Society in Britain, 1700–1900* (New Haven: Yale University Press, 1993), p. 246.
60 Derbyshire Record Office, D 1658/11/3, Derbyshire asylum case book 1856–57.
61 Derbyshire Record Office, D 1658/11/3, Derbyshire asylum case book 1856–57, entry of 8 January 1857.
62 Derbyshire Record Office, D 1658/11/3, Derbyshire asylum case book 1856–57, entry of 23 October 1858.
63 Derbyshire Record Office, D 1658/11/3, Derbyshire asylum case book 1856–57, entry of 12 July 1856.
64 Derbyshire Record Office, D 1658/11/3, Derbyshire asylum case book 1856–57, entry of 16 February 1860.
65 Gale and Howard, *Presumed Curable*, pp. 60, 80, 95, 126.
66 Gloucestershire Archives, HO 22/63/37 Gloucestershire asylum admissions book for private patients 1845–1906; HO 22/70/3 Gloucestershire asylum casebook for male private patients 1852–55.
67 St Andrew's Healthcare Archives CL 13 St Andrew's asylum case notes.
68 Devonshire Record Office, 3992F/H/15/2–3 Wonford House case books 1847–58; see also Staffordshire Record Office D 5379/2/4 Staffordshire asylum case book 1848–59, entry for patient Walter Scott.
69 St Andrew's Healthcare Archives CL 11 St Andrew's case notes.
70 St Andrew's Healthcare Archives CL 9 St Andrew's asylum case notes; the case of Angus Cameron at Warwick is given more fully later.
71 Shepherd, '"One of the best fathers"', pp. 5–6.
72 On undermined masculine identity, see also Chapter 6 and the case of William Whitfield Edwardes.
73 Gloucestershire Archives, HO22/70/8 Gloucestershire asylum case book male private patients 1852–55.
74 Borthwick Institute, CLF 6/5/1/10 North Riding asylum case notes 1887–92.
75 Warwickshire Record Office, 1664/624 Warwickshire asylum case book 1875–78.
76 I am very much indebted to Len Smith for directing me to Fox's case; see also L. Smith, *Cure, Comfort and Safe Custody. Public Lunatic Asylums in Early Nineteenth-Century England* (London: Leicester University Press, 1999), p. 215.
77 R. Thorne, 'Sir Charles Fox', *New Oxford Dictionary of National Biography* (Oxford: Oxford University Press, 2004), www.oxforddnb.com viewed on 13 November 2015; Derbyshire Record Office Derby St Werburgh

parish registers, baptisms 1668–1812, burials 1722–1805 and 1806–37; 'A description of an improved cupping-glass', *The Lancet* 8:195 (1827), pp. 238–9, and later editions; 'Gas', *Derby Mercury* 12 January 1831 p. 2 and later editions.

78 Derbyshire Record Office, D 1190/2/7 Derbyshire Royal Infirmary minute book 1833–36.

79 *The Satirist* was a scandal-sheet published from 1831 until 1849 when it was suppressed; G.C. Boase, 'Barnard Gregory', *New Oxford Dictionary of National Biography* (Oxford: Oxford University Press, 2004), www.oxforddnb.com viewed on 13 November 2015. The journal took up the cause of investigating madhouses and printed a series of articles later published as R. Paternoster, *The Madhouse System* (London: Richard Paternoster, 1841); W.L. Parry-Jones, *The Trade in Lunacy. A Study of Private Madhouses in England in the Eighteenth and Nineteenth Centuries* (London: Routledge and Kegan Paul, 1972), p. 228.

80 Fox did not become a high profile member of the Alleged Lunatics' Friend Society, despite his common cause with Paternoster and their combined presence in *The Satirist*; N. Hervey, 'Advocacy or folly: the Alleged Lunatics' Friend Society, 1845–63', *Medical History* 30 (1986), pp. 245–75.

81 'Madhouses and their Management', *The Satirist* 23 December 1838, p. 403, 6 January 1839, p. 2, 13 January 1839, p. 10, 20 January 1839, p. 18.

82 'Madhouses and their Management', *The Satirist* 20 January 1839, p. 18.

83 'Private Madhouses', *The Satirist* 25 November 1838, p. 374.

84 N. A., HO 44/32/91, Home Office domestic correspondence letter of 28 June 1839.

85 Derbyshire Record Office D1190/2/8 Royal Infirmary minute book 1837–42, minutes of February–April 1838 finding irregularities in the conduct of the master and matron.

86 N.A., HO 107/1337/32, HO 107/1481/50; 'To the Editor of the Derby Mercury', *Derby Mercury,* 5 December 1838, p. 2; death certificate of 22 January 1860.

87 'The Derbyshire General Infirmary', *Derby Mercury* 17 November 1869, p. 5.

88 See among other reports 'The Army', *Caledonian Mercury* 18 August 1836, p. 1.

89 Elsewhere it certainly inspired extreme irritation; see E.T. Hurren, 'Remaking the medico-legal scene: a social history of the late-Victorian coroner in Oxford', *Journal of the Social History of Medicine* 65:2 (2009), pp. 207–52, on pp. 220–1.

90 St Andrew's Healthcare Archives, CL 17 St Andrew's hospital case book 1885–87; death certificate of 23 December 1916.

91 General Medical Council, *The Medical Register* (London: General Medical Council, 1887), p. 145 and subsequent editions to 1915.
92 'Deaths', *The Times* 26 December 1916, p. 1.
93 See, among other articles, 'Birmingham Blue Coat School', *Birmingham Daily Post* 22 April 1876, p. 6.
94 'Suicide of a Medical Man at Bath', *Bristol Mercury and Daily Post* 27 July 1878, p. 4.
95 'Inquests', *The Times* 22 July 1878, p. 7.

6

Despairing doctors: professional stress and suicide

Mortality among the members of the nineteenth-century medical profession was high in relation to other professions and to non-professional occupations.[1] The level of risk was greatest for young men, and the career-young (up to age forty-five), when mortality among practitioners was significantly higher than for men of the same age in the general population.[2] Suicide made a small contribution to this picture, since it accounted for 1.4 percent of all practitioner deaths 1873–82, but it was a more prominent cause of death among those aged forty-four and under, where it accounted for 2.9 percent.[3] Furthermore, medical men at all ages continued to suffer a higher risk of suicide than other adult men into the 1890s and beyond. Young men aged thirty-four and under were particularly vulnerable, although the differential between practitioners and the population was decreasing by the start of the twentieth century.[4] In this fatal respect, medical men stood out from their professional and generational peers.

Robert Woods' analysis of these statistics highlights the emphasis placed on these findings by nineteenth-century contemporaries. Medical men, like chemists, had easy access to poisons and therefore the means to hand in moments of distress. They were also regarded as vulnerable by reason of the mental stress of their professional work, unpredictable daily work patterns, and physically gruelling conditions of attendance. Added to this they were thought by contemporary medical statistician William Ogle to suffer 'that over-sensitiveness to the ills of life, which is the tax paid in return for the advantages of education'.[5] This expresses the gentler, updated, nineteenth-century version of a much older argument that suicide was the consequence of misplaced pride.[6] Woods endorses the conclusion that risk was exacerbated by proximity to poison but does not explore the question further, being chiefly interested in mortality and its relation to morbidity rather than suicides' motives.[7]

This chapter picks up where Woods leaves off, to look in more depth at the phenomenon of practitioner suicide. Rather than starting with contemporary statistics, it assumes that data is best sought in the evidence of coroners' inquests and specifically by a systematic analysis of suicide verdicts reported in the press. The records of coroners' courts do survive for a number of locations, and some were used by Olive Anderson in her study of suicide in Victorian and Edwardian England, but combing these solely for inquests on practitioners would yield a poor return on research time.[8] In contrast, newspaper articles enjoy a double advantage, namely a capacity to span all counties and the opportunity to feature commentary beyond simple reporting of the evidence and verdicts recorded by the courts. They do not contain the same information as the legal records of inquests, and as Rab Houston has pointed out they may present a story to emphasise key didactic points.[9] They do show how newspapers chose to depict such events, and how contemporaries beyond the inquest proceedings learned about practitioner suicide. At the same time they offer embedded data, incomplete but not necessarily inaccurate, about individuals' experience of the drivers and circumstances of such suicides.

Neither court documents nor newspaper articles on their own can remove the biggest challenge for studying suicide, namely its successful concealment for social and financial reasons. Families, co-residents, and others might see their own best interests as tied to a claim of natural or at worst accidental death, and it is generally assumed that in historic cases the more prosperous the survivors the more facility there was for avoiding a suicide verdict.[10] As members of a professional group who were firmly embedded in the middle class by the later nineteenth century, practitioners' families were perhaps highly motivated to opt for concealment and unusually well placed to achieve it. There was a clear risk that deaths deemed to have been 'accidents' by inquests might have concealed suicidal intent. Therefore, as in the other chapters of this book, the analysis that follows is based on the conclusions that can be drawn from minimum counts of suicide discoverable by these means.

For a variety of reasons, this methodology cannot establish the 'real' rate of suicide among practitioners, and it is likely that press coverage was particularly weak in the early nineteenth century when there could be a substantial shortfall of suicides reported against inquests held.[11] Its efficacy as an indicator of registered suicide can be checked for the later nineteenth century, however, against the statistics compiled by William Ogle for 1873–82. Local registrars in England and Wales were required to send notification of practitioners' deaths to the Medical Register Office, to ensure that the published *Register* governed by the General Medical Council was updated, and Ogle used these returns to determine that fifty-five practitioners were deemed to have killed themselves in this decade. The newspaper searches find forty-two instances of inquests considering suicide among apparently qualified medical men in the same period (so excluding the thirteen suicides reported as by medical students or assistants, and four instances giving a formal verdict of misadventure). This suggests that newspaper searches underestimate suicides by qualified medical men by around 24 percent. It remains entirely possible that there was additional slippage for the registrations counted by Ogle and deaths reported in newspapers, whereby both cohorts are incomplete and miss relevant deaths. Even so, it seems that, for the 1870s at least, there is a measure of coincidence between the cases of medical suicide counted by both methods; the majority of instances counted by Ogle are identified by keyword searches in the press.

The newspaper articles about medical suicide relate decisively to the twin themes running through this book: the dimensions of medical masculinity and the challenges of the medical marketplace. Practitioners reflected on both in their suicide notes, and while references to impugned masculinity are implicit in fears of financial failure, allusions to competitive practice are quite plain. The latter are particularly concerned with intra-generational conflict, where established medical men allegedly strove to curb the incomes, energies, and opportunities of medical students or junior colleagues.

This chapter therefore first examines the role and visibility of the inquest in determining acts of suicide in nineteenth-century England and Wales. It then looks in more detail at the 285 medical deaths investigated or reported as suicides between 1800 and 1890, with particular reference to the behavioural patterns, methods, and motives that emerged in inquest evidence. It concludes with the case of William Whitfield Edwardes, whose suicide in 1883 generated intense social commentary and presented the consolidating medical profession with a quintessential dilemma.[12]

Suicide inquests and ideological change

Deaths thought to be by the individual's own hand demanded an inquest, and in the late eighteenth and nineteenth centuries juries technically had three viable verdicts for use in cases of suicide. They might conclude that the person was suffering from temporary insanity (distinct from technical lunacy), or that the state of their mind could not be known. If, however, the jury took the view that the suicide was conducted rationally and with malign intent (perhaps by a person they considered guilty of an additional criminal offence), they might take the view that the suicide was a felony, and return a verdict of *felo de se*.[13] This punitive verdict was intended to place a deep stain on the posthumous reputation of the suicide, and disable his family from inheriting his estate – since all property under this verdict was forfeit to the Crown. The Crown frequently returned, or failed to demand, such property in the nineteenth century, but the principle remained in law until 1870 and was occasionally asserted.[14] In the eighteenth century there were additional penalties imposed around the burial of suicides, since the law sanctioned burial in unconsecrated ground and even the mutilation of the corpse (traditionally a stake through the heart). An Act of 1823 forbade staking and allowed burial in consecrated ground, but up to 1882 a verdict of *felo de se* might still require that the suicide be deprived of the prominent features of a Christian burial. This process involved interment between 9 o'clock in the evening and midnight, without benefit of religious observance or other ceremony.

Penalties for felonious self-murder were rarely observed by 1800, however, when the vast majority of suicides were judged to have acted during a period of temporary insanity. MacDonald estimates that verdicts of *felo de se* accounted for just 1.4 percent of judgments in London 1760–99, and Anderson gives the figure of 3 percent in London 1788–1829, meaning that public condemnations of suicide were entirely overshadowed by the exoneration of poor mental health.[15] Insanity verdicts could still be strongly deprecated by some contemporaries. The 'forbearance' of juries in this respect was even blamed in some quarters for the supposed rise in suicide rates.[16] Nonetheless, the verdict of temporary insanity became established as the norm for the overwhelming majority of suicide cases, and was shored up by evolving ideas about the significance of suicide for individuals and communities. Some of these ideas emanated from medical men who arguably had a substantial vested interest in the medicalisation of suicide. James Cowles Pritchard, for example, coined the phrase 'irresistible impulse' which contributed to moderating the opprobrium formerly attaching to suicide and also to unfolding debates around criminal insanity.[17] This did not mean that practitioners thinking about the subject of suicide withdrew all at once from a traditional, judgemental stance. Forbes Winslow in his pioneering book described it, contradictorily, as both a moral offence and a phenomenon with comprehensible medical causes.[18] Henry Maudsley's work was characteristic of a compassionate strain in medical writing, and an emphasis on social context, in the 1870s and after.[19] Debates about suicides' insanity or criminality extended across the Victorian period but, whether driven by professional elites or public opinion, many coroners became firmly persuaded by the case for insanity.[20] In 1885 a jury proved unusually harsh in wishing to find that Doctor Edwin Canton had killed himself wilfully, but the coroner Henry Wakley would not permit a verdict of *felo de se*.[21] Canton was not thought to have committed any crime or been guilty of wrongdoing, so it would have been out of line with custom and practice to find *felo de se*, but it was still overstepping the coronial role to overrule the verdict.[22] Nonetheless Wakley argued that 'everyone was insane more or less' (or that 'every suicide was insane more or less' depending on the newspaper), and his intervention appears to have inspired no protest.[23]

An unknown number of inquests avoided a suicide verdict altogether and instead pronounced the death accidental, and there was social pressure to ensure that his happened in specific cases. Negative attitudes to the commission of suicide were supposed to have been enhanced in the nineteenth century by three factors. The rise of a 'suburban spirit' allegedly diminished the idea of suicide as a sin but instead intensified social opprobrium. Furthermore, the emphasis on insanity as a medical explanation for suicide meant that this cause of death acquired some of the taint and hereditary implications of madness. Finally, the familiarity of narratives that linked suicide to poverty risked conferring additional stigma on the individual who died.[24] This meant that any changes of attitude towards suicide in terms of verdicts delivered, from punitive to pitying, could collapse in the face of personal experience, so families, friends, and colleagues of successful suicides might well experience feelings of shame, guilt, fear or revulsion.[25] Some communities were particularly likely to develop and then retain intensely negative ideas about suicide, such as those in remote, rural locations.[26] It is not surprising, then, that sympathetic coroners might help to occlude the literal circumstances of death to ameliorate survivors' experience.[27]

Another unknown quantity is the number of middle-class or elite deaths that did not attract an inquest at all, either because relevant deaths were not reported to the coroner or because social pressure or even bribery encouraged coroners to ignore selected deaths.[28] Some families took the view that an inquest would be tantamount to an accusation of some kind and undertook vocal protest if coroners insisted on acting.[29] It is entirely reasonable to suppose, if impossible to verify, that some coroners took the decision not to act, effectively to forestall complaints from their social peers or superiors.

Understanding suicide: nineteenth-century reporting practice

The press of around 1800 was generally unsympathetic to suicide. Andrew has described this as a rejection of inappropriate behaviour that undermined the rule of law and its ultimate sanction, namely execution by the state.[30] When practised by those above the working sort and labouring poor, it constituted a fashionable vice that could be bracketed with gaming, adultery, and duelling. These activities were all morally pernicious and legally damaging for a society founded on a shared assumption of the pre-eminence of self-preservation.[31]

That said, reporting of suicides, and of coroners' inquests more broadly, was not a core part of newspapers' business at the end of the eighteenth century. Increasing revenue from advertising, the declining role of the political subsidy, and a desire to demonstrate editorial independence rather than partisanship were the priorities of newspaper management into the early nineteenth century.[32] Provincial newspapers made a regular, if infrequent, feature of suicides by 1800, when approximately one in every eight of each of the northern English papers studied by Houston included a suicide report. This meant that suicide stories may have become a recognised component of the news while not occupying even 1 percent of the available space.[33] These reports might be quite brief, and coverage focused on unmarried working people rather than middling sorts. Even so, they managed to deliver morality lessons on both spiritual and worldly conduct. They also displayed a parochial sense of security and probity, given that suicides beyond the newspaper's locality might be retailed to emphasise that 'odd things could happen to those who went to London or anywhere else far away'.[34]

The conduct of inquests remained tangential to the press's core objectives in the early decades of the nineteenth century, but shifting priorities meant that they became established as a regular feature in some newspapers. The development of longer, more frequent, publications encouraged the inclusion of fuller local sections in provincial newspapers, for instance, which tended to boost the number of suicides reported.[35] From the 1840s, the column inches devoted to inquest reporting proliferated as one source of miscellaneous information characterised by 'human interest', with relatively little relevance to issues of commerce or party politics. This journalism appealed to the growing popular readership of daily and weekly newspapers that was in turn spurred by the reduction and eventual abolition of stamp duty. The trend towards increased reporting did not go unnoticed, and was strongly deprecated by commentators who did not make their living from newspapers when it became clear that successful suicides of all occupations could inspire copyists.[36] The second half of the century saw periodic pulses of supposed 'suicide mania'.[37]

As the nineteenth century progressed, suicide reporting became less socially selective, less consistently didactic, and more ameliorative in tone. Narrative motifs in reporting suicides co-opted the language of shock, tragedy, pity, and melancholy rather than the available alternatives for framing a suicide (such as judgement on evil, an inquiry into the bizarre, or a rueful but comedic story).[38]

The London newspapers reported suicide in accordance with the supposed interests of their readerships. Anderson found that in the 1860s the *Daily Telegraph* reported inquests on suicides more fully than its competitors, and also published short pieces about suicide as a phenomenon (aside from coverage of specific cases). She attributed this characteristic to a reading public drawn from the lower-middle class seeking family entertainment as well as information on political and commercial matters.[39] Notable cases were reported ubiquitously, but other newspapers tended to be more selective or sparing in reporting everyday cases of suicide. Thus the *Daily News* might feature male suicides, while the *Morning Post* with a readership among the social elite ignored the majority of all these events entirely. Cheap Sunday newspapers with working-class readers reported suicide in the widest variety of genres, from pathetic to gruesome, but the lower-middle-class *News of the World* gave the topic the most column inches.

The increase in the quantity of newspaper print in the final third of the nineteenth century gave scope for more space to be devoted to increasingly diverse subject matter. The provincial press developed more numerous titles, moved from weekly to daily production, and increased circulation. At the same time Sunday newspapers proliferated, and these thrived on the popularity of crime and scandal as entertainment.[40] This meant that there was more capacity to cover suicide, and attend to it in detail, than had been the case earlier in the century. Suicide inquests increasingly had to compete with other forms of content, however.

The 'New Journalism' characterising the final quarter of the nineteenth century, emerging in the 1860s but consolidated in the 1880s, drew on American styles of press publication. This diversified the varieties of content in British newspapers to include interviews, letters, fiction, puzzles, humorous features, and other genres. These additions appealed to people who had benefited from the spread of elementary education but who lacked the skills to decode the denser, traditional style and content of some newspapers. The 'new' approach was most prominently (notoriously) available in the *Pall Mall Gazette* under the editorship of W.T. Stead, employing cross-headings (for reading by scanning), illustrations, and campaigns for socially progressive causes.[41] The spread of this new style meant that suicide reporting became more melodramatic, but also meant it came to occupy less space than it had in the 1860s. Anderson argues that, by the end of the nineteenth century, suicide was effectively crowded out by a range of new stories and layouts. When suicides were reported in the halfpenny press they were represented strongly both in terms of sensational prose and striking presentation, but fewer cases were included overall.[42]

Medical suicides: masculinity, means, and motives

The relationship of medical personnel to the inquest has so far been characterised in the historiography as one of tradition, reform, expertise, and modernity. The medical-political implications of coroners' elections were central to the professionalising agenda.[43] Studies of medical men as the main actors or subjects of the nineteenth-century inquest have characterised them either as keen to appropriate the process for professional medicine, a campaign spearheaded by Thomas Wakley in *The Lancet*, or as an active agent in deaths under anaesthesia.[44] Similarly, the role of medical men in suicide has been construed as one of prevention with particular reference to institutional populations, in practitioners' official capacities such as prison surgeons and asylum superintendents. Thus suicide opened up another avenue for medical specialism and the display of professional skill.[45] This chapter up-ends these perspectives and puts the medical man in the position of the corpse. This was a non-professional, non-expert, culturally feminised role, and as such it was deeply problematic for practitioners, the developing middle class, and the press.

Throughout the century, and across most publications, there was a glaring disparity between the incidence of suicide and its depiction in terms of gender: male suicides tended to outnumber female suicides by three to one, but the narratives and imagery employed in the newspaper and periodical press clustered around the suicide of young women.[46] Barbara Gates has argued persuasively that the reading public wanted to believe in the ideological rationale for female suicide.[47] This might have been expected to render male suicide in general and practitioner suicide in particular intensely problematic for newspapers. How should they describe and account for an act that was ideologically feminised but committed by men who, by virtue of their professional aspirations, had spent their lives advertising their desire for middle-class masculine respectability? The answer lay in a retreat into sorrow and an emphasis on the overwhelming nature of temporary circumstance. The masculinity of the practitioners was never openly impugned by the newspapers. The victims were not characterised as either criminal or cowardly (except in the cases of the three men judged *felo de se*), nor were they castigated as effeminate for their self-murder. The closest these reports ever came to this sort of conclusion, which on the basis of Gates' research would in any case have proved highly unpalatable to readers of all stripes, was to explain practitioner suicide by reference to temporary weakness.

The difficulties that medical suicide posed for multiple groups in the early nineteenth century is best witnessed in the aftermath of Sir Richard Croft's death by shooting. Croft had been the presiding practitioner at the delivery of Princess Charlotte's baby son, and so was the obvious target for recrimination and blame when first the infant and then the Princess herself died. He shot himself on 12 February 1818 and, while the event was reported, Andrew still judges the coverage a 'hush-up'.[48]

The social barriers and conflicts inherent in reporting practitioner suicide might have reduced this research to a thin and cursory survey; in the event, it was surprisingly successful in yielding as many as 285 cases for closer investigation. These cases were found by seeking the word 'suicide' in close proximity to the occupational descriptors for practitioners used throughout this book. Synonyms of suicide such as 'self-murder' were not found to be helpful; this specific term might plausibly have emerged among the searches conducted for Chapter 4 for 'murder', but in practice no such cases were found. Reports of a legal forum, such as an inquest, were perhaps likely to use the formal, Latinate 'suicide' rather than a more colloquial term. Similarly, the popular phrase 'to make a hole in the water' is found in the newspapers, but never in relation to a practitioner (Table 6.1).[49]

Table 6.1 Hits found for practitioner suicide using a proximity measure of ten, 1800–90*

	Physician	Surgeon	Doctor	Medical	Total
'Suicide' within 10 words	254	1,312	661	practitioner 34 student104 man 199 officer 112 total 449	2,676
Cases for study	39	164	21	61	285

* British Library Newspapers, www.find.galegroup.com/bncn/, was searched on 8 September 2010 and subsequently.

It quickly becomes apparent that the years 1800–20 yield very few cases. Only eight examples of practitioner suicide fell in this period, of whom one was unnamed and one was Croft. In the 1820s the collective press contained only single instances of such suicide each year, but in the 1830s the numbers began to rise with between three and six medical examples each year. From the 1840s to the end of the period there were between three and nine medical suicides typically reported annually. The figure never reached as many as ten in any individual year, but the five-year moving average indicates that the 1850s and 1880s were the high points of reported incidence (Figure 6.1).

It seems highly unlikely that this distribution bears a meaningful relation to the number of medical suicides committed across the period, particularly in the decades 1800–40, and it is most probable that it is a consequence of reporting strategies. The measure of alignment between the totals secured from newspapers and Ogle's figures quoted at the start of this chapter suggest that, by the 1870s, there was some equivalence between suicides determined by inquest verdict and suicides reported in at least one newspaper in the British Library's database. Even so, there could be no justification for defending a Durkheimian argument about the rise of medical suicide from these figures. It was rather their increased visibility that was pertinent for readers.

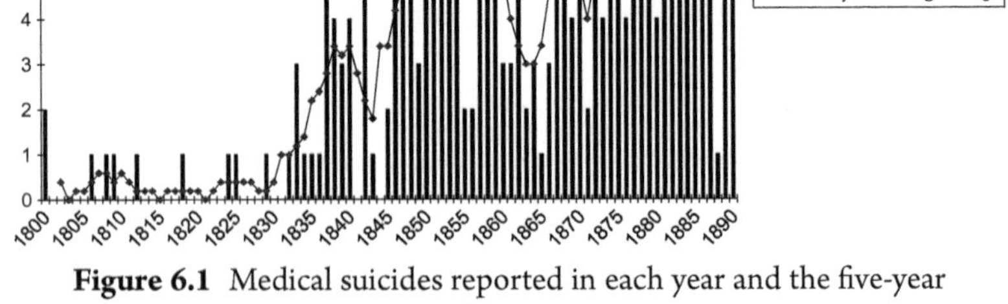

Figure 6.1 Medical suicides reported in each year and the five-year moving average

The reported incidence of medical suicide was much more infrequent in the medical press. The names of men found in the lay press were cross-referenced with the obituaries and notices printed in the *British Medical Journal* and *The Lancet*. In both publications, unsurprisingly, the majority of suicidal deaths were not noted but there was some significant variation between the two periodicals.[50] The *British Medical Journal* and its predecessor publications were produced from 1840, but obituaries only became a regular feature from 1853. Of the 257 deaths occurring 1840–90, just forty-three were included and, of those, twenty did not specifically mention that the practitioner had killed themselves (although it was sometimes implied). *The Lancet* was more likely to notice a death, but its willingness to refer to suicide varied according to the decade; of the 278 deaths that occurred from 1823 onwards (so after *The Lancet* commenced publication) at least ninety-three attracted some notice. Medical suicides were apparently reported with some readiness in most years, with the exception of the period 1869–79 when no deaths were found that to be explicitly ascribed to self-destruction (although one man was said to have been 'a victim to the want of a holiday').[51] Entries in both journals were often brief, although obituaries lengthened over the period and became more fulsome in praise of the deceased and his career.

The format of inquest coverage in the lay press became sufficiently routine, particularly in the fifty years of 1840–90, to enable the collection of standard data including the name and address of the deceased, their age and manner of their death, the approximate date of their demise, and the inquest verdict. Longer reports might contain extended accounts of witness evidence, a transcript of any suicide note, or expressions of regret (in general or attributed to a particular commentator) on the events leading to the death. These characteristics can be used to chart the circumstances and motivations for practitioner suicide.

There was seasonality to suicidal behaviour *per se*, and practitioners were as much subject to this as other groups. June was by far the most prominent month, with the half-year May to October exhibiting much higher concentrations of medical suicide than November to April. This pattern adheres to the seasonality of all suicides found by Ogle for London 1865–84 (Figure 6.2).[52]

Age was recorded less consistently than other types of data, meaning that the age of 25 percent of men is unknown, but from this limited

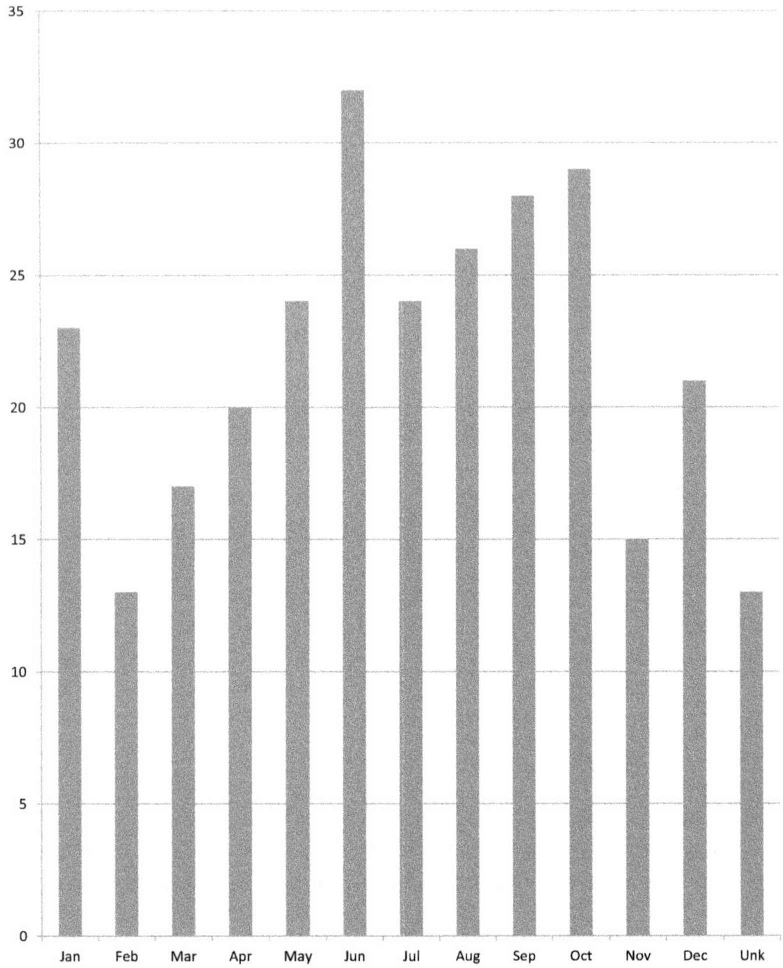

Figure 6.2 Medical suicides by calendar month

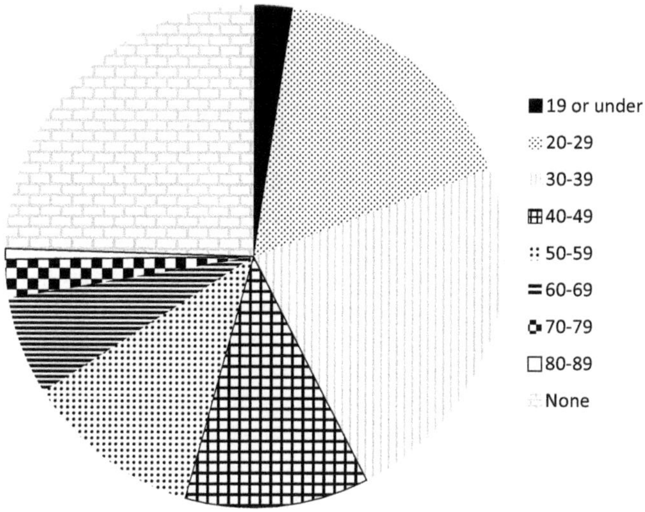

Figure 6.3 Age distribution of medical suicides

evidence medical suicide reported in newspapers across the century conforms with Ogle's findings for 1873–82. Young men, or the career-young, were most likely to present as suicides, with the age group thirty to thirty-nine most prominent (Figure 6.3).

Also like non-medical suicides, practitioners inspired imitation, both beyond the profession and within it. Dr Dickson killed himself in Northumberland in March 1874 on the eve of his marriage, but the news was reported in the locality of his home in Jersey where a woman copied his actions in December of the same year. They both bled to death having made wounds in their arms, the unnamed woman stating that she had 'followed the example of the doctor'.[53] The most deadly of these developments was not explicitly imitative, but identical actions by three men in the same practice within three years cannot have been entirely coincidental. Assistant surgeon Henry Baker killed himself with poison in November 1848, whereupon his employer Robert Rouse of Fulham recruited Samuel Rowland as a replacement. Rouse died by his own hand in January 1850, while Rowland committed suicide in the same way in June 1851. The motives of the three men were apparently very different (respectively: romantic disappointment, overwork compounded by fears of impoverishment, and previous trauma in the form of repeated shipwreck) but in seeking relief from despair they took their cues from each other.[54]

A third of the suicides reported did not include confirmation of the inquest verdict, but practitioners clearly participated in the same blanket assumptions of temporary insanity conferred on the population at large. Over 85 percent of those cases where a verdict is known recorded that the deceased was suffering from temporary insanity, also termed in the press as an unsound mind, aberration of mind, delirium or derangement. Open verdicts accounted for the rest, with the exception of just three men found guilty of *felo de se*, all of whom were suspected of theft, manslaughter or murder.[55]

Of course, insanity could be cited both for men who suffered a genuinely fleeting malady and for those regarded as formerly or persistently mad. The case of Angus Cameron is discussed in Chapter 5, but he was not alone. William Bell cut his throat while he was visiting his wife and family in Cheltenham, having been given temporary permission to leave the Sandywell Park lunatic asylum. The reason for his admission nine months earlier had been his suicidal lunacy.[56] Henry Myers had been discharged from Hoxton asylum for over three months when he died by his own hand in 1860.[57]

The search for suicides, and the propensity of some reports to feature discussion of suicide when a different verdict was ultimately recorded, means that seven instances of misadventure or similar verdicts were found for practitioners. These few cases serve as further reminders of the potential for porosity between suicide and accident. They also go some way to justify the inclusion of the 30 percent of cases where no verdict has been discernible, because it was quite usual for the public to learn about these medical deaths as 'supposed suicides' whatever the eventual verdict.[58] Robert Glover's inquest exhibited a strong *prima facie* case for suicide, but delivered a verdict that was rather more in accordance with the wishes of his surviving brother and colleagues.[59] Glover, who died from an overdose of chloroform, had suffered multiple physical and emotional injuries. He had served in the Crimea where he contracted dysentery, and since his return in 1857 he had felt compelled to take 'opium and stimulants' as a consequence. He was married about six weeks before his death, but separated from his wife after only a week, referring later to his marriage as a 'bad affair'. His wife was subsequently admitted, or rather readmitted, to Colney Hatch lunatic asylum. The coroner (as it happens, Thomas Wakley) revealed in his summing up that he personally had spoken to Glover at about the time of his marriage concerning the possibility of Glover himself entering an asylum. Against these multiple reasons for depression, though, Glover's brother and fellow doctors asserted his unremitting cheerfulness. On the day of his death he had allegedly enjoyed lively conversations, reflected on his marriage without its affecting his mind, and protested 'he was never better in health'. He was also said to have spoken strongly against suicide in the past. The jury concluded that he had taken an excessive amount of chloroform, but was seeking intoxication rather than self-destruction.

Poisoning was the predominant method to procure suicide chosen by medical men. This was the case in 1873–82 when 60 percent were found to have died by this cause, and the same percentage is found among these 285 cases.[60] Moreover this preference was a matter of popular apprehension: '[poisons] have gone out of fashion; scarcely any one but doctors, chemists, or washerwomen use them now, and they, according to their calling, swallow opium, arsenic, Prussian blue or salts of copper. What a falling off from the days of hemlock!'[61] This was in contrast to the male population in general, among whom hanging and strangulation were most prevalent and for whom poison was the choice of just one in ten.[62] Practitioners, of course, had occupational access to poisons throughout the period, even after the passage of the 1868 Poisons and Pharmacy Act.

Men who took poison, whether medical or in other occupations, were likely to choose the same substance. Prussic acid was the contemporary term for hydrocyanic acid in aqueous solution, and it was used by 30 percent of all men who died by self-administered poison and by 70 percent of all poisoned practitioners.[63] It had a number of advantages for the individual determined to achieve their own demise. Prussic acid was highly toxic and so was a relatively certain method of self-poisoning, and depending on the concentration of the chemical it could take effect very quickly, rendering its victim unconscious in seconds and dead in a few minutes. Moreover this efficacy was well advertised to nineteenth-century practitioners because the effect of prussic acid poisoning was a matter of some discussion in the medical press. The *Provincial Medical and Surgical Journal* even published three cases in the 1840s of self-poisoning specifically committed by men with medical training, debating whether the effects of prussic acid were instantaneous.[64] This poison enjoyed the additional advantage, for coroners and juries, of being readily identifiable by dint of its aroma, or that of its 'antidote'. Prussic acid has a distinctive smell of bitter almonds that was often said to have been detected on a dying breath, or in the opened stomach, of the deceased. Ammonia was thought to counteract its fatal effects, and this too could be recognised by its scent (where men had either been treated by a fellow professional before death, or where the victim himself had tried to avert death at the last minute).[65]

In practice, the toxicity of prussic acid could vary according to the solution meaning that death was not always swift, entailing some practitioners in additional suffering. The strength recommended in the *London Pharmacopoeia* in 1836 had only a third of the potency of 'Scheele's' strength, but it was the latter that was in 'universal use'.[66] Scheele's preparation was often specified at inquests, presumably signalling to those in the know that the solution had been purposefully concentrated rather than dilute. It was also understood, though, that prussic acid could decompose, particularly in its purest form, giving rise to occasional instances of suicide which should have been speedy but in the event were slow and dramatic.[67] William Marsden of Balsall Heath near Birmingham lived for some time after swallowing at least one bottle of prussic acid between midnight and 1 am on 18 June 1868. Having told his wife 'Ettie, I have done it, I have taken it' he staggered out to the grass in front of his house. His wife and two of his children followed him. A passer-by went to his assistance and the police and a surgeon were called. He was taken back into the house but died in his own surgery at about a quarter to two. The surgeon who attended Marsden implied that the poison's lack of freshness was relevant to the protracted nature of the death.[68]

Practitioners were perhaps at higher risk of dying from an overdose of prussic acid than they were from some other poison because it was a common substance for self-dosing in non-fatal quantities. It was notably used as a sobering agent by men who had enjoyed a drink but who were then called upon to act in a professional capacity.[69] Charles Porter was reputed to have been 'addicted to drink' for fifteen years before his death, but had used prussic acid for himself and for patients who needed to regain sobriety quickly. On the night he died he was tipsy, but rather than the ginger beer brought for him by his wife he drank from one of the other bottles in his surgery. He then threw himself on the couch and announced 'if this is prussic acid, I am a dead man'.[70] Porter's death may not have been literally intentional, but the close connection in medical minds between alcohol consumption and the supposedly sobering capacity of prussic acid was fatal in a number of cases and its usage when inebriated was clearly very risky.[71]

Regrettably, practitioners throughout the nineteenth-century perceived multiple benefits from having prussic acid readily to hand for use in minor ailments such as headaches, bodily pains, and indigestion.[72] Daniel Holmes was in the habit of 'touching his tongue with the cork of that bottle'.[73] Henry Heywood always kept some in his dressing room or bedroom, but disastrously kept chloral (to aid sleep) in a similar bottle.[74] Doctors prescribing poisons for themselves to give them respite from professional stress could find themselves courting disaster. The habit of self-dosing with prussic acid certainly meant that the fine line between suicide and accidental death was blurred still further in the case of practitioners, and gave juries space to interpret the cause of death as misadventure rather than self-murder.[75]

In deliberating their verdicts, inquest juries or the witnesses they heard typically tried to ascribe the practitioners' distress to one or more causes. Newspapers reported their conclusions in 70 percent of medical cases and, while practitioners suffered their share of unhappy relationships, alcoholism, and physical ill health, it was professional and financial worries that were allegedly the most prominent motives.[76] Over half of the medical suicides with causes ascribed came under one or both of these headings.[77] Fear of financial failure arising from inadequate professional returns serves to echo the findings of MacDonald and Murphy, who argued that shame and poverty were the most typical prompts for eighteenth-century suicides.[78] The nineteenth century saw a persistence of these patterns, not least because, as I suggest in Chapter 1, the threat of public exposure for a failing such as insolvency, whether literally under insolvency law, by bankruptcy, or by some other means, was a major challenge to middle-class Victorian masculinity. To fall short of respectable solvency was to miss one of the many yardsticks which were increasingly evident to aspiring medical men.

The evidence of Chapter 1 suggests that medical financial failure was more common than might be supposed, with a minimum of twenty-five men per year undergoing insolvency, bankruptcy or composition arrangements from the mid 1820s. It is important to stress, however, that the men already experiencing financial process were not those most likely to resort to suicide; only 2 out of 1,075 practitioners can be found to have committed suicide after due process had been advertised in the *London Gazette*.[79] Instead, the vulnerable practitioners were those men anticipating failure but who had not yet failed (or had not yet had the fact of their failure publicised). Impending 'pecuniary embarrassment' or the first signals of legal action for debt proved crisis points for men who fell foul of this 'unhappy and soul-thrilling reflection of the present'.[80] A small run of medical suicides explained by reference to imminent financial failure was published in the 1850s, for instance. Surgeon John Smith of Wheatley in Oxfordshire was not merely imagining the risk of imprisonment for debt. He received at least one letter threatening him with gaol, and on the morning of the inquest Mrs Smith took receipt of his summons at the suit of a Mr Evans, a tailor in Oxford.[81] The arrival of bailiffs or others authorised to secure property against debt was also a dangerous event for the sensitive practitioner.[82]

Overwork, the loss of employment, or failure to gain a particular post, all had implications for both income and status and were identified as precipitating suicide in numerous instances. Overwork provided both a cognate pretext for suicide and a means to laud the practitioner after they were dead by drawing attention to their dedication to duty. This gives additional weight to the idea that doctors felt pressure to appear disinterested to the point of self-destruction. Alexander Thom's level of overwork was depicted as severe, but simultaneously was idealised. The account of his inquest was deemed to be too impersonal by a 'friend', who responded with a long letter which held up Thom as the perfect medical man. His legwork in attending scattered patients' homes, his selfless anxiety on their behalf, his philanthropic wisdom plus his refusal to resort to legal action to retrieve debts, were all catalogued with approving hyperbole; 'He fell a martyr to his profession: his incessant application broke a physical constitution of iron strength.'[83] Charles Ford's death did not attract the same sort of hagiographic obituary, but then he had a different problem; he had not secured enough work. His wife confirmed at the inquest that he had been 'very much depressed' at failing to win the surgeon's appointment for one or more of the clubs (in other words, Friendly Societies) in his locality of Bedworth in Warwickshire.[84]

These cases provide tacit proof of the challenges of the medical marketplace, but occasionally suicides were allegedly prompted by the kind of covertly competitive behaviour discussed in Chapter 1. One strategy was to drive other practitioners out of the locality, but another was to keep them so overburdened with work and so poorly remunerated that they became locked into a subordinate position, both professionally as an assistant and socially as a menial adjunct to the local medical scene. James Cavan felt that this was his lot when he killed himself in Sunderland in March 1879. His suicide note explained 'I owe my death to my master and his friends. I am too proud and sensitive to mention names … for the last six months I have been driven amid frost and snow to destruction and death single-handed. He owes me five months' salary, for which I have worked hard day and night, doing the work of two.'[85] Cavan sought to address an allegation of patient neglect and a claim that he had failed to return his accounts, but wherever the chief responsibility lay for his despair (with his employer's behaviour or his own), the case reveals otherwise obscured possibilities for quietly crushing one's medical competitors.

Not all stress connected with the profession was related to performance or finance; there was intellectual pressure too, particularly for trainees or men seeking to enhance their qualifications. The decade 1874–84 alone saw ten reports of medical suicide where the alleged cause was over-study or anxiety about examinations. An examination failure, and preparation for a retake, could prove exhausting and demoralising, while a second failure could inspire immediate despair.[86] Medical students had a reputation for wildness and instability, but even so a spate of suicides did prompt some questions and self-searching in the profession, which was noticed in the lay press.[87] Reporting the suicide of an unnamed student at Guy's Hospital, the *Medical Press and Circular* was said to have observed 'considerable dissatisfaction exists at several of the large London medical schools amongst the students, on account of the refusal of the teachers to "sign up" a man, unless morally certain that he will pass the college. This is notably the case at Guy's, where this otherwise sensible course is said to be carried to extremes. We would counsel the authorities to investigate the matter.'[88] This suggests that in addition to statutory regulation and growing concern about the demands of the medical curriculum, access to a medical professional identity was guarded fiercely by individuals. This was perhaps simply a late-nineteenth-century expression of economic protectionism which had a very long tradition among skilled trades and professions alike, but arguably it had been given added impetus by memories of acute professional overcrowding (which would have been a feature of the early careers of men responsible for teaching the students of the 1870s and 1880s). Is it too much to postulate that the surplus of practitioners between the 1820s and the 1840s continued to have indirect consequences for medical recruits in successive generations?

Intellectual pressure and external confirmation of failure were damaging, but so too was negative self-judgement. The impact of self-scrutiny and denigration is very difficult to witness in the most personal of writings, even suicide notes, so this is not a prominent theme among practitioners' known motives. The writings found on the body of Thomas Morton, however, supply a rare view of the potentially relentless and corrosive effect of self-criticism. Morton was a high achiever by all professional and social criteria, holding successive surgical appointments at the North London Hospital, later to become University College Hospital, and at the Queen's Bench prison. He was a noted anatomist with a roster of publications to his name. Therefore his death in October 1849 came as a shock to the profession as a whole and 'was a great blow to the prestige of the College.'[89] He left two letters (one directed to his wife, the other resigning from his post at the hospital) but these were not especially revealing. It was the informal diary he had kept which indicated the cause of his desperation. The notes loosely dated June to October 1849 comprised a series of rules for behaviour and remarks of self-reproach on the subject of household expenditure and consumption, with a heavy emphasis on the avoidance of alcohol. He repeatedly urged himself to avoid drink, on occasions when he might be encouraged by others to drink, and chastised his lapses from these self-imposed high standards; 'When I fail it is by thoughtlessness and want of firmness.'[90] These writings were read by some contemporaries as confessions of repeated drunkenness, but there was little or no confirmation from his peers that he had been routinely intoxicated. Rather, and with hindsight, these notes seem to be evidence of an overly rigid personal code of behaviour that made no allowance for lapses.

Perhaps the most hurtful circumstances of all were those where a practitioner was said to be guilty of shameful wrong-doing, particularly if committed in the course of their professional duties, such that external and internal judgements became aligned. Chapter 3 examined charges of neglect in some detail, finding that consequent manslaughter prosecutions were rarely successful, and Chapter 4 argued that medical men stood a good chance of being acquitted of serious sexual assault and subsequently congratulated if they could endure the trial. For some men, though, the disgrace attached to allegations alone could prove too much to endure. As MD and professor of chemistry Augustus Matthiessen wrote succinctly just before his death 'I have been charged with an indecent assault on a lad, and, although innocent, yet it will blight all my future prospects, and therefore I have resolved to resign all.'[91]

Suicide under such circumstances could constitute an act of protest and, to some extent, self-vindication. If one's reputation was permanently forfeit in life, then perhaps in death it could be retrieved, where suicide could be construed as an expression of sincerity – either of repentance or of innocence. There were literary models for suicide as an act of self-redemption, and practitioners exhibited their equivalents.[92] David Morris, for example, who was accused of impropriety with a female servant and dismissed from his post, killed himself in the presence of his wife. He announced his intention quite clearly, commenting on his future inability to support his dependents and concluding with the words 'This is trouble indeed.'[93] Supposed sexual misconduct, his employers' endorsement of the claim by their discharging him, and the loss of income proved a lethal combination for Morris as it undermined both his sense of self as a professional breadwinner and his public identity as a respectably employed married father. Yet, when Morris killed himself he also made a mute appeal to the wider community for compassion and recognition, and in this he was posthumously successful. The coroner at his inquest was at pains to record that Morris had been 'universally respected' and his funeral was attended by 'an immense concourse of people'. Suicide was personally destructive, but could rehabilitate a reputation.

Morris's basic circumstances were replicated in almost every detail in the professional experience and sudden death of William Whitfield Edwardes in 1882. What had changed in the interim, though, was the medical profession's reputation, which raised the stakes still higher for the suicide and for the practitioners who survived him. The result was the most famous medical suicide of the nineteenth century and the case which brought the realities of the professionalised medical marketplace into their sharpest focus.

Riotous scenes: William Whitfield Edwardes and the perfect storm of professional pressure[94]

William Whitfield Edwardes was born in Llanfyllin in Montgomeryshire in early 1851, one of at least five sons born to Thomas Edwardes, a member of the Royal College of Surgeons and a general practitioner.[95] His career was solidly successful; a student at St Mary's Hospital, he secured his LSA in 1877, MRCS in 1878, and an MD from Brussels.[96] His personal life was seemingly ideal; he married in 1878 and quickly witnessed the birth of two healthy sons.[97] But Edwardes' decision to buy into a partnership in Hounslow in October 1881 can be seen in hindsight as a mistake. He invested the enormous sum of £1,800 in a half share of a practice with Michael Whitmarsh in expectation of receiving £800–1,000 a year in income, an act of optimism that was not borne out by his subsequent receipts from the business (which were nearer £200 a year).[98] Thus far, Edwardes' experience was not dissimilar to that of Richard Hunter, the partner of bankrupt John Steight examined in Chapter 1. In both cases the inducement to make an ambitious investment did not prove justified. It is likely that by October 1882 Edwardes was experiencing considerable disquiet about his own financial future, which his wife thought amounted to his being very depressed. Furthermore, the men's relationship soured to the extent that Edwardes was once said to have turned Whitmarsh out of his house. This action (confirmed by Whitmarsh) was bold but incautious given that Edwardes was the less-established man. Their shares in the practice may technically have been equal, but Whitmarsh was the senior by virtue of both age and public recognition, holding appointments with local Friendly Societies and the Poor Law Union.

What happened next is unclear, despite the wealth of press reporting. Either Edwardes indulged himself in a relatively minor impropriety, or he was falsely accused by a patient (acting alone or with the subsequent encouragement of Whitmarsh). It was later claimed that he attended Rose Bignell at her house on 22 December 1882, who was possibly being treated for post-partum hysteria, and that he kissed her forcibly and repeatedly. This was reinterpreted in some accounts as attempted or actual indecent or criminal assault. Bignell, a young married woman aged nineteen, subsequently retracted her allegations in writing witnessed by Whitmarsh, and Edwardes' anxiety diminished although he considered prosecuting Bignell for libel. But this was not the end of the matter. Rather Whitmarsh sent for Edwardes and told him that Bignell's retraction did not prove decisively that her claims had been untrue. He then offered to buy Edwardes out of the partnership so that Edwardes could start again elsewhere – for just £500. Whitmarsh further compounded Edwardes' situation by assuring him that he would speak against him rather than in his support if the events with Rose Bignell led to a trial.

Whitmarsh seems not to have concealed his pleasure at having found a way to dissolve an unhappy business relationship, and with some financial profit to himself. Edwardes suspected that there had been collusion between Whitmarsh and Bignell, so he sought legal advice on bringing a charge of conspiracy against Whitmarsh, but he was not at all confident of clearing his name. Edwardes was well aware what such a trial for sexual assault could mean, but was overly pessimistic about the likely outcome. On the night he died he said to his wife, 'I would not hesitate to face the trial and five years' imprisonment if it were not for you. You might then be the wife of a convict.' He was entirely accurate that he might potentially face a five-year term for a successful prosecution if the charge was rape, but as the examples in Chapter 3 illustrate, the risk of a criminal trial – let alone a successful conviction against a practitioner – was very slim. Nonetheless Edwardes was not mollified either by the odds in favour of acquittal or by his wife's confidence in his innocence, believing instead that the accusation was sufficient on its own to ruin him. He decided that to accept Whitmarsh's money would be to leave behind a dishonoured name, a reaction which chimes with descriptions of his demeanour as sensitive, nervous, and reserved.

Edwardes, like Morris before him, took prussic acid and died in the early hours of 27 December 1882. Unlike Morris, he wrote a letter which he addressed to the local press, presumably with the intention of securing high-profile public notice of his own perspective. This document passionately asserted the falsity of Rose Bignell's allegations and argued the impossibility of retrieving his reputation. But Edwardes reserved his most outspoken comments for Michael Whitmarsh, 'that fiend in human form', for the mercenary advantage he tried to obtain using Bignell's evidence as leverage. Unlike Cavan in 1879, Edwardes did not balk at naming names. The inquest which followed inspired strong *post hoc* expressions of support for Edwardes' plight by the residents of Hounslow. The funeral was held on the morning of 1 January 1883 with full military honours observed by the 8th Middlesex Rifles (in which Edwardes had been a lieutenant). Shops were closed and the road leading to the cemetery was lined with spectators. The same evening 2,000 people (it was claimed) convened at a water drinking fountain near to Whitmarsh's house shouting and throwing stones until all of the house windows were broken. The crowd then burned an effigy of Whitmarsh, and provoked similar disturbances on successive evenings – to the extent of injuring police officers on 4 January (Figure 6.4).

Figure 6.4 Newspaper portraits of Michael Whitmarsh and Rose Bignell. 'Dr Michael Whitmarsh' *The Penny Illustrated Paper and Illustrated Times* 13 January 1883, p. 17 and 'Mrs Bignell' *ibid.* 20 January 1883, p. 40

The inquest was conducted over five separate days and evolved from an inquiry into a cause of death into the trial of the surviving actors by public opinion. According to one commentator, the atmosphere was less that of a court of law and more one of a 'semi-theatrical bear garden.'[99] The eventual verdict was one of temporary insanity, with a rider from the jury that Edwardes had been driven to his death by the pressure generated from Whitmarsh's manipulation of Bignall's allegations. The Middlesex coroner Dr Thomas Diplock was criticised widely for allowing the inquest to become so protracted, and for permitting extended questioning of witnesses on tangential matters (including the marital history of Edwardes' and Whitmarsh's assistant). A quieter counter-current in the press observed that Diplock had been right to permit a full airing of local grievances, in order to dispel the 'miasma' of rumour.[100]

The strength of support for Edwardes among his former neighbours and patients made a very substantial impression on popular sentiment, on the reading public nationwide, and on the medical profession. Popular feeling was captured in the production of more than one poem on the subject. A broadsheet-style ballad has not apparently survived in full, but extracts were printed in the London and provincial press. Naturally enough this sketched out a story of a clever, kind doctor subjected to slander and whose death was 'a scandalous shame.'[101] More obviously politicised and educated readers could turn to *Punch*, which printed an alternative set of verse from the perspective of a fellow practitioner. 'The Doctor's Dream' presents an idealised version of the medical lifestyle in as much as it lionises the 'splendid mission' of the average practitioner while emphasising the struggles he may have endured to maintain his professional identity.[102] Indeed it goes a long way to pin down professional aspirations in the 1880s. At the conclusion of the poem the speaker has cause to reflect on 'that brother-in-arms who's gone and utter – well, something loud and deep!' This is the poem's only reference to Edwardes, and it remains fairly oblique, but readers of *Punch* in January 1883 could not have been ignorant of the man who was so recently 'gone', or the debate that was being engaged.

The Hounslow tragedy, as it was repeatedly styled in the press, was reported throughout Great Britain in January 1883. It gave rise to at least 320 separate articles or notices in fifty newspaper titles including Scottish and Irish examples and two Welsh-language publications.[103]

The *Middlesex Chronicle* reported that the *Daily Telegraph* and *Daily Chronicle* had each sent three representatives to report on the inquest, and that the Press Association was present on behalf of sixty-three provincial newspapers.[104] It was a national *cause celebre*, likened in one article to the Tichborne case, wherein public sympathies lay largely with Edwardes but some newspapers promoted different angles.[105] *Reynolds's Newspaper* invited its readers to endorse the jury's opinion wholesale, where the scope for sensationalism trumped the journal's otherwise radical agenda.[106] The London correspondent of the *Ipswich Journal* took a more sceptical view, dubbing Edwardes 'weak-minded' for having killed himself and intimating that public opinion would have swung against him if he had lived.[107] The *Daily News* emphasised instead the dangers that medical men were exposed to from female patients' accusations.[108] Public interest was intense but of relatively brief duration, since the case was subsequently forgotten outside of Hounslow.[109]

The medical profession could not remain ignorant of these events, and nor could it get away with maintaining total silence. The *British Medical Journal*, *The Lancet*, and *Medical Times and Gazette* were all effectively compelled to offer some coverage of the case, if not direct commentary on the actions of Edwardes and Whitmarsh. Their dilemma lay in what attitude to adopt. Edwardes was possibly a wronged man, but he was dead; Whitmarsh was being construed in the lay press as a villain, but he was very much alive and arguably deserving of some defence from his professional brethren. The result was that the professional journals exhibited a much less decided stance than the lay press, with a quiet emphasis on Whitmarsh's claims to a fair hearing beyond the highly charged atmosphere of the inquest.

The Lancet and the *British Medical Journal* published notice of the inquest at its outset, but left the expression of opinion to correspondents. Letters then tended to steer away from controversy to find common ground on which readers would be unlikely to disagree. The barrister James Greenwood used the occasion as a reminder of 'the ever present and real danger … of charges of immorality or indecency bring brought … by hysterical and erotic female patients'.[110] Greenwood connects Edwardes to public fears of sexual predation by medical practitioners and to professional fears of reputational risk that held such important consequences for men accused of rape. In a different vein, well-known campaigner for medical causes Joseph Rogers thought that the best way to respond to the 'sense of moral reprobation under which the two principal actors lie' was to raise money for Edwardes' widow and children.[111] His suggestion was overruled, however, by Edwardes' relations and by the medical press. First Edwardes' brother wrote to assure the profession that the family was amply provided for, perhaps thinking to divert posthumous implied criticism of the dead man's capacity as a provider (irrespective of his widow's level of need). Second, there were expressions of caution on the grounds that a fund might tend to act as a judgement on Whitmarsh, or an endorsement of an inquest verdict that was insufficiently substantiated.[112] By the second week in February, letters on the subject had disappeared.

The most vocal occupational journal in respect of Edwardes' case was the *Medical Times and Gazette* which urged caution until the inquest was concluded and then offered a long and reflective discussion that judiciously found evidence of some fault on both sides.[113] Edwardes was guilty of losing 'all power of cool judgement' while Whitmarsh failed to support him against a 'hysterical woman'. The article went on to deplore the violence of the public response in Hounslow, and thereby found a means to assert that 'Dr Whitmarsh deserves some credit for the quiet way in which … he endeavoured to lead the coroner to keep order in court.' It concluded that Whitmarsh had undergone severe punishment and, while this was in line with the evidence before the inquest, the journal would be glad to see his character cleared. In this manner the analysis shifted readers' focus from obligations to the dead man, towards reproach for his hasty action and optimism about the rehabilitation of his reviled but surviving partner. This argument served to add a further responsibility to the burden already borne by practitioners, namely the requirement to withstand accusations of wrong-doing with calm appraisal.

The behaviours of Edwardes and Whitmarsh illustrate the contradictory faces of medicine at this time. The covert competition which was a some-time product of the constrained medical marketplace is present in this case, but so is the sensitivity of a professionalised man towards reputational assault. The protracted investigations of the inquest exposed the extent of Whitmarsh's occupational protectionism. He had brought charges against Dr Henry Sydney of Hounslow in 1881 concerning the death of one Mrs Woodward, which generated a counterclaim of libel. The action only ceased when Whitmarsh apologised to

Sydney, a fact he readily admitted in his own testimony.[114] Given that Sydney was only five years older than Edwardes, and Whitmarsh was both their senior by at least a decade, this comprises circumstantial evidence that Whitmarsh was in the habit of trying to bully younger medical men in his vicinity by one means or another.[115] Nonetheless, the inquest also revealed Edwardes' vacillations, prompted by economic survival on one hand and the maintenance of honour on the other. Should he accept Whitmarsh's offer of £500? Should he attempt to prosecute the Bignells for libel or keep silent? He apparently changed his mind several times on both questions, giving some contemporary credence to claims that he had proved 'weak'.

In retrospect, however, the intentions of both main actors matter less than what the particular event of the suicide reveals about the context in which it was conducted. Both men were aspiring to be prudent businessmen and respectable professionals, when the building and maintaining of a solid reputation were hampered by messy facts of life such as stuttering cash-flow and unpredictable relations with patients and colleagues. The demands imposed from without might be unsustainable on their own, and force competition into unexpected channels, but the addition of exacting personal standards from within (meaning both inside the profession and in the minds of individuals) could render a situation literally unbearable. In Edwardes' case this amounted to a refusal to live with a public allegation of sexual incontinence that could feasibly conclude in a criminal conviction, and while many of the men in this chapter met their breaking points under different circumstances, there is a common theme among them of the thwarted pursuit of an unimpeachable professional identity. Suicide was one way to exert autonomy over this pursuit by ending it, while at the same time making some sort of claim to justification (either silently or via the medium of the suicide letter). In this way self-destruction provided both a powerful if necessarily nihilistic form of protest against a hostile working environment and evidence of damaging self-criticism.

Conclusion

Ogle's historic and straightforward juxtaposition of medical suicide with access to poison, reiterated by Woods, can now be elaborated in a number of ways. First, habits of self-dosing were probably ubiquitous, certainly unregulated, and even continued when already under the influence of alcohol or other intoxicants. This meant that the line between suicide and accident, always a permeable one, was eroded altogether for some practitioners. Second, financial difficulty was widespread in medical practice, and while only a couple of the men who underwent bankruptcy or insolvency could be specifically identified among medical suicides, the fear of financial failure could prove a powerful motive for self-destruction. The prospect of future or imminent exposure as a debtor, rather than the fact of current or past exposure, was what proved fatal for these men's self-conception. Third, and consequent upon financial fear, nineteenth-century practitioner suicide can routinely be construed as a consequence of, and comment upon, the stresses of the medical marketplace. Sometimes this comment was oblique, as in the cases of Alexander Thom and Charles Ford, while at other times it was spelled out pithily in suicide notes. Loss of post, exhaustion, the anticipated or actual criticism of one's professional peers, an allegation of wrong-doing, or even worse any combination of these challenges, could undermine men's resilience swiftly and decisively. There is no clear indication that suicidal responses became more consistent, or more reliably associated with assaults on professional identity, over the period. The relatively even distribution of practitioner suicides across decades and the commonality of their motives over 1840–90 make this impossible. What is clear is that Edwardes' case in 1882–83 was emblematic of deep feeling among practitioners about the life of a medical man, both what it should be and what it could not legitimately become. Risk-taking was acceptable but only when accompanied by an ability to surmount the prospect of failure with objectivity, at a time when failure cut to the heart of both public and private personas. Squarely facing one's trials figuratively or literally in a courtroom was laudable; permitting your wife to become the spouse of a convict was not. This generation of exceptionally high expectations within the profession about the acceptance and management of stress makes practitioner suicide entirely comprehensible and even predictable.

Notes

1 R. Woods, 'Physician, heal thyself: the health and mortality of Victorian doctors', *Social History of Medicine* 9:1 (1996), pp. 1–30, on pp. 7–9.

2 Woods, 'Physician, heal thyself', p. 10.
3 Woods, 'Physician, heal thyself', p. 13.
4 Woods, 'Physician, heal thyself', pp. 15–16; V. Bailey, *'This Rash Act'. Suicide Across the Life Cycle in the Victorian City* (Stanford: Stanford University Press, 1998), p. 189 for confirmation of surgery as a high-risk occupation in Hull. High levels of risk continued to pertain for health professionals in the twentieth and twenty-first centuries; see J. Charlton, S. Kelly, K. Dunnell, B. Evans, and R. Jenkins, 'Suicide deaths in England and Wales: trends in factors associated with suicide deaths', *Population Trends* 71 (1993), pp. 34–42, on p. 35, and H. Meltzer, C. Griffiths, A. Brock, C. Rooney, and R. Jenkins, 'Patterns of suicide by occupation in England and Wales: 2001–2005', *British Journal of Psychiatry* 193 (2008), pp. 73–6, on p. 74.
5 W. Ogle, 'Suicides in England and Wales in relation to age, sex, season and occupation', *Journal of the Statistical Society* 49 (1886), pp. 101–35, on p. 111.
6 D. Andrew, 'Debate. The secularization of suicide in England, 1660–1800', *Past & Present* 119 (1988), pp. 158–65, on p. 162.
7 Proximity to dangerous substances as an aspect of risk remains a feature of the literature; K. Hawton, A. Clements, S. Simkin, and A. Malmberg, 'Doctors who kill themselves: a study of the methods used for suicide', *Quarterly Journal of Medicine* 93 (2000), pp. 351–7.
8 O. Anderson, *Suicide in Victorian and Edwardian England* (Oxford: Clarendon Press, 1987).
9 R.A. Houston, *Punishing the Dead? Suicide, Lordship, and Community in Britain, 1500–1830* (Oxford: Oxford University Press, 2010), chapter 7.
10 Woods, 'Physician, heal thyself', p. 17; Ogle, 'Suicides in England and Wales', p. 102; M. Zell, 'Suicide in pre-industrial England', *Social History* 11:3 (1986), pp. 303–17, on pp. 306–7. There was even an assumption in the late eighteenth century that coroners were bribed; see W. Black, *An Arithmetical and Medical Analysis of the Diseases and Mortality of the Human Species* (London: C. Dilly, 1789), p. 243. I am indebted to Kevin Siena's work for this latter reference.
11 Anderson, *Suicide*, p. 2. Three-fifths of suicides subject to inquest in Cumberland 1774–1824 were omitted from the *Cumberland Pacquet*, and married members of the middling sort were much more likely to be left out than single, working people; Houston, *Punishing the Dead*, pp. 333–4.
12 The chapter does not consider attempted, unsuccessful suicide. The evidence for attempted suicides must generally be sought beyond the press because they were reported quite patchily. If no inquest was necessary,

then there was no imperative for anything to be reported or even known beyond the intended suicide's family and their own medical attendant (if any was called). The admissions records of asylums have been used instead to gain some view of the propensity to suicide; see A. Shepherd and D. Wright, 'Madness, suicide and the Victorian asylum: attempted self-murder in the age of non-restraint', *Medical History* 46 (2002), pp. 175–96. Around 13 percent of the medical men whose case notes were analysed in Chapter 5 concerned men who were reputed to be suicidal. Even so, the evidence for attempted suicide among practitioners is very thin.

13 M. Macdonald, 'Debate. The secularization of suicide in England, 1660–1800', *Past & Present* 119 (1988), pp. 165–70, on p. 169. Houston argues that the criminality or marginality of acts judged *felo de se* was emphasised to comfort readers, see Houston, *Punishing the Dead*, p. 336.

14 33 & 34 Vict., cap. 23. The Act of 1870 abolished forfeiture for all felonies, and suicide was not mentioned in debates; Macdonald, 'Debate', p. 168.

15 MacDonald, 'Debate', p. 169; Anderson, *Suicide*, p. 221.

16 Andrew, 'Debate', p. 160

17 J.C. Pritchard, *A Treatise on Insanity and other Disorders Affecting the Mind* (Philadelphia: Carey and Hart, 1837), p. 284 and *passim*; B.T. Gates, 'Suicide and the Victorian physicians', *Journal of the History of the Behavioural Sciences* 16 (1980), pp. 164–74, on pp. 165–6.

18 F. Winslow, *The Anatomy of Suicide* (London: Henry Renshaw, 1840).

19 H. Maudsley, *The Physiology and Pathology of Mind* (London: Macmillan, 1868), pp. 345, 347; Gates, 'Suicide', p. 169.

20 G. Laragy, '"A Peculiar Species of Felony": suicide, medicine, and the law in Victorian Britain and Ireland', *Journal of Social History* 46:3 (2013), pp. 732–43.

21 In press reports the coroner's name is given only as Wakley. They probably referred to Henry Membury Wakley (d. 1902), son of Thomas Wakley and a deputy coroner of Middlesex.

22 P. Fisher, 'The Politics of Sudden Death: The Office and Role of the Coroner in England and Wales 1726–1888', unpublished PhD thesis (Leicester University, 2007), p. 119 quoting James Brooke-Little that a coroner must accept even an absurd verdict if the jury insists.

23 'Inquests', *The Standard* 29 September 1885, p. 6 or 'A Singular Coincidence', *Dundee Courier and Argus* 2 October 1885, p. 6 for 'everyone' or 'The Suicide of Dr Canton', *Lloyd's Weekly Newspaper* 4 October 1885, p. 10 for 'every suicide'. The case was also reported in 'The Suicide of Dr Canton', *Daily News* 29 September 1885, p. 3; 'Supposed Suicide of an Eminent Physician', *Western Mail* 29 September 1885, p. 3; 'Suicide of a

Medical Man', *Berrow's Worcester Journal* 3 October 1885, p. 2; 'Shocking Discovery at Hampstead', *Illustrated Police News* 3 October 1885, p. 3; 'Sad Death of a London Doctor', *Manchester Times* 3 October 1885, p. 6 and 'Death of Mr Canton', *The Era* 3 October 1885, p. 9 all without reference to the jury's preference for the *felo de se* verdict.

24 Anderson, *Suicide*, p. 193

25 P. Michael, 'From Private Grief to Public Testimony: Suicides in Wales, 1832–1914', in A. Borsay (ed.), *Medicine in Wales c. 1800–2000* (Cardiff: University of Wales Press, 2003), pp. 40–64, on p. 40.

26 Michael, 'From Private Grief', p. 40.

27 J.H. Rumsby, 'Suicide in the British Army, c. 1815 to c. 1860', *Journal of the Society for Army Historical Research* 84:340 (2006), pp. 349–61, on p. 350.

28 Bribery may have been commonplace in the eighteenth century, see D.T. Andrew, *Aristocratic Vice. The Attack on Duelling, Suicide, Adultery and Gambling in Eighteenth-century England* (New Haven: Yale University Press, 2013), p. 105.

29 Fisher, 'The Politics of Sudden Death', p. 216.

30 Andrew, 'Debate', pp. 160, 164. MacDonald and Murphy argue that the press actively fostered a more tolerant view of suicide; see *Sleepless Souls*, pp. 301–2. Andrew's and Houston's more recent research argues persuasively, though, that this was not the case; see Houston, *Punishing the Dead*, p. 358 and Andrew, *Aristocratic Vice*, p. 92 and *passim*.

31 Andrew, 'Debate', pp. 164–6.

32 Conboy, *Journalism*, pp. 109–19.

33 Houston, *Punishing the Dead*, p. 329.

34 Houston, *Punishing the Dead*, pp. 332, 336.

35 Houston, *Punishing the Dead*, p. 328.

36 B.T. Gates, *Victorian Suicide. Mad Crimes and Sad Histories* (Princeton: Princeton University Press, 1988), pp. 38–45.

37 The phrase 'suicide mania' secured 159 hits in the British Library Newspapers database on 11 November 2013. These were associated most frequently with places but also with occupational groups; see, for example, 'Suicide Mania Amongst School Teachers', *North-Eastern Daily Gazette* 1 April 1892, p. 2.

38 Anderson, *Suicide*, p. 195 offers four basic genres for suicide reporting: sad, wicked, strange or comic.

39 Anderson, *Suicide*, p. 217.

40 K. Williams, *Read All About It! A History of the British Newspaper* (London: Routledge, 2010), pp. 117, 119.

41 Conboy, *Journalism*, pp. 166–70.

42 Anderson, *Suicide*, pp. 252–3.

43 Inquests and their associated processes, such as the election of coroners, were of somewhat less interest to the lay press of the 1820–60s than they were to the specialised professional journals. See Chapter 3.

44 I.A. Burney, *Bodies of Evidence. Medicine and the Politics of the English Inquest, 1830–1926* (Baltimore and London: Johns Hopkins University Press, 2000), chapter five.

45 Anderson, *Suicide*, chapter 11; Shepherd and Wright, 'Madness, Suicide, and the Victorian Asylum'. The delivery of low suicide rates in asylums was as much attributable to ancillary workers like attendants as it was to practitioners; S. York, 'Alienists, attendants and the containment of suicide in public lunatic asylums, 1845–1890', *Social History of Medicine* 25:2 (2011) pp. 324–42.

46 Anderson, *Suicide*, chapter 2; L.J. Nicoletti, 'Morbid Topographies: Placing suicide in Victorian London', in L. Phillips (ed.), *A Mighty Mass of Brick and Smoke: Victorian and Edwardian Representations of London* (Amsterdam: Rodopi, 2007), pp. 7–34.

47 Gates, *Victorian Suicide*, chapter VII.

48 Andrew, 'Debate', p. 161.

49 Anderson, *Suicide*, p. 210. A search for 'a hole in the water' occurring on the same page as the word 'surgeon' yielded twenty-six hits for the period 1800–90 (search conducted 7 November 2013). None of the hits pertained to practitioner suicide.

50 Both the *British Medical Journal* and *The Lancet* are available full text online; death notices and obituaries were sought digitally rather than manually in the month following the death. Searches in the *Journal* could be conducted by month and so were chronologically limited. Searches in *The Lancet* were by volume and so encompassed six months for each search giving rise to many more spurious 'hits'; to make these searches more focused and viable, notices of deaths by suicide were only sought in the 'Medical News', 'Births Marriages and Deaths' and 'Obituary' sections of *The Lancet*.

51 This was said of Michael Harris; 'Deaths', *The Lancet* 106:2719 (1875), p. 545.

52 Ogle, 'Suicides in England and Wales', p. 117. This seasonal pattern had long roots since it also featured in sixteenth-century England, when the quarter April to June was the most risky; Zell, 'Suicide', p. 311.

53 For Dickson see 'Suicide of a Physician at Berwick', *York Herald* 6 March 1874, p. 6 and *ibid.* 7 March 1874, p. 7; for the unnamed woman see 'Shocking Suicide in Jersey', *Bradford Observer* 21 December 1874, p. 4.

54 'Suicide of a Medical Gentleman at Petersham', *Morning Post* 20 November 1848, p. 3; 'Melancholy Suicide', *Daily News* 29 January 1850, p. 3;

'Lamentable Suicide of a Surgeon', *Hampshire Advertiser and Salisbury Guardian* 14 June 1851, pp. 3 and 8.

55 The case of *felo de se* Alfred William Warder is discussed at length in Chapter 4. The retention of open verdicts among the cohort studied here is given additional justification by studies of twentieth-century practitioner suicide; Hawton et al., 'Doctors who kill themselves', p. 351.

56 'Melancholy Suicide', *Morning Post* 27 March 1850, p. 3.

57 'Suicide of a Medical Man with Prussic Acid', *York Herald* 8 December 1860, p. 2.

58 In Ireland it was even possible for people (not incidentally medical professionals) to leave notes of their intention to kill themselves and for the inquest jury to find an effectively open verdict; see G. Laragy, 'Suicide and Insanity in Post-Famine Ireland', in C. Cox and M. Luddy (eds), *Cultures of Care in Irish Medical History, 1750–1970* (Basingstoke: Palgrave Macmillan, 2010), pp. 79–91, on p. 83. Modern studies of sudden practitioner death have conflated those deaths labelled as suicide with those where cause of death was ultimately undetermined or accidental; see J.C. Ritchings, G.S. Khara, and M. McDowell, 'Suicide in young doctors', *British Journal of Psychiatry* 149 (1986), pp. 475–8, on p. 476 which takes as its cohort fifty-five deaths, comprising thirty-six suicides, eight undetermined, and eleven of accidental poisoning.

59 Glover's inquest was reported in multiple journals and in the medical press; all references in this paragraph are taken from 'The Late Melancholy Death of Dr R Mortimer Glover', *Morning Chronicle* 14 April 1859, p. 2.

60 Woods, 'Physician heal thyself', p. 21. The second most popular method for practitioners was bleeding of some kind, ranging from opening a blood vessel to cutting the throat. The preference for self-poisoning followed by self-cutting persisted into the late twentieth century; see Hawton et al., 'Doctors who kill themselves'.

61 'Peculiarities of Suicide', *The Blackburn Standard: Darwen Observer, and North-East Lancashire Advertiser* 5 June 1880, p. 2 quoting 'Suicide', *Blackwood's Magazine* (June 1880), pp. 719–35.

62 Ogle, 'Suicides in England and Wales', p. 118.

63 Ogle, 'Suicides in England and Wales', p. 119; women who died by poison were more likely to use laudanum or 'vermin killer'.

64 'Case of Poisoning with Hydro-Cyanic Acid', *Provincial Medical and Surgical Journal* 25 September 1844, pp. 398–9; [untitled] *ibid.*, 30 June 1847, pp. 349–51, and 'History of a Case of Poisoning by Prussic Acid', *ibid.*, 9 August 1848, p. 428–31. Debate about the action of prussic acid was spurred in 1844 by the trial of surgeon James Belany for poisoning his

wife; see Chapter 4. This gave rise to extensive coverage of the poison's effects in the same journal in 1845.

65 For self-dosing with ammonia, see the inquest on Dr Nesbitt of Yeovil: 'The Lamentable Death of Dr Nesbitt', *Hampshire Advertiser and Salisbury Guardian* 30 September 1848, p. 6. For medical authority to use ammonia in cases of poisoning by prussic acid, see 'Case of Poisoning with Hydro-Cyanic Acid', *Provincial Medical and Surgical Journal* 25 September 1844, pp. 398–9.

66 C. and J. Watt (eds), *The Chemist; or, reporter of chemical discoveries and improvements* 1 (London: R. Hastings,1840), p. 96. Karl Wilhelm Scheele (1742–86) was the first person to isolate prussic acid.

67 'Lectures on Materia Medica Lecture XIX Hydrocyanic Acid', *London Medical Gazette* 6 February 1836, p. 716.

68 'The Suicide of Dr Marsden', *Birmingham Daily Post* 20 June 1868, p. 3.

69 This form of usage was reported, for example, at the inquest held on surgeon James Smythe by the doctor called to attend him; 'The Supposed Suicide of a Surgeon', *Birmingham Daily Post* 16 October 1886, p. 6.

70 'The Supposed Suicide by a Birmingham Surgeon', *Birmingham Daily Post* 14 August 1876, p. 5.

71 The use of a highly toxic poison to tackle inebriation in the nineteenth century is in some ways a foreshadowing of the clear recognition in the twentieth century of the relationship between alcohol or drug misuse and suicide; Charlton et al., 'Suicide deaths in England and Wales', p. 37. Alcohol was mentioned as a factor in at least forty of these 285 suicides.

72 See, for example, the inquest on George Sidley: 'Supposed Suicide of a Naval Surgeon at Southampton', *Nottinghamshire Guardian* 19 May 1853, p. 8.

73 'Suicide by a Medical Man', *The Standard* 30 January 1845, p. 1 (quoting material gathered from the *Wiltshire and Gloucestershire Standard*). A similar case occurred in Bath thirty-five years later; see the inquest on Evan Evans: 'Painful Death by Misadventure', *The Bristol Mercury and Daily Post* 31 January 1880, p. 8.

74 'A Pendleton Surgeon Poisoned', *Liverpool Mercury* 20 August 1880, p. 6.

75 See, for example, the uncertain verdict at the inquest for Henry Bishop in 1881; J.M.T. Ford, 'John Gorham 1814–1899. Victorian Medicine in Tonbridge' unpublished PhD thesis (Exeter, 2009), pp. 254–5. Self-dosing alone was arguably highly risky and a prelude to addiction; see J.V. Kragh, 'Women, Men and the Morphine Problem, 1870–1955', in T. Ortiz-Gómez and M.J. Santesmases (eds), *Gendered Drugs and Medicine. Historical and Socio-cultural Perspectives* (Farnham: Ashgate, 2014), pp. 177–98.

76 Siena has prioritised bodily illness, injury, and pain as a motive for rational suicide in the eighteenth century; K. Siena, 'Sickness and Suicide in Eighteenth-Century London' unpublished paper from the international conference on the history of suicide held at McMaster University 18–19 August 2006.
77 The motives of 199 men were apparently identified, of whom 108 were driven by financial or professional anxiety. This foreshadows evidence of practitioner suicide from 1991–93, when twenty-five of a cohort of thirty-eight successful medical suicides (men and women) had 'significant problems related to work'; see K. Hawton, A. Malmberg, and S. Simkin, 'Suicide in doctors. A psychological autopsy study', *Journal of Psychosomatic Research* 57 (2004), pp. 1–4, on p. 1.
78 MacDonald and Murphy, *Sleepless Souls*, pp. 259–300.
79 These were John Hemming, bankrupt in 1880 who died in 1884, and Frank Williams, insolvent 1825 and 1830, who died in 1858.
80 'History of a Case of Poisoning by Prussic Acid', *Provincial Medical and Surgical Journal* 9 August 1848, p. 431.
81 'Melancholy Suicide at Wheatley', *Jackson's Oxford Journal* 30 October 1852, p. 3.
82 See the inquests on physician John Stokes, 'Suicide of a Physician', *Daily News* 8 August 1853, p. 6, surgeon John Edwards, 'Melancholy and Determined Suicide by a Surgeon', *Daily News* 16 September 1853, p. 5, and surgeon William Ashcombe, 'Suicide of Two Gentlemen', *Birmingham Daily Post* 20 August 1858, p. 1.
83 'The Late Mr Alexander Thom Surgeon', *Huddersfield Chronicle and West Yorkshire Advertiser* 19 July 1856, p. 5.
84 'Suicide of a Medical Man', *Birmingham Daily Post* 19 September 1887, p. 5.
85 'Suicide of a Yorkshire Surgeon', *Leeds Mercury* 5 April 1879, p. 5.
86 See the cases of medical student William Bower, 'Suicide by a Medical Student', *Reynolds's Newspaper* 22 November 1874, p. 7, medical assistant George Sargent, 'Distressing Suicide of a Surgeon at Melton', *Supplement to the Ipswich Journal* 25 December 1875, p. 1, medical student Thornton Cape, 'Suicide of a Medical Student', *Huddersfield Chronicle and West Yorkshire Advertiser* 30 June 1877, p. 3, an unnamed medical student, 'Suicide of a Guy's Hospital Student', *Weekly Supplement to the Leeds Mercury* 2 February 1878, p. 1, Dr Frederick Atwood, 'The Suicide of a Gentleman on Hampstead Heath', *The Standard* 16 April 1879, p. 6, medical student Thomas Pemberton, 'Miscellaneous News', *North Wales Chronicle* 17 May 1879, p. 3, Dr George Holt, 'Suicide of a North Country Physician', *York Herald* 26 November 1881, p. 8, Dr Edward Robertson, 'Suicide of a

Surgeon', *North-Eastern Daily Gazette* 9 July 1883, p. 3, and medical student Charles Blunden, 'Suicide of a Medical Student', *North-Eastern Daily Gazette* 27 February 1884, p. 3.

87 K. Waddington, 'Mayhem and medical students: image, conduct, and control in the Victorian and Edwardian London teaching hospital', *Social History of Medicine* 15:1 (2002), pp. 45–64 on the reputation and reform of medical students' behaviour.

88 'Suicide of a Guy's Hospital Student', *Weekly Supplement to the Leeds Mercury* 2 February 1878, p. 1.

89 D'A. Power, 'Morton, Thomas (1813–1849)', rev. Patrick Wallis, *Oxford Dictionary of National Biography*, Oxford University Press, 2004; online edition, May 2008 www.oxforddnb.com/view/article/19376, viewed on 13 December 2013.

90 The abbreviated contents of Morton's notes were widely reported in the lay press, but they were given in full in 'Inquest on the Body of the Late Mr Morton', *The Lancet* 54:1367 (1849), pp. 512–15, on pp. 514–15.

91 'Suicide of a Professor of Chemistry', *Morning Post* 8 October 1870, p. 6.

92 Gates, *Victorian* Suicide, pp. 70–2 for a discussion of Sydney Carton's effectually suicidal self-sacrifice in *Tale of Two Cities.*

93 'Distressing Suicide at Hounslow', *North Wales Chronicle* 2 September 1854, p. 4.

94 Unless otherwise stated, the details for this discussion are drawn from reports of Edwardes's inquest which opened on 30 December 1882, and continued in adjournments held on four additional days until its conclusion on 18 January 1883. The articles are numerous, but for good examples of the accounts of each day's business see 'Painful Suicide of a Surgeon', *Lloyd's Weekly Newspaper* 31 December 1882, p. 1; 'The Suicide of a Surgeon at Hounslow', *Bristol Mercury and Daily Post* 5 January 1883, p. 8; 'The Suicide of a Surgeon at Hounslow', *Morning Post* 11 January 1883, p. 2; 'The Hounslow Poisoning Case', *Daily News* 17 January 1883, p. 2; 'The Suicide of a Surgeon at Hounslow', *Reynolds's Newspaper* 21 January 1883, p. 3.

95 N.A., HO 107/2499/372.

96 General Medical Council, *The Medical Register* (London: General Medical Council, 1879), p. 228 for his LSA and MRCS qualifications; his status at St Mary's Hospital was reported following his death. Edwardes signed himself MD Brux in his suicide note.

97 Marriage of 24 September 1878, 'Marriages', *The Standard* 27 September 1878, p. 1; births of Harold Edwardes in the September quarter of 1879 and William Edwardes in the December quarter of 1882 www.freebmd.org.uk viewed on 29 November 2013.

98 Practice prices in 1876 ranged from £100 to over £1,000; M.J. Peterson, *The Medical Profession in Mid-Victorian London* (Berkeley: California University Press, 1978), p. 99.
99 'Crowner's Quest-Law', *The Saturday Review* 20 January 1883, p. 71.
100 'The Use of Inquests', *Spectator* 56 (20 January 1883), pp. 78–9.
101 See the stanza included in 'London Letter', *Western Mail* 19 January 1883, p. 2.
102 'The Doctor's Dream', *Punch; or, the London Charivari* 20 January 1883, p. 36. It was later reprinted in C.W. Scott, *Poems for Recitation* (London: Samuel French, 1884).
103 This is based on a digital search of the British Library Newspapers database on 21 September 2010 for the word 'Edwardes' alone or for the combination of 'Edwards' AND 'Hounslow', owing to the high probability that the victim's surname might not be rendered accurately in its distinctive form. Each hit was checked to ensure against false positives.
104 'The Hounslow Poisoning Case', *Middlesex Chronicle* 20 January 1883, p. 5. This newspaper is not included in the British Library Newspapers database; I am indebted to the staff of the Hounslow archives for their assistance in obtaining copies of relevant editions.
105 'Our London Correspondent', *Ipswich Journal* 20 January 1883, p. 5.
106 'The Hounslow Case', *Reynolds's Newspaper* 21 January 1883, p. 4.
107 'Our London Correspondent', *Ipswich Journal* 20 January 1883, p. 5.
108 'The Verdict in the Hounslow Case', *Pall Mall Gazette* 19 January 1883, p. 12.
109 A search of the British Library Newspapers database for the name Edwardes within twenty words of either 'Hounslow', 'suicide', 'Whitmarsh' or 'inquest' yielding no relevant hits 1884–1900 (searched 2 December 2013). Only the phrase 'Hounslow tragedy' sought on its own found two hits in 1885, both reporting legal action taken by Whitmarsh in relation to a promissory note but otherwise unconnected to Edwardes's death. The events of 1882–83 were revisited seventy years later in the local press, and were considered at length by W.C. Cunnington in about 1960; see Hounslow Local Studies VF 942.192 and '70 Years Ago Whitmarsh Riots', *Middlesex Chronicle* 26 December 1952, p. 7. *The Lancet* reprinted the poem 'The Doctor's Dream' in 1900, which generated brief reflections about authorship; *The Lancet* 155:3998 (1900), pp. 1105–7 and 155:3999 (1900), pp. 1179–81.
110 'Charges Against Medical Men', *The Lancet* 121:3098 (1883), p. 65.
111 'The Hounslow Tragedy', *British Medical Journal* 27 January 1883, p. 183.
112 'The Hounslow Tragedy', *British Medical Journal* 3 February 1883, pp. 228–9. Edwardes's estate was valued at £1,092 in probate granted 3

February 1883; probate register 1883 https://probatesearch.service.gov.uk/Calendar#calendar viewed on 6 November 2015.

113 'The Hounslow Tragedy', *Medical Times and Gazette* 27 January 1883, pp. 92–3.

114 'The Hounslow Poisoning Case', *Middlesex Chronicle* 20 January 1883, p. 7.

115 The men's relative ages are given in the 1881 census; N.A., RG 11/1338/112 and RG 11/1338/31 gives Sydney and Whitmarsh respectively as living in Hounslow while RG 11/197/80 gives Edwardes in St Pancras.

Conclusion

Medical misadventure was frequently a matter of public record, but some forms of career turbulence were more readily acknowledged than others. Practitioners who served in India, for example, and who were later thought to suffer from unsoundness of mind, were in effect exonerated from personal culpability. Their derangement was simply marked down as the fault of the heat. The cause of Frederick Fletcher's insanity, when he was admitted to the Northampton asylum in 1867, was given succinctly as 'Indian climate', while the coroner who directed the inquest following Samuel Argent's suicide in 1882 sympathetically thought that Argent 'had evidently been affected, as most Europeans were, by such a climate and such a career'.[1] Assumptions like these formed part of a wider discourse of Western susceptibility to tropical environments, and provided a smooth explanation for disturbing divergences from the professional type without raising awkward questions about systemic flaws.[2] Yet most instances of career turbulence were not so easy to construe by the profession, by newspapers, or by the public as blameless misfortune besetting disinterested and manly professionals in a smoothly functioning polity.

This research offers a fine-grained analysis of the challenges to medical careers based on multiple case studies featuring a measure of 'failure' and the questions this also raises about the nature and construction of medical masculinity. Retrieving these cases has swept up over 1,800 men who encountered one or multiple difficulties. The majority of these practitioners – over 1,000 – were identified in the context of financial hardship, but large cohorts were also uncovered among men thought to have committed suicide, and men accused of neglect. These represent confirmed minimums rather than estimated totals.

Professional challenge, interruption, and failure were therefore not rare exceptions in medicine, but the experience of many and the justified apprehension of many more.

These rich case histories move the debate about the professionalisation of medicine away from established narratives of medical reform and social progress and towards a more complex landscape of conflict, frustration, and stress. They imply that the combined force of the professionalisation process and the distorting effect of an artificially constrained medical market had profound consequences for multiple individuals and particularly their masculine identity. The relationship between medicine and money is revealed as particularly vexed, and one that can be charted throughout all of the chapters here from bankruptcy onwards. From the 1820s, practitioners were increasingly caught in a double bind: the need to engage in appropriate conspicuous consumption to inspire trust in their patient clientele was unhelpfully underpinned when the same high spending relative to income encouraged creditors to extend undue trust for future payment. These encouragements to live beyond one's means were met, also increasingly from the 1820s, by an overcrowded pool of trained practitioners who could not operate in a free-market capacity. Therefore, doctors' notional aspiration, to move entirely away from a commercial morality towards a professional one, confounded men throughout the remainder of the century. Whether they were striving for a lucrative career in England and Wales, or whether they sailed for India, individual practitioners were discomfited and occasionally appalled by the necessary pursuit of money and the stratagems it demanded. Social and literal injunctions against advertising or self-promotion forced men quietly to submit to impecunious livelihoods, to go to the wall without protest, or to explore alternative methods to jostle for public attention and income. 'Covert' competition took a number of forms and could include private contracts between practitioners and their assistants to protect established medical practices, which only became public when disputes broke beyond surgery walls. Criminal prosecutions, particularly those for abortion and some high-profile accusations of murder, revealed only limited scope for legitimate condemnation of rivals.

This constitutes a forcible repositioning of the 'medical market' as a concern for practitioners into the second half of the nineteenth century and beyond. Professionalising forces did not quell and then over-write competition narratives in medicine. Instead they drove competition underground and created different sorts of pressure point. The 1860s have emerged here as a decade of anxious defence of the professional persona. The passage of the 1858 Medical Registration Act did not professionalise medicine overnight, but provided a basis from which initial statutory reform of the profession mediated medical status, both between peers and with the public. It did so in the aftermath of Palmer's execution for murder. This event cast a long shadow over the profession that was revived in the media attention given to Pritchard and Warder in 1865–66. Medical reputations were further complicated by the Contagious Diseases Acts, which first appeared to endorse medical intervention for the good of public health but then attracted outspoken opposition to compulsory examination. In this way, medical professional authority was rendered highly unstable in the 1860s despite, and partly because of, legal change deriving from a professionalising agenda.

At the same time professionalising forces presented enormous conflicts to medical masculinity, where the latter was always at variance with the norms of middle-class expectation. In the mid nineteenth century, when the domestic ideal was paramount, medical men could not achieve the separation of work and home granted to others, since surgeries frequently lay within households and patient groups included doctors' wives, children, and servants. In the later part of the century, as dominant masculinity rejected the domestic circle in favour of homosocial settings – including the professional worlds of hospital and laboratory – practitioners were asked to exhibit continued commitment to homes, particularly patient homes. Evident breeches of right feeling rarely seem to have broken beyond household walls, except where harsh words were used to the poor and union officials were entitled to take an interest (and were possibly keen to exercise the right to reproach).

Multiple poignant narratives confirm that the suppression of agitation and distress was widespread and could pave the way to crisis and tragedy. The melodrama of William Marsden's suicide, played out in front of his wife and children in the street outside his home, was perhaps excessive, but the same despair characterises many men's attempts to balance professional probity and private respectability. The performance of medicine as a display of disinterested, regulated skill, became literally too much to ask of middle-class men whose sense of self was inherently bound up with their own material survival and their intimate emotional lives. This came to the fore most painfully for men who could not save the lives of their own children, but is most frequently visible among men whose anxiety and depression prompted obsessive patterns of thought around professional slight or injury. By the late nineteenth century, the apparently self-confident profession was striated with distress.

Yet occupational and personal stress was not purposeless. Failure was functioning to mark the boundaries of professional behaviour, and was sporadically manipulated by those within and without the profession to act as an imperfect mechanism of professional evolution and governance. There was no united voice emanating from orthodox medicine, and the public took different views on medical demeanour depending on the specifics of each case and the perspective of the observer. Consequently, there was more contradiction than consensus, but some broad patterns emerge. There was no need for explicit opprobrium in the face of outright financial failure. The combined force of authoritative calls for disinterest and the private struggle to make ends meet comprised a sufficient schooling in personal finance, and quiet recovery was common. Reticence on all sides was also reserved for doctors who were ill, and poor mental health was met with sympathetic silence from almost all quarters. Neither lay nor professional interests were served by drawing attention to practitioner incapacity. By contrast, harsh words used in the course of poor-law work could be widely advertised in the newspapers. Dismissive or offensive language was made the focus of particular scrutiny, but in such a way as to invoke reproach rather than legal penalty. The loss of a poor-law appointment was conceivable, but prosecutions for manslaughter were reserved for extreme cases. Similarly, egregious crimes against the body which demanded a prosecution gave rise to one or two exemplars of scape-goating, but more frequently generated a widely approved acquittal.

Medical suicide was the most problematic phenomenon for shaping professional conduct. It was routinely brought to public attention via inquests, but generated responses beyond grief or shock, and forestalled the opportunity for a regretful blanket of silence. Questions were asked about the rigours of medical training, the terms and conditions of assistants' employment, and effectual fitness to practice. These queries were raised by coroners, witnesses, jurymen, and most potently by the doctors themselves in the testimonial status accorded to their suicide notes. The extreme commitment of the doctor to his own point of view, maintained to the point of self-destruction, rendered the suicide inquest a dangerous time for dispassionate defence of emerging professional protocols.

Failure was decisively a component of the professionalising process in medicine, but the dogmatic insistence on disinterest made the consequences of failure more shattering than they needed to be. In its anxiety to shed commercial mores and personal weaknesses, the profession was arguably too aggressive in ignoring, sidelining or explaining away the incidence of failure rather than normalising it. By setting up barriers to the ideological admission of failure, and by using its rude intrusion as a foil either to demonise or extenuate the actions of specific medical men, both the public and the profession inhibited doctors from interrogating systemic challenges (such as those posed by seeking promotion in Indian service) or from better accommodating failure and the prospect of failure. Medical professionalism and masculinity would have been more gently guided by an acceptance of inadequacy or limitation, to 'counsel the adoption of what might be termed a "modest" approach to the affairs of life'.[3] Ultimately, acknowledgement of this more sceptical tradition might similarly have been made by the generations of doctors since 1890. Medical misadventure is inevitable, but if the experience of nineteenth-century practitioners is at all illustrative, its deployment for setting professional boundaries has been misconceived.

Notes

1 St Andrew's Healthcare Archive, Northampton, CL4 Northampton General Lunatic Asylum case notes 1862–67, p. 502; 'The suicide of a Birmingham surgeon', *Birmingham Daily Post* 12 June 1882, p. 5.

2 M. Harrison, '"The Tender Frame of Man": disease, climate, and racial difference in India and the West Indies, 1760–1860', *Bulletin of the History of Medicine* 70:1 (1996), pp. 68–93.

3 J. Malpas and G. Wickham, 'Governance and failure: on the limits of sociology', *Australian and New Zealand Journal of Sociology* 31:1 (1995), pp. 37–50, on p. 45.

Select bibliography

Ackroyd, M., Brockliss, L., Moss, M., Retford, K., and Stevenson, J. *Advancing with the Army. Medicine, the Professions and Social Mobility in the British Isles 1790–1850* (Oxford: Oxford University Press, 2006).

Anderson, O. *Suicide in Victorian and Edwardian England* (Oxford: Oxford University Press, 1987).

Andrews, J. 'Case notes, case histories, and the patient's experience of insanity at Gartnavel Royal Asylum, Glasgow, in the nineteenth century', *Social History of Medicine* 11:2 (1998), pp. 255–81.

Bailey, J. '"I dye [sic] by Inches": locating wife beating in the concept of a privatization of marriage and violence in eighteenth-century Engand', *Social History* 31:3 (2006), pp. 273–94

Bailey, V. *'This Rash Act'. Suicide across the Life Cycle in the Victorian City* (Stanford: Stanford University Press, 1998).

Bayly, C.A. *Indian Society and the Making of the British Empire. The New Cambridge History of India* (Cambridge: Cambridge University Press, 1988).

Bingham, A. 'The digitization of newspaper archives: opportunities and challenges for historians', *Twentieth Century British History* 21:2 (2010), pp. 225–31.

Boddice, R. 'The manly mind? Revisiting the Victorian "sex in brain" debate', *Gender and History* 23:2 (2011), pp. 321–40.

Brown, M. 'Medicine, Quackery and the Free Market: The "War" against Morison's Pills and the Construction of the Medical Profession, c. 1830–c. 1850', in M. Jenner and P. Wallis (eds), *Medicine and the Market in England and its Colonies, c. 1450–c. 1850* (Basingstoke: Palgrave Macmillan, 2007).

Brown, M. *Performing Medicine: Medical Culture and Identity in Provincial England, c.1750–c.1850* (Manchester: Manchester University Press, 2011).

Brown, M. '"Rats, Bats, and Barristers": *The Lancet*, libel and the radical stylistics of early nineteenth century medicine', *Social History* 39:2 (2014), pp. 182–209.

Burney, I.A. *Bodies of Evidence. Medicine and the Politics of the English Inquest 1830–1926* (Baltimore: Johns Hopkins University Press, 2000).

Burney, I.A. *Poison, Detection and the Victorian Imagination* (Manchester: Manchester University Press, 2006).

Burnham, J.C. *How the Idea of Profession Changed the Writing of Medical History* (London: Medical History Supplement, 1998).

Cardwell, M.J. 'Royal Navy Surgeons, 1793–1815: A Collective Biography', in D.B. Haycock and S. Archer (eds), *Health and Medicine at Sea 1700–1900* (Woodbridge: Boydell Press, 2009), pp. 38–62.

Conley, C.A. 'Rape and justice in Victorian England', *Victorian Studies* 29 (1986), pp. 519–36.

Conley, C.A. *The Unwritten Law. Criminal Justice in Victorian Kent* (Oxford University Press: Oxford, 1991).

Crawford, C. 'Patients' rights and the law of contract in eighteenth-century England', *Social History of Medicine* 13:3 (2000), pp. 381–410.

Crawford, D.G. *A History of the Indian Medical Service 1600–1913* (Calcutta: Thacker, Spink & Co., 1914).

Crowther M.A. and M. Dupree, *Medical Lives in the Age of Surgical Revolution* (Cambridge: Cambridge University Press, 2007).

D'Cruze, S. *Crimes of Outrage. Sex, Violence and Victorian Working Women* (London: University College of London Press, 1998).

Digby, A. *Making a Medical Living: Doctors and Patients in the English Market for Medicine, 1720–1911* (Cambridge: Cambridge University Press, 1994).

Digby, A. *The Evolution of British General Practice, 1850–1948* (Oxford: Oxford University Press, 1999).

Donnison, J. *Midwives and Medical Men. A History of Inter-professional Rivalries and Women's Rights* (New York: Schocken Books, 1977).

Duffy, I.P.H. *Bankruptcy and Insolvency in London during the Industrial Revolution* (New York: Garland, 1985).

Eigen, J.P. '"I answer as a physician": Opinion as Fact in pre-McNaughtan Insanity Trials', in M. Clark and C. Crawford (eds), *Legal Medicine in History* (Cambridge: Cambridge University Press, 1994), pp. 167–99.

Ferner F.E. and McDowell, S.E. 'Doctors charged with manslaughter in the course of medical practice, 1795–2005: a literature review', *Journal of the Royal Society of Medicine* 99 (2006), pp. 309–14.

Finn, M. *The Character of Credit. Personal Debt in English Culture, 1740–1914* (Cambridge: Cambridge University Press: 2003).

Flinn, M.W. 'Medical Services under the New Poor Law', in D. Fraser (ed.), *The New Poor Law in the Nineteenth Century* (London: Macmillan, 1976), pp. 45–66.

Foyster, E. *Marital Violence. An English Family History, 1660–1857* (Cambridge: Cambridge University Press, 2005).

Gale, C. and R. Howard (eds), *Presumed Curable. An Illustrated Casebook of Victorian Psychiatric Patients in Bethlem Hospital* (Petersfield: Wrightson Biomedical Publishing, 2003).

Gates, B.T. 'Suicide and the Victorian physicians', *Journal of the History of the Behavioural Sciences* 16 (1980), pp. 164–74.

Gates, B.T. *Victorian Suicide. Mad Crimes and Sad Histories* (Princeton: Princeton University Press, 1988).

Ghosh, D. and Kennedy, D.K. 'Introduction', in D. Ghosh and D.K. Kennedy (eds), *Decentring Empire: Britain, India, and the Transcolonial World* (Hyderabad: Orient Longman, 2006), pp. 1–15.

Goodman, H. '"Madness and Masculinity": Male Patients in London Asylums and Victorian Culture', in T. Knowles and S. Trowbridge (eds), *Insanity and the Lunatic Asylum in the Nineteenth Century* (London: Pickering and Chatto, 2015), pp. 149–65.

Haagen, P.H. 'Eighteenth-century English Society and the Debt Law', in S. Cohen and A. Scull (eds), *Social Control and the State* (1983), pp. 222–47.

Hammerton, A.J. *Cruelty and Companionship. Conflict in Nineteenth-Century Married Life* (London: Routledge, 1992).

Haynes, D.M. 'Victorian Imperialism in the Making of the British Medical Profession: An Argument', in D. Ghosh and D.K. Kennedy (eds), *Decentring Empire: Britain, India, and the Transcolonial World* (Hyderabad: Orient Longman, 2006), pp. 130–56.

Hobbs, A. 'The deleterious dominance of *The Times* in nineteenth-century scholarship', *Journal of Victorian Culture* 18:4 (2013), pp. 472–97.

Hodgkinson, R.G. *The Origins of the National Health Service. The Medical Services of the New Poor Law, 1834–1871* (Berkeley: University of California Press, 1967).

Houston, R.A. *Punishing the Dead? Suicide, Lordship, and Community in Britain, 1500–1830* (Oxford: Oxford University Press, 2010).

Hurren, E.T. 'Remaking the medico-legal scene: a social history of the late-Victorian coroner in Oxford', *Social History of Medicine* 65:2 (2009), pp. 207–52.

Inkster, I. 'Marginal Men: Aspects of the Social Role of the Medical Community in Sheffield 1790–1850', in J. Woodward and D. Richards (eds), *Health Care and Popular Medicine in Nineteenth Century England* (London: Croom Helm, 1977), pp. 128–64.

Jackson, M. *The Age of Stress: Science and the Search for Stability* (Oxford: Oxford University Press, 2013).

Jackson, W. *Madness and Marginality. The Lives of Kenya's White Insane* (Manchester: Manchester University Press, 2013).
Jenner, M.S.R. and P. Wallis, 'Introduction', in M.S.R. Jenner and P. Wallis (eds), *Medicine and the Market in England and its Colonies, c.1450–c.1850* (Basingstoke: Palgrave Macmillan, 2007), pp. 1–23.
Kennedy, D.K. 'Diagnosing the Colonial Dilemma: Tropical Neurasthenia and the Alienated Briton', in D. Ghosh and D.K. Kennedy (eds), *Decentring Empire: Britain, India, and the Transcolonial World* (Hyderabad: Orient Longman, 2006), pp. 157–81.
Keown, J. *Abortion, Doctors and the Law. Some Aspects of the Legal Regulation of Abortion in England from 1803 to 1982* (Cambridge: Cambridge University Press, 1988).
Kjaergaard, P.C. 'Competing allies: professionalisation and the hierarchy of science in Victorian Britain', *Centaurus* 44 (2002), pp. 248–88.
Knight, P. 'Women and abortion in Victorian and Edwardian England', *History Workshop Journal* 4 (1977), pp. 57–69.
Kragh, J.V. 'Women, Men and the Morphine Problem, 1870–1955', in T. Ortiz-Gómez and M.J. Santesmases (eds), *Gendered Drugs and Medicine. Historical and Socio-cultural Perspectives* (Farnham: Ashgate, 2014), pp. 177–98
Laragy, G. '"A Peculiar Species of Felony": suicide, medicine, and the law in Victorian Britain and Ireland', *Journal of Social History* 46:3 (2013), pp. 732–43.
Lee, T.A. 'The professional journal as a signal of movement to occupational ascendancy and as legitimation of a professional project: the early history of The Accountant's Magazine 1897–1951', *Accounting History* 11:1 (2006), pp. 7–40.
Lemmings, D. 'Introduction: Criminal Courts, Lawyers and the Public Sphere', in D. Lemmings (ed.), *Crime, Courtrooms and the Public Sphere in Britain, 1700–1850* (Ashgate: Farnham, 2012), pp. 1–22.
Lester, V.M. *Victorian Insolvency. Bankruptcy, Imprisonment for Debt, and Company Winding-up in Nineteenth-Century England* (Oxford: Clarendon Press, 1995).
Lincoln, M. 'Medical Profession and Representations of the Navy', in G.L. Hudson (ed.), *British Military and Naval Medicine 1600–1830* (Amsterdam: Rodopi, 2007).
Loudon, I. *Medical Care and the General Practitioner, 1750–1850* (Oxford: Oxford University Press, 1986).
Loudon, I. 'Some International Features of Maternal Mortality, 1880–1950', in V. Fildes, L. Marks, and H. Marland (eds), *Women and Children First. International Maternal and Infant Welfare 1870–1945* (London: Routledge, 1992).

Loudon, I. *Death in Childbirth. An International Study of Maternal Care and Maternal Mortality 1800–1950* (Oxford: Clarendon, 1992).

Loudon, J. and I. Loudon, 'Medicine, Politics and the Medical Periodical 1800–50', in S. Lock and R. Porter (eds), *Medical Journals and Medical Knowledge: Historical Essays* (Routledge: London, 1992), pp. 49–69.

MacDonald, H. 'Procuring corpses: the English anatomy inspectorate 1842–1858', *Medical History* 53:3 (2009), pp. 379–96.

MacDonald, M. and Murphy, T.R. *Sleepless Souls. Suicide in Early-modern England* (Oxford: Clarendon Press, 1990).

MacKenzie, C. *Psychiatry for the Rich. A History of Ticehurst Private Asylum, 1792–1917* (London: Routledge, 1992).

MacKenzie, J.M. 'The Imperial Pioneer and Hunter and the British Masculine Stereotype in Late Victorian and Edwardian Times', in J.A. Mangan and J. Walvin (eds), *Manliness and Morality. Middle-class Masculinity in Britain and America, 1800–1940* (Manchester: Manchester University Press, 1987).

McLaren, A. 'Women's work and regulation of family size: the question of abortion in the nineteenth century', *History Workshop Journal* 4 (1977), pp. 70–81.

McLaren, A. *Reproductive Rituals; the Perception of Fertility in England from the Sixteenth to the Nineteenth Century* (London: Methuen, 1984).

McLaren, A. '"Not a stranger: a doctor": Medical Men and Sexual Matters in the Late Nineteenth Century', in R. Porter and M. Teich (eds), *Sexual Knowledge, Sexual Science. The History of Attitudes to Sexuality* (Cambridge: Cambridge University Press, 1994), pp. 267–83.

Malpas, J. and Wickham, G. 'Governance and failure: on the limits of sociology', *Australian and New Zealand Journal of Sociology* 31:1 (1995), pp. 37–50.

Mangan, J.A. and Walvin, J. 'Introduction', in J.A. Mangan and J. Walvin (eds), *Manliness and Morality. Middle-class Masculinity in Britain and America, 1800–1940* (Manchester: Manchester University Press, 1987).

Marriner, S. 'English bankruptcy records and statistics before 1850', *English Historical Review* 33 (1980), pp. 351–66.

Melling, J. and B. Forsyth, *The Politics of Madness: The State, Insanity and Society in England, 1845–1914* (London: Routledge, 2006).

Micale, M.S. *Hysterical Men. The Hidden History of Male Nervous Illness* (Cambridge: Harvard University Press, 2008).

Oppenheim, J. *Shattered Nerves. Doctors, Patients and Depression in Victorian England* (Oxford: Oxford University Press, 1991).

Peterson, M.J. *The Medical Profession in Mid-Victorian London* (Berkeley: California University Press, 1978).

Porter, R. 'Rape – Does it Have a Historical Meaning?', in R. Porter and S. Tomaselli (eds), *Rape. An Historical and Cultural Enquiry* (Oxford: Basil Blackwell, 1986), pp. 216–36.

Price, K. *Medical Negligence in Victorian Britain. The Crisis of Care under the English Poor Law, c.1834–1900* (London: Bloomsbury, 2015).

Reiter, P.J. 'Doctors, detectives, and the professional idea: the trial of Thomas Neill Cream and the mastery of Sherlock Holmes', *College Literature* 35:3 (2008), pp. 57–96.

Richards, J. 'Passing the Love of Women: Manly Love and Victorian Society', in J.A. Mangan and J. Walvin (eds), *Manliness and Morality. Middle-class Masculinity in Britain and America 1800–1940* (Manchester: Manchester University Press, 1987), pp. 92–122.

Roberts, M.J.D. 'The politics of professionalisation: MPs, medical men, and the 1858 Medical Act', *Medical History* 53:1 (2009) pp. 37–56.

Roper, M. and Tosh, J. 'Introduction', in M. Roper and J. Tosh (eds), *Manful Assertions: Masculinities in Britain since 1800* (London: Routledge, 1991), pp. 1–24.

Rowbotham, J. and Stevenson, K. 'Causing a Sensation: Media and Legal Representations of Bad Behaviour', in J. Rowbotham and K. Stevenson (eds), *Behaving Badly. Social Panic and Moral Outrage – Victorian and Modern Parallels* (Ashgate: Aldershot, 2003), pp. 31–46.

Rowbotham, J., Stevenson, K., and Pegg, S. *Crime News is Modern Britain. Press Reporting and Responsibility, 1820–2010* (Basingstoke: Palgrave Macmillan, 2013).

Scull, A. *The Most Solitary of Afflictions. Madness and Society in Britain, 1700–1900* (New Haven: Yale University Press, 1993).

Scull, A. 'Museums of Madness revisited', in *The Insanity of Place/The Place of Insanity. Essays on the History of Psychiatry* (London: Routledge, 2006).

Shave, S. '"Immediate Death or a Life of Torture are the Consequences of the System": the Bridgwater Union Scandal and Policy Change', in J. Reinarz and L. Schwarz (eds), *Medicine and the Workhouse* (Rochester: Rochester University Press, 2013), pp. 164–91.

Shepherd A. and D. Wright, 'Madness, suicide and the Victorian asylum: attempted self-murder in the age of non-restraint', *Medical History* 46 (2002), pp. 175–96.

Shepherd, A.C. 'Mental Health Care and Charity for the Middling Sort. Holloway Sanatorium 1885–1900', in A. Borsay and P. Shapley (eds) *Medicine, Charity and Mutual Aid. The Consumption of Health and Welfare in Britain, c. 1550–1950* (Aldershot: Ashgate, 2007), pp. 163–82.

Simpson, A.E. 'The "Blackmail Myth" and the prosecution of rape and its attempt in 18th century London: the creation of a legal tradition', *Journal of Criminal Law and Criminology*, 77 (1986), pp. 101–50.

Smith, L.D. 'Social Class in the Lunatic Asylum', in O. Ashton, R. Fyson, and S. Roberts (eds), *The Duty of Discontent* (London: Mansell, 1995), pp. 142–66.
Smith, L.D. *Cure, Comfort and Safe Custody. Public Lunatic Asylums in Early Nineteenth-Century England* (London: Leicester University Press, 1999).
Smith, R.G. *Medical Discipline. The Professional Conduct Jurisdiction of the General Medical Council, 1858–1990* (Oxford: Clarendon Press, 1994).
Snell, E. 'Trials in Print: Narratives of Rape Trials in the Proceedings of the Old Bailey', in D. Lemmings (ed.), *Crime, Courtrooms and the Public Sphere in Britain, 1700–1850* (Ashgate: Farnham, 2012), pp. 23–42.
Stebbings, C. 'Tax and Pharmacy: A Synergy in Professional Evolution', in P. Harris and D. De Cogan, *Studies in the History of Tax Law* 7 (2015), pp. 153–69.
Stevenson, K. '"Most Intimate Violations": Contextualising the Crime of Rape', in A-M. Kilday and D. Nash (eds), *Histories of Crime. Britain 1600–2000* (Basingstoke: Palgrave Macmillan, 2010), pp. 80–99.
Sullivan, S. 'Spectacular Failures: Thomas Hopley, Wilkie Collins, and the Reconstruction of Victorian Masculinity', in M. Hewitt (ed.), *An Age of Equipoise? Reassessing Mid-Victorian Britain* (Ashgate: Aldershot, 2000), pp. 84–108.
Tomkins, A.E. 'Fragility and resilience in a middle-class family: Jeremiah Ginders (1777–1845) and his kin', *Staffordshire Studies* 13 (2001), pp. 79–108.
Tomkins, A.E. 'Mad doctors?: the significance of medical practitioners admitted as patients to the first English county asylums up to 1890', *History of Psychiatry* 23:4 (2012), pp. 437–53.
Tomkins, A.E. 'Casenotes and Madness', in M. Jackson (ed.), *The Routledge History of Disease* (London: Routledge, 2016).
Tosh, J. *A Man's Place. Masculinity and the Middle-Class Home in Victorian England* (New Haven: Yale University Press, 1999).
Tosh, J. 'Gentlemanly politeness and manly simplicity in Victorian England', *Transactions of the Royal Historical Society* 12 (2002), pp. 455–72.
Waddington, K. 'Mayhem and medical Students: image, conduct and control in the Victorian and Edwardian London Teaching Hospital' *Social History of Medicine* 15:1 (2002), pp. 45–64.
Walker, G. 'Everyman or a monster? The rapist in early-modern England, c. 1600–1750', *History Workshop Journal* 76:1 (2013), pp. 3–31.
Walton, J. 'Casting Out and Bringing Back in Victorian England: Pauper Lunatics, 1840–70', in W. Bynum, R. Porter, and M. Shepherd (eds), *The Anatomy of Madness: Essays in the History of Psychiatry* (London: Tavistock, 1985), pp. 132–46.

Wiener, M.J. 'The Victorian Criminalisation of Men', in P. Spierenburg (ed.), *Men and Violence. Gender, Honor, and Rituals in Modern Europe and America* (Columbus Ohio: Ohio State University Press, 1998), pp. 197–212.

Weiner, M. 'Domesticity: A Legal Discipline for Men?', in M. Hewitt (ed.), *An Age of Equipoise? Reassessing Mid-Victorian Britain* (Aldershot: Ashgate, 2000), pp. 155–67.

Woods, R. 'Physician, heal thyself: the health and mortality of Victorian doctors', *Social History of Medicine* 9:1 (1996), pp. 1–30.

Wright, D. 'The Discharge of Pauper Lunatics from County Asylums in mid-Victorian Britain. The Case of Buckinghamshire, 1853–1872', in J. Melling and B. Forsythe (eds), *Insanity, Institutions and Society, 1800–1914* (London: Routledge, 1999), pp. 93–112.

York, S. 'Alienists, attendants and the containment of suicide in public lunatic asylums, 1845–1890', *Social History of Medicine* 25:2 (2011), pp. 324–42.

Index

EU authorised representative for GPSR:
Easy Access System Europe, Mustamäe tee 50,
10621 Tallinn, Estonia
gpsr.requests@easproject.com

www.ingramcontent.com/pod-product-compliance
Ingram Content Group UK Ltd.
Pitfield, Milton Keynes, MK11 3LW, UK
UKHW021834100926
8556IPUK00004B/333
* 9 7 8 1 5 2 6 1 1 6 0 7 9 *